The Bandido Massacre

PETER EDWARDS

THE BANDIDO MASSACRE

A TRUE STORY OF BIKERS, BROTHERHOOD AND BETRAYAL

HARPERCOLLINS PUBLISHERS LTD

The Bandido Massacre
Copyright © 2010 by Peter Edwards.
All rights reserved.

Published by HarperCollins Publishers Ltd.

Originally published in a hardcover edition
by HarperCollins Publishers Ltd: 2010
This mass market paperback edition: 2011

HarperCollins books may be purchased for educational, business, or sales
promotional use through our Special Markets Department.

HarperCollins Publishers Ltd
2 Bloor Street East, 20th Floor
Toronto, Ontario, Canada
M4W 1A8

www.harpercollins.ca

Library and Archives Canada Cataloguing in Publication data
is available upon request.

ISBN: 978-1-55468-045-0

Printed and bound in the United States

OPM 9 8 7 6 5 4 3 2 1

To Barbara, Sarah and James

For family

CONTENTS

PART III: HUNTERS TO HUNTED

Now Cain said to his brother Abel, "Let's go out to the field."
And while they were in the field, Cain attacked
his brother Abel and killed him.
GENESIS 4:8

He who makes a beast of himself
gets rid of the pain of being a man.
SAMUEL JOHNSON

He was complaining about having to do all of the
wet work—that's referring to killing somebody.
POLICE AGENT "M.H." DESCRIBES
WAYNE (WEINER) KELLESTINE OF THE BANDIDOS

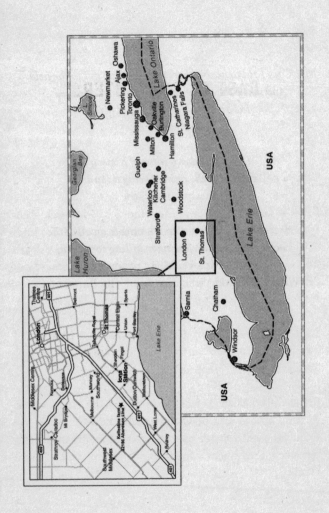

CAST OF CHARACTERS

BIKERS AND ASSOCIATES

Cameron Acorn: Member of the Bandidos Motorcycle Club from the small Ontario town of Keswick, north of Toronto. Pled guilty in January 2008 to manslaughter for the death of drug dealer Shawn Douse as well as three counts of armed robbery and three counts of forcible confinement for robbing a motorcycle shop.

Jason Addison: President of the Bandidos in Australia and an often-sharp critic of the Bandidos' headquarters—or "mother chapter"—in Texas.

Remond (Ray) Akleh: Former secretary of the Hells Angels in the Ontario city of Oshawa, who transferred to the Ottawa-based Nomads chapter after a bitter dispute with fellow club members, especially chapter secretary Steven Gault.

Pierre (Carlito) Aragon: Full member of the No Surrender Crew (the nickname for the Toronto Bandidos), who worked at a strip club on The Queensway in Toronto, providing security for lap dancers. Often seen in the company of hard-looking Spanish-speaking strippers.

Marcelo (Fat Ass) Aravena: Mixed-martial-arts fighter and junior Bandido from Winnipeg.

Carleton (Pervert) Bare: National secretary of the Bandidos in Texas, who was disgusted by what he considered the low-level criminal activity of some of the Bandidos in Canada.

Maurice (Mom) Boucher: Leader of the Montreal Hells Angels Nomads chapter, now in prison for first-degree murder for ordering the murders of prison guards.

Alain (Red Tomato) Brunette: First president of Bandidos Canada and an early supporter of the No Surrender Crew.

David (Dred) Buchanan: Sergeant-at-arms of the West Toronto chapter of the Hells Angels, whose duties included enforcement of club discipline.

Dana (Boomer) Carnegie: Former minor pro-hockey player and former member of the West Toronto Hells Angels.

Donald Eugene (Mother) Chambers: Former U.S. Marine who founded the Bandidos Motorcycle Club in Texas in the mid-1960s.

John (Big John) Coates: Massive biker from Sherbrooke, Quebec, pled guilty to conspiring to assault and cause bodily harm to Wayne Kellestine in October 1999, after Kellestine had survived a drive-by shooting near his farm. For this, Coates was sentenced to four months in custody. His brother James pled guilty to the same crimes and received no jail time in addition to the year he had spent in pre-trial custody.

Ernie Dew: President of the Winnipeg Hells Angels who was sentenced in 2008 to thirteen years in prison for cocaine trafficking and possessing property obtained through crime, after a former friend was paid more than $525,000 to turn police agent. The Manitoba Court of Appeal ordered him a new trial in 2009 because Dew couldn't afford to have a lawyer present every day for what the court called "a serious and complex case."

Jamie (Goldberg) Flanz: Prospect (as in junior) member of the Toronto Bandidos, who ran a small computer consulting firm north of Toronto. The only Jew in the Canadian Bandidos. Had only been a prospect for six months at the time of the murders.

James Albert (Ripper, Rip, Old Troll) Fullager: Longtime Toronto biker who was a founding member of the Wild Ones Motorcycle Club in the early 1960s and who moved on to the Black Diamond Riders, Loners and, finally, the Bandidos.

Brett (Bull, Beau) Gardiner: Winnipegger who was just twenty-one years old when he was charged with eight counts of first-degree murder after the Shedden Massacre, although he didn't shoulder a rifle during the slaughter.

Steven Gault: Fraud artist, drug dealer, drug user, thief, thug and one-time secretary of the Oshawa Hells Angels, who joined the club for the sole purpose of selling the members out. He received more than a million dollars from police for his efforts. Living under a new name somewhere now. Not a nice guy.

George (Pony) Jessome: Also known as George Jesso. Tow truck driver in the Toronto suburb of Etobicoke and member of the Bandidos, who had terminal cancer. He had few, if any, enemies. Only became a prospect in the club in May 2005, less than a year before the murders. Some members of his family spell their last name "Jesso."

Wayne (Weiner) Kellestine: Nazi-loving Bandido who had an extensive gun collection at the time of the Shedden Massacre, even though he was under two lifetime bans on possessing firearms. He signed his name with lightning bolts, a boast that he was an underworld killer.

George (Crash) Kriarakis: Bandidos' Canadian national secretary and Toronto chapter member, who was given his nickname because he drove a tow truck, responding to highway crashes. He also called himself "Gus"—his father's name—when meeting people he didn't fully trust. He had a strong marriage and no criminal record. He was one of the few members of the No Surrender Crew who actually rode a motorcycle. Privately, he wanted out of the club. He was a favourite of the American mother chapter of the Bandidos because of his stability.

Frank (Cisco) Lenti: Toronto-area former member of the Satan's Choice, Diabolos, Outlaws, Loners, Rebels, Bastone and Bandido clubs and the target of an alleged Hells Angels murder plot.

Joey (Crazy Horse) Morin: Also known as Joey Campbell. Was briefly a Bandido in Edmonton. Fearless, non-druggy and good with his fists.

Giovanni (John, Boxer) Muscedere: Toronto Bandido who was Canadian club president at the time of the massacre. Also known as "Prize" and "Prize-fighter" for his brief stint as a boxer. Father of five and grandfather of three, he worked for twenty years for an auto-parts maker in Tilbury, in southwestern Ontario.

Dwight (Big D, Dee) Mushey: Secretary-treasurer of the Winnipeg Bandidos and second-degree black belt in the Korean martial art of tae kwon do.

Robert (Peterborough Bob) Pammett: Member of the Toronto chapter of the Bandidos, whose decision not to attend his chapter's emergency "church" meeting at Weiner Kellestine's farm likely saved his life.

Mario (The Wop, Mike) Parente: Former national president of the Outlaws. Joined the Satan's Choice as an eighteen-year-old, and switched to the Outlaws when they moved into Canada nine years later, in 1977. Considered a true old-school outlaw biker, or a "one percenter." Sometimes called "a one percenter's one percenter" for his refusal to compromise on outlaw biker rules. His Outlaws got along with the Bandidos but had an often-tense, sometimes hostile, relationship with the Hells Angels.

Robert (Donny) Petersen: Spokesperson for the Ontario Hells Angels who was fired from his government post as a motorcycle safety expert because of his Hells Angels membership. A former boxer and successful Toronto motorcycle dealer, he is considered a voice of reason in the outlaw biker world.

Jeffrey Pike: Texas-based biker who became international president—or *El Presidente*—of the Bandidos in 2005. Sharp critic of the Toronto Bandidos. Had final veto power over Bandidos matters. Earned a legitimate, six-figure income from the Texas oil fields.

Luis Manny (Chopper, Porkchop) Raposo:,Full-patch member of the Toronto Bandidos, who beat charges in Quebec of participating in a criminal organization and trafficking marijuana and cocaine. Opposed granting full-chapter status to the probationary Winnipeg chapter of the Bandidos. Didn't like to say much on the phone.

Frankie (Bam Bam, Bammer) Salerno: President of the Toronto Bandidos, who talked privately of retiring from biker life after the birth of his son in the spring of 2006. His strong marriage helped him battle heroin, gambling addictions and obesity.

Michael (Taz, the Tazman, Little Beaker, Poo Bear) Sandham: Former Canadian Forces infantryman who was forced to resign from his job as a Winnipeg-area police officer after Ontario police learned of his ties to the Outlaws biker club. Attempted to forge ties with the Texas-based mother chapter of the Bandidos to further his ambitions of becoming an outlaw biker boss. Lied his way into the biker world by claiming he wasn't ever a member of the police.

Bill (Bandido Bill) Sartelle: *El Secretario* of the Bandidos worldwide. Second only to Jeff Pike in the club's pecking order. Also earned a legitimate, six-figure income working in the Texas oil industry.

Paul (Big Paul) Sinopoli: Secretary-treasurer of the Bandidos' Toronto chapter, who talked of quitting biker life for a while to get his massive weight under control.

Wolodumyr (Walter, Nurget) Stadnick: Former national president of the Hells Angels, now in prison for multiple counts of conspiracy to commit murder, gangsterism and drug trafficking. Considered a shrewd judge of talent and the architect of the Hells Angels' expansion across Canada. Carefully guards secrets, including the meaning of "Nurget."

"Stone": Toronto Bandido prospect, whose nickname came from his druggy demeanour.

Mary Thompson: Prosecution witness in the case against four Bandidos and associates who were charged with murdering drug dealer Shawn Douse of Keswick, Ontario. Not her real name.

M.H.: Bandido turned police agent who is now in a witness protection program. Because of a court order, his real name cannot be published. Often stone-faced, but capable of tears.

Mike (Little Mikey, Mikey T) Trotta: Full member of the Bandidos' Toronto chapter, who had been connected to the club only fourteen months at the time of the murders. A close friend of Bam Bam Salerno.

Carlo Verrelli: Promoted to full-patch status in the West Toronto Hells Angels after he showed bravery in helping a dying fellow biker, during an incident in which he was severely injured himself.

George Wegers: U.S.–based *presidente* of the Bandidos in the early 2000s, during their expansion drive into Canada.

Jailed in 2005. From Washington State, and considered a tad liberal by some Texas Bandidos.

David (Concrete Dave) Weiche: Son of Martin Weiche, a wealthy businessman who tried to restart the Nazi party and who hosted Ku Klux Klan rallies on his London, Ontario–area property in the 1970s. Concrete Dave moved from southwestern Ontario to the Bandidos' Bellingham, Washington, chapter. Considered a friend of Wayne Kellestine, except when it was to his benefit to be otherwise.

Edward (Connecticut Ed) Winterhalder: Senior American Bandido sent to Canada to help organize new Bandidos chapters. Believes much of Canada's Bandido troubles stemmed from methamphetamine use and trafficking.

LAWYERS, JUDGES AND POLICE

Detective Inspector P.A. (Paul) Beesley: Senior Ontario Provincial Police homicide investigator, given the job of investigating the Shedden Massacre.

Detective Sergeant Mick Bickerton: Excellent interviewer for the Ontario Provincial Police.

Tony Bryant: High-profile Toronto criminal lawyer whose former clients included schoolgirl sex killer Paul Bernardo.

Heather Carpenter: London lawyer who was part of Sandham defense team.

Don Crawford: Longtime southwestern Ontario lawyer who represented Michael (Taz) Sandham.

Gordon Cudmore: Another member of Sandham's defence team, a lawyer held in particularly high regard in the legal community in southwestern Ontario. Measured, reasonable and likeable, he was stuck with a thoroughly unlikeable client. He had about as much chance of winning as legendary jockey Willie Shoemaker would have had if he'd tried to ride Mister Ed in the Kentucky Derby.

Timothy Diack: Winnipeg police officer who knew biker M.H. before the Shedden massacre.

Detective Constable Jeff Gateman: Member of the Ontario Provincial Police Biker Enforcement Unit who spent much time with police agent M.H.

Louie Genova: Lawyer for Toronto-area biker Frank (Cisco) Lenti.

Kevin Gowdey: Unflappable head of the prosecution team in the Bandido mass-murder trial.

Mr. Justice Thomas Heeney: Superior Court judge who ably oversaw the trial of eight Bandidos in London, Ontario, in 2009, a task much harder than herding cats uphill.

Fraser Kelly: Crown in the Bandido mass-murder trial. Has an encyclopedic and quick mind.

Detective Sergeant Mark Loader: Member of the Ontario Provincial Police Biker Enforcement Unit who spent much time with police agent M.H.

Detective Inspector Ian Maule: In charge of massive forensic file for the murder mega-trial.

Clay Powell: Lawyer for convicted killer Wayne (Weiner) Kelles-tine,and former top prosecutor who put hockey mogul Harold Ballard of the Toronto Maple Leafs behind bars for fraud. As a defence lawyer, he kept Keith Richards of the Rolling Stones out of prison after the guitarist's heroin bust.

David Steinberg: Original defence lawyer for Frank Mather, one of the men found guilty in the Shedden Massacre.

Mr. Justice Ross Webster: Motorcycle-riding judge at the preliminary hearing into the Shedden Massacre. Nicknamed "Ross the Boss."

Peter Westgate: Senior Crown attorney in Newmarket, Ontario, who prosecuted Frank (Cisco) Lenti for second-degree murder in the shooting of Hells Angel David (Dred) Buchanan of the West Toronto chapter.

Serve Somebody

At one point during the trial of Michael Sandham et al. for the Shedden Massacre, *London Free Press* reporter Jane Sims said it sounded like the He-Man Woman Haters Club from the old *Little Rascals* television series. She was right. With its grandiose rituals and overblown mythology, the Bandidos Motorcycle Club can seem more the stuff of fantasy and macho escapism than something from the real world. Of course, things became horribly real on the morning of April 8, 2006, in a farmyard west of London, Ontario. And to this day, the tears that flowed, the numbness and loss felt by the family members of the victims of the slaughter, remain only too real.

There was no great public outcry of sympathy when the bodies of the eight bikers were found, riddled with bullets. Instead, the general feeling among the public and the media was a combination of revulsion and curiosity, as if the bodies of aliens had suddenly appeared on the edge of a tidy farm community. Over the past three years, I found, however, that the dead men were deeply loved by their friends and families, who often also disapproved of their biker lifestyle. One of my strongest memories from this project is the raw emotion of their sobbing loved ones during the preliminary hearing and trial.

I covered the Shedden Massacre from the day of the slaughter to the present, with an assortment of related trials and preliminaries, sometimes on my own time and often through my work reporting for *The Toronto Star*. I spoke on the telephone with mass murderer Wayne (Weiner) Kellestine hours after the murders, although the attempt for an interview that day brought nothing more than a pithy three-word response. Only the middle word— "my"—was reprintable in a family newspaper.

Since the massacre, I have also spoken several times, and at great length, with many others in the outlaw biker world who knew the cast of characters in the massacre. These include Frank (Cisco) Lenti in the fall of 2007, while he was awaiting trial for second-degree murder for killing Hells Angel David (Dred) Buchanan of Toronto; Normand Brisebois and Gilles (the Kid) Lalonde, both now in witness protection programs after fighting for the Dark Circle in the biker wars; "J.B." of the Prairie Bandidos; Mario (Mike, The Wop) Parente, former national president of the Outlaws; and Kerry Morris, who was at Wayne Kellestine's farm hours after the murders. A particularly intelligent person I had the pleasure of meeting while preparing this book was Glenn (Wrongway) Atkinson, former secretary of the No Surrender Crew. I also talked with several Ontario Hells Angels, all of whom said they were stunned at the wild turn things had taken at Shedden. In an unguarded moment, one Hells Angel told me,

"It's a great morning when you wake up and find out your enemies have killed themselves." My most valuable source was Julian Carsini (not his real name), who was grieving the loss of close friends. He was extremely open, with the sole condition that his true identity not be published.

The Shedden Massacre was not the work of criminal masterminds. As a whodunit, the story could be told in a few sentences. But look at it as a *why*dunit, and it becomes a mystery of fascinating complexity. Not even the outlaw biker insiders have an easy answer for this. Police, family members, even rival gangs can only shake their heads. On the surface, the slaughter is patently absurd. In order to gain control of the club in Canada, the killers destroyed it. Instead of expediting their dreams of wild freedom and rough-hewn glory, the crimes quickly landed the ambitious Bandidos in prison. It was as though the killers were fighting for a bigger share of nothing. An agonizing irony is that several of their victims secretly wanted to quit the club anyway, but stayed on under the threat of violence. All they would have had to do was hand in their patches, and all the men who converged on that blighted farm on the night of April 7, 2006, both the betrayers and the betrayed, would today be leading the lives they dreamed of. But some shared underworld code doomed them all. Because the unfolding of this tragedy is so pointless, the *why* is that much more poignant.

Like other outlaw bikers, the Bandidos portray themselves as motorcycle enthusiasts who are systematically misunderstood and abused by police and the rest of the public, whom they refer to dismissively as "citizens." The

Shedden slaughter demonstrates they have much more to fear from their own ranks than from anyone else, including their supposed rivals in the Hells Angels. One might argue that self-loathing proved a far greater danger than enemies with guns. Many police may despise outlaw bikers, but there's no record of a Canadian police officer actually executing one of them.

There have been literally hundreds of bikers murdered in Canada by fellow bikers over the past quarter-century, with most of the violence taking place in the province of Quebec—or the "Red Zone"—in the 1990s and early 2000s. Even against this bloody backdrop, the Shedden Massacre stands out. It's the world's largest known biker massacre and the biggest mass murder in the province of Ontario since 1832. That earlier tragedy—which took place between the hamlets of Vanessa and Waterford, less than an hour's drive east of Shedden—involved a different sort of family.[1] A hard-drinking farmer named Henry Sovereign (also spelled Sovereene and Sovereen) slaughtered his wife and seven children. The courthouse yard where a crowd turned out, in the midst of a cholera epidemic, to watch Sovereign's one-way walk to the gallows on August 13, 1832, is less than a ten-minute walk from the high-tech courtroom where the trial of the men charged in the Shedden Massacre was held 167 years later.

Throughout my research, I found no evidence that anyone in the province of Ontario ever became rich by joining the Bandidos. If anything, membership in the club made the bikers poorer, through court costs and time away from legitimate work, where they might earn regular wages. Given the lack of real money that came from club membership in Ontario, one can't help but marvel at the intensity of the emotions that were triggered in the bikers by the struggle to wear distinctive "Fat Mexican" patches of cloth on their backs.

During the more than three years of interviews and trial coverage to prepare this book, I often thought of the irony of how many rules it takes to run a club devoted to freedom and life outside the law. In the end, the Bandidos were as bound by rules as the rest of us, and perhaps more so. Often as I typed what appears in these pages, I couldn't help thinking of the lyrics of Bob Dylan's "Gotta Serve Somebody," where he notes that everyone, from barbers to presidents, inevitably ends up serving someone or something. He could have added outlaw bikers to his list, without diluting the song's meaning.

Perhaps the best explanation I could find for the carnage that came to light in Shedden comes from the writings of cultural anthropologist Ernest Becker. He wrote in his Pulitzer Prize–winning book *The Denial of Death* that much of what men do—from fathering children to attempting to produce timeless art to death-defying acts of heroism—is an attempt to win some illusion of immortality. Becker convincingly argued that men routinely join groups where they can feel uplifted by shared heroic dreams, and which promise an intoxicating rush of power and heroism. Some join sports teams, political parties, faculty clubs, fraternities or religious sects, while some write books. Others, like the men who met at midnight at Kellestine's barn, join one percenter motorcycle clubs.

Becker obviously wasn't speaking of Kellestine or Taz Sandham, or their compulsions to wear the patch of an outlaw gang, but he described them nonetheless when he wrote of how "cherished narcissism feeds on symbols." I also thought of Nazi-loving Kellestine when I read Becker's discussion of how Hitler's Nazis used murder in an attempt to cement brotherhood, and defined the act with the term *Blutkitt*. A reading of Becker also helped me deal with a central irony of outlaw biker clubs like the Bandidos, and how their efforts to defy mortality often end in the very thing they fear the most: death.

Not everyone in the Bandidos or other one percenter clubs has the madness or cruelty of a Wayne Kellestine. Far from it. Men like George (Crash) Kriarakis, George (Pony) Jessome and Michael (Little Mikey) Trotta had far different motivations for joining the club. They worked hard and stayed out of crime and often seemed to me to be better suited to a men's service club like the Lions than a biker brotherhood. The Bandidos, Outlaws, Pagans and Hells Angels are all self-identified as one-percenter or "outlaw" motorcycle clubs. Police biker experts such as Staff-Sergeant Jacques Lemieux of the RCMP have testified in court that this means they do not want to abide by society's laws, and that they should be regarded as criminal organizations, although no court has ruled this to be the case for the Bandidos. Either way, for members like Kriarakis, Jessome, Trotta and others above them in the Bandidos Texas Mother Chapter, being a one-percenter was an attitude rather than an actual need to exhibit criminal behaviour. Giovanni (John, Boxer) Muscedere was far more hard core, but it became clear that he too had been driven into the club by a longing for brotherhood and a place where he could feel secure and powerful. He may have been an outlaw, but I don't consider him a criminal, and I continue to marvel at the heroism he showed in the final moments of his life.

In the pages that follow, no conversations have been invented. All dialogue is reproduced either through electronic records or through the memories of reliable participants. There was a court-ordered ban on publishing the real name or any identifying traits of M.H. The only other thing I have deliberately changed in these pages is the name of the female witness to the murder of Shawn Douse in Keswick, Ontario. Neither her real nor assumed name is "Mary Thompson," which is how she is identified in this book. Hopefully, she's proud of her courage and is easing into a productive new life, under a new name, as this book goes to print.

Also, as this book goes to print, all of the six men convicted of first-degree murder in the Bandido massacre have filed notices of their intention to appeal the verdicts against them. Among other things, they argue that Mr. Justice Thomas Heeney should have allowed more latitude in cross-examining the Crown's star witness, who can be identified only as "M.H." Marcelo (Fat Ass) Aravena argues that he should have been allowed to advance a defense that he was under duress from armed members of the club on the night of the killings. In his appeal notice, Michael (Taz) Sandham sounds indignant, writing that the verdicts were "perverse" and "make no sense." For his part,

Wayne (Weiner) Kellestine writes that the judge shouldn't have allowed his collection of Nazi paraphernalia, including "the German swastika flag" shown hanging in his barn, to be introduced as evidence. Kellestine also takes a swipe at his former Bandido brother Sandham, arguing that the judge should have given "a warning on the dangers" of Sandham's evidence. And so the in-fighting that characterizes the group continues in a new forum.

PART I

MIDNIGHT VISIT

CHAPTER 1

Church

It is now dead midnight.
Cold fearful drops stand on my trembling flesh.
RICHARD III, ACT 5, SCENE 3

Kill 'em all, let God sort it out
SIGN IN WAYNE (WEINER) KELLESTINE'S WINDOW

Jamie (Goldberg) Flanz didn't suspect a thing when the surveillance car slipped behind his luxury sport utility vehicle as
he drove out of Keswick, north of Toronto. With him in the
grey Infiniti FX3 was Paul (Big Paul) Sinopoli, a gargantuan full-patch member of the Bandidos Motorcycle Club,
and when Big Paul was around, it was hard to notice anything or anybody else, since he all but blocked out the sun.

Flanz had just been a prospect member of the Bandidos, the lowest rung on the club's ladder, for six months.
His lowly status meant he was required to be on call for
round-the-clock errands like fetching hamburgers and
cigarettes or chauffeuring full members like Big Paul. Pro-

spective members like Flanz generally performed such grunt work without complaint, in hopes that they too would someday be allowed to wear a "Fat Mexican" patch on their backs to announce that they were full members in the second-largest motorcycle club in the world, behind only the Hells Angels.

Given their difference in rank, it made sense that Flanz had the chore of driving Big Paul to the emergency club meeting at Wayne (Weiner) Kellestine's barn in tiny Iona Station (population 100) in rural southwestern Ontario on the evening of Friday, April 7, 2006. Club meetings were called "church," "holy night," "the barbecue" or "dinner," and attendance at this particular gathering was mandatory, much to Big Paul's chagrin. Weiner Kellestine's barn was a couple hours' drive from the Greater Toronto Area, where most chapter members lived, and Big Paul was only attending because senior members had made it clear that if he didn't, he would likely be kicked out of the club.

The York Regional Police surveillance team had been quietly tailing Flanz and Big Paul for almost four months, since shortly after a man walking his dogs in neighbouring Durham Region on December 8, found the body of a small black male bound, gagged and badly burned in a forested area near the York-Durham Region Line. The grisly corpse was all that remained of small-time drug dealer Shawn Douse. The reason Flanz and Big Paul were on the police radar was a simple one: the last time Douse was seen alive, he was stepping out of a cab late on the night of Tuesday, December 6, to attend a party at a townhouse in Keswick owned by Flanz.[2]

In many respects, Goldberg Flanz seemed an unlikely target for a police surveillance crew probing a particularly grubby and violent murder. With his shaved head, goatee, pirate-styled hoop earring and muscled-up football line-man's physique, Flanz looked intimidating enough. However, if you stopped to look into his eyes, the tough-guy effect quickly evaporated. Once you saw his smile and his eyes, his bruiserish appearance seemed nothing more than a carefully constructed persona, much like the performance of his namesake—the professional wrestler Goldberg. He was only playing tough.

Flanz was the rare Toronto-area outlaw biker who didn't have blue-collar roots or a trade that involved soiling his hands. In real life, he had far more money and social status than his biker mentor, Big Paul. Flanz's father, Leonard, was a senior partner in a prestigious Montreal law firm, specializing in insolvency cases, while Goldberg ran a small computer consulting business that provided on-site technical support to companies. While most of the Ontario Bandidos didn't qualify for credit cards and lived on the brink of having their cellphones cut off, Goldberg owned a couple of properties, one for his real family and another as a hangout for his Bandido friends. His "Goldberg" nickname was a not-so-subtle reminder that he was Jewish, which also made him an odd fit in his circle of friends in the outlaw biker world. It was hard to think of any other Jews in Canada's outlaw biker world, but there were hardcore anti-Semites, including the man they were going to visit that night, Weiner Kellestine, who once ran a gang called the Holocaust.

Weiner Kellestine was under two lifetime weapons bans, but remained an enthusiastic collector of Nazi memorabilia and military weapons, including machine guns, pistols, bayonets, knives and explosives. He encouraged rumours that he was a biker assassin by signing his name with lightning bolts resembling the insignia of Adolf Hilter's *Schutzstaffel,* the Nazi murder squad more commonly referred to as the SS. Lest that not be unsettling enough, Kellestine surrounded himself with skinhead white supremacists and once cut a massive swastika onto his farm field with a scythe. He ran a business called Triple K Securities, a not-so-subtle nod to the initials of the Ku Klux Klan. Triple K offered "complete electronic privacy," "telephone taps," "home intrusion alarms," electronic sweeps for hidden recording devices and "discreet professional service." When he gave Goldberg a business card, Kellestine wrote "SS" on the back with his phone number.

Many members of the Bandidos are considered by police to be criminals, but there was no sound business purpose for Flanz to be cozying up to the Bandidos. Truth be told, the Toronto Bandidos may have had the ambition, but most of the profitable crime was being committed by members of other groups, who worked hard at being criminals. Part of Goldberg Flanz's appeal to the Toronto-area Bandidos was that they could borrow money from him. The attraction the Bandidos held for Goldberg was harder to define. He might be a whiz with computers and have solid business sense, but he saw himself as more complex than that, and something about the dangerous image of an outlaw motorcycle club appealed to him in a way he himself couldn't fully understand.

Aside from Kellestine, most of Goldberg Flanz's GTA biker buddies didn't have a problem with the fact that he was a Jew. They might have cringed, however, had they read his profile in an Internet chat room, where he looked for love under the code name BigDaddyRogue. At the very least they would have teased him mercilessly had they read how he wrote, using horrible grammar and spelling: "If you are stong [*sic*] enough to love you have more strength then most. I have that strength, the will, and the confidence to give what I expect in return. IM a diehard romantic who beleives in giving all of HImself when he finds that somone special." He went on to describe himself as "a strong Man" who was searching "for something most seem to have forsaken . . . true love." He didn't exactly describe himself as an outlaw biker, but came close, writing, "This Man comes with a Harley." He also said in the online profile that he believed in happy endings, writing of himself, "He is a romantic diehard who still believes in finding His fairy tale."

There was no record of his friend and mentor Big Paul Sinopoli also being a diehard romantic, unless one counted an enthusiastic love affair with large plates of food and biker brotherhood. Big Paul was thirty years old, but still lived with his folks in a basement apartment of their ranch-style home, set among a thicket of trees in Jacksons Point, north of Toronto.

No one could remember Big Paul ever having a long-standing girlfriend, or any friends at all, for that matter, apart from other bikers. He was chummy with a few local Hells Angels, but kept this quiet, as Bandidos and Hells Angels were supposed to be mortal enemies. A one-time security guard and salesman at a sporting goods store, Big Paul dabbled in selling drugs, but didn't make enough money at it to move out into a place of his own. Those who knew him appreciated his quick, easy sense of humour and apparent absence of ego. Those qualities made his bulk less threatening, and some women who knew him called him "the big teddy bear." Once, he pointed to a black Bandidos T-shirt that was tightly stretched across his abdomen, smiled broadly and asked biker cops who were standing nearby, "Does this make me look fat?"

Privately, Big Paul was extremely insecure about his massive weight, estimated at somewhere on the hefty side of four hundred pounds. He had been teased about it since his childhood, when he emigrated to Canada from his birthplace of Argentina. He had occasionally talked wistfully about returning to South America to rediscover his roots, but his more immediate concern was shedding a couple of hundred pounds to stave off what seemed to be an inevitable heart attack.

Although Big Paul was a full member of an outlaw motorcycle club, he wasn't particularly interested in motorcycles, and still hadn't paid off his second-hand Harley-Davidson. He was rarely seen on it, since it was in no better shape than Big Paul. Perhaps he also knew he would look like a bear in the circus riding it. While Big Paul didn't love motorcycles, he revelled in his version of the biker lifestyle, which offered massive men like himself the prospect of respect, in addition to ridiculous nick-names like "Tiny" rather than the "Fatso" or "Hey you" they might hear in the outside world. A Bandidos patch had a way of covering over some pretty glaring imperfections. As fellow club member Glenn (Wrongway) Atkinson noted, "How many guys that weigh four hundred pounds get laid that often?"

That evening, Goldberg Flanz, Big Paul and the police surveillance team snaked their way south down Highway 404, west on Highway 407, and then onto Highway 401. When the Infiniti pulled close to the town of Milton, north-west of Toronto, the York Regional officers peeled off, leav-ing the pursuit to a team of five officers from neighbouring Durham Region. Those officers were in a minivan and tow trucks and took turns travelling in front of and behind the Infiniti, making them hard for the bikers to pick out, even if they had been looking.

The surveillance team lost sight of the Infiniti for almost half an hour, before finding it again at an Esso sta-tion just west of Woodstock at 9:30 P.M. The bikers were none the wiser, and when the officers spotted Goldberg once again, he was talking with two other men. A police officer pumped gas into his tank nearby as the two men got into a silver Volkswagen Golf. Flanz didn't bother to fill his tank, as he also drove away. The Volkswagen was already familiar to the Durham Region officers working on Project Douse, and they knew it was registered to Luis Manny (Chopper, Porkchop) Raposo, a full-patch mem-ber of the Toronto chapter of the Bandidos, who grandly called themselves the No Surrender Crew. Chopper was with another man they would later learn was Giovanni (John, Boxer) Muscedere, Canadian president of the Bandidos Motorcycle Club.

Chopper Raposo was a different sort of biker than Big Paul or Goldberg Flanz. Even though he was considerably smaller than the other two men, his eyes could take on a glassy, crazed quality, and at those times he looked like a man who would shoot first, and often. Chopper Raposo could be painfully polite and respectful, especially on the phone, but whenever he was photographed in biker social settings, he always seemed to be grinning dangerously and giving someone the finger.

It was a hard-edged image for a forty-one-year-old who still lived at home with his parents, in the upper floor of their brick home in Toronto's Kensington Market area. With its big-screen television, glass chandelier, full bathroom and kitchen, Chopper's place seemed like a tony urban loft, and it didn't hurt things that his parents paid for his motorcycle insurance as well. Chopper was a good-looking man, and there had been a number of women in his life, but none rivalled his mother for strength or love, although no one would dare call Chopper Raposo a momma's boy.

Raposo held the rank of *El Secretario*, or secretary-treasurer, of the club's Toronto chapter, the only full chapter of the Bandidos in Canada. Despite his druggy demeanour, there was no doubt that he took Bandido club business extremely seriously—and personally. That night, his briefcase contained club paperwork, including a membership list with the nicknames of all of the No Surrender Crew, as well as "Taz" and "D," referring to Michael Sandham and

Dwight Mushey of Winnipeg. There was also a chart showing who owed what in terms of club dues, and a printout of an insulting email he had recently received from Taz Sandham, president of the probationary Winnipeg Bandidos chapter. Also in Chopper's briefcase was a loaded sawed-off shotgun, which looked a lot like a pirate's oversized pistol. Club rules forbade such weapons at "church" meetings, but some instinct told Chopper he was justified in carrying hidden and deadly firepower this night.

Boxer Muscedere had agreed for the meeting to be held at Kellestine's barn, even though it was an inconvenient drive for the Torontonians. The No Surrender Crew didn't have a clubhouse to call their own, and Kellestine had pushed hard for the meeting to be held in his barn. Boxer and Kellestine had been friends for almost a decade, and Boxer was loyal to a fault where his friends were concerned. In Boxer's world view, Kellestine was his brother, warts and all, and nothing trumped brotherhood. Boxer could sense Kellestine was tense about something, but didn't seem too concerned. Kellestine was often tense about something. Unlike Chopper Raposo, Boxer went unarmed to the farm that night.

Somewhere west of Woodstock, Chopper got a call on his cellphone from Cameron Acorn, another chapter member, who was in jail at the Central North Correctional Centre in Penetanguishene, north of Toronto, awaiting trial on robbery charges. A wistful Acorn asked Raposo to send him a picture of himself "cruising, giving the finger."

When Raposo agreed, Acorn told him he loved him.

"I love you too," Raposo replied, and then laughed. "I

love you even though we haven't written. We're lazy cock-suckers." Raposo passed the phone to Muscedere, saying, "Talk to Boxer."

"I love you, bro," Boxer said.

In the biker world, too many "love you, bros" is often a sign that something nasty is in the wind, but Boxer was not about to ruin the jovial mood with worries or accusations. They were all adults. They didn't need to be reminded of the power of words of love, especially for those who are plotting betrayal. "I hear disturbing news, but I love you," was all Boxer said. At this point, it would have been wholly natural for Acorn to inquire what the disturbing news might be. Instead, Acorn let the statement hang in the air, as if he had already divined the problem and didn't want to press things further. It's a cardinal rule that an outlaw biker is supposed to support his president, but Acorn kept quiet that night about any unsettling rumours of upheaval he may have heard, and Boxer didn't press him. Instead, he offered fatherly advice to Acorn, who, at twenty-six years of age, was twenty-two years his junior. Boxer sounded like a concerned coach as he advised the young biker to make productive use of his time behind bars. "Don't become like those deadbeats in there."

Acorn then asked them to remember him and write him letters: "I'll call you guys next weekend. Make sure Chopper doesn't forget about that picture."

"I'm gonna fucking tape it to his forehead," Boxer laughed.

In the few minutes that they spoke, Acorn said "Love you, bro" to Boxer and Chopper thirteen times before he finally hung up the phone. Not once did he offer a warning to the men he called his brothers.

For a time, the Infiniti and Volkswagen seemed to be travelling in tandem through the dark towards the farm. Then they separated, and the police surveillance team stayed with Flanz's Infiniti. They suspected the Volkswagen was dropping behind them, in the type of counter-surveillance often used by more organized outlaw biker clubs. But they couldn't do much except drive on.

West of London, the Infiniti turned off Highway 401 onto Iona Road, past the Cowal-McBride Cemetery and then left down the dirt road called Aberdeen Line, to the rusty iron gate in front of number 32196. A stone gateway with a BEWARE OF DOG sign opened onto the potholed driveway to Kellestine's dirty white farmhouse. It would have been next to impossible for the visitors to see the electric fence that ringed the property, and there was no evidence that Weiner Kellestine's farm actually housed any livestock. There were no more than a few trees along the laneway, as Kellestine had cut the rest of them down years before, so that no one could creep up on him. It was after nightfall now, and the only movement on the unlit laneway up to his farmhouse came from shadows in the moonlight.

Up near the house, inside a second chain-link fence that stood eight feet tall and was topped with barbed wire, were the rusty shells of a half-dozen old cars and an equally rundown shed, garage and porta-potty. Behind them was the unpainted barn, and it was too dark to see the wall that had been painted with a white circle that enclosed a white fist in chain mail grabbing a lightning bolt from the sky. It was the symbol of Kellestine's old gang, the Annihilators, and if the barn had been better lit, the police surveillance team might have seen that the lightning bolt was in the shape of the jagged SS emblem so loved by the Nazis. The old farmhouse might have been charming in the hands of someone else, but Kellestine's presence gave it a sinister, hillbilly-gothic feel. In a window facing the laneway was a sign welcoming visitors with the words, "Believe in Life after death? Trespass and find out."

The land around the Kellestine farm was too flat to provide much of an observation spot, and police had no warrant to lawfully enter the property anyway. The Durham team had been following Flanz off and on for months, and they didn't want to be seen and compromise their operation. They pulled over on a darkened lane a couple of kilometres away and waited in the troubled silence. They weren't biker cops and didn't know Kellestine's history of membership in outlaw motorcycle gangs. Nor had they heard the local folklore, of bodies that had been buried in nearby fields in the night after summary executions by Weiner Kellestine.

A few minutes behind Chopper Raposo's Volkswagen was a tow truck driven by George (Pony) Jessome. Beside him sat George (Crash) Kriarakis, the Bandidos' Canadian national secretary, or *El Secretario*. At age twenty-eight, Kriarakis was the second-youngest member of the No Surrender Crew. He had no criminal record, and wasn't involved in typical biker sidelines like selling drugs, running strippers or acting as muscle for hire. His dramatic

nickname of "Crash" may have rung with typical biker bravado, but it came from his day job as a tow truck driver,
not from outlaw deeds or misdeeds. His choice of dog was
decidedly unbikerish as well: Crash was the affectionate
owner of a snow-white teacup bichon frise.

Crash clearly didn't have the inner sadness or anger
or self-loathing of some bikers, and it was easy to think
that his club membership was no more than a youthful
phase. Inside the club, it was a given that he would attend
Sunday dinners with his family. Despite plenty of chances
to carouse with strippers and biker groupies, he invariably shunned them for the company of his wife, Diane. To
those he truly trusted, Crash sometimes confided that he
wanted to quit the Bandidos altogether, in order to spend
more time with Diane. They had been married for less
than a year and she was the type of smart, loving, successful woman many of the other Bandidos could only dream
about meeting themselves. Those Bandidos who thought
about such things considered Crash and Diane to be soul-
mates.

Crash's driver for the evening, Pony Jessome, was a fellow tow truck driver who lived out of a dirty white trailer
behind a chain-link fence in the yard of his employer,
Superior Towing of Etobicoke. Although he was a full
member, Pony didn't actually own a working motorcycle,
which wasn't unusual in the Toronto Bandidos. At fifty-
two, Jessome also seemed a little old, and a lot sickly, for
the biker life, and he didn't talk much about how he had
been diagnosed with a terminal form of cancer. He wasn't
looking for sympathy, just the opportunity to sip a beer

in the corner of a room in the final stage of his life, surrounded by men he could call brothers.

Also on the road that evening en route to Weiner Kellestine's farm was a Pontiac Grand Prix carrying Mike (Little Mikey, Mikey T) Trotta and his close friend Frankie (Bam Bam, Bammer) Salerno, the Toronto chapter president. Tiny as they were, the Bandidos had two overlapping hierarchies, with Boxer above Bam Bam, and holding the national presidency. It sounded grand, but there were plenty of titles and a dearth of members. Trotta, a full Bandidos member, worked as a used trailer salesman, and went home each night to his wife and two-year-old son. He had been with the club for about eighteen months, and still didn't really look like a biker. With his wisp of a goatee, Little Mikey looked more like the type of person you'd see keeping score at a coed slo-pitch game.

His friend Salerno was a man with plenty of vices and inner conflicts, many of which were detailed in his criminal record, which included more than thirty convictions for offences like fraud and theft.[3] At least one friend traced his troubles back to his childhood, when his parents split up. His father ran a successful car dealership north of Toronto and was eager to set him up in business, but Bam Bam preferred to try to find his own way. His early efforts at self-discovery in outlaw biker clubs had been less than impressive. He had been kicked out of the Loners Motorcycle Club for heroin use, and once he accidentally burned down the Loners' clubhouse when he fell asleep while he was supposed to be standing guard and tending the wood stove.

The Bandidos gave him a fresh start in the outlaw biker

world, but he almost blew that too, once getting suspended for non-payment of dues. He often talked with his wife, Stephanie, about getting out of the club and the outlaw biker life altogether. Bam Bam and Stephanie were celebrating the birth of their first child just a month before, a son they'd named Mario, and Bam Bam had never seemed so happy. He was forty-three years old, and they had wanted a baby for years, but he told Stephanie it wasn't easy to leave. "Do you think this is like a bowling club?" Bam Bam asked her. "Do you think I can just walk away?"

He had been deathly afraid, since the birth of his son, because whenever things went well in his life, they always seemed to be followed by a sickening crash. In the months before his ride to Kellestine's, he'd had the chilling feeling that he didn't have much longer to live. He took out an insurance policy on his life and counselled Stephanie that it was his wish that she remarry, should he meet an early death. He carried a .32 pistol as protection against the nameless threat that dogged him, but he couldn't have been too worried that night, as he left it on the back seat of his old BMW back in Oakville before catching a ride with Little Mikey.

Only a three-quarter moon lit their way as they drove up the laneway. Somewhere in the dark, Kellestine's German shepherd, Kisses, was barking. At 10:15, Goldberg Flanz called Boxer and repeated that he was going to approach the farmhouse first. Flanz was eager to prove he had the balls to deserve his full-membership patch. The other vehicles would enter the farmhouse area in ten-minute intervals, once Goldberg determined the coast was clear. They might all be biker brothers, but they were also dangerous men, and their host was the most dangerous of all.

As he made the first approach in the dark to the farmhouse, Goldberg told Boxer he was keeping his cellphone on. He wanted Boxer to keep his phone on too, so he could listen in for potential trouble. Boxer okayed the plan, but he cautioned Goldberg that it might be best to wait for them outside the farmhome. For some reason, cellphones never seemed to work inside Kellestine's farmhouse. Boxer didn't say that much of its interior resembled a shrine to Nazism, but did say Goldberg could expect some troubles.

"You're going to have some bad reception over there, so you might have to stay outside," Boxer said. His friends would later debate whether these words referred to the bad cellphone reception in the area or troubles from inside the farmhouse. Whatever the case, Boxer's voice sounded uncharacteristically nervous on what threatened to be the longest—and last—night of his life.

PART II

BOXER'S BROTHERHOOD

CHAPTER 2

Bandido Nation

What are these
So withered, and so wild in their attire,
That look not like the inhabitants o' the earth
And yet are on't?
MACBETH, ACT 1, SCENE 3

There are only two types of people,
those who are brothers and those who are not.
HANDOUT TO PROSPECTIVE BANDIDOS MEMBERS

The oldest member of the No Surrender Crew, James Albert (Ripper, Rip, The Old Troll) Fullager, didn't attend the meeting at Wayne Kellestine's farm that night. He remained at home, too sick with cancer to make the two-hour drive, oblivious to the looming betrayal of the men and principles the veteran biker held dear.

Most days, Ripper could be found inside his home in Toronto's east end with his glasses on, reading *Time* magazine or *Reader's Digest* and looking like a particularly rumpled, weather-beaten grandfather. Keeping him company in the house were his common-law wife and her ex-husband, whom he treated like a brother; his chihuahuas Chi Chi and Harley (the latter shared a name with Bammer Salerno's collie and numerous sons and pets of one percenter bikers); and a menagerie of pet birds. For all their outwards disdain of the world around them, outlaw bikers like Ripper Fullager are essentially conservative people. There was a Union Jack and a picture of the Queen, and sometimes also an Ulster flag, in Ripper's home, and the only day when there wasn't a small Canadian flag outside the front door was on July 1, Canada Day, when Ripper replaced it with a particularly large one. Ripper was a diehard fan of the Maple Leafs and Argonauts, while he despised American politics and the National Football League. He wouldn't consider attending a Buffalo Bills game, even if he were somehow allowed to cross the border.

But Ripper was no ordinary grandfather. Other bikers loved to gather in his kitchen or backyard, sip a beer and listen to his gruff Ripper-speak, in which sleeping was "horizontal Zs" and a con man was someone with "slidey fucking ways." In a world where many people nursed petty grudges, Ripper believed in speaking his mind and dealing with things out in the open. Typical Ripper advice was "Say what you've got to say and be done with it." He wasn't rich, but supplemented his pension by dealing hashish out of his home, and made an effort to pay his bills on time and in full. When a Toronto utilities worker suggested on the phone that Ripper was a deadbeat because he had fallen behind on a bill, Ripper called up a biker known as

"Big Gus," who stood about six foot six and weighed in the neighbourhood of four hundred pounds. Ripper and Big Gus visited the utilities worker in person at his office, and the harsh, bureaucratic tone softened dramatically.

Ripper was a biker historian of sorts, although he didn't write things down for outsiders to study. It might be a stretch to call Ripper a sage in outlaw biker society, or a relic from the golden age of motorcycle clubs, but it wouldn't be an outright lie either. When he held court in his backyard, by a painted wooden sign with a huge "Fat Mexican" logo, Ripper was a living, breathing, cussing, drinking touchstone of things that seemed important and lasting in his world.

Fullager was just six years old in 1947, a defining year in outlaw biker history. That was the year a group of motorcycle riders who called themselves the Pissed Off Bastards of Bloomington rioted after the arrest of one of their members for disorderly conduct at a race in Hollister, California. In an attempt at public relations, the president of the American Motorcycle Association told the press that 99 percent of motorcyclists were law abiding.[4]

The Pissed Off Bastards gleefully seized on the quote, and soon began sporting diamond-shaped patches on their leather jackets and vests that read "1%er." It was a proud declaration that they were among the one percent of motorcyclists who chose to live outside the law as free men, as opposed to the spunky and often annoying lawyers and students and housewives who just revved up their bikes on weekends. They were delighted to be the kind of people other riders went out of their way to say they were not. In the end, the name "Pissed Off Bastards" must have seemed inadequately menacing or disgruntled: a year after the Hollister riot, they changed their name to the Hells Angels. The name had been used before, but never as successfully as a branding exercise.

Fact and fiction played off each other in the movie *The Wild One*, which was based on the Hollister riot and came out in 1953, when Ripper was an adolescent. From their very beginnings, biker gangs have fascinated mainstream society, and director Laslo Benedek, producer Stanley Kramer and screenwriter John Paxton attempted to capture that early outlaw biker spirit on film. When Marlon Brando's sullen character is asked, "What are you rebelling against?" he has a petulant reply ready at hand: "What have you got?" But for the true outlaw biker, the real hero of *The Wild One* isn't the Brando character, but rather Chino, played by Lee Marvin. Chino is based on the real-life figure of Willie (Wino Willy) Forkner of the Boozefighters Motorcycle Club, and he rides an American Harley-Davidson, not a British Triumph like Brando. The Boozefighters' rallying cry was "Jesus died so we could ride," and it wasn't meant entirely as a joke. (And, just to be clear, the club adopted its name because its members loved their booze too much, not too little. Forkner founded his new club after he was kicked out of another group, called the 13 Rebels, for boozing a little too much. Today, the Boozefighters bill themselves as "a drinking club with a motorcycle problem.")

The Bandidos were conceived in the summer of 1965, when former U.S. Marine Donald Eugene (Mother) Chambers and a group of fellow dockworkers with military backgrounds began hanging around together after work and on weekends in the fishing village of San Leon, in the Texas Gulf area, and clattering around on their bikes. The next summer, Chambers began organizing regular meetings and calling his group the Bandidos.

Marketing and reality converged again the summer after that, when Frito-Lay came up with the idea of promoting their corn chips with an animated character named the Frito Bandito, conjured up by Frederick Bean (Tex) Avery, the legendary creator of Bugs Bunny and Daffy Duck. Avery enlisted the talents of Mel Blanc, the voice of Bugs Bunny, Daffy Duck and Porky Pig, among others, to sing out, to the tune of the traditional Mexican folk song "Cielito Lindo": *Ay, ay, ay, ay / I am the Frito Bandito / I love Fritos corn chips / I love them I do / I love Fritos corn chips / I steal them from you!*

Protests from Hispanic groups pushed Frito-Lay to make their Bandito character less threatening and stereotypical, and they stripped away his holstered six-guns, trimmed his stubble, flattened his gut and softened his heavy Mexican accent. Within a few years, Frito-Lay gave up altogether and bailed out on the advertising campaign.[5] Meanwhile, Chambers and his biker buddies revelled in the very qualities that made Hispanic people cringe. Chambers appropriated the troubling little bandit, and consciously made the bikers' version even more offensive, adding a scowl, an overhanging paunch, and placing a pistol in one hand and a machete in the other. They stitched his likeness onto the backs of their leather vests, lovingly calling him "The Fat Mexican." There was something both menacing and childlike about the image, and the same might be said for members like Ripper Fullager and Boxer Muscedere.

Many of those early "one percenters" were working-class veterans of World War II who had seen the very worst of civilization's dark side while in uniform and balked at the idea of blending quietly into the sweeping conformity and consumerist ebullience that marked civilian society at the war's end. (The Hells Angels' red and white colours were drawn from the Third Pursuit Squadron of the United States Army Air Force, the Bandidos' red and gold from the Marine Corps.) To them, a return to postwar life often meant being swallowed up into anonymous factory jobs, and they cringed at being nothing more than cogs in machines. Unable or unwilling to reintegrate into the society they had left behind when they enlisted, they found some of the brotherhood they had known on the battlefields of Europe and the Pacific in the ranks of the colourfully named motorcycle clubs that sprang up across the continent. A unifying glue to all such groups was a common quest for rebellion, adrenalin and the company of other men who felt alienated from their own society.

And, of course, a shared love of Harley-Davidsons. They may be loud, heavy and cripplingly expensive; they may be uncomfortable and they may vibrate so much that they will eventually rattle themselves apart. But if you want to give the world around you the finger, chugging around on a Harley is not a bad way to go about it. Deafening other motorists with a totally customized chopper is even better. At a time when industrialization threatened to emasculate the blue-collar worker, especially those stuck working shifts in factories, the Harley was a loud, public phallic symbol—seven hundred pounds of highly personal raw power growling between a biker's legs. Cars were seen as confining, and one of the Bandidos' first rules was that members were not to wear club colours inside a vehicle: "No colours in a cage."

Members of one percenter clubs are required to own a Harley-Davidson, and it can be off the road for a maximum of thirty days a year, or the member has to pay the club a five-hundred-dollar fine. One percenter bikers who are too large to ride a Harley—like Big Paul Sinopoli or gargantuan Paul (Sasquatch, Sas) Porter of the Hells Angels' Ottawa Nomads chapter—were expected to own one of the motorcycles nonetheless. Porter, whose weight was estimated to be in the range of four to five hundred pounds, maintained a Harley, while taking to the roads on a custom-welded machine, suitably braced to hold up his bulk. As a further sign of his commitment to the club, rules call for a probationary Bandido to pledge his Harley to the national office of the club for a year, to be forfeited if he grievously breaks club rules. In other words, if you don't have a Harley, you're not a real biker, and if you're not a real biker, you just lost your Harley.

Honda, Suzuki and Kawasaki produce lighter, faster motorcycles, but one percenters dismiss them as "rice burners" and "Jap crap." Honda spent millions of dollars in an attempt to defuse the outlaw stigma associated with riding a motorcycle by advertising, "You meet the nicest people on a Honda." One percenters countered with T-shirts with slogans like "Honda, Suzuki, Yamaha, Kawasaki, From the People Who Brought You Pearl Harbor" and "Fuck off, I've got enough friends."

Like many original hard-core bikers, Ripper Fullager was a veteran of the Canadian military, having served as a peacekeeper in Cyprus. He became a one percenter in the 1960s, during what might be considered a golden age of motorcycle clubs. Ripper could trace his personal biker ties back to 1960, when, as a teenager, he had helped design the crest of the Toronto Wild Ones (a gang with an obvious debt to Hollywood).[6] Back then, Ripper's apartment on Sorauren Avenue in Toronto's Parkdale district doubled as the Wild Ones' clubhouse. Somewhere on Ripper's body, in between his various tattoos, was a scar from a gunshot wound, suffered back when he was a member of Johnny Sombrero's Black Diamond Riders. The scar was a souvenir of a nasty scuffle, when the BDR tried, unsuccessfully, to level the clubhouse of the rival Canadian Lancers (an outlaw club with rather less flair than most when it came to choosing a name). It was also a badge of honour, not so different from the Fat Mexican patch he sported on his back in his final years.

Clubs were like a new home for Ripper, who grew up in a string of foster homes in the Greater Toronto Area, from Highland Creek to Port Credit. He was already a member of the Black Diamond Riders when he got word that his younger sister was being mistreated in a foster home. Years later, Ripper liked to tell how he arrived at the foster home with Sombrero and a collection of other BDR members. They carried furniture and liquor from the house out onto the front lawn, where some members sat on the couch and treated themselves to complimentary drinks while others roared back and forth on the lawn on their motorcycles. When the foster father finally arrived, Ripper liked to recall, the young biker bloodied his nose and told him to expect far worse if he didn't start treating his little sister better.

There was another story involving his family, about something that happened far later, that Ripper clearly didn't enjoy telling. It was the story of how he rode his Triumph motorcycle across the continent to British Columbia in search of his father. He apparently found him somewhere on the streets of Vancouver, but the meeting didn't go well. Ripper rode back to Toronto, unimpressed, and the two men never spoke to each other again. He would search out his family in other places now, and find comfort in an association of brothers from different mothers. When Ripper Fullager called a fellow biker "bro"—for "brother"—it was his highest term of endearment.

Club membership means riding in a pack and brotherhood, and nothing is more important than brotherhood in the one percenter world. The Bandidos' founder, Donald Chambers, summed up a biker's priorities unambiguously: "Look at your brother next to you and ask yourself if you would give him half of what you have in your pocket or half of what you have to eat. If a citizen hits your brother, would you be on him without asking why? . . . Your brother isn't always right but he is always your brother."

It would be difficult to exaggerate the allure of joining a band of powerful, swaggering brothers, or the seduction of finding a new identity in the one percenter ranks. Fullager was called "Ripper" for the way he loved to rip about town on his Harley (though it can't have hurt that his nickname echoed the initials etched on gravestones: R.I.P.). Only those who knew him particularly well were allowed to call the five-foot, six-inch biker with the bushy grey beard and ponytail "The Old Troll." Such nicknames provided a symbolic break from a biker's past—Chambers became known as "Mother" for founding the Bandidos. His successor as Bandidos national president—or *El Presidente*—Ronald Jerome (Ronnie) Hodge, was called "Stepmother." In a club list of Ripper's Toronto Bandidos from January 2005, not one member is listed by his full name, but rather by nicknames like "Bammer," "Rooster," "Irish," "Beaver," "Crow," "Lucky," "Grumpy," "Wrongway" and "Pony." The Canadian Bandidos had two "Choppers" at one point, while the Loners in Woodbridge, north of Toronto, had both a "Fat Mario" and an "Ugly Mario." Bam Bam Salerno had toyed with the nickname "Babar," but it was ultimately deemed too cutesy for an outlaw biker. Identification with nicknames is so strong that many club members don't even know their brothers' birth names—they aren't considered relevant.

But it takes more than a truculent attitude and a Harley-Davidson to be deemed fit to wear a diamond-shaped "1%er" patch over your heart. Every family has its rules, especially families consisting entirely of brothers. While outlaw bikers love to portray themselves as rebels and rugged individualists, they have, ironically, developed a highly structured world, with a strict, feudal chain of command. Members can vote on important issues, but their president—called "Supreme Commander" in some clubs—embodies the club's beliefs and has absolute veto power. One percenter rules became so all-encompassing that they didn't just govern how club members live but also how they die. For example, suicide is forbidden under the official Bandido by-laws—"Any Brother who commits suicide, WILL NOT be allowed to have a BANDIDO funeral."

Many one percenter rules are explicit, and even intrusively trivial. Handouts to prospective Bandidos spell out the expectations that will be placed upon them, should they be chosen to enter the one percenter life. Monogamy, of a sort, is promoted: members are cautioned not to steal another member's "Ol' Lady," for example, and to be careful of associating with women who were close to other clubs.

A prospect Bandido was expected to adhere to a code of conduct nearly as complex as the rules governing the behaviour of samurai in feudal Japan:

- If two or more Patchholders are having a private conversation, don't approach them within earshot, especially if they are talking with a Patchholder of another club. If you need to interrupt, put yourself in a place of visibility and wait to be acknowledged. If it's important that you interrupt, ask another Patchholder to break in for you.
- Always show respect to a Patchholder of another club. Even though he's with another club, he's earned his patch; you haven't.
- Never ask when you may be getting your patch.
- Never call a Patchholder "brother." He's not your brother.
- Never call a Patchholder of another club "brother." He's not your brother either.
- At an open function, never turn your back to a Patchholder of another club. This is not so much for safety reasons, but as a show of respect.
- Never be quick to walk up to a Patchholder of another club in a public setting, even if you know him well and the clubs are on friendly terms. If you want to greet him, walk up slowly and wait for him to indicate that he wants such a public display to take place. He may be on some club business and may not want to give the general public the impression that the clubs are on such friendly terms. If he looks like he's

going to ignore you, accept it and keep your distance. The best approach is always to wait for them to come to you, and to let everyone else see that.

Some of the principles sounded almost Biblical, in an earthy, biker way: "You should be aware of the 'Golden Rule' of conduct while travelling in club circles: If you give respect, you'll get respect. If you act like an asshole, you'll be treated like one."

Other rules can be harder to articulate, particularly for men more comfortable expressing themselves with actions rather than words, but for the true one percenter, the so-called 110-percent one percenter, the code of the biker brotherhood is a complete ethical norm that can be substituted for the rules mainstream society lives by. Mario (The Wop, Mike) Parente, the former national president of the Canadian Outlaws Motorcycle Club, had simple, strong reasons for wanting to be in a one percenter motorcycle club when he joined the Satan's Choice at age eighteen: "Be free. Ride the bike. That's it. And being with a bunch of individuals that wanted to help each other out." For Parente, this meant he refused to aid the police or prosecutors no matter what, preferring to settle his problems by himself, as he and his peers thought a man should. He maintained his silence with authorities even when a mob tried to shoot him in Hamilton, Ontario, and when a prisoner in jail there tried to gouge out his eyes with a sharpened toothbrush. "It's my—how do you say?—my honour," Parente said. "My respect. I wouldn't be able to look in the mirror if on my account somebody was in jail. I wouldn't be able to look in the mirror and feel good about myself."[7]

To a true-blue one percenter, the biker ethos is something rigorous, if often pretty rough-hewn. When one club member pleaded destitution and kept mooching money from fellow members, Ripper counselled another in the Bandidos' fold, "Maybe you can punch him in the face, for the principle." It was one thing to scam or sponge off a "civilian," but quite another to treat another Bandido with such disrespect. As Ripper explained, "When you become a one percenter, or are trying to be, you don't do it that way." As for subterfuge or scheming, such things were beneath the dignity of a guy who lived by the biker code. When asked to keep a secret from someone else in his club, Ripper could be expected to snort derisively and reply, "What am I? A fucking high school girl?"

Frank (Cisco) Lenti, perhaps the closest thing to a member of the one percenter aristocracy, has ridden a Harley as a member of the Satan's Choice, Rebels, Diabolos, Outlaws, Loners, and a club he founded himself, called the Bastone (named for the suit of clubs in an Italian deck of cards), as well as the Bandidos. Asked to define what it means to be a one percenter, Lenti replied, "To me, it means that you're a man . . . How else could you explain a one percenter? When the shit hits the fan, you don't back down. When you back down, you're a punk."[8] You give people what you sense you'll receive from them. Treat a true one percenter with respect, and you can be assured of courtesy in response; threaten him, and you can count on a hard fist to the face, a thumb to the eye, or worse. Being a one percenter, to men like Lenti, doesn't mean that you are of society's outcasts. To the contrary, it means that you have gained entry into something very exclusive.

Nothing represents the exclusivity of a one percenter club as boldly as the "patch," the lurid symbol a biker wears on his back. Like heraldic emblems or regimental insignia, the patch stands for the brotherhood a club member is expected to live and die by. It may be no more than a few square inches of cloth, but it embodies the meaning of a one percenter's life.

Each member is allowed only one, smaller patch for a significant other, showing that she is his "property." There are also strict rules outlining when and where that "old lady" can wear the patch. "If she rides her own bike it is NOT to be worn while riding with or around Patcholders [sic] or Prospects," the by-laws explain. "It should not be worn in public without her old man in view." No one, not even an outlaw biker's wife, can touch his patch, and his colours, the term for the assortment of crests and patches on his jacket or vest, are not to be left unattended in public. Bernie Guindon of Oshawa, a founding member of the Satan's Choice of Canada and later a Hells Angel, once flew into a rage when a fellow club member left his colours on the back of a chair at a club function, even though everyone in the hall was a Hells Angel and the colours were only a few feet away. Wearing club colours could have the same effect as holding a cocked shotgun—it is just never a good idea to leave a loaded weapon unattended.

Banished members of one percenter clubs are expected to immediately hand in their patches and all paraphernalia bearing club crests, and to remove club tattoos from their skin, something that will be done—roughly and painfully—*for* them if they do not act quickly enough. Asked how a former member's tattoo would be forcibly removed, Hells Angels turncoat Steven Gault of Oshawa replied, "I've heard everything from a cheese grater to burning it off to a knife." Others in the club would dismiss the comments as nothing more than the utterances of a rat, and not to be believed.[9]

A biker's status can be determined by a quick glance at his colours, just as a soldier's rank is manifested in stripes on his or her uniform. True to the clubs' military roots, a sergeant-at-arms is appointed to enforce the rules, and sometimes to supply weapons to club members. The rigid club structure was considered essential for an individual member's survival.

In similarly militaristic fashion, non-members are referred to as "civilians," marking a radical distinction between one percenters and the world around them. As a Bandidos handout for new members states: "There is never any doubt which comes first. Though most things in life can let him down, he knows that his club and his brothers will always be there because he is always committed to being there himself . . . A Patch-holder has the attitude that there are only two types of people, those who are brothers and those who are not."

But this relationship to the "civilian" world is not as simple as the club rules make it seem. Just as these groups devoted to the wildest forms of freedom contentedly submit to military-style rules of conduct, they also fret over what mainstream society thinks of them, even as they insist they don't care. The names they give themselves boldly flaunt their taste for violence and mayhem, yet they also go out of their way to claim they are simply misunderstood motorcycle enthusiasts and unfairly persecuted free spirits.

One of Ripper's functions in the No Surrender Crew was to coach prospective members on how to be taken seriously by mainstream society, even while disrespecting its laws. He passed out notes to prospective Bandidos that explained that their displays of brotherhood should bring enhanced status from the general public, who might otherwise disdain or ignore them:

> Those who are less informed only see the surface. They see the vigilance of mutual support. They see the potential danger of invoking a response from a well-organized unit that travels in numbers and is always prepared for confrontation. They know that one can't provoke one club member without being answerable to the whole club, and that such an answer is a point of honour that must come, to the last man. The type of respect that this generates is one born out of fear . . .
>
> It stands to reason that cultivating a relationship with these people is important, and to be perceived by them as "Biker Scum" would not be advantageous to the club. We therefor [sic] will conduct ourselves as upstanding citizens in every way . . . "good neighbours" so to speak. The goal is to be admired by the general public rather than feared.

Even as he advises new members to be good neighbours, he can't help celebrating the dangerous glory of a quasi-military unit that makes it a point of honour to respond to any confrontation with heedless violence.

A one percenter does not necessarily think of himself as against the law; he just wants to be outside it. He may not feel that he has to obey society's rules, but he is under no obligation to break them, either. In its most philosophical form, the one percenter ethos seems to offer a courageous man the opportunity to wrestle with the meaning of right and wrong on his own terms, without mainstream conventions muddying the waters.

But not many bikers are philosophers.

If there was a single day when the flirtation between liberals and outlaw bikers expired, it was December 6, 1969. That's when the Rolling Stones gave a free concert at the Altamont Speedway in northern California. Hells Angels were hired as security for the event, and their payment was beer. When Angels hurled full beer cans into the rowdy audience and stabbed to death a young African-American man who had been carrying a gun, many writers took it as nothing less than the symbolic death of the 1960s youth culture. As they saw things, peace and love had been clubbed senseless with pool cues.

But outlaw bikers had never really been liberals, or members of the youth culture. In the 1960s, as memories of World War II faded somewhat, just as popular culture began its love affair with peace, some bikers began sewing patches onto their vests and jackets with the Nazi SS symbol. Others wore "FF," for "Filthy Few." The Bandidos came up with a similar patch of their own, with the words "Expect No Mercy" inside a circle. Angels would sometimes say that a Hells Angels Filthy Few patch-wearer was the first to arrive at a party and the last to leave. A police explanation for Filthy Few, SS and Expect No Mercy patches was much more sinister: they were awards for bikers who had committed murder for the club and gotten away with it.

Chambers originally hoped that his Bandidos would be folded into the Hells Angels, who didn't have a chapter in the Texas Gulf area. That blending of the clubs never happened; instead, the Bandidos expanded throughout Texas, and into Alabama, New Mexico, South Dakota and Washington State. In those early, exuberant years, members increasingly collided with the law as they became more involved in motorcycle theft, running prostitution rings and drug dealing. Chambers himself went to prison in 1972 after he and two other Bandidos forced three drug dealers to dig their own graves in the desert before shooting them and shovelling the dirt back into the holes. The drug dealers' capital offence was selling the Bandidos baking soda and calling it methamphetamine. It didn't take long for people in the drug world to realize it wasn't smart to cheat a guy wearing a Fat Mexican patch. It also wasn't wise to cut in on their drug-dealing turf. Some bikers like Frank Lenti were fundamentally opposed to drugs, but others leapt into the drug trade with both boots. The brotherhood that made clubs closely knit also made them near-perfect networks for crime.

As the Bandidos Nation grew, they became friendly with the Outlaws, another one percenter gang, who laid claim to being the oldest outlaw club in the world. Founded in 1935 in the Chicago area—in a bar along the storied Route 66—as a racing, touring and partying club, they were strongest in the Midwest. It was common knowledge in the outlaw biker world that the Outlaws and Hells Angels didn't mix well, as was reflected by the Outlaws' saying of ADIOS (Angels Die In Outlaw States). Soon, there were also dangerous rifts between the Hells Angels and Bandidos.

By the early 1980s, there was plenty of pressure from authorities, after a federal judge was assassinated and an assistantU.S. attorney was shot and wounded by Bandidos in San Antonio, Texas. Long gone were the days when authorities considered the Bandidos nothing more than a collection of sometimes surly good old boys who guzzled beer and smoked pot down by the Texas docks.

The Bandidos Nation, as they liked to call themselves, changed forever in 1983 with the visit of Arthur Mark (Snodgrass, Snotgrass) Spencer of Sydney, Australia's Comanchero Motorcycle Club to Texas to pick up Harley-Davidson parts. Soon he was meeting with the Bandidos' national president—or *El Presidente*—Ronald Jerome Hodge and the Texas Bandidos, and the conversation included plenty of talk about international brotherhood.

Spencer and Hodge shared military backgrounds and a heightened need for a sense of fraternity in the civilian world. Hodge had served in the Marines, while Spencer had enlisted in the Australian navy at age seventeen, the minute he could escape from an orphanage.

Some Texas Bandidos saw business opportunities in a closer association with the Australians. The Texans were increasingly involved in selling amphetamines, and noted that P2P, one of the main ingredients necessary for its manufacture, was legally available in Australia. The Bandidos had twenty-eight chapters at that time, all of them based in the United States. The Australian Comancheros had just one chapter, formed in 1966, which was very much a reflection of their leader and founder, Scottish-born former serviceman William George (Jock) Ross. A sign inside the Comancheros' clubhouse bluntly encapsulated their guiding philosophies: "If it's white, sniff it / If it's female or it moves, fuck it / If it narks—kill it."

In time, a rift grew between Ross and Spencer, as one might expect between an overbearing parent and a naturally rebellious child. The Comancheros split into two chapters in August 1983, with one headed by Ross and the other by Spencer. But it was the new affiliation with the Bandidos that set the stage for real strife between the former friends. In November 1983, Spencer told Ross that he and fellow members of his chapter were quitting the Comancheros to sew on the Fat Mexican.

Things were ready to explode by September 2, 1984—Father's Day in Australia—when the new Bandidos chap-

ter planned a motorcycle-parts swap meet in the parking
lot of a tavern in the Sydney suburb of Milperra. Ross
and his Comancheros crashed the event, decked out in
club colours and armed with guns, machetes and metal
pipes. There were some five hundred people in the parking lot when the shooting started. When it was over, three
Comancheros, three Bandidos and a fourteen-year-old
girl lay dead and fourteen ambulances were needed to
haul away the wounded. What began as a quest for brotherhood ended in bloodshed and betrayal, a pattern that
was painfully familiar in the one percenter world.

For Spencer, the sense of loss was too much to bear,
and he hanged himself in custody in April 1985. He knew
that one percenters were forbidden from taking their own
lives, but he slipped the noose around his neck anyway.
"I want my bros to not think of me as weak, but as tired
of fighting for the well being of the club," he wrote in his
suicide note. "I have failed maybe I don't know. But I do no
[*sic*] someone will do the right thing for the club."

In 1989, the Bandidos gained their first toehold in
Europe when the MC Club de Clichy became the Mar-
seilles Bandidos. Two years later, the chapter's vice president was killed in a drive-by shooting, and a year after
that, eight Hells Angels were arrested for the murder. The
Bandidos Nation had gone international, but the cost was
steep.

CHAPTER 3

Canadian Push

That I essentially am not in madness,
But mad in craft.
HAMLET, ACT 3, SCENE 4

It was greed . . . They killed their own brothers. Money talks.
BIKER ENFORCER NORMAND BRISEBOIS
ON THE QUEBEC BIKER WARS

It's impossible to talk for long about Boxer Muscedere's Bandidos without noting the influence of the Hells Angels, the world's largest biker club. The Hells Angels planted a flag in Canada on December 5, 1977, when a Montreal-based gang called the Popeyes patched over—or switched allegiances—to the U.S.-based biker club. The move was aided by New York State Hells Angels, who stood to gain a tighter drug-trafficking network north of the border. It also offered the American Angels a firm base in Canada for further northern expansion. In time, other strong clubs in Canada might join the Angels too, falling like dominos as the club went global.

For the Popeyes, the patchover promised dominance over other local clubs with whom they had been warring for drug turf. Since the Angels were international and careful about whom they let into their ranks, the Quebecers could be confident that they wouldn't be ripped off in drug deals by their new brothers, even if they didn't know them personally. There was also the power of the Angels patch. The Popeyes may have been a tough, sometimes murderous group, but for anyone looking to intimidate a rival, it's hard to beat the Angels' winged-skull logo and its implication of far-reaching, international muscle.

Among the founding members of the Canadian Hells Angels was five-foot, six inch, 135-pound Yves (Apache, The Mad Bumper) Trudeau, who also became the first Canadian to sew a Filthy Few killer's patch onto his leather jacket. (He preferred the old-school look of a leather jacket to the more modern vests.) The bantam-sized biker wasn't particular about his victims; he killed enemies, total strangers and fellow Angels with an equal disregard for human life, as long as the price was right.

In time, Apache Trudeau was recognized as too unruly and dangerous for even the Angels. He narrowly escaped murder himself, when members of his Montreal North chapter were invited to a "church" or club meeting at the Lennoxville clubhouse, home of the Sherbrooke Hells Angels, only to be slaughtered by their brothers. The bodies of the five visitors were wrapped in sleeping bags, weighted down with barbell plates and dumped into the club's unofficial graveyard, the dark, cold waters of the St. Lawrence River. Such is the fate of bikers accused by their brothers of excessive drug use, violence and stealing money from the gang. "With the values we had at the time, it was the only solution," the massacre's architect, Réjean (Zig-Zag) Lessard, would later say. Years later, an invitation to the Lennoxville clubhouse would still provoke a certain chill in even the hardest one percenter. Don't worry, the Quebec Angels would say in a display of dark humour, you don't need to pack a sleeping bag for the trip.

Many police officers speculated hopefully that the Lennoxville slaughter—and the police round-up that followed—meant the Hells Angels had hit the end of the road in Canada. Surveillance was cut and police priorities shifted. What happened next was a biker version of Darwinism, as the surviving Canadian Hells Angels morphed into something much more dangerous in the early 1990s. Under a new leader, Maurice (Mom) Boucher, the Montreal Hells Angels began working out in gyms and refrained from heavy drug use, especially crack cocaine or anything that involved the use of a needle. Boucher, who was himself a recovering drug addict, wanted his members to be loyal to the club, not to narcotics habits, and also realized that drug use made them weak and more likely to chat with police.

The revitalized, fitter Hells Angels pushed out from their old strongholds in the Montreal suburbs and into the city's downtown core, where there was plenty of money to be made dealing drugs. Under Boucher, the Montreal Hells Angels became big business, developing direct ties to South American drug suppliers. Before long, they invested with the Mafia as equal partners in massive cocaine and hashish shipments. Gone were the days when the Hells Angels in Quebec merely peddled other peoples' illegal merchandise or acted as muscle for hire.

There were fundamental differences between Mom Boucher's Hells Angels and the organization run by Vito Rizzuto, the most powerful man in the Canadian Mafia. Both groups moved cocaine and hashish for profit, but Rizzuto took the standard Mafia pose that he wasn't a criminal, just a misunderstood businessman. For years, Canadian mobsters even denied that there was such a thing as the Mafia, outside of Hollywood movies. Carmine Galante, a New York mobster who hid out in Montreal in the 1950s, once told a reporter, "Between you and I, all I do is grow tomatoes." Outlaw bikers take an entirely opposite tack. They wear uniforms to announce they don't respect the law and bluntly challenge authorities to catch them.

In downtown Montreal, some independent drug dealers tried to find a middle ground between the styles of the Mafia and *Les Hells* when they formed a club of their own, the Rock Machine, in 1989. It wasn't really a motorcycle club at all: members didn't have to own a bike to join. What brothers Giovanni (Johnny) and Salvatore Cazzetta sought to create was a cohesive confederation of drug-dealing groups, with a lower profile than bike clubs like the Hells Angels. Some Rock Machine members even committed the cardinal biker sin of riding Japanese sport bikes—faster, sleeker and more anonymous than Harleys.[10] Rock Machine members also chose not to wear leather vests or jackets emblazoned with gang crests and colours, since they didn't want to make themselves easy targets for police to photograph and identify. Instead, they sported diamond-studded gold rings with an eagle's-head design. "If you put patches on your back, it was like saying, 'Chase me, man,'" said Gilles (the Kid) Lalonde, an enforcer with the Dark Circle gang, a heavy-duty collection of experienced bikers who were aligned with the Rock Machine.

Still, early Rock Machine members were nothing if not cocky. They set up their bunker-like Montreal clubhouse just three blocks from the headquarters of the provincial police, the Sûreté du Québec, as if to taunt the cops. They invested ninety thousand dollars to buy the brick house and several times that amount to fortify and furnish it. On its inner walls, a few rules were posted. One forbade members from using cocaine, although they could smoke marijuana or hashish. Another rule was that members were expected to kick back a percentage of the money they made from drug dealing to the club. Yet another rule was that biker "brothers" inside the Rock Machine must be respected. In those early, hopeful days, there was also a sticker on the wall referring to a group the Rock Machine founders still considered friends: "Hells Angels Forever."

Johnny Cazzetta knew Hells Angels boss Mom Boucher from the 1980s, when they were members together in a small bike gang called the SS. Others in the Rock Machine had golfed and gone to boxing matches and strip clubs with Boucher and Vito Rizzuto. They assumed their friendships would continue with the birth of the new club, and at first, things were chummy, as Rock Machine members were happy to deal drugs supplied by the Hells Angels.

In the early 1990s, Rock Machine members could strut into the Castel Tina, a strip club on Jean-Talon Street East in Montreal that was run by Rizzuto's close associate, Paolo Gervasi. There, they would sit at their own private table on the main floor, where Vito Rizzuto sometimes dropped by to sip grappa and talk business. Through Gervasi, Rizzuto hired bikers connected to the Rock Machine to do security work and dirty enforcement jobs. The pay scale for trashing a bar so that it went out of business was between $5,000 and $10,000 cash, and the Mafiosi always paid on time. On a larger scale, Rizzuto was concerned about the growing power of *Les Hells*, but didn't want to go to war with them himself. It was in his interest to prop up the Rock Machine, to a point, while not angering the Hells Angels enough to provoke them. It was a delicate balancing act, but such brokering was Vito Rizzuto's forte, and he considered himself a mediator, not a gangster. In Vito Rizzuto's perfect world, the Rock Machine would be strong enough to blunt the Angels' power, but would also lack the clout to challenge his Mafia.

There wasn't widespread alarm when the Hells Angels killed a couple of Rock Machine members in the early 1990s. But a few more murders brought the chilling realization that Boucher wanted all of the drug profits from downtown Montreal for his Angels, even if it meant killing off his former golfing buddies. In the opinion of Normand Brisebois of the Dark Circle, the bloodletting was unnecessary, as there were easily enough drug users to make all of them wealthy. While a philosopher might say that there was enough sun for everyone, drug dealers had their own expression. "As we say in the business, the apple pie was big enough for everybody," Brisebois later said. "It was greed . . . They killed their own brothers. Money talks."[11]

Within a few years, any pretense of fraternity between the Hells Angels and Rock Machine was washed away with blood. By the summer of 1997, there was a sickening regularity to the funerals in Quebec, as the body count approached one hundred. Each murder drove Boucher wilder, and he raved about his desire for hits on cabinet ministers, judges, journalists and prison guards, in addition to rival bikers. He revelled in the imminence of his own impending death, as he drafted funeral cards of himself perched on a Harley-Davidson.

But it wasn't a fair fight. The Rock Machine's Dark Circle hit squad was lethal, but was outnumbered almost five-to-one by the Hells Angels. "The Hells Angels were ten times more powerful and organized than us," Brisebois later said in an interview. "The Rock Machine was more like [just] drug dealers," Lalonde said. "They weren't much of an organized club. The Hells Angels was more like a big business."

The best the Rock Machine could hope for was a bloody standoff in a never-ending war, unless they dramatically altered the battlefield by enlisting powerful allies. Rock Machine founders Johnny Plescio, Fred Faucher and Robert (Tout Tout) Léger flew to Sweden to forge ties with Scandinavian members of the Hells Angels' arch-enemies, the Bandidos.

If anyone could go toe to toe with the world's biggest

motorcycle club, it was the Fat Mexicans. The Rock Machine leadership had been impressed by the fighting spirit shown by the Nordic Bandidos in their own very public war against the Hells Angels, which was fought not with fists and broken beer bottles, but with machine guns, grenades and rocket launchers. Eleven people were murdered and ninety-six were injured between 1994 and 1997. With friends like that, the Rock Machine might be able to turn the tide.

Young members of the Rock Machine were eager to patch their club over into the Bandidos' fold. Perhaps the lure of Bandido membership would help them recruit other young bikers. Or maybe the increased firepower would convince *Les Hells* to back off. As they attempted to pull closer to the Bandidos, the Canadians didn't give much thought to their new club's strict set of bylaws or their love of Harley-Davidsons. "They thought they would have more people join them to fight the Hells," Brisebois says. "I don't think it was anything else."

The centre of Bandido power remained in the U.S., and George (Bandido George) Wegers, who held the dual posts of international president and U.S. national president, visited Quebec in October 1997 to meet the suitors face to face. Wegers was from Whatcom County, Washington, well outside the Bandidos' centre of power in the Gulf states. Aside from Texas, the Bandidos also claimed Washington and Montana as their territory, meaning other clubs had to get their permission to set up chapters there. By Bandido standards, Wegers was considered liberal, which was a relative thing. It meant he stopped members from wearing racist patches and outlawed stealing from junior members or beating them without real cause. He also favoured international expansion, feeling that if an organization isn't growing, it's dying.

There wasn't time to say much more than hello before someone tipped off authorities and Wegers was ordered out of the country. On his way out, Wegers advised the Canadians to strengthen their relationships with American Bandidos, to win over their support. The Rock Machine's task would be to convince the Americans who ran the club that they were indeed outlaw bikers, and not just gangster drug dealers who occasionally roared about on motorcycles.

The topic of the Rock Machine cozying up to the Bandidos was high on the agenda when Canadian Hells Angels west coast officers met in November 1997. Club minutes recorded that they had a video of Wegers meeting with the Rock Machine. The Bandidos still had no chapters in Canada, but the Hells Angels were watching them with more than a little concern. The Bandidos weren't the only one percenters contemplating expansion.

Even a veteran biker cop would have gasped at the sight on Highway 401 in June 1993. Heading westbound into Ontario was a formation of Hells Angels, stretching back as far as the eye could see. Police tallied up ninety-four

Hells Angels and associates from junior affiliate clubs like the Satan's Guard, Rowdy Crew and Evil Ones. At the front of the pack, perched on one of his Harleys, was the club's national president, Walter Wolodumyr (Nurget) Stadnick. At his side was road captain David (Wolf) Carroll, who also wore a "Filthy Few" crest above his heart.

The bikers rode en masse to the resort town of Wasaga Beach on Georgian Bay, north of Toronto, where they were greeted by members of the Loners Motorcycle Club. Yellow tape was used to cordon off a strip club, some motels and cottages on the town's low-rent east side, close to the main beach and a half-dozen blocks from the Ontario Provincial Police detachment. Five dozen Harleys were parked in neat rows outside the club, where the establishment's regular sign was covered with a black flag featuring the Hells Angels logo. Anyone not invited by the bikers was ordered to stay on the outside of the tape. Among the privileged few allowed into the makeshift inner sanctum were strippers, who gamely climbed over the tape in high heels, carrying their costumes in plastic grocery bags.

Inside the yellow tape, Frank (Cisco) Lenti of the Woodbridge Loners posed for a picture with Stadnick and Carroll, the latter wearing a T-shirt bearing the slogan "Filthy Few Denmark" and two lightning bolts to underline the fact that he was considered a killer on two continents. The front of Stadnick's vest featured a rocker and the word "World," another reminder of the scope of his club. Both Hells Angels had their arms around Lenti, who sported a Loners T-shirt adorned with a Confederate flag. Wolf Carroll stared straight at the camera without smiling, while

Stadnick grinned and Lenti looked a little uncomfortable, like the meat in the Filthy Few sandwich. Perhaps, as the photo was taken, Lenti was thinking back a half-dozen years, to when he was in the Outlaws, a traditional enemy of the Angels. Back then, there were rumours that Satan's Choice members were plotting to murder him and another Outlaw, to impress the Hells Angels.

Things took an ugly turn later that weekend at Wasaga Beach. As is often the case in the outlaw biker world, as in more mainstream family squabbles, it was a small thing that threatened the attempt at civility. A senior British Columbia Hells Angel asked a Loner to get him a beer, and the Loner rudely suggested that perhaps the Hells Angel should get it himself. In about the time it takes to say "Molson Canadian," more than twenty bikers began pushing, shoving and telling each other to fuck off. Somehow, violence was averted, but the Angels seem not to have forgiven the insult. A year later, they flexed their muscles more effectively than they could have done in the bar, ordering the Loners to change their club patch, which featured a red Confederate flag. The Angels said the Loners' use of red made it too close to their own "death head" patch of a grinning, winged skull. The Loners complied, although some members privately bristled. Bristling publicly about the Hells Angels can be a dangerous game.

However, it would be another five years before the Red and White publicly showed their strength again in Ontario. The Loners' club "rodeo" north of Toronto in August 1998 promised a weekend of brotherhood, booze and bikes in the mud by Lake Simcoe. Members of the Para-Dice

Riders, Red Devils, Vagabonds, Last Chance and Satan's Choice clubs were in attendance, sharing laughs. Some bikers competed in a "slow race," in which the goal is to be the last to cross the finish line; riding a lumbering Harley as slowly as possible, without falling over, is no easy feat. In another test of skill, a biker would ride under a weiner, which dangled by a string, while a woman perched on the back of his Harley would try to bite it. The champion was the woman with the biggest chunk of weiner in her mouth.

The mood that summer weekend abruptly turned frosty when members of the Hells Angels Nomads chapter from Quebec rode in. Almost immediately, the Vagabonds club from downtown Toronto got on their bikes and left, obviously still not forgiving the Angels for the murder of club president Donald (Snorko) Melanson a decade earlier over unpaid cocaine debts. Like many others in small Ontario clubs, Melanson had been a partier, not a businessman, earning his nickname for the prodigious amounts of cocaine he could snorkel up his prominent nose. But not everyone rode off in protest. Some of the Ontario bikers were impressed with the Quebec visitors that afternoon by Lake Simcoe, and asked if they could take pictures of them, with their "FF" patches. The Angels complied, though they demanded that they be given the negatives once the film was developed.

That weekend's rodeo marked a turning point of sorts in the Ontario outlaw biker scene. Until *Les Hells* rode in, there had been a healthy social scene between varied Ontario biker clubs. Brotherhood, even between clubs, was more important than business. The existing clubs had also used their collective muscle to keep the Angels from squeezing in and dominating things. After the 1998 Loners rodeo, things were decidedly more tense. From that moment, it seemed as though every development in the biker world was seen through the lens of how it affected the Hells Angels. Bikers were expected to decide whether they were for or against them; the middle ground disappeared as the Red and White tide advanced. It was hard to escape the feeling that the sun was setting on a kind of golden age for Toronto outlaw bikers.[12]

That year, a half-dozen Quebec Hells Angels quietly moved into the Greater Toronto Area and made themselves visible by frequenting the area around Weston Road and Highway 7 in Woodbridge, north of Toronto. The Hells Angels were still courting the Loners, but it wasn't an easy relationship. The following summer, the Toronto-based Para-Dice Riders were the Hells Angels' preferred group.

In May 1999, Glenn (Wrongway) Atkinson received a fax at the collection agency where he worked, inviting him, Pietro (Peter, Peppe) Barilla and other notable Loners from the GTA to a party at the notorious headquarters of the wealthy Sherbrooke chapter of the Hells Angels in Lennoxville, about 140 kilometres east of Montreal.

Unknown to the Toronto-area bikers, there was a business agenda that drove the invitation. The Angels wanted to discuss the strained relations between the Loners and the Para-Dice Riders. The Angels were now close to the Para-Dice Riders and wanted the Loners to explain themselves.

Wrongway Atkinson and the Loners rode their Harleys through what the Angels considered enemy territory that was thick with Rock Machine members and arrived at the clubhouse in the middle of the night after wandering lost in the darkness. Locals they asked for directions shied away, afraid to become involved in the doings of the Angels and this group of menacing outsiders. Finally, a police cruiser pulled them over, and the cops offered to lead them to the compound.

What the Loners saw was completely beyond their experience of biker clubhouses. The Angels' headquarters are set on an eleven-hectare lot, situated defiantly on a hill atop the killing ground of the five Angel brothers, with 465 metres fronting the thoroughfare. Rather than retreat from the ground where their one-time brothers had been slaughtered, the Angels seemed to celebrate the grim deed and the reforging of the club that followed. The central, sprawling, multi-level building looks like a hotel on steroids. At the very pinnacle of the main building, above the bright red steel roof, a red flag emblazoned with the club's grinning winged-skull "death head" symbol flies like a Jolly Roger.

To get to its fortified front door, the visitors had to pass guard dogs, floodlights and burglar alarms. (Anyone approaching through the surrounding woods has to brave hidden bear traps.) At the front door, a biker politely but firmly told Atkinson and his cohort not to bring illegal drugs inside. "If you have anything like that, leave it in the hotel," he said in heavily accented English. "Do not bring it inside." Inside, a large room was like a nightclub, with loud techno music playing, a sharp change from the Lynyrd Skynyrd, Who and Led Zeppelin popular in Toronto-area clubhouses. Some of the older Angels seemed a bit annoyed at the sound, but it was clearly the playlist of choice for the younger, well-dressed, weight-lifter types that made up the majority.

Former national president Walter Stadnick greeted the travellers at the door, addressing Atkinson by his first name: "Hey Glenn, how are you doing?" The men had never met before, but, like any biker, Atkinson knew of Stadnick, who played the role of convivial host. "Our house is your house," Stadnick said, "except for one room."

The Ontarians had shown they were true bikers by making the trip from Ontario, despite the tiring ride and daunting destination. The biker wars with the Rock Machine were raging, and the Angels were themselves cautious about riding in public in their colours. So the Loners were treated with the respect one percenters show other true bikers, which included a well-stocked buffet of food and nubile off-duty strippers. The bar was as extensive as anything you'd see in a high-end nightclub, and one wall of a living room was entirely covered with a map of the world, with LED lights showing all of the Angels' 190 clubhouses from Oakland, California, to Auckland, New Zealand, from Costa Del Sol, Spain, to West Rand, South Africa. In the bathrooms were photos of mirrors with lines of cocaine. Around the pictures of the cocaine was a red circle, and another red line ran through it, the universal symbol not to do something. Bikers may be attached to the idea of doing whatever they want, but it can prove hazardous to want to do a line of coke in a bathroom owned by the Hells Angels.

All of the compound was spotless, even the two-storey garage, where there was a television, stereo, lifts for working on bikes and racks of replacement parts. The Loners were free to use whatever they wished. "Help yourself, just clean up when you're finished," an Angel told them.

A Quebec police study once found that Hells Angels in the province were shorter than the average male Quebecer. Perhaps the goal of the study was to support a hypothesis that the Angels laboured under a Napoleon complex, in which physically small men overcompensate for what they see as their own shortcomings with excessively aggressive, controlling behaviour. Whatever the case, Stadnick, who stood just five foot four, transcended the theory. Despite his compact frame, there was something undeniably huge about the man and the clubhouse where he played host. It was about big crime, big money, big stakes, big risks and big profits, and in this world, there was no one bigger than the lord of the Lennoxville manor, Walter Stadnick.

Stadnick was low-key and genial as he asked Atkinson about common acquaintances. But it quickly became clear to the Ontario bikers that their smiling host was not just making small talk. Stadnick knew exactly where Atkinson and other bikers in the GTA lived. He was privy to many intimate details of their lives, like the names and activities of their girlfriends and spouses. He didn't say such things in a threatening manner—he didn't have to. The very walls of the Lennoxville clubhouse spoke of the possibilities of murder.

Moreover, Stadnick was sitting with henchman Wolf Carroll, himself a living, breathing threat to anyone at cross-purposes to the Angels. Carroll was genial and soft-spoken at first. Then his tone changed as he asked the visitors about Gennaro (Jimmy) Raso, the Loners' president. He wanted to know why Raso hadn't come to Quebec with the others. His tone was insolent, as if goading the visitors to defend their absent leader. As Carroll's anger built, he called Raso a pussy and a man with no balls, and it became easy to envision Raso as more fish food at the bottom of the St. Lawrence.

It was understandable that the Hells Angels coveted the GTA, where there were more than five million residents and no Angels or Bandidos chapters to provide them with illegal drugs. The Angels bristled at news of a party at the Loners' Richmond Hill clubhouse in June 2000 that was attended by about five dozen "machinists," the Loner nickname for the Rock Machine. Machinists outnumbered Loners two-to-one at their own party, and it was clear something was brewing between the two clubs that the Angels wouldn't like.

The Hells Angels' pointman in Toronto was Dany Kane, a junior member with the Angels' Quebec support club, the Rockers. Unbeknownst to the Angels, Kane was working as a paid police agent, and his notes for that month stated that Wolf Carroll wanted him to kill members of the Loners named Jimmy and Peter, who were considered the club's top leadership and muscle. (Jimmy and Peter were certainly Raso and Peppe Barilla.) Kane was given photographs of club members to identify his targets, and paid a visit to a former Loner who had moved on to the Para-Dice Riders. Shortly afterwards, Kane told his police handlers that Carroll aborted the murder plan, saying that too many people knew about it.

But the Hells Angels' real business was not with small clubs like the Loners. There was only one real challenger for turf in Canada, and that was the Bandidos.

On November 28, 2000, Richard (Dick) Mayrand of the elite Nomads chapter of the Hells Angels in Quebec telephoned Wegers of the American Bandidos, identifying himself only as "Dick from the Hells Angels." Mayrand needed to meet face to face to sort some things out. He couldn't enter the United States because of his criminal record, while Wegers had already been expelled from Canada because of his biker ties. They agreed to sit across from each other at a picnic table straddling the Canada–U.S. border in Peace Arch Park, between Blaine, Washington, and Surrey, British Columbia. The cross-border park had been named "Peace Arch" as a tribute to lasting amity between the two countries. That day, however, things looked anything but peaceful as the senior bikers sat face to face, each flanked by bodyguards, with Mayrand sitting in Canada and Wegers in the United States.

The agenda for the meeting was short enough, but it was not likely the two leaders were going to reach a consensus. Mayrand wanted to discuss troubling reports that the Bandidos were about to grant membership to Canadian members of the Rock Machine, while Wegers gave little sign that he was inclined to see things from his rivals' point of view. For over an hour Mayrand talked, while Wegers sat still and listened, poker-faced.

He delivered his response three days later: the equivalent of giving Mayrand and the Hells Angels the finger. At a banquet hall in Woodbridge, the Bandidos granted probationary status to forty-five members of the Rock Machine. The ceremony was so rushed that no Fat Mexican patches were ready to hand over to the new members. Even though there were no crests, the message was clear: the Bandidos Motorcycle Club had now officially planted its flag in Canada.

Wegers probably didn't expect the Hells Angels in Quebec to accept the provocation meekly, and in late December of 2000 they loudly answered back. Some 168 members of established Ontario clubs—including the Satan's Choice, Para-Dice Riders, Lobos, Loners and Last

Chance—arrived at the Hells Angels' bunker-like club-house in Laval, outside Montreal, in sport utility vehicles. A van brought an industrial-strength sewing machine to stitch the Angels' grinning skull patch onto the vests of the new members, who gave up their old clubs for member-ship in the world's biggest biker gang. The club dropped its standard probationary status for new members, which they usually depended on to screen out the unfit and potential informers.[13]

With that massive stitchery, the Greater Toronto Area was suddenly home to the largest concentration of Hells Angels chapters in the world—a half-dozen within an eighty-kilometre radius. It was an audacious gambit, but it seemed to have come straight out of Sun Tzu's *The Art of War*. "Generally in war the best policy is to take a state intact; to ruin it is inferior to this," that classic book of mili-tary strategy, written in the fourth century B.C., advises. Whether Nurget Stadnick or other senior Hells Angels were taking a page from Sun Tzu's playbook, or just responding to a slap in the face from the Bandidos the only way they knew how, they had pulled off a major coup. The Red and White had finally captured the Greater Toronto Area, with-out a shot being fired.

CHAPTER 4

Brothers by Different Mothers

I am bound to thee forever.
OTHELLO, ACT 5, SCENE 2

You're my brother. I should be able to trust you.
WAYNE (WEINER) KELLESTINE TO FELLOW BIKER
GLENN (WRONGWAY) ATKINSON

Ortensia and Domenico Muscedere were expecting their first child when they stepped off the ocean liner in Halifax in 1957, ready to start their new life in Canada. They had left behind their home in Vicalvi-Pozzuoli, Frosinone, in the central Italian region of Lazio, near Rome. They chose Canada to start their family after hearing it was ripe with opportunities for people like themselves who weren't afraid of hard work. First, they stayed in Windsor, Ontario, with relatives who had sponsored them. Two years later, they moved with their first-born, Giovanni (John), to Sarnia. Baby Giovanni was the first Canadian in the family.

John's younger brother Cesidio (Joe) remembered

John as a high-spirited but protective child. "He always made sure I stayed out of trouble, did my homework and never missed school. All the things he didn't do," Joe later recalled. "One memory that stands out in those days was in Grade 3, when we saw John run by our classroom door being chased by two nuns, one carrying a strap. I came to find out later that John, about to get the strap, moved his hand and Sister hit her own thigh."

Protestant bullies gave young John an even tougher time than nuns with poor strapping skills, and they would often chase him for sport. One day, when John had enough of running, he turned and faced his attackers, swinging back at the biggest of the gang. It wasn't an artistic success as far as fights go, and there were plenty of tears. But by the time it was over, the Protestant bullies had decided it was best to find someone to pick on other than the future president of the Bandidos.

His parents learned some English through their family-run restaurant, but Italian remained the language of their home and John was often teased for his Italian accent. Eventually, John managed to hide it with a mumble that sometimes sounded like his mouth was full of marbles, making him sound somewhere between Sylvester Stallone's character from the Rocky movies and Don Corleone from *The Godfather*. Years later, a friend from his early childhood years said she felt that John didn't really want to open up verbally, and be mocked more by others, and so he came up with his mumble, which covered his accent and gave him an air of mystery. "It was almost like he really didn't want to share his voice with people," she said.

In time, John developed a tough outer facade, but those who really knew him felt he was just actively cultivating a persona, to protect the vulnerable Giovanni inside. "He didn't really want to be somebody anybody could look down on," the friend said. "He wanted respect." It wasn't just his accent that he wanted to hide from others. It was also his aversion to being dominated or controlled. "His real voice was not commanding enough," she said. "His real voice was actually kind of soft."

When John was twelve, the Muscederes moved again, this time to Chatham. By now, the family included a younger sister, Lucy. It was while living in Chatham that he found he loved spending time in the gym. And he loved boxing most of all. In the ring, you were judged by your heart and your actions, not the sound of your voice. Training was almost like a religion for him, and Joe shared his passion, driving in a car to accompany him as he did his roadwork. In John's first amateur fight, the guy in the other corner looked big and threatening, but John was able to knock him out of the ring and onto a ringside table, just like something you'd see in the movies. His family would never forget the thrill of watching John stand up to the tough-looking opponent and actually win. He went on to fight tougher guys, and had his share of victories, but John's most memorable bout was a loss. He ventured into the ring with a four-time national champion, and though he wasn't the guy with his gloves in the air when the fight was over, promoter and ringside announcer Harry Marshall called it the best amateur fight he had seen in twenty years.

In time, John's friends came to know him as "Boxer," "Prize" and "Prize-fighter." Even after he stopped fighting, as family obligations replaced training, he still carried himself with an athlete's easy confidence. And whenever he could, he enjoyed helping others train and being in the corner for them when they fought, feeling fully alive and armed with nothing more than two fists and a lot of heart.

Boxer wasn't a complicated man, but he was a strong one, having developed a simple ethos of hard work and honesty from his family and the gym. He saw that life might not be fair, but it could be great nonetheless. As Boxer grew into manhood, he mirrored his parents and always worked. For twenty years, he showed up for his shifts at a brake factory in nearby Tilbury, and was grateful for the opportunity, even if the actual work was mind-numbing and repetitive. He couldn't understand how some men could simply lie around and sponge off others. Such men weren't really men at all.

In time, Boxer married, then divorced, then married and divorced again. He loved his children and stepchildren dearly and couldn't understand how some men, even after a bad marriage, could just walk away from their child support obligations as if their children didn't exist. Such men didn't deserve his respect. He had his own pet phrase for them: "A cumshot that should have stayed in the toilet."

He chose pit bulls for pets, and thought they were a good influence for his children. A child who studies a pit bull isn't a child who is going to be picked on, the way he had been when he was little Giovanni Muscedere, running from the Protestant kids in the schoolyard. Pit bulls are also fiercely loyal. Those who knew Boxer were struck by the absolute devotion he displayed to those he considered his friends. Some also worried that this quality would someday prove to be a fatal flaw. John sometimes blindly defended others who didn't deserve his friendship, just because he felt they needed his protection. "He was all or nothing," said an old Chatham friend. "If he liked you, he liked you, and if he didn't like you, you knew."

Just as boxing is a combination of disciplined hard work and adrenalin, so was Boxer's life. While the factory represented confinement and security, a brand new 1984 Honda V65 he bought promised freedom on two wheels. He had never ridden a bike until the day he bought one, but in his first year with the Honda, he rode it thirty thousand kilometres, the equivalent of almost five trips across Canada. "On many occasions he would return home absolutely frozen but with a big smile on his face," Joe later recalled.

In later years, Boxer Muscedere didn't talk much, even to close friends, about how he had drifted into motorcycle clubs in the late 1990s, when he was forty years old. Boxer was a tough man, but, even years after the breakup with his wife, it was difficult for Boxer to tell that story of how he had gotten down on his hands and knees and begged her to stay for the sake of their children. She left him anyway, and not long afterwards, Boxer became a one percenter biker, riding an orange Harley Fat Boy and surrounding himself with a second family of biker brothers like Wayne (Weiner) Kellestine. He saw clubs as representing camaraderie and a love of motorcycles, and what could be wrong with that? People who didn't leave meant a lot in Boxer's world, and he found it easy to forgive their sins. As Boxer rose through the outlaw biker ranks, he didn't talk much anymore about his marriage failures, and when he did open up to a friend, he confided that watching his wife go felt a lot like dying.

Boxer's quest for brotherhood often brought him to the property at 32196 Aberdeen Line on the outskirts of tiny Iona Station, which sits on flat and fertile farmland just off Highway 401, about a half-hour's drive west of London, Ontario. Wayne Kellestine moved there in 1982 from Thorndale, a short hop east of London on the 401, near the hamlets of Cobble Hill, Silvermoon and Friendly Corners. Kellestine's new residence cost just fifty thousand dollars, and included 1.11 hectares of property. That made it far too small for real farming, but it did promise quick highway access and a measure of privacy.

Kellestine was almost a decade older than Boxer, and gladly acted as a mentor to the tough, trusting newcomer to the outlaw biker world. Kellestine might seem strange and quirky, but he also knew how to laugh, and he played the role of benevolent big brother to the hilt. In time, the Kellestine farm became something of a sanctuary for Boxer, a world away from his workaday, factory life. And if Kellestine resented his visitor's genuine sense of honour, he kept his feelings hidden.

For many years, Boxer's new friend had been the source of lively whispers in Elgin County. It was hard not to notice that bodies began turning up in shallow graves in the farm fields around Kellestine's property shortly after he moved in. From a distance, the dirty white two-storey clapboard farmhouse that was home to Kellestine, his first wife and first daughter looked much like almost every other home around Iona Station, including the property on Hogg Lane where liberal economist John Kenneth Galbraith was born in 1908. (It was believed that the second *g* in Hogg had been added as an attempt at refinement, before the name was later changed altogether to Thomson Line.)

In time, the yard of the Kellestine property began to reflect its owner. It was far more unkempt than most farms in the area, with a half-dozen cars in the yard, including an ancient Chevrolet Monza coupe and an even older Packard sedan. An in-ground swimming pool had been added, but in time it was so neglected that a thicket of trees sprouted out of the deep end.

The *real* difference between the Kellestine home and other neighbouring farms, however, would have been hard not to notice for anyone who ventured inside. On the main floor was a shrine of sorts to violent losers. There were Confederate and Nazi flags, and a massive collection of Nazi memorabilia that included helmets, arm bands, daggers and eagles. For some reason, he also hung up a Union Jack. Displayed prominently on the wall was an old cavalry sword. Hidden inside the walls, under a sink, even under shingles on the roof, was a vast arsenal of pistols and rifles that Kellestine couldn't display in the early 2000s, when he was under two court-ordered, lifetime firearms bans. For some guys, one lifetime ban is not enough.

Despite the odd furnishings, there was a certain normalcy to the farmhouse. The kitchen was nicely refinished in unpainted pine, and the downstairs family room had an attractive floor-to-ceiling stone fireplace. In the basement, partially buried in the clutter, were a pool table, sauna and cedar hot tub. Family photos marked the way up the stairs to the second floor, where one bedroom was just what you'd expect for a little girl: pink walls, Shrek and Homer Simpson posters and a Cat in the Hat rug. In the master bedroom, there was a four-poster bed covered with a quilt. It gave off a certain cozy, bed-and-breakfast feel, if you could get past the military gas mask on the bed, the wonky toilet with a sign warning users not to flush and the legions of wood ticks.

There was no hay or farm equipment inside the large wooden barn. Instead, Kellestine had packed the place tightly with junk—mattresses, fridges, a broken pop cooler that had once been used in a corner store, an obsolete television set, a riding lawn mower, and a dirty yellow ball cap with the letters KKK embroidered across the front. On the walls of the barn were moderately risqué pictures of women from calendars, two Confederate flags, a chair with the crest of his beloved Montreal Canadiens hockey team and a flag with the legend POW-MIA. In the main room were several stolen signs, one of which read PROVINCIAL OFFENCES COURT. Close to the barn was a porta-potty, and by that, a wooden shed, its doorway covered with a stiffened old piece of burlap. Inside, under a tarp, was an old motorcycle, the only one on the premises of the longtime outlaw biker.

To his neighbours, Kellestine exuded a gruff, folksy good humour. Others in the community, with no criminal ties, didn't find it a scandal to share the occasion beer with him at a nearby hotel. He was also a hit at the fair in the nearby hamlet of Fingal, where he once bought up all of the baked goods in sight, then returned to heartily praise the baker. "Where's Rose?" he had boomed amidst the church ladies and grandmothers, who clearly enjoyed the attention of the swaggering, pie-loving biker.

Until Weiner Kellestine's arrival, the few times Iona Station had made the newspapers were in profiles of its best-known son Galbraith, who had long since departed for Harvard University. In 1967, when Galbraith published his bestselling *The New Industrial State*, Kellestine was an unruly local eighteen-year-old, kicking off an adult criminal record with a spree of violence that brought him three convictions for assault and assault causing bodily harm. By 1978, when Galbraith was drawing the ire of conservative economic theorists with his newly published books *The Age of Uncertainty: Points of Departure* and *Almost Everyone's Guide to Economics* (with Nicole Salinger), Weiner Kellestine was being fingered to police by a thug as the killer of Toronto clothing store owner John DeFilippo. The story was that Kellestine had posed as a pizza delivery man in Toronto, bursting in and opening fire when the door was opened. The exact reasons for the murder were unclear, perhaps known only to the killer and the victim. Whatever the case, police didn't have enough evidence to prosecute Kellestine for the killing.

The Outlaws Motorcycle Club expanded from the United States into Canada in the summer of 1977, the same year the Hells Angels absorbed the Popeyes. When an Outlaws chapter appeared in East London, Kellestine had hopes of becoming a member, but soon was written off as too unstable and too visible to police to keep in the fold. Even a gang named after its contempt for the law figured Kellestine was too unruly. His personality was bizarre enough when he was straight, and far, far worse when he was pumped full of cocaine or methamphetamine.

Perhaps Kellestine had read that his hero, Adolf Hitler, kept himself pumped up in the final stages of World War II with a combination of caffeine and methamphetamine. Maybe Kellestine had also read reports that the nostrils of the Führer were swabbed regularly with cocaine and that chocolates dosed with methamphetamine were widely distributed to Nazi airmen and tank crews to torque their aggression and courage. Whatever the case, like Hitler, Kellestine would have known that amphetamines killed his fatigue and jacked up his alertness, flooding him with waves of grandiosity and euphoria. After a time, however, such highs were overtaken by jags of suspiciousness, irritability and persecution, not unlike the characteristics displayed by a paranoid schizophrenic.

When it was clear he wasn't getting an Outlaws patch, with its skull and crossed pistons, Kellestine founded a small outlaw motorcycle club of his own called the Holocaust. The Holocaust's defining symbol was a white skull and a lightning bolt, like those on the uniforms of Hitler's Waffen-SS. Its members included Brian Beaucage, a bad man from a good farm family, whose frightening mood swings were blamed in part on his enthusiastic use of steroids and speed. Beaucage's life ended on March 3, 1991, in a boarding house on Lansdowne Avenue in Toronto. He was almost beheaded by a fellow club member after a night of cocaine and porn, in what became known in biker circles as "forty hacks with an axe."[14]

By 1988, the Holocaust had fizzled and Kellestine became president of the Annihilators, a motley but tough motorcycle club in the Outlaws' orbit. Their headquarters was a dirty pink-brick building on Mondamin Street in a residential area of nearby St. Thomas. Its windows were covered with steel plates, and security cameras recorded activity at its doors. Locals used it as a "booze can," where they could play pool, buy stolen goods like jewellery, tools and camera equipment, and often get cheap cigarettes from the nearby Chippewa of the Thames reserve.

Toronto Outlaw Frank (Cisco) Lenti considered the place little more than a glorified chicken coop, made worse by Kellestine's annoying habit of sprinkling roofing nails on its parking lot and the nearby road. The idea was to flatten the tires of curious police officers; the problem was that Kellestine tended to forget exactly where he had dropped the nails, which meant he often also flattened the tires of many of his guests and customers. It became common practice for bikers to slowly walk the parking lot, looking for nails, before venturing inside for a drink.

The expression the Outlaws used for men like Kellestine was "heat score," meaning someone who continually drew police attention. In 1989 they were reminded why it made good sense to keep Kellestine out of their ranks, when he wandered about a London motorcycle show drunk and spat in the face of a police officer. Things only got worse when Kellestine and another biker attempted to flee in a limousine, dragging the off-duty officer alongside the limo. Kellestine dashed into the nearby Outlaws clubhouse on Egerton Street, five minutes from the central police station. Once things settled down, there was another assault conviction on Kellestine's record, unwanted attention for the Outlaws from the police and no real gain for anybody.

In June 1991, Kellestine's name was in the news after a well-known local biker, Thomas Harmsworth, was dropped off at St. Thomas-Elgin General Hospital by four of his friends, bleeding from five bullet wounds. Luckily for Harmsworth, a heart surgeon was in the hospital and available to patch the gaping hole in his chest. Not long afterwards, Weiner Kellestine was charged with attempted murder, and he faced the very real prospect of his first stretch of serious prison time. The case collapsed when Harmsworth, who was on parole from Collins Bay medium-security penitentiary in Kingston, refused to cooperate with police. In fact, Harmsworth, an old-school one percenter biker, even provided Kellestine with an alibi. No motive for the shooting was ever given, by the shooter, victim or witnesses, as Harmsworth took the outlaw biker code to its extreme, siding with his would-be killer rather than authorities.

Kellestine was back on the police radar shortly after September 19, 1991, when Ingersoll Police Constable Scott Rossiter was fatally shot with his own service revolver in the parking lot behind the Ingersoll police station, about a half-hour's drive east of Kellestine's farm. Immediately, a manhunt began for David Kenneth (Sparky) O'Neil, a handyman who fixed and sold motorcycles out of a weather-beaten barn. Police cautioned O'Neil's biker friends that they faced serious criminal charges themselves if they helped the fugitive hide out. Police even took to the airwaves, featuring the case on the popular American television show *Unsolved Mysteries*.

O'Neil annoyed Kellestine and the rest of the Annihilators by showing up at his Aberdeen Line farmhouse and their St. Thomas clubhouse while on the lam, running the risk of drawing a firestorm of police heat. In January 1992, the hunt for O'Neil ended at a shallow grave in a cornfield near Kellestine's farm. The body had several bullet holes in the head, and Michael Simmons, the younger brother of local Outlaws president Andrew (Teach) Simmons, had no doubt—although he didn't witness the murder himself—that O'Neil had been killed for bringing unwanted attention to the Annihilators. "He wouldn't stay put," Michael Simmons later said in an interview. "So they put him on ice."[15] Kellestine might have felt lucky the Outlaws didn't treat him the same way.

Shortly after O'Neil's murder, Kellestine and three other Annihilators members began wearing new patches on their leather club vests with a lightning-bolt/SS design, indicating they were underworld killers. Word drifted through the area that it was Weiner Kellestine who had directed police to O'Neil's body, and that his reward was a pass on some outstanding charges. The rumours may have been false, but they were effective nonetheless.

For his part, Weiner Kellestine basked in the belief that he was a bona fide underworld killer who had risen above the law. When writing to fellow bikers, Weiner Kellestine now proudly signed his name, "Your brother always, Weiner, 1%er, SS."

Still, it would be naive to blindly accept Kellestine's claim to have executed a wayward biker, when so little of what he said was remotely credible. While Boxer was as honest as a child, Kellestine couldn't seem to stop himself from lying. One of his favourite confabulations was that he had once served in the Canadian military, in a unit that had since been disgraced—an unmistakable hint that he had belonged to the once-elite Canadian Airborne Regiment that had been disbanded for cruelty to civilians in Somalia. In reality, he had never been a member of that unit, or any other. Kellestine also liked to boast that he was descended from the line of Hessian mercenaries who fought alongside the British in the American Revolutionary War. Perhaps that explained the British flag in his home. It was a romantic notion for Kellestine to think that he was descended from fearless fighting stock, though the Hessians weren't so much soldiers for hire as debtors and petty criminals pressed into action for nothing but food, and the only ones left behind in North America after the Revolutionary War were those the Germans didn't want back. Kellestine also held himself out to be a proud Nazi, and the fact that thousands of members of the Canadian Forces died fighting the Nazis apparently didn't register on him. It was the willingness to kill, not the cause, that mattered most.

Kellestine's unpredictable violence was fuelled by a fierce paranoia. He could make people laugh, but there were some things Weiner took very seriously, even if those who knew him did not. There was something fun and exciting about having to wait at his locked gate on Aberdeen Line until you were buzzed in through the intercom, when it was working, as a video camera recorded everything, on those days when *it* was working. It was as if visitors must be going to see someone important. "Who would think he'd be famous or infamous one day?" one guest later asked.

Motion-detecting cameras and alarms were installed to ward off sneak attackers. Once, when bikers were snorting cocaine with straws and playing pool, Kellestine came flying down the stairs in an arctic combat suit, armed with an Uzi submachine gun. A motion detector had been set off, and Kellestine braced himself for an attack, possibly from police. He ordered someone to start a fire in the fireplace, so that the cocaine could be destroyed. "Fuck that! Just hand out the straws," one of the bikers shouted, refusing to burn the stash. Moments later, Kellestine returned from the cold to report that the motion detector had been set off by a frost buildup on its electronic eyes, and the party continued.

Another time, when entertaining company at the house, Kellestine shot his then-wife Linda in the back with an air pistol, just for a joke. He once pointed a .45-calibre pistol at informant Michael Simmons's big toe and asked for permission to blow it off. Simmons's reply was that he would prefer to be shot between the eyes, as he didn't like pain. It was apparently the right answer, as Kellestine smiled, laughed and lowered the handgun.

In March 1992, in part as a result of Simmons's under-cover work, police laid drug and weapons charges against Kellestine and fourteen others, including Simmons's older brother Andrew (called Teach because he had once been a substitute schoolteacher), president of the London chapter of the Outlaws. When police raided Kelles-tine's farmhouse, they found him asleep on a couch with a loaded handgun within reach. Kellestine had sold cocaine, pills and a handgun to undercover police and eventually pleaded guilty to trafficking in narcotics, trafficking in the proceeds of crime, possession of a prohibited weapon, pos-session of an unregistered weapon, delivering a firearm to a person without a firearms acquisition permit, care-less use of a firearm, and possession of property obtained by crime. For all of this, he was sentenced to six years in prison, his first federal prison stint, at the age of forty-two.

People become criminals for many reasons, some of them even worthy of sympathy. But Kellestine was no victim of circumstance. On January 11, 1993, a prison psychologist reported that Kellestine appeared altogether comfortable in his criminal lifestyle. "Criminality appears to be a matter of choice of lifestyle," the psychologist reported, adding that the "subject's responses drew a portrait of guardedness and evasiveness." Narcissists often feel persecuted, and Kellestine certainly fit that pattern. A January 26, 1994, parole report reads: "Denies guilt. Says he was set up and betrayed by others." A preliminary risk assessment done on that day argued against granting him unescorted temporary absences: "Police describe subject as a very violent person who uses intimidation to gain control of others. Describes him as a 'Soldier of Fortune.'" On May 6, 1994, Kellestine was turned down for full parole; a prison report noted that he "claims to own a construction company and security firm but Police report indicates these were not legitimate businesses and were fronts for criminal activity."

Still, he was freed on parole later in 1994, and not long after that, the body of London resident Cynthia Cywink was found at the Southwold Earthworks, a National Historic Site about five kilometres from his farmhouse. Cywink's killer was never found, but there were persistent rumours that she had done something to annoy Weiner Kellestine shortly before her murder.

On April 27, 1998, his parole was revoked after London-area police told corrections officers that he had "been associating with known and active criminals." He told his parole officer that he would rather remain in prison than live back at his farm under the constant scrutiny of police. In a letter to him, the board noted, "You stated that you did not want another conditional release and your only interest at present is in the huge party to be thrown following your Warrant Expiry Date."

Once he was finally released, rumours started up again about unholy things happening around the property on Aberdeen Line. In December 1998, the body of thirty-five-year-old millionaire Salvatore (Sammy) Vecchio was found by a trapper on a seldom-used dead-end road a few kilometres north of Iona Station in Southwold Township, in a swampy area on the banks of the Thames River, near where Cywink's body was discovered. Vecchio, a habitué of bars and strip joints popular with local bikers, had been only half buried. His head was left sticking out of the ground and had been clubbed repeatedly, which police suggested was an attempt "to deliver a message" to others. Exactly what the message meant, or who was supposed to be receiving it, was unclear, as Vecchio had a dizzying circle of tough friends in biker circles and the Hamilton mob. After all the clues were examined, police hadn't arrested anyone and still wondered if it was just a coincidence that his semi-burial took place virtually in the backyard of the area's most notorious outlaw biker.

But not all rumours depicted Kellestine as a remorseless tough guy. Bikers laughed as they recounted how he had been bitch-slapped by a husky woman in a London-area roadhouse after he ordered her to remove a T-shirt that supported the Hells Angels. Instead of doffing the offending T-shirt, the woman told him to fuck off. Kellestine didn't back down, so she rained a volley of lefts and rights on him as he sputtered "Stop it!" repeatedly until others got in the middle and broke things up.

It was around this time that Kellestine first met up with Boxer Muscedere, fresh from his ugly divorce. Boxer never took to carrying a gun, even as his friend Kellestine kept expanding his own personal arsenal and tally of victims. Boxer would have known that Kellestine was a bit crazy and definitely violent, but he also talked frequently about brotherhood and loyalty. Boxer didn't have a criminal record and wasn't looking to become a big-time criminal—or even a small-time one. He also didn't share Kellestine's Nazi views, but he valued loyalty, especially to friends who called him "brother."

The party at the Woodbridge clubhouse of the Loners Motorcycle Club, on Rutherford Road at Highway 400, was in full swing on Wednesday, June 2, 1999, when a loud, whooping sound could be heard from inside the farmhouse. The people celebrating were Wayne Kellestine, Boxer Muscedere and their friend John (J.J.) Victor. The noise peaked and the three bikers burst outside, tossed their Annihilators Motorcycle Club crests into a metal garbage can and ignited them. The fire heralded the end of the Annihilators and the birth of the London-area chapter of the Loners, with Kellestine as its leader.

To the Toronto-area Loners, many of the newcomers seemed like little more than hayseed rowdies. The worst of the bunch was Kellestine, with his shoulder-length grey hair and slightly unsettling nickname. "Weiner" was bestowed upon him because he apparently had a particularly large slab of manhood, or so Kellestine told the story. The Toronto bikers simply took his word for it, as none of them was especially interested in seeing proof. While Weiner and his crew weren't particularly impressive catches, warm bodies were in demand, as the Loners wanted to boost their numbers as a buffer against the westward push of the Hells Angels. The Angels were better organized than other Ontario clubs, and far more aggressive. They sought nothing less than a coast-to-coast-to-coast presence in Canada. Smaller clubs like the Loners also had to grow, or risk being swallowed up or swept aside altogether. In the face of the Hells Angels' advance, lowering their standards to include Weiner Kellestine seemed like a worthwhile risk for the club.

The Loners weren't the big time of one percenter biker life, but the club was certainly a step up from the small-town Annihilators. They had Ontario chapters in Woodbridge, Richmond Hill, Toronto, London and Windsor, as well as Italian chapters in Reggio Calabria, Messina, Brolo, Avellino, Isernia, Naples and Salerno and a Portuguese chapter in the Azores. They were small, but they were international, and Boxer, Weiner and J.J. were thrilled to join their ranks.

Weiner Kellestine celebrated with a party at his farm, at which a pig was roasted on a spit and bikers listened to live rock music. He was able to pull in more than a hundred people, many of whom paid twenty dollars for commemorative

T-shirts that read LONERS ROCK & PIG FEST '99 and depicted a grinning skull with two crossed rapiers, a Confederate bandana and a crumpled hillbilly cowboy hat. At the party, Kellestine badly wanted to impress the Toronto-area Loners with just how wild and dangerous he could be. Within minutes of meeting Glenn (Wrongway) Atkinson, Kellestine led him to a shed beside his weather-beaten barn and swung open the lid of a crate to reveal a cache of automatic weapons and handguns.

Atkinson was annoyed rather than impressed. "That's a little foolish," he admonished. "You don't even know who I am, man."

Atkinson hadn't really wanted to go to Kellestine's party in the first place. He had just started seeing a new girlfriend, and the prospect of spending the afternoon with Kellestine's crew instead wasn't something he relished.

"I could be an undercover cop, as far as you know," Atkinson continued.

"You're my brother," Weiner Kellestine replied, his feelings a little hurt. "I should be able to trust you."

On the drive home, Atkinson turned to a friend and asked, "Can you believe the type of people we're attracting?"

But in time, the Greater Toronto Area Loners came to see Kellestine's good points. His farm was a good place to get bogus passports and fake First Nations status cards, although some Loners were annoyed by Kellestine's never-ending barrage of advice.

The Sherbrooke chapter of *Les Hells* wasn't caught up in the bloody biker war that consumed the energies of its Montreal and Quebec City chapters. While the other Quebec chapters bombed and shot and schemed, the Sherbrooke chapter quietly made overtures to expand its influence into Ontario.

The Sherbrooke Hells Angels announced their presence in Weiner Kellestine's neighbourhood with the arrival of Big John Coates, a six-foot, seven-inch, three-hundred-pound gang associate. Coates's older brother Jimmy was a member of Kellestine's Loners, and Big John wanted to pull Jimmy and his friends over to the Angels. Many of the younger Loners were all for patching over if they got the chance. But Kellestine had everything to lose if Big John Coates succeeded, as there was virtually no chance that he would be offered an Angels death-head patch. Like the Outlaws, the Hells Angels took business seriously and weren't eager to admit "heat scores." A patchover would leave Kellestine a loner in more than just name.

But putting yourself in the way of the Hells Angels' plans is not without its risks. Tensions with the world's largest biker gang still simmered on October 22, 1999, the date of the wedding ceremony of Wayne Frederick (Jake) Connor, the hefty president of the Loners' Richmond Hill chapter. Boxer Muscedere and the rest of the London Loners were at the wedding party that evening, when the celebration was interrupted by a buzz.

"What's going on?" one of the guests asked.

"Shootout," a biker replied. "One of our guys."

A few hours before, as Weiner Kellestine had turned

onto Iona Road, a red Mustang pulled up alongside his four-by-four. Kellestine had been heading to Connor's wedding and might have recognized one of the men in the car that approached him as Dave (Dirtbag, Dirty) McLeish, a fellow Loner and former member of his Annihilators club. With McLeish was Phil (Philbilly) Gastonguay, who was friendly with the Sherbrooke chapter of the Hells Angels but not a member. Within seconds, the windows of Kellestine's white Chevrolet Blazer were shattered by bullets, but somehow Weiner sped away unscathed. Kellestine had been in the Loners less than four months, and already he had attracted gunfire from the Angels.

When police caught up with Big John Coates in Woodbridge, they searched his car and found an information package on various members of the Loners. Sûreté du Québec biker expert Guy Ouellette would later testify that Big John was in Ontario to murder some bikers there. Weiner Kellestine's feelings of persecution and grandeur were even more pronounced now; he may have been paranoid, but it turned out that people really *were* out to get him. It was all the worse that one of his would-be killers was a former biker brother.

Kellestine was even edgier and more unpredictable now, but one constant in his life was Boxer Muscedere's loyalty. Certain things about Boxer were absolutes, including the fact that he would never betray a friend, even a crazy one. If that friend was like an extended family member, the bond was tighter still. Boxer also wouldn't abandon what he considered his responsibilities. Even as Boxer slipped deeper into the one percenter biker world, he kept his job at the Tilbury brake factory and fed his family with his paycheque, not crime. And although he was an outlaw biker with access to deadly weapons, Boxer still preferred to to settle disputes with his fists, like a man. His friend Weiner Kellestine tried for a far different image, when Boxer introduced him to his younger brother Cesidio (Joe).

"I'm Wayne Kellestine," Weiner announced. "I sell drugs and I kill people."

CHAPTER 5

Sea of Fat Mexicans

We few, we happy few, we band of brothers;
For he to-day that sheds his blood with me
Shall be my brother; be he ne'er so vile,
This day shall gentle his condition . . .
HENRY V, ACT 4, SCENE 3

I've never seen so many Fat Mexicans in my life.
It was a sea of Fat Mexicans.
BANDIDO PIETRO (PETER, PEPPE) BARILLA
DESCRIBES HIS TRIP TO THE U.S.

It didn't take long for the investigation into the murder attempt on Weiner Kellestine's life to lead the police to some interesting information about the plot's intended victim. Investigators seized some forty weapons from his farm, including shotguns, fifteen hunting knives, Chinese bayonets, antique swords and a rocket launcher. At fifty, Weiner Kellestine was headed back into custody. But the Loners weren't the only people who were going to miss him: some of his neighbours complained to the press that, with Weiner and his weapons out of commission, thefts in the area were going up.

Unlike Weiner, Boxer Muscedere was more interested in brotherhood than weapons or ambition, and others in the club generally found him likeable, solid and passionate in a non-psychotic way. In December 1999, Boxer Muscedere gave an interview to Katie McCrindle of *The Chatham Daily News*. At the time, Boxer was trying to keep the police at bay by handing them cards bearing portions of the Charter of Rights and Freedoms. He also tried to allay local concerns after the Loners bought a hall in the tiny southwestern Ontario hamlet of Electric, under the improbable name of the Universal Life Church. Boxer truthfully told McCrindle that he was a hard-working forklift driver, not an international drug baron. "I'm not Al Capone. I've been working in a Tilbury factory for twenty years." Boxer also told the reporter that he was in the Loners for "comradeship, loyalty and honour." With no apparent trace of irony, Boxer continued: "We're Loners. We get along with everybody."

The Angels' push into Ontario was unrelenting. On April 12, 2001, they set up a prospect chapter in London, Ontario, in Boxer and Weiner's neighbourhood, under the guidance of Georges (Bo-boy) Beaulieu of the rich, aggressive Sherbrooke chapter. The Angels' Ontario officers' minutes showed they had hopes of setting up more chapters in Pickering, Guelph, Sudbury and Hamilton in the near future.[16] In the face of the Angels' expansion, stasis didn't seem an option for Boxer's Loners. There was growth, and there was decay and death, with precious little safe ground in the middle. It was as though all of the clubs were like sharks, and the only way to stay alive was to keep moving.

The Angels pressured the Loners to drop the word "Ontario" from the backs of their vests, which the Loners took as a slap in the face—a taunt that the Loners were nothing more than a regional club in Ontario. The Loners responded with more courage than foresight. They had had loose contact with the Bandidos since December 1999, when American Bandidos sent a Christmas card up to the club. On Tuesday, May 22, 2001, Boxer, Weiner and a dozen other members of the Loners' Richmond Hill and Woodbridge chapters agreed to become probationary Bandidos. It was bold and perhaps foolish, and the Bandidos blithely accepted Kellestine, even though the Outlaws and Hells Angels wouldn't consider letting him into their ranks. The Bandidos' immediately priority was numbers, not quality, and the Angels were big and getting bigger, while the Bandidos were scrambling to stay on the map in Canada.

The move meant Jimmy Raso was losing his brotherhood, and one of his former members, who assumed Raso would be joining his old brothers from the Loners in the Bandidos, tried to console him in an email sent on May 24. His comments echoed the optimistic views of many, including Boxer: "I suppose perhaps maybe you're going through a little bit of a mourning period which would be understandable. The thing is though we didn't change the biking world. It changed all around us. It was either get with the times or sink like a rusted out vessel . . . We now not only have those members we always have had with strength-

ened loyalties and ties, but now, we have a multitude of new
brothers . . . The Bandidos Motorcycle Club are good solid
brothers, who really believe in the whole ideology and con-
cept of BROTHERHOOD."

A few days later, Boxer's club marked the move to the
Bandidos with a party at the old Loners clubhouse on
Jane Street in Toronto. The clubhouse was close to the
street, and it was hard not to think how vulnerable it was,
should the Angels in Ontario feel the kind of urge clubmates so often felt in Quebec. Boxer and Peppe Barilla,
president of the Loners' Woodbridge chapter, welcomed
Canadian Bandidos president Alain Brunette; Robert
(Tout Tout) Léger, the Canadian secretary, or *El Secretario*; Sylvain (Sly) Grégoire, the Bandidos' webmaster
(the club had no grandiose Spanish name for this post)
and others. That day, Brunette particularly enjoyed his
meeting with Woody, the eight-hundred-pound Afri-
can lion who was the Loners' mascot. Woody's original
owner, Guerrino (Woody) Siriani of Woodbridge, had
liked to say that he would rather live a day as a lion than
a thousand as a lamb. After Seriani's death in a motorcycle accident, Woody was adopted by the club as a living,
breathing, sometimes growling, reminder of that credo.
Dejectedly pacing his twenty-five-metre-by-twenty-five-
metre chain-link pen, however, Woody might just as well
have stood for some of the more troubling ironies of the
biker life. As menacing as he was, Woody was anything
but free.

For his part, Boxer was nothing less than giddy. On
June 18, he left a jubilant message on his new club's web-

page: "On our first ride together as brothers it was great we will make a mark in history together only we can appreciate the freedom of riding in the wind . . . ride free forever."

On the other side of the great divide of the biker world, the Angels didn't have a pet lion, but they were organized. And they were well informed. The club put together a file containing the names of 614 people who had been connected to the Rock Machine and Bandidos in Quebec and Ontario. The dossier contained a wealth of information: names, dates of birth, addresses, licence plate numbers, social insurance numbers, driver's licence identifications, addresses of wives and mistresses, favourite haunts, physical descriptions, photos and their status in the club. Disseminated as a CD-ROM, the file also contained information on more than a dozen businesses friendly with the Bandidos in Ontario and Quebec, in addition to others in the criminal underworld, including the Outlaws motorcycle gang and the Sicilian Mafia. It was a Michelin guide of sorts for hitmen working for the Angels. With their decision to move into the Bandidos camp, Boxer and his friends joined the list of potential targets. The Angels would have to update their records.

Not long after he found the disc, Grégoire was shot to death in his Montreal car dealership, Automobiles Sans Tracas, which translates into "automobiles without trouble." His murder came just eight months after that of the Bandidos' previous webmaster, Réal (Tintin) Dupont. In the biker world, as in mainstream business, information was power, making the post of webmaster a dangerous one.

Two months after the Jane Street party, Chopper Raposo, Peppe Barilla and four other former Loners rolled up to the annual Sturgis bike rally in the Black Hills of South Dakota, near Mount Rushmore and just a few kilometres from the town of Deadwood, where frontier lawman Wild Bill Hickock was gunned down in 1876 while playing poker. As usual during the biker rally, the town of Sturgis (population just over six thousand) swelled to more than half a million people, most of them leather-clad. What interested the carload of Canadians most was the sight of five or six hundred members of the Bandidos, decked out in full colours. When they returned to Toronto, Barilla reported to Boxer and the others in the club that he was duly impressed by the Bandidos' presence. "I've never seen so many Fat Mexicans in my life," he told his biker associates, in his Italian accent. "It was a sea of Fat Mexicans."

Tout Tout Léger had thought of joining them on their pilgrimage to South Dakota. Shortly before the bikers headed south, he changed his mind, deciding instead to honour his bail conditions, which barred him from leaving Canada or associating with criminals. And so he went with his family for a quiet holiday at his cottage in Ste-Catherine-de-Hatley in the Eastern Townships. Ironically, his decision to obey the law made him an easy target for a crew of Hells Angels hitmen. The Ontario Bandidos would later hear that when their new friend

Tout Tout saw the Angels' murder squad coming, he stepped in front of his wife and children, shielding them from the gunfire.

Outlaw bikers often belong to clubs with gleefully satanic names and imagery, but generally, when one of their numbers dies, they gather quietly in churches, get down on their knees and pray to the same god as everyone else. Many outlaw bikers, like Frank Lenti, consider themselves good Christians, though they take a decidedly Old Testament view of theology. At Tout Tout's funeral, the body was dressed in a suit, his Bandidos colours folded neatly beside him in the casket.

Boxer Muscedere, Crash Kriarakis and Chopper Raposo attended Tout Tout's funeral, and the chapter sent a wreath of flowers ordered from a shop in Verdun. Bandidos secretary Wrongway Atkinson was mortified to hear that the florist had made up the wreath in red and white, the colours of the Hells Angels. It was either a bad joke or a monumental gaffe by the florist. Whatever the case, the red and white flowers only made a bad situation worse.

The bloodshed and danger didn't scare Boxer away from his new club and new brothers. If anything, it only served to make him more fiercely loyal, as if they were now bound together by spilled blood. Though Boxer had worn the Fat Mexican on his back since May, he truly became a Bandido at that moment. He had BANDIDOS WORLDWIDE tattooed across his belly, along with a sketch of a Harley-Davidson motorcycle and a Fat Mexican. On his vest, he had three patches over his heart: BANDIDOS, OUR COLOURS DON'T RUN, and JUST GOOD OL' BOYS.

Quebec was a danger zone for Boxer now, and he rode directly into the heart of it in full Bandido colours. Sometimes soldiering through the rain, Boxer, Barilla and a Bandido named Josh rode 1,600 kilometres on the round trip from Chatham to the funeral. His Bandidos in Ontario were scrambling to establish themselves, at the same time that the Quebec Hells Angels were doing so well financially that Walter Stadnick had set up an incorporated property management firm with computerized accounting systems in two apartments, money-counting machines and a heavy-duty safe, to launder tens of millions of dollars in drug profits.

That day, as Boxer rode to Quebec with the wind in his face, he felt totally alive. He didn't care that he didn't have drugs or power or a private army, like leaders of the Quebec Angels. He did have a loving family, as well as his extended family in the Bandidos. The Angels should have scared him, but somehow he felt exhilarated. It was clear that Boxer was head over heels in love with his new life as a Bandido.

A few months later, when Boxer arrived home on his Harley Fat Boy from a get-together at the Kingston clubhouse, he again sounded enraptured as he described the 1,100-kilometre round trip. He typed this note on the Bandidos Canada website, in his typically horrible grammar and spelling:

> ya i got caught in the rain but man i had a great ride
> your good company bro flying the colours made the
> rain dry as soon as it hit me all you have too do is
> beleave and i beleave in the bandido nation love

Frank (Cisco) Lenti sandwiched between Hells Angels David (Wolf) Carroll (left) and Wolodumyr (Walter Nurget) Stadnick in Wasaga Beach, Ontario, in 1993. Note the "Filthy Few" patches on the vests of Carroll and Stadnick. Police say the patches are sometimes given to bikers who had killed for the club, while bikers sometimes say they're for members who party particularly hard. PETER EDWARDS PHOTO

Pietro (Peter, Peppe) Barilla and James (Ripper) Fullager when they were both members of the Loners in the 1990s—back when outlaw bikers actually rode bikes. JULIAN CARSINI PHOTO

T-shirt sold at Weiner Kellestine's 1999 pig barbecue to celebrate his Annihilators club joining the much bigger Loners club.

PETER EDWARDS PHOTO

Entering the big time of the outlaw biker world in December 2001: Boxer Muscedere (far left) and Frankie (Bam Bam) Salerno (second from left), with Bandidos national president Alain (Red Tomato) Brunette (third from left, standing). JULIAN CARSINI PHOTO

Ripper Fullager (far left) plays host to (from left to right) Cisco Lenti, Dennis (Chief) Cada and Boxer Muscedere at his home in Toronto's South Riverdale district. JULIAN CARSINI PHOTO

Cisco Lenti (left) and Ripper Fullager gave the club links to the old one percenter tradition. Fullager loved to call Lenti "Old Frank," even though Lenti was the younger man. JULIAN CARSINI PHOTO

Brief taste of glory: Former Alberta Rebels, sporting spotless new Fat Mexican patches, celebrate patching over to the Bandidos in July 2004. A few months later, they would switch allegiance yet again, this time to the rival Hells Angels. JULIAN CARSINI PHOTO

When former Rebels club members entered the Bandido fold in Edmonton in July 2004, there was a procession. Bandidos Canada members took the lead, followed by probationary and then prospect members. Bringing up the rear were members of the Death's Hand Motorcycle Club from Calgary. JULIAN CARSINI PHOTO

Well-respected Joey (Crazy Horse) Morin (third from left) hooked up with the No Surrender Crew in June 2003. With him in Ripper Fullager's backyard are Fullager (far right), Glenn (Wrongway) Atkinson (back left standing), Cisco Lenti (sitting), Boxer Muscedere (red hat), Chief Cada (on Boxer's left) and George (Crash) Kriarakis (crouching). JULIAN CARSINI PHOTO

Uneasy biker brothers: (from left to right) Chopper Raposo, Boxer Muscedere, Weiner Kellestine and Michael (Taz) Sandham in the fall of 2005, months before the massacre. CROWN EXHIBIT

Boxer Muscedere (left) and Weiner Kellestine share a Christmas hug.

A Christmas card prepared by the Toronto (No Surrender Crew) Bandidos to spread good cheer to their biker brothers around the world. JULIAN

The softer side of Boxer Muscedere: The father of five, and grandfather of three, stands by a photo of his daughter Angelina. CROWN EXHIBIT

Boxer Muscedere and Nina Lee, visiting Weiner Kellestine's farm less than a year before the murders. CROWN EXHIBIT

Nazi sympathizers nest: Weiner Kellestine in his farm home, surrounded by his beloved Nazi memorabilia. PETER EDWARDS PHOTO

Murderer's embrace: Weiner Kellestine (left) hugs Chopper Raposo at Kellestine's farm in June 2005. CROWN EXHIBIT

respect loyalty respect too all brothers be safe til we meet we are getting stronger.

Boxer hugged Frankie (Bam Bam, Bammer) Salerno on Saturday, December 1, 2001, in the ballroom of the Kingston Travelodge, which looked particularly festive decked out with a Christmas tree and red and yellow balloons, a passable approximation of the club's gold and red colours. The reason for the celebration was that the Bandidos had just granted forty-five full memberships in four new Canadian chapters. At the ceremony, Boxer and his Bandido brothers were given their CANADA bottom rockers to sew onto their vests, meaning they had become full members of the Bandidos Nation in just six months—half the usual waiting period. The reason for the accelerated promotions wasn't that they were twice as good as the average candidates for membership. The truth was that the club was getting desperate and badly needed to boost its ranks in the face of the Hells Angels' relentless growth.

For Boxer and the rest of the Loners, sewing the patches onto their backs meant they were passing a point of no return, publicly aligning themselves against the Hells Angels, the world's most powerful biker club. If they had been content to remain as Loners, they could have continued to drink beer and smoke pot and go to bike rallies and pig roasts with no real risk. Now, they were taking sides in what threatened to be a war.

Boxer and his old Loner clubmates didn't dwell on negative things that afternoon. Peppe Barilla hoisted a Bandidos Canada vest, while national president Alain Brunette savoured the moment, and a feeding of ribs and seafood. Boxer picked up a full patch for his longtime friend Weiner Kellestine who, owing to bail stipulations, couldn't associate with known criminals as he awaited trial on new weapons and drugs charges. Like all new members, Kellestine was given a personal information form, which included a space to fill in a description of his motorcycle. Club rules call for all members to have working motorcycles, but Weiner Kellestine thumbed his nose at the requirement. In the space, Kellestine scribbled that he owned a 1903, single-cylinder, 49-cubic-centimetre bike with no brakes, no lights and "drop out lubrication." When Boxer filled out his form, he proudly noted that he was the owner of a Harley-Davidson Fat Boy.

Despite Kellestine's quirks—such as his attempts at humour on the form—Boxer remained loyal to him, but Boxer had also grown close to Frankie (Bam Bam, Bammer) Salerno, who lived in the upscale Toronto suburb of Oakville. Boxer and Bam Bam shared Italian heritage and seemed to understand each other instinctively, as *paesani* sometimes do. Often, they would slip into speaking Italian to each other without seeming to even realize it, each searching for exactly the right word or phrase to express his feelings. Kellestine was quick to feel offended or abandoned, but kept any feelings he had about the Boxer–Bam Bam friendship to himself.

When they joined the Bandidos, Weiner, Boxer, Bam Bam and the other new members were handed the twelve-page set of Fat Mexican by-laws. One new requirement was that they were expected to file monthly reports to the mother chapter in Texas, or face fines. Soon, the former Loners were sending the Texans messages about parties in Kingston, Toronto and Montreal with other groups, including the support club the Killerbeez (whose motto was "Keep the Hive Alive") and the Palmers, a Montreal organized crime association.[17]

Three days later, Eric (the Red) McMillan, the sergeant-at-arms of the newly formed Kingston Bandidos, walked out of the strip club in the basement of the Dynasty Inn in Oshawa after last call. That night, McMillan had been called to a meeting with the rival Hells Angels, amidst reports that the Toronto Bandidos were flexing their muscles in Oshawa and cutting into the Angels' business of running strippers. As Eric the Red stepped onto the parking lot, he was quickly surrounded by three Hells Angels. One ran a knife into his stomach, slitting his skin from his chest to his belly.

Doctors patched Eric the Red back together, and he recovered amidst media pronouncements that the parking-lot bloodletting meant that the Quebec biker war had officially expanded into Ontario. The headlines may have been exaggerated, but the knife that carved up Eric McMillan was a sharp message to Boxer Muscedere and his fellow Ontario Bandidos: Party time was over and survival was anything but guaranteed.

The Toronto Bandidos were clearly outnumbered and surrounded. The Central Region of the Hells Angels' Canadian empire included chapters in West Toronto, East Toronto, Downtown Toronto, North Toronto, Thunder Bay, Simcoe, Windsor, Oshawa, Niagara, Kitchener, Keswick and Woodbridge, as well as the Ottawa-based Nomads. Minutes for a Hells Angels Central Region officers' meeting for January 2002 showed that the one percenter clubs in the province were still anxiously watching each other, like gaggles of teenagers at a high-school dance. One note from the minutes reads: "The Outlaws were invited to the Bandido Xmas party in Tweed. They did not attend." Another states, "The Bandidos sat with the Outlaws in the bar at the bike show."

The minutes also hinted at tensions anticipated for another motorcycle show scheduled for the next month in London, Ontario. The organizer of the London Motorcycle Show at the Western Fair Progress Building was Larry Pooler of the Downtown chapter of the Hells Angels, and the Outlaws apparently planned to crash the event. As Angels club minutes stated, "Outlaws are having a National Run to the London Bike Show on Feb. 1/2/3 . . . Big Squeeze?"

As the show began on Saturday, February 2, 2002, a police officer told Pooler what sounded like alarming news: thirty Bandidos and their supporters were on their way to the Progress Building. The police officer seemed to want guidance on how to stave off an ungodly rumble.

"Tell them to all buy tickets," Pooler said.

Around three in the afternoon, about twenty Bandidos

and their supporters began marching slowly through the Progress Building, past displays of motorcycles and bike parts, all the while glaring at about forty Hells Angels. The Angels on site weren't people to be trifled with—they included Remond (Ray) Akleh of the elite Nomads chapter; Paul (Sasquatch, Sas) Porter, the Nomads' behemoth president; and Oshawa president Mark Cephes Stephenson. The Bandidos badly needed to show they weren't afraid and that they too deserved respect.

The Bandidos who strutted through the Progress Building all wore their black leather vests with their CAN-ADA bottom rockers. Bikers are as territorial as wolves, and the Bandidos would scarcely have been more provocative if they had actually urinated on the Angels' turf. London city police turned out in force, along with Ontario Provincial Police tactical officers, attempting to keep peace while filming the event for future study. Police video caught Boxer Muscedere front and centre, grinning and looking a little manic in his new red and gold colours. With his dangling Fu Manchu moustache, he looked like a personification of the Fat Mexican logo, though his black woollen tuque gave him a distinctly Canadian look.

Police noted that some of the bikers wore bulletproof vests, while others carried knives. As a show of anti-Angel solidarity, Bandidos publicly hugged Outlaws, including Mario (The Wop, Mike) Parente, their stocky, handlebar-moustached Canadian president. The Bandidos and Outlaws remained separate clubs, but their mutual dislike of the Angels pulled them closer. Ordered off the fairgrounds, Boxer and his fellow Bandidos complied, while grumbling like schoolboys that it wasn't fair that the Hells Angels were allowed to stay while they had to go. Not long afterwards, the dance was repeated, with slightly less intensity, as about thirty Outlaws made a slow march through the centre of the Progress Building. When the afternoon was finally over, it didn't feel as though bloodshed had really been avoided; rather, it had been postponed until a later date.

The red Pontiac Sunfire with Quebec plates was speeding as it headed west on Highway 401, approaching Kingston at 10:05 A.M. on Sunday March 10, 2002. An Ontario Provincial Police cruiser pulled it over, and when an officer approached the car, its driver, Marc Bouffard, and passenger, Daniel Lamer, let on that they couldn't speak any English. Lumpy outlines could be seen beneath their jackets, the types of impressions made by bulletproof vests.

The police officer called for French-speaking backup and summoned Bouffard to sit in the back of his cruiser. The OPP officer certainly couldn't know at the time that Lamer was en route to Kingston, the home of Alain Brunette, national *presidente* of the Bandidos, or that Lamer didn't intend to return home until Brunette was a dead man.

It seemed like just another routine traffic stop until

Lamer walked towards the cruiser, pulled out a pistol and squeezed off eight quick rounds. One of them caught Constable Dan Brisson squarely in the back, but his bulletproof vest deflected the bullet, which grazed his neck and head. Lamer was hit five times as police returned fire, including a kill-shot to his head.

Inside the Sunfire, police found four handguns, a silencer, handcuffs, a balaclava and pictures of Brunette and his vehicle. They also found pictures of several members of the Toronto chapter of the Bandidos, suggesting Boxer and his friends were also in the killers' sights.

The Hells Angels in Ontario remained far more restrained than their Quebec brothers, but the Quebecers clearly weren't worried about crossing the border and asserting their will. Minutes of the Angels' Central Canada officers' meeting in March 2002 noted the formation of a "committee to recommend policy to presidents." "This 'think tank' committee should look at the big picture and plot our options for the Presidents to make decisions," the minutes noted. Minutes of the officers' meeting a month later called for peace with the Outlaws and Bandidos. The Ontario Hells Angels clearly didn't share the bloodlust of their Quebec brothers. "No one wants to be friends with the Bandits but we want to avoid problems if possible," the minutes stated. "We are not going to start trouble but everyone feels that we deal with situations as they arise."

Weiner Kellestine was still behind bars on his gun charges when Boxer Muscedere was promoted by Brunette to vice *presidente* of Ontario in the spring of 2002.

Boxer replaced Barilla, who was locked up in Ste-Anne-des-Plaines penitentiary on gangsterism, drug trafficking and conspiracy charges. The promotion called to mind Woody Allen's joke that "eighty percent of success is just showing up." All Boxer really wanted was brotherhood, but he now held a serious title in a serious club, almost by default. Boxer was forty-five years old, and had just five years' experience as a member of one percenter clubs. By comparison, Walter Stadnick of the Hells Angels had been in his club for two decades.

By late June 2002, as the result of a massive police sweep called Project Amigo, Brunette and some sixty-five Canadian Bandidos were either locked up or on bail awaiting charges that ranged from drug trafficking, to gangsterism, to conspiracy to murder Hells Angels. The project began with an investigation into a series of arsons on low-end bars in southwest Montreal, as Bandidos tried to muscle in on the Hells Angels' drug-pushing locales. In one day of the sweep, police scooped up almost two hundred kilograms of hashish, eight kilograms of cocaine, four firearms and a silencer. It was clear that Boxer's new club was being quickly depleted by prosecutions. It was also clear that their ranks didn't just include good old boys like Boxer, but also heavy-duty criminals who ran strippers, dealt drugs—and killed rivals when they felt the need or impulse.

Another half-dozen Bandidos, including Chopper Raposo of Toronto, were on the run from Project Amigo police, who accused Chopper of trafficking in Viagra and ecstasy. That left just over a dozen Bandidos from the Toronto chapter who were free and on the streets. So when Brunette was denied bail, there wasn't much competition or fanfare when Boxer Muscedere was promoted by Brunette yet again, this time to the lofty post of national *presidente*.

It was clearly a caretaker position, but it was an honour and an obligation nonetheless, and it also made Boxer a target. Boxer could expect more attention from the Hells Angels and the police, but probably wasn't worried about how the promotion would upset men he considered his brothers. For the first time, Boxer outranked his old friend Weiner Kellestine. Weiner liked followers, like the old Boxer. He wasn't comfortable with equals, even though he might call them "brother." As a rule, Weiner Kellestine treated his superiors with contempt bordering on hatred.

His superiors in the Bandido Nation also posed challenges for Boxer. While it sounded impressive that Boxer was the national president, he was still under the American secretary in the club's pecking order. He wasn't supposed to directly contact *El Presidente* Wegers; he had to go through Wegers's son, who acted as a private secretary of sorts. Meanwhile, Wrongway Atkinson and Crash Kriarakis of the Toronto Bandidos were allowed to call Wegers any time, day or night. There was no official reason for this state of affairs: Wegers just seemed to like talking with Atkinson and Kriarakis more than talking with Boxer, despite his title. It was infuriating and more than a little humiliating for Boxer. He bristled again when German Bandidos sent Atkinson a gift of a black leather bomber jacket, but included nothing at all for Boxer; and again when Jason Addison, the Australian Bandidos president, sent Atkinson a box of support shirts and stickers, also ignoring the Canadian president.

That July, as Boxer Muscedere settled into his new role, Kellestine was back in court, pleading guilty to twenty-two charges related to a cache of weapons and ammunition found by police at his Aberdeen Line farm. He was also accused of selling a kilo of hashish to an undercover police officer. Some of the weapons found on his farm were stolen and others were prohibited, and he wasn't supposed to be around any of them, since he was already under a court-imposed lifetime weapons ban.

Appearing in court gave Kellestine a chance to be the centre of attention, as he tied his long hair back and put on his shiny silverish suit, so that he looked a little like a hayseed version of New York gangster John Gotti. His lawyer, Michael Epstein, told the court that there was some debate whether his fifty-three-year-old client was "attempting to extricate himself from certain motorcycle people" at the time he was the target of the failed murder plot.

"The accused's position is that he has," Epstein told the court. "The Crown would have a different view, I think. But it is safe to say that he certainly has no affiliation with the Annihilators, Outlaws or Hells Angels." That was all true as far as it went, but Kellestine wasn't sharing his future plans with his lawyer or the judge. They couldn't be expected to know that he was now a full-patch member of the Bandidos, the chief worldwide rival to the Hells Angels.

CHAPTER 6

No Surrender Crew

Why, then, I do but dream on sovereignty;
Like one that stands upon a promontory,
And spies a far-off shore where he would tread,
Wishing his foot were equal with his eye . . .
HENRY VI, PART III, ACT 3, SCENE 2

They all have a mother. People are who they are. They just
have to be given respect. Look at how people look at us.
BOXER MUSCEDERE EXPLAINS WHY HE HAS NO PROBLEM
WITH NON-WHITES AND GAYS

Boxer Muscedere had seemed happy enough when Weiner Kellestine was above him in the biker hierarchy in the Annihilators, Loners and the early months of the Canadian Bandidos. In time, however, Boxer also grew to enjoy holding the title of Bandidos national *presidente* for himself. Members generally preferred him too, despite his increasingly volatile temper—made worse by snorts of cocaine— and his almost total inability to manage money. He could be a gentle, even sweet, appreciative man, or violent and unforgiving, but he was always trustworthy and genuinely tried to embody the old-school one percenter ideal of bikes and brotherhood. With Boxer, everything was from the heart, and he often punctuated his sentences with the phrase "top left," which was his way of saying "from the heart" without sounding too mushy. Members found him easier to read than Weiner Kellestine, with his mercurial mood swings and stream-of-consciousness rantings, in which he somehow equated the Confederacy, the American Revolution and Nazism with goodness and Canada. Boxer Muscedere could barely read and write and didn't bother playing historian, but he was straightforward, honest, fearless and loyal to a fault, which was just fine with them.

Despite Weiner's strange and violent ways, Boxer wasn't about to abandon the man who had brought him into the outlaw biker fold. During Kellestine's frequent stays behind bars, Boxer would pass a hat for donations to help pay the mortgage and utilities at Weiner's farm. Others in the club grumbled that they weren't entitled to such largesse when they were in custody, but they didn't dare challenge Boxer on it, more out of respect for his hard knuckles than for Weiner's financial well-being. For his part, no one gave more to Kellestine than Boxer, so he didn't see why his other brothers shouldn't help out too.

As Boxer assumed the Bandidos' top Canadian post, he found he was always defending his old friend to other members. There was the embarrassment about the time that Weiner crashed a gay pride march on Richmond Street in downtown London, flanked by white supremacists with shaved heads and black T-shirts with a clenched white fist logo on their backs. It was a public display by the Bikers Against Pedophiles group founded by Concrete Dave Weiche, the biker son of local Nazi Martin Weiche. In a symbolic message that only he could understand, Kellestine waved a Confederate flag in front of the news cameras and made a great show of moral rectitude. Toronto-area clubmates shuddered at the unseemly media freak show of Kellestine attempting to mock gays. There is an understanding that a one percenter club shouldn't get involved in any political cause, unless it was something that directly affects them, like motorcycle helmet laws. The idea is that they are supposed to be freedom-loving rebels, not bigots who try to impose their values on others. The Greater Toronto Area Bandidos worried that things like the Pride Parade debacle only destroyed whatever mystique they might have built up, and would inevitably make them targets of jokes themselves. "It makes you look like small-town hillbillies," one former Toronto area Bandido grumbled. "If you keep your mouth shut, you keep some mystique." Boxer also veered away from gay-bashing, just as he made it clear he wasn't a racist or anti-Semite. For someone who looked like a good old boy, he could be surprisingly liberal and tolerant. "They all have a mother," Boxer told a club friend. "People are who they are. They just have to be given respect. Look at how people look at us."

But not only did Kellestine not worry about what mainstream society thought about him, he didn't seem to care even what his biker brothers thought, either. Some club members quietly noted that Kellestine still didn't have a working Harley on the road, a pretty clear-cut violation of the Bandido bylaws and a complete mockery of the one percenter lifestyle. And although he didn't ride a bike himself, Weiner somehow still felt entitled to call for the expulsion of others for the same infraction of club rules. Members also bristled at how Kellestine would whine to Boxer until meetings were rescheduled at the last minute from Toronto to his ramshackle barn, so that he would be spared the two-hour drive into Toronto. When Boxer complied, Weiner wasn't sheepish. Instead, he loudly called for discipline against any members who balked at attending. He also didn't appear at all grateful to Boxer, who had made his mortgage and utilities payments several times. Instead, he still seemed to smoulder with jealousy about Boxer's success, and treated such preferential treatment as his due, not as a favour. "He was Boxer's buddy, so he could pretty much get away with anything," a former member said. "He thought absolutely nothing of inconveniencing other people . . . He'd moan like a baby if he had to do something that wasn't to his liking."

It was hard to take Weiner Kellestine totally seriously, even if he signed his name with SS and clearly had a backer in Boxer. When he wasn't there, others in the club would sometimes chuckle over stories of him sobbing and begging for forgiveness back in the late 1970s, when he was accused of murdering Toronto clothing store owner John DeFilippo, allegedly showing up at the retailer's door posing as a pizza delivery man. No matter how many weapons he stockpiled, he only seemed to be *acting* nuts. "I don't think he's as crazy as he let on,"

Atkinson later said. "He'd always have the advantage figured out—how he could do anything to his advantage. Crazy people don't think like that."

Despite Kellestine's bizarre antics, this was a time of growth and potential. Any Friday the 13th is a special day for one percenter bikers to get together, and on Friday, September 13, 2002, some twenty members of Killerbeez West Side, the Bandidos' Keswick-based junior support club, arrived en masse at a stag thrown for Bam Bam Salerno at a banquet hall on Highway 27 on the Mississauga-Toronto border. The Killerbeez West Side were a force on the streets of small-town Keswick, where they outnumbered the local Hells Angels by a half-dozen members. That night at Bam Bam's stag, there wasn't anything too wild going on, out of respect for his fiancée, Stephanie, but it was an impressive show of brotherhood and muscle nonetheless.

The stag gave Bam Bam a chance to settle an old debt, through raffle tickets sold on a forty-two-inch plasma television. Bam Bam whispered to some guests that he could greatly improve their chances of winning if they'd only pay him an extra twenty dollars. "Trust me, I'll make sure your number has a better chance of coming up," he told them. As he pocketed the extra twenties, word sifted out to a few guests that Bam Bam had sold the real winning ticket a couple of weeks before to cover a debt, then fixed the raffle so that the draw would have the appearance of fairness. That evening, as the man who bought the winning ticket was outside smoking a cigarette, Bam Bam quickly called out the winning number. Bam Bam refused to allow friends of the winner to run out to get him, so that he could collect his prize. Instead, Bam Bam drew yet another ticket, belonging to a relative who had also been promised the win. There was something about Bam Bam that made such petty scams seem almost endearing, as he constantly sought out angles that might somehow help him, without really hurting anyone else. "Salerno had more angles than a geometry class," an old friend said, chuckling at the memory of the television draw scam.

The Ontario Hells Angels continued to be acutely aware of the movements of the Toronto Bandidos, although the two clubs still hadn't clashed significantly. In the agenda for the Central Canada officers' meeting in November 2002, Robert (Donny) Petersen, the region's secretary, noted a meeting between an unidentified Bandido and Paul (Sasquatch, Sas) Porter, who had defected to start up a chapter of the elite Hells Angels Nomads in the Ottawa area. The Angels' minutes used a mocking, condescending tone to discuss their supposed rivals:

> BANDITS:
> A Bandit approached Sas [Porter] during a chance meeting at a gas station. The Bandit wanted to talk about peace. We didn't know we were at war . . .

THE BANDIDO MASSACRE 119

Some Toronto Bandits want to leave and become Loners again.

It took a lot of optimism to imagine a day when Boxer's Bandidos might reach the level of the Ontario Angels. Hells Angels chapters like the ones on Ortono Avenue in Oshawa or on Eastern Avenue in downtown Toronto had computers with encrypted Internet systems, reinforced steel doors, security cameras and listening devices to alert them to unwanted visitors, as well as fully stocked bars to entertain visitors. The Eastern Avenue clubhouse even had a metal sculpture of the club's trademarked winged skull on its property. Unlike most biker clubs, the Toronto Bandidos still didn't have a clubhouse, or even regular nights for church meetings. They met randomly in members' homes on Saturday afternoons, Sunday nights and pretty much any evening, although they liked to keep Fridays free for fun.

The profile of the Toronto Bandidos rose significantly in late 2002 with the addition of Frank (Cisco) Lenti, who was by now in his mid-fifties and a survivor of more than four decades of gang activity. Lenti's demeanour could be ultra-polite, like a maître d' who lives to serve, or he could work his face into a nightmarish intensity, like Charles Manson on steroids. He preferred to be genial, which belied the fact that he had been a genuine force to be reckoned with in the Greater Toronto Area underworld for decades. It was Lenti who had introduced Cecil Kirby of the old Satan's Choice to powerful criminal Cosimo Elia Commisso for enforcement jobs back in the late 1970s and early 1980s. As he did this, Lenti warned the mobster, "Remember, he's not one of us," meaning Kirby wasn't of Italian heritage. When Kirby turned informant, claiming that his family was under threat from the mob, Lenti distanced himself from Canadian authorities by quickly relocating to the Italian city of Perugia, north of Rome, for two years, sometimes riding his Harley-Davidson Soft Tail with Italian Hells Angels.[18]

After his return to Canada, Lenti was on good terms for a time with the local Hells Angels. He was then in the Loners, and the Hells Angels provided intelligence that two Loners members were police informants. It was as if the Angels knew more about the Loners than the Loners knew about themselves. While Lenti appreciated the heads-up, he didn't like how the Hells Angels also seemed compelled to micromanage Loners business. It was tough for a man like Lenti not to bristle at the Angels' arrogance, and even more maddening that they were generally right about things. So in 1994, when some senior Hells Angels visited the Loners clubhouse and offered Lenti membership in their worldwide organization, he had a rude surprise for them: a cordial invitation to join the Loners instead. Not surprisingly, the Hells Angels stormed out.

By August 1995, Lenti was running his own club, the Diabolos. He placed the initials MG, for Motorcycle Gang, after the club's name, rather than the standard, more politically correct MC, for Motorcycle Club. While other clubs shunned the word "gang," Lenti embraced it wholeheartedly, boasting, "I'll show them who the real fucking gang is." There was a buzz during the summer of 1995 that

Lenti was about to fold his Diabolos to set up his own Woodbridge chapter of the Satan's Choice, which would be a direct insult to the Woodbridge Loners.

On the morning of Thursday, August 25, Lenti was just settling into the driver's seat of his Ford Explorer in the driveway of his Woodbridge home when someone nearby pushed down on a detonator button. The explosion that followed blew off a chunk of Lenti's buttock and leg, crushed his pelvis and covered him with burns.

It was something of a miracle that he lived to wake up in a hospital, to hear a doctor say he would never walk again. Lenti proved the prediction wrong, although riding a motorcycle would be extremely painful. Police and bikers alike strongly suspected that the pipe bomb had been planted by a Woodbridge Loner, who would later become a Hells Angel, but no one was ever prosecuted for the crime. The only charges from the attack were against Lenti himself, as police found a loaded submachine gun and a 9-millimetre semi-automatic handgun in the wreckage of the Explorer. After regaining consciousness, Lenti tried to reassure York Regional Police Detective Angelo DeLorenzi that the weapons were no threat to public safety. "I was using them for my kinda people," Lenti told the detective. "I wasn't using them for law-abiding citizens."

The pipe bombing wasn't enough to kill Frank Lenti, but it did slow him down a little. When the weather turned cold or damp, he complained of pain in his joints, although he could still take his Harley-Davidson Road King out for spins. There had been a rumour that the explosion had torn off his testicles, but Lenti proved that to be a lie.

Almost a decade after the blast, the limping grandfather fathered another son. There were also stories that he had a heavy-duty metal cane, which could serve as a club, and another with a sword hidden inside. The tales about the canes were considered more reliable than the myth that he had lost his balls.

Lenti's mystique grew as he survived the bomb blast, and his membership in the Bandidos offered the promise of steering the club to glory days in the not-so-distant future. Ripper Fullager affectionately called him "Old Frank," even though he was, in reality, a few years older than Lenti. Ripper clearly enjoyed having Lenti around, although he grimaced when Lenti insisted on calling the club a gang. The semantic disagreement wasn't enough to seriously strain their friendship, but it always got a rise out of Ripper nonetheless.

In addition to a tough, seasoned new member, Boxer's Bandido chapter also now had a grand nickname: the "No Surrender Crew." The name was the idea of Wrongway Atkinson, who had lived for a couple of years in Belfast and proudly announced his heritage with a Celtic-braid tattoo on his left forearm. Atkinson noted that a branch of the Irish Republican Army was nicknamed the "No Surrender Crew," and if it was good enough for them, it also worked for Boxer Muscedere's homeless bunch.

Low-key and literate, Atkinson was as strong a diplomat as Lenti was a warrior. He found parallels between Irish politics and those of the outlaw biker world, and appreciated the old joke that the first order of business for a new Irish political organization is how to deal with the inevitable split. He had lived in Ireland shortly after leaving high school, and toured Britain as a rock drummer, a youthful fantasy job but not a great way to make a living. He returned to Ireland in 1999 with Wayne (Jake) Connor of the Loners to meet with members of the Irish Alliance. The Alliance was a confederation of independent motorcycle clubs that were loosely pulled together by a desire to keep international clubs like the Hells Angels off their turf, in much the same way that small independent clubs had managed for years to present a united front and block the Hells Angels from moving into Toronto.

In the late 1990s, the Loners also had Irish connections through Pluto, a member (and tattoo artist) who lived in Dublin, and another member named Ivan who had also lived there. Back before the patchover to the Bandidos, Loners president Jimmy Raso had sent Atkinson and Connor to Ireland in an effort to reach out to the Devil's Disciples, in hopes of expansion. The Loners had socialized with the Devil's Disciples for a couple of nights in Belfast and Dublin, where they stayed in the clubhouse and a gutted city bus that served as a mobile party place. There was also partying north of Dublin in the seaside town of Skerries, where the Irish bikers had their own scaled-down version of the Sturgis bike rally. When the visit was over, however, the Devil's Disciples remained independent, as the Canadians had dramatically underestimated how strongly the Irish bikers opposed an invasion by international clubs, whom they seemed to regard as nothing more than modern-day Huns. It was during that trip that Wrongway Atkinson was given his nickname after once getting lost and ending up in the wrong town.

Boxer's Bandidos also entertained grand thoughts of international expansion, and Atkinson was back in Ireland in 2003 with a British Bandido known as "Mick the Nomad" in an unsuccessful attempt to persuade the Irish Alliance to become Bandidos. By this time, Atkinson had risen to become *El Secretario* of the Bandidos in Canada. Despite his high rank in the club, there were times when others in the No Surrender Crew found him decidedly unbikerish, such as when he sat immersed in literary works like James Joyce's *The Dubliners* while other Bandidos partied. No explanation was needed for a chapter member to dig his nose into a line of cocaine, but burying it in a book was quite another matter. "What the fuck are you doing?" a Bandido named Beaver had asked. For Atkinson's part, the works of Joyce seemed to fit in with his biker life. "He [James Joyce] was an outsider in his own community," Atkinson later said. "I felt like that myself."

In January 2003, the No Surrender Crew seemed primed to take on another high-profile member, Joey (Crazy Horse) Morin from Edmonton. Morin had been in email contact with the club since October 2001, when he sent a message signed only "John Doe XXX." In it, he wrote hopefully: "I believe now is a very good time. I am a very educated and influential individual who's quite familiar with Biker Politics. There are more of us, whom are very interested in claiming territory with you. But for now I am doing the initiating. We have to start somewhere." In time, he and Wrongway Atkinson developed a friendly correspondence. Like Boxer Muscedere, Morin had also been a pugilist, but unlike Boxer, he shunned cocaine use. Still in his early thirties, Joey Crazy Horse was relatively young, intense, strong and tough, and he didn't suffer fools well. He also didn't brag about how, in 1991, he had been awarded a medal of bravery from the Governor General for helping pull a man and two boys from a flame-filled truck. He showed fearlessness of a different sort when he printed up stickers to mock a group of former Rebels club-mates who had gone over to the Hells Angels. The ink was in the old Rebels' colours of red and black and read, SUP-PORT ME, MYSELF AND I, a bold, public statement that he considered his old clubmates to be sellouts.

Joey Crazy Horse arrived in Toronto in early 2003 with a few Rebels from Alberta for a meeting with the No Surrender Crew. He clearly had some unexplained prob-lem with the Hells Angels that was pushing him towards the Bandidos fold, but the visitors weren't taking any possible move towards the Bandidos lightly, as they had plenty to lose. And it was clear that the days of the strong, small independent clubs seemed to be numbered. Up to that point, western Canada was considered "red and white," or Hells Angels territory, and clearly the Angels wouldn't welcome an attempt by their rivals to plant a flag there. The Rebels also had jobs, bank accounts, credit cards and motorcycles—all things in painfully short supply among the No Surrender Crew. As they met, it seemed that each of the Rebels was wearing fifty thou-sand dollars or so worth of jewellery, while most of the Torontonians couldn't afford Harleys and some still lived with their parents. If the Albertans signed on, then Boxer's club would gain a few thousand dollars a month in dues, as well as immeasurable prestige. What the Rebels stood to gain was far harder to measure.

That weekend, there was a party at Kellestine's farm, and the Torontonians could only shudder at the impression made by the garrulous hillbilly. Worse yet, Boxer lost his temper with a Toronto club member over something trivial. He worked himself into a fury and took a swing at the guy, in plain view of the Albertans. Chopper Raposo was floating around the farm stoned, which was also bad form. As he left for home, an Alberta Rebel confided to someone he trusted that he wasn't crazy about the idea of paying dues to drug addicts.

In Joey Crazy Horse, Boxer saw nothing less than a chance for a great western expansion. The party at the Kellestine farm certainly wasn't a success, but it didn't kill Boxer's dream either. He flew out to the Prairies that spring, to continue to woo Joey Crazy Horse's group, but when he returned home, his mood was somewhere between angry and depressed. Boxer hated flying at the best of times, and he especially hated flights with a stopover, as he reasoned this doubled his chances of dying in a crash during takeoff or landing. More unsettling was what Boxer saw when he landed in Alberta. The westerners were even better organized than he had expected, even though they didn't belong to an international—or even a national—club. Why they might want to join his Bandidos was a mystery.

That spring, the No Surrender Crew deemed Big Paul Sinopoli and Cameron Acorn—whom Fullager called "the fat one and the skinny one"—worthy of their prospect patches. Boxer seemed particularly impressed by Acorn. Maybe it was his energy and natural leadership ability, or maybe it was that Acorn still listened to his mother, who called herself "Moma Bee." Whatever the case, Boxer trusted him enough to put him on a fast track to full-patch status.

The Victoria Day weekend in May traditionally marks the commencement of riding season for Canadian bikers. When the big weekend rolled around in 2003, the weather was perfect for striking out as a pack on their Harleys, but only Lenti, Boxer, Wrongway Atkinson and Crash Kriarakis actually had working motorcycles. Lenti was livid. He had a good excuse for not riding, since he had been blown almost in half by a bomb, yet he was still gamely riding his bike. A few days later, only about ten of eighteen club members showed up to a barbecue in Ripper's backyard. If they weren't about motorcycles or big on brotherhood, it was natural to wonder what exactly was the point of the Toronto Bandidos chapter. Certainly, none of them was making money as big-time criminals.

Although the club lacked money, members and motorcycles, Boxer still often mustered up a swagger on the streets and was especially cocky in Internet chat rooms. He loved to goad and mock the Hells Angels, calling them losers and making veiled threats. Perhaps that was on the mind of Woodbridge Hells Angels in mid-June 2003, when they heard that Crash Kriarakis of the No Surrender Crew had been spotted sitting alone in a Woodbridge restaurant, wearing Bandidos gear. The two sides had reached an agreement of sorts in Woodbridge, whereby the Bandidos could wear their colours on the west side of Highway 400, which bisected the town, while the Angels could openly wear their colours on the east side. That afternoon, Crash was dining alone on the wrong side of town.

For the most part, the Greater Toronto Area Hells Angels ignored the Bandidos or treated them with contempt. But Crash's appearance at the restaurant on their side of town was too provocative to ignore. In their eyes, it was nothing less than a public insult. A half-dozen Hells Angels quickly arrived, including a particularly beefy specimen known as Mr. Meaney. Crash was no match for Mr. Meaney, even if he had wanted to fight.

And he was no fighter. He had been an enthusiastic high school rugby player, but he was too bound by ideas like fair play and kindness to be an effective, down-and-dirty brawler. So when the Hells Angels interrupted Crash's solitary meal to tell him they wanted to speak with him immediately in the parking lot, he panicked and refused, calling a friend for help. That friend instantly telephoned Frank Lenti, who lived just a few minutes away.

Although he was almost sixty and walked with a pronounced limp, Lenti didn't ask how many Hells Angels were at the restaurant or wait for backup when he got the call. He simply hopped in his tow truck and roared over to help his biker brother. When he got there, the Angels were gone and the police were just arriving. Crash was still in the restaurant, with a fresh black eye that bore the imprint of a large ring worn by one of the Angels. Lenti was beside himself with anger. Outlaw bikers aren't supposed to call the police, no matter what the threat. They are supposed to take care of business themselves. It had been nervous restaurant staff who called the police, but it still looked bad, as if Crash was somehow a rat. If Crash had gone outside to settle things up with the Angels, he might have taken a beating, but a few bruises were immeasurably preferable to this public embarrassment.

An emergency meeting was called that night at Ripper Fullager's, followed by a sit-down with the Eastern Avenue Hells Angels. In the end, most of Boxer and Lenti's anger was directed at Crash. The Angels had done exactly what you'd expect a one percenter club to do: they had marked their turf and protected their brand. Crash's behaviour wasn't so forgivable. "You should have fought like a man," Boxer told him, more than once. Not long after his beating, Crash moved from Woodbridge down into Toronto, into a luxury condominium with proper security. He told a few close friends of the move, but not a word was said to Frank Lenti or Boxer Muscedere. They may have been his brothers, but they were now brothers he didn't want dropping by.

Joey Crazy Horse was back in Toronto that June, at the time of Crash's restaurant debacle. The more he saw of Boxer's No Surrender Crew, the more doubts he nursed about it. During that visit, he attended a get-together at the Club Pro Adult Entertainment Lounge in Vaughan, where Lenti worked in a loosely defined security capacity. While the strippers were plentiful and accommodating, Joey Crazy Horse remained uneasy about linking his fate

with that of the Torontonians. There was something exciting about the potential here, but they needed to build on
Lenti's muscle, Atkinson's brains and Boxer's fearless loyalty. Otherwise, they could expect more beatings, or worse.

CHAPTER 7

Visitor from the West

In following him, I follow but myself.
OTHELLO, ACT 1, SCENE 1

He's hiding something.
FRANK LENTI COMMENTS ON PROSPECTIVE
BANDIDO MEMBER MICHAEL (TAZ) SANDHAM

Part of the appeal of a growling Harley-Davidson motorcycle is that it can make a weak man feel strong, and Michael (Taz, Tazman, Little Beaker, Poo Bear) Sandham had plenty of failure to put behind him as he rode up the potholed dirt road to Weiner Kellestine's farm in June 2003. If things went well, Sandham might finally become somebody. If things slipped in the wrong direction, another disappointment was almost too much for him to contemplate.

Sandham's last shot at redemption was the Bandidos.

Sandham had taken a twisted road to get to the dirty white farmhouse on Aberdeen Line. He had served in the Second Battalion of the Princess Patricia's Canadian Light Infantry in Winnipeg from the age of twenty until twenty-four. With no tours of duty overseas, it was a secure if low-paying job for a young man with serious family responsibilities and ambitions that greatly outstripped his abilities. At twenty, he had married a woman he had known for only six months, and by the time he was honourably discharged, there were two young children to support and a marriage on the brink of collapse.

Sandham later claimed that his military work included time with the elite Special Intelligence Unit, working on top-secret operations, and that he had served for a time in combat in Bosnia. Like his host, Weiner Kellestine, Sandham liked to lie that he had been a commando with the Canadian Airborne Regiment before it was disbanded in disgrace. When Sandham left the military as a private in June 1994, he immediately bought himself a business suit and said he was going to work for the Canadian Security Intelligence Service on top-secret projects. A second career as a spy sounded impressive, but it was hard to believe his yarn about working for CSIS when he was selling vacuum cleaners on commission and living in a modest rented townhouse he could not afford. He was too proud for his wife, Cynthia, to go to work, but not too proud for her to accept donations from a food bank or borrow money from her grandmother.

Sandham's next plan was to draw upon his military training to open up a martial arts school. He had taken some combat training in the military, but now held himself out to be nothing less than an international fighting phenomenon and a virtual one-man army. He pretended, in pamphlets he had printed up, to have black belts in several fighting styles, as well as a 12–0 record (with eleven knock-outs) in full-contact hand-to-hand combat matches in Canada, the U.S. and Korea. He wrote that he had achieved a sixth-degree black belt in hwa rang kempo, a fourth-degree black belt in tae kwon do, a black belt in jiu-jitsu and a red sash, signifying master's status, in wing chun kung fu. As if all that weren't enough, he wrote that he had attended "many self-defence seminars throughout the world hosted by such famous people as Chuck Norris, Steven Seagal, Bill 'Superfoot' Wallace and Dan Inosanto (the only person certified by Bruce Lee)." And to hear him tell it, these were the least of his fighting accomplishments. He claimed his speciality was an unknown martial art he had founded himself, in which he anointed himself with a ninth-degree black belt and the exalted title of "Grand Master." He described his new fighting art as a harmonious melding of mind and body and a "modern day warrior style," and promised to teach his students "psychology, fear management, and sound tactics." The new sport was named after himself: "Sando."

Sandham wrote that world leaders sought him out to avail themselves of his unique understanding of tactics, weaponry and bare-knuckle combat skills. Describing himself in the third person, he wrote: "He is a VIP Protection Specialist and has protected such persons as former Chief of Staff General DeChastelane [sic], former Prime Minister Brian Molruney [sic], Princess Patricia and various other higher military staff. Mr. Sandham was also involved in crowd security during the Princess Diana and Prince Charles visit to Canada."

Illegal steroid injections made "Sando Grand Master"

Sandham look somewhat bigger and more powerful than his natural self, which still wasn't all that big or powerful. The drugs also had a predictable effect on his temper. Soon, Cynthia was complaining that he was physically and emotionally abusive, sometimes spitting on her and the boys.

Not long after that, Cynthia moved out, and Sandham was ordered by the court to pay a hundred dollars a month in child support. By this time, the former couple was no longer on speaking terms. Among his last words to her, Cynthia later said, was a threat that if he couldn't have her, no one could, since he would kill her.

Despite his impressive brochures, Sandham's plans for the martial arts studio didn't pan out, and in 1998 Sandham filed for bankruptcy. But while he might not relish discussing his financial failures, bankruptcy was something the No Surrender Crew might have been expected to view sympathetically. But they would have been a lot less accommodating had they ever found out what had come next in Sandham's life. As he made his way to Kellestine's farmhouse, Taz brought with him a secret that, if discovered, could prove fatal for himself or the club—or both.

The secret would be hard to keep, since Frank Lenti had already caught a whiff of it. He had heard from an old friend in the Outlaws that Sandham had already tried to join that club and been turned down. And it hadn't been a difficult decision. Some people said that he had once been a cop. Former police officers and prison guards were automatically barred from joining any one percenter club. Lenti's friend advised him to carefully check that rumour out before accepting the Winnipegger into their fold. Lenti called Weiner Kellestine in Iona Station and told him about the ambitious candidate for membership in the No Surrender Crew and the troubling rumours that accompanied him. As the club's *sargento de armas,* or sergeant-at-arms, Kellestine was responsible for such security assignments.

"I'll pick his brain," Kellestine promised. "I'll pick his fucking brain."

Kellestine seemed to be the ideal man to check out the membership candidate. A paranoid's paranoid, Kellestine held himself out to be an intelligence expert with his business, Triple K Securities. If there was a member of the No Surrender Crew with the skills to suss Michael Sandham out, it was Wayne Kellestine.

For a guy like Kellestine, Sandham should have been a gold mine. Because Sandham *had* been a cop. Maybe not quite a real cop at first—he found work as an auxiliary officer for the police force in Ste. Anne, east of Winnipeg, as he recovered from bankruptcy—but a cop all the same, particularly in the eyes of a one percenter. He then went to police college, and finally seemed to have found his calling. He was tops in his class in marksmanship, and showed a keen interest in weapons and street gangs. His police college records noted he was "an active team member" and "co-operative and friendly."

When he applied for work in the nine-officer rural East St. Paul police force, twenty kilometres outside Winnipeg, Sandham wrote that he was profoundly influenced by his four years in the Canadian military, writing, "the elimate [*sic*] of discipline was always their [*sic*]." He also praised his police college studies, but "of course the discipline may not be as high as the military." Neither strong spelling nor modesty were qualities East St. Paul was in a position to insist upon, and Sandham was hired.

His policing career came to an abrupt end in October 2002, after he appeared in a surveillance video shot by the Ontario Provincial Police Biker Enforcement Unit at the funeral of Outlaws club member William (Wild Bill) Hulko in Sault Ste. Marie. At the time, Sandham had told his chief that he was going to Vancouver for the funeral of a relative. Immediately after the service in Sault Ste. Marie, he had requested a sick leave, then headed to the Outlaws clubhouse in Woodstock, Ontario, where he hung out for a week. Once his chief caught wind of his lies, Sandham quickly resigned rather than face a firing. Despite the unfortunate connection to the Outlaws, the tiny force's chief still wrote a letter of reference for Sandham, which helped him land a job with a private security and investigation firm. This meant Sandham still at least looked like a cop, as he patrolled the Manitoba back roads as a not-so-glorified security guard.

To Frank Lenti it wouldn't have mattered whether Sandham was a security guard, a dog catcher or a meter maid. If he had ever been a cop, there was no way he was joining the Bandidos. Ex-cops and former prison guards were, by definition, untrustworthy. Such men were only after power, not brotherhood, and they'd crack if put to the test. Worse yet, they could be feeding information to their police friends. In the one percenter world, there were few people more dangerous than a lamb in wolf's clothing.

So Lenti was more than a little surprised when he paid Kellestine and Sandham a visit and found the *sargento de armas* relaxed and sucking on a beer. It looked more like a drinking party than an interrogation session.

"I thought you were picking his fucking brain," Lenti said.

"I'm about done," Kellestine replied.

Still, Lenti and another biker friend had their own queasy feelings about Sandham. He sat quietly and didn't interact with others at Kellestine's farm, and seemed like the kind of guy who tattled in school or sucked up to the school bully in hopes of manipulating him to fight his battles. Even his voice was squeaky, as if someone were squeezing his nuts.

"Have you noticed that when you talk to him, he turns red?" Lenti asked his friend.

"Yeah."

"He's hiding something," Lenti said.

There was also something a little odd about Sandham's total lack of tattoos. Lenti's massive arms are like pictographs, telling stories of the rise and fall of clubs in Ontario since the early 1970s. They bear the devil ensigns of his old clubs the Satan's Choice and Diabolos, crossed Confederate flags for the old Rebels club, and a single Confederate flag for the Loners. There had been a three-inch skull on his right forearm to signify his time with the Outlaws, which was transformed into a psychedelic inferno after he left that club. His arms also bore images of a dancing skeleton, a nude woman, triangles with the "1%er" legend, and his own personal symbol, the "bastone," or baton—representative of the club suit in an Italian deck of playing cards. His right forearm featured a sombrero to signify the Bandidos, and the number 13 for the letter *M*, the thirteenth letter of the alphabet. The *M* stood for marijuana, motorcyclism, murder and mother in the biker world.

By contrast, Sandham's stubby arms were as bare as Lenti was suspicious of him. He would have to pass several tests before he would be allowed to ink the Fat Mexican on them, if the veteran one percenter had any say in the matter.

Between sips of beer, Kellestine offered to go to Winnipeg and live there for a while, to further investigate Sandham's background. Lenti feared this would just mean more partying, at club expense. "We can't afford that," Lenti said.

But neither could the Bandidos afford to let the wrong guy into the club. The Bandidos may not have had much, but they had the certainty of their rough-hewn fraternity. Whether a club has as much to lose as the Hells Angels, or as little as the Bandidos, the rules are the same. It is common practice for one percenter clubs to run intense background checks on prospective members. Some police officers grumble that bikers carry out tougher screening than police forces do for their own recruits. What happened when Michael Sandham came calling, however, was inexplicable: Boxer's friend, Weiner Kellestine, was asleep at the wheel. From that moment, things would never be the same for the No Surrender Crew.

CHAPTER 8

Growth

Idle weeds are fast in growth.
RICHARD III, ACT 3, SCENE 1

*It's like the police. There are some are honest
and some who are corrupt.*
CHOPPER RAPOSO

In July 2003, Luis Manny (Chopper) Raposo of the No Surrender Crew was in jail in Laval, north of Montreal, when justice officials approached him with an offer. He had been behind bars for thirteen months on drug charges—including conspiracy to buy Viagra and ecstasy—laid as a result of Project Amigo. The deal: he could immediately walk free, if he would plead guilty to gangsterism. "I'm not guilty and I'm not going to plead guilty," Chopper told a judge on July 18. "It's not a crime to go to parties or to go to funerals. Yes, I am a member of the Bandidos, but it's like priests in the Catholic church. There are some who are pedophiles, and others who are not. It's like the police. There are some who are honest and some who are corrupt."

By the time Chopper delivered his courtroom lecture, the Crown's case against him was crumbling. Informer Eric (Ratkiller) Nadeau, who held the rank of *secretario* or secretary of the Montreal chapter of the Bandidos, was proving to be an erratic police witness. The Crown's case was so thin that a judge set Chopper free before his scheduled trial. Pure defiance turned out to have been a brilliant legal strategy.

Chopper Raposo returned to Toronto a bitter man. He valued one percenter brotherhood, and it stung him that fellow chapter members hadn't visited or written him, leaving him all alone in the largely francophone jail, deep in Hells Angels territory. In their defence, several members were under strict bail and parole stipulations that barred such contact, and Wrongway Atkinson had visited Chopper's mother every two weeks to run errands for her. Still, Chopper was in a foul mood as he moved into the upstairs loft of his parents' home. His grumbling became so loud that Boxer and the rest of the No Surrender Crew fully expected him to turn in his club colours at a church meeting one evening. Instead, Chopper relented, and agreed to stay on despite his bruised feelings, in a decision that immediately added muscle to the club. Chopper had no way of knowing how the decision would change his life.

Crash Kriarakis made a trip to Greece that summer, and took a detour on the way home to visit Germany, where he spent a few weeks with the Bandidos' Eastgate chapter on the outskirts of Berlin. Crash posted messages on the Internet describing how the German Bandidos were a strong and efficient bunch of brothers. They were a motorcycle club that actually rode motorcycles, and also didn't seem to have a bad reputation with the general public. They were an example of what the No Surrender Crew could be, if they learned some discipline and restraint. Boxer loved to read Crash's positive Internet postings, and was excited about the possibilities for the No Surrender Crew. When Crash returned home to Toronto, he presented Boxer with a German souvenir Bandido T-shirt. Caught up in the spirit of internationalism and efficiency, Lenti printed up a batch of "I support the Bandidos worldwide" T-shirts.

In July 2003, Boxer approved a plan by Alain Brunette to end Quebec's bloody biker wars over the Montreal cocaine trade, which had lasted almost a decade and killed some 170 people. The arrangement with the Hells Angels looked a lot like unconditional surrender. The Bandidos agreed to fold in Quebec altogether in July 2003. In return, the Hells Angels guaranteed that Bandidos in prison and on the streets could go on living.

Although Boxer had agreed with the plan, he was soon dismissing the Quebec Bandidos who made the deal as cowards. All future expansion would have to be to the west, and Boxer clearly wanted to be the one leading that drive to the Pacific. Members said privately that Boxer didn't understand the pressures of life behind bars for men like Brunette, since he hadn't ever been in prison himself. They also worried that Boxer seemed to be changing. He had once been a jovial buddy, but now showed traces of megalomania. Did he think he was doing them all a favour, coming in from Chatham to lead them?

Throughout the summer, Boxer continued to bask in

his role as national *presidente*. Despite the growing pains, including the dearth of members who actually rode motorcycles, Boxer remained optimistic that the Bandidos could expand and become a truly national brotherhood.

Club spirits were dampened somewhat that summer when two bicycle patrol officers became suspicious about the beer and brotherhood they spied while riding past Ripper Fullager's backyard. They immediately notified the Biker Enforcement Unit, who crashed the event. From that point on, Ripper's backyard barbecues could only be visited by people without bail or parole stipulations, which put a decided crimp in his guest list.

That summer, Crash Kriarakis encouraged a biker—known as "Mr Clean" for his bald pate—to shake his dependence on percodan, a prescription painkiller that gave him an artificial glow of contentment. Crash's efforts appeared to be going well until Mr. Clean slipped up during a church meeting held in Ripper's home and called Ripper a drunk. Mr. Clean was almost ten years younger than Boxer, but that didn't stop the president from tattooing Mr. Clean's face with a volley of lefts and rights, making a crisp and sickening *whack, whack, whack* sound. Boxer was loyal to Ripper and demanded that others respect the senior biker as well. Once the punches subsided, Mr. Clean fled the church meeting in his truck, never to be seen again. It was painfully clear that Ripper was a man to be respected and Boxer was someone to be feared. Thoughts of the purplish welts on Mr Clean's face were a reminder to others in the crew of what they might expect if they provoked the wrath of Boxer.

In August, records for the Central Region of the Hells Angels pointed out that the Ontario Angels hadn't agreed to the truce reached in Quebec with the Bandidos. The notes also hinted at possible future tensions in Ontario: " . . . at the Canada Run we received a message that the Banditos [*sic*] in Quebec were handing in their patches, disbanding, & the members that wanted to stay in the club were told they could move to Ontario with the blessing of the Hells Angels, we sent back a message that this was not approved by any of us."

For his part, Boxer continued to look westward in hopes of expansion, glory and dues money. In late October, Boxer and a Bandido named Chief flew out to British Columbia, where they met in Surrey with Robert Charles Simpson, who worked in a local motorcycle shop, and a couple of other prospective members. The province seemed ripe for the Bandidos, especially since members in Tacoma and Spokane were close enough to provide support. Then, on November 7, 2003, Boxer and a dozen others from the No Surrender Crew met with about eight Edmonton bikers— led by Joey Crazy Horse—at a hotel near the Toronto airport. The topic again was moving west.

Back on the home front, there was also cause for Boxer to be optimistic. His crew still didn't have a clubhouse to call home, but they were able to wangle permission to meet once a week in the basement of a Greek restaurant in south Riverdale, near the intersection of Broadview Avenue and Queen Street East, in the grotty shadow of Jilly's strip club.[19] The restaurant owner didn't know anything about outlaw motorcycle clubs, but he did take an instant liking to Crash Kriarakis. He seemed like a nice, polite Greek boy. How bad could it be if a group of his friends met once a week in his basement?

Though the arrangement was certainly better than continuing to hold random meetings in members' homes, it still paled in comparison to the Hells Angels' fortified downtown clubhouse, with its welded steel sculpture by the reinforced front door, a five-minute drive away. The restaurant's basement—which was musty, poorly lit and littered with cases of empty beer bottles, food boxes and old tables and chairs—looked shabbier still compared to the hilltop compound of the Sherbrooke Hells Angels, with its high security, private forest and welcoming strippers. But it was better than nothing.

Perhaps someday in the future, Boxer's crew might have a separate meeting place of its own. In the meantime, there were niggling day-to-day concerns that slowed down the club's quest for expansion. Frank Lenti grumbled about how tough it was to get Christmas cards and red and gold stickers made up. Prices were high, and craftsmanship was low. Making things worse, no one seemed to be able to agree on what would make a good Christmas card. It was hard to imagine the nearby Hells Angels, in their stylish bunker, getting into a flap over a task that should have been simple and fun.

One suggestion was that the No Surrender Crew could try something that involved having their pictures taken in sombreros, like the ones Pierre (Carlitto) Aragon of the Killerbeez sometimes wore. The Bandidos often sported them when visiting a Mexican restaurant near King Street

West and Spadina Avenue in downtown Toronto, and they always seemed to get a laugh. Or perhaps they could try something similar to what Crash's new friends in the Berlin Bandidos had done: they had mailed out Yule greetings that showed club members, all dressed in black and looking suitably tough but tidy in their Fat Mexican club colours. In front of them were a pair of naked—and fat-free—women, wearing little more than Santa tuques.

That November there was yet another insult, when Boxer and a half-dozen No Surrender members went to a downtown Toronto strip club for an afternoon of beer and table-top entertainment. Once there, they were told they would have to remove their colours or leave the club. Boxer led them away in a huff, grumbling that they would take their business elsewhere. A few days later, the insult was compounded when they heard that the same strip club had let in a party of Hells Angels, wearing full club regalia.

Things weren't going so well at their temporary clubhouse, either. On one particularly embarrassing day, Bam Bam Salerno skipped out of the restaurant upstairs without paying for a hamburger. Confronted with his deed, Bam Bam turned indignant and insisted he had every intention of settling his tab soon. But despite his optimism and his frequent assurances that he was good for the money, Salerno was in debt to clubmates. He also owed a mechanic $400 on a clunker of a BMW he'd bought for $2,000. One thing he didn't want was a repeat of the humiliation of being kicked out of the club for thirty days for non-payment of dues. He talked of finding a real job of his own, and not just making money on petty scams like smuggling cigarettes from First Nations reserves, but he always seemed to be saying things like that. It went without saying that it would be difficult to find good, honest work, even if he truly wanted it, because he couldn't seem to stay out of trouble—his criminal record was pockmarked with some thirty convictions, most of them for drug and theft offences.

Still, Bam Bam would say hopefully that all he needed was one employer who wanted his services. "All you need is one spot," he told a friend. Working in an office, as another drone in the workforce, sometimes didn't sound so bad. He confided that he was even willing to cut his hair and shave his beard, if that was what it took to get him employed. That a member of the No Surrender Crew would have to contemplate a "civilian" job to pay off the debts he had incurred as a biker is some indication of the Toronto Bandidos' success as criminals.

There was no stronger constant in Bam Bam's life than the support of his wife, Stephanie. There had been a time when Bam Bam was so fat that he wheezed when he walked, like Big Paul Sinopoli, but Stephanie had quietly enlisted the portly biker in the Jenny Craig weight-loss program. Now, there was just a little jiggle to his gait, and Bam Bam was a happier man for it. And while Bam Bam waited for his big break, he cleaned and cooked and fretted in the spacious Oakville home paid for by Stephanie, who ran a beauty salon. "I feel like a loser," he told a friend. "My wife's the one making the money. I do all of the housework."

Bam Bam's very presence in the windowless basement, amidst the cases of beer bottles and stacks of old chairs, seemed to provoke Frank Lenti into chastising him. A man like Lenti could never follow a leader like Salerno, whom he deemed a pussy. It came as no surprise that there were often ugly confrontations between the two. Bam Bam was battling heroin addiction, while Lenti didn't even smoke cigarettes and made it a point of honour that he never dealt drugs. Lenti even had bikers spy on his own children, to make sure they didn't smoke or use drugs. Lenti once confronted Bam Bam about a *bastone* tattoo he saw on Salerno's arm. Lenti considered that his own personal marker. He never got tired of pointing at the tattoo on his own arm and joking, "I always have something up my sleeve." Here was Bam Bam, cutting in on his brand by getting the same tattoo. Lenti gave Salerno a day to do something about it, or he would personally, and roughly, remove the ink *for* him. Bam Bam foolishly ignored the threat, and suffered a beating. Soon afterwards, the tattoo was gone.

At another meeting, Lenti confronted Bam Bam about a rumour that Bam Bam was speaking to the police. The tone of Lenti's voice made it clear that blood would soon be splattered in the small, dank basement if Bam Bam didn't provide the proper answer, and quickly. "You have no proof," Bam Bam protested. Lenti pressed on, saying that a prison source said that Bam Bam was a rat. Salerno protested that the prisoner was simply telling a lie to turn his biker brothers against him. Things calmed somewhat, with Lenti telling Bam Bam that he must confront the source once he was released from prison. "You settle that beef when he gets out," Lenti ordered.

At still another meeting, Lenti exploded about disrespectful and anonymous messages he had just read on the Bandidos' website. The gist of the accusations was that Lenti placed himself above the club, and Lenti didn't take such comments lightly. "Some piece of shit has been writing shit on the guest book," he fumed. His voice was low and threatening as he banged on a table and continued, "I have proof."

Lenti then announced that he had traced the "piece of shit" to an IP address that had the distinct smell of Bam Bam Salerno. He called Salerno a liar and a thief who should be kicked out of the club. Anyone who knew Frank Lenti knew that, when angry, he gouged eyes, and so the pressure was on Salerno to quickly pacify him.

The best Salerno could do at first was blubber, "Please, please, please." He frantically denied the accusation. He insisted that someone with advanced computer skills had infiltrated his email. High-tech demons were trying to divide and conquer their crew. Most likely it was an Outlaw who'd broken into his house and tapped into his computer, he continued.

"Wasn't me, bro," he protested, between tears. A few days later, Bam Bam produced a letter from his Internet provider, which he said offered irrefutable proof that the accusations against him were groundless. It was only natural to wonder how much Bam Bam had bribed a cable company employee to provide the letter. Or perhaps it was just a forgery, which was cheaper than a bribe and would have the same effect. Most likely, Salerno was being chatty while stoned on painkillers.

Once again, it had appeared that all hell would break loose in the basement, and once again, things eventually subsided. These meetings were like family squabbles: full of drama, but often ending with something that at least resembled warmth.

In December, Bam Bam Salerno announced that he was climbing out from under a few thousand dollars' worth of debt to his clubmates. In a proud, almost buoyant mood, he told a friend that putting family and biker "brothers" first was the right way to run his life. "You'll never have to go to a stranger because your family will back you 100 percent," Bam Bam said, sounding like a proud child.

It was a particularly happy Christmas for Boxer. That November, he had met Nina Lee, the friend of a Bandido named Chief, and crew members noted quietly that she was quite a catch, while the grizzled Boxer was no Brad Pitt. By the time the No Surrender Crew held its Christmas party in a Woodbridge restaurant that year, Boxer was clearly in love. His passions rivalled his early days in the Bandidos, when he rode alone in the rain. That evening, Nina sat on his lap and they necked like high school kids. It was a new public side of Boxer that his friends found unsettling. It was natural to wonder if he might mellow and lower his guard.

The new year promised great things for Boxer's crew. An email sent on December 20, 2003, by Nina's friend "Bandido Chief 1%ER," bubbled with brotherhood and optimism that things were finally headed in the right direction:

Just wanted to say i had a great time last night. good to see most of my brothers Crash Beaver Boxer Chopper frenchie circlehead and the one with the red and smelled like diesel fuel you know who you are. Bam Bam i know you were working to bad i know we would have cracked jokes all night L.L.R [Love. Loyalty. Respect] Cisco fucking site looking great . . . i love it.Good to see our friends and hanga-rounds Had a great time Love.Loyalty and Respect B.F.F.B. [Bandidos forever, forever Bandidos] .

The year 2003 ended with a New Year's party at Ripper Fullager's. Over a few beers, the No Surrender Crew decided to disband their junior support club, the Killerbeez. Valued brothers were needed in the big club, where they could be prospects, or junior members. Boxer worried that some of the kids who wanted to join the Killerbeez weren't even of legal drinking age. His club needed an influx of proven men, not boys, if it was going to survive.

CHAPTER 9

Shot of Reality

O, beware, my lord, of jealousy;
It is the green-eyed monster which doth mock
The meat it feeds on . . .
OTHELLO, ACT 3, SCENE 3

The puppet has cut his strings.
FRIEND OF BOXER MUSCEDERE DESCRIBES
TENSIONS WITH WEINER KELLESTINE

The No Surrender Crew was homeless again in January, after the owner of the Greek restaurant had second thoughts about the bikers meeting in his basement. No businessman is eager to turn away patrons, and there wasn't anyone else vying for use of the basement, but the restaurateur had heard bad things about one percenter clubs and politely asked them to stay away. Boxer was more offended than angry, but respected his wishes and moved his crew on.

He was still infatuated with his grand plans for expansion. The idea was to shore up his American support, while pushing into the west. Perhaps Taz Sandham from Winnipeg could open some doors for them. Weiner Kellestine certainly seemed comfortable enough with him, even though Sandham was a newcomer to one percenter life.

One of Boxer's ideas was to fly to Detroit on a small private plane, since his biker profile made it hard for him to cross the border via regular channels. Although Boxer was a white-knuckle flyer, it was still worth the aggravation. Once in the U.S., he would drive to Colorado to meet senior American Bandidos face to face. They would discuss such matters as Boxer's expansion plans, but the main point was that they meet face to face, man to man. That plan fell through when Boxer couldn't find a pilot who would take him across the border on the sly. The rejection didn't hit him too hard, since it would have been difficult to scrape up money for the flight—or even a car rental in the U.S.—anyway.

There's a truism in organized crime that you don't have to worry about your enemies, because it's your friends that will do you in. A criminal's killer is often the last guy he had a cup of coffee or a beer with. Whether or not Joey (Crazy Horse) Morin had been drinking with the men who shot him in the parking lot of Edmonton's Saint Pete's strip club a half-hour before midnight on Friday,

January 30, 2004, he apparently knew them. They managed to walk right up to him and open fire on him and his associate, Robert Simpson, at close range. The encounter ended with Morin and Simpson lying on the pavement in pools of their own blood. Simpson died on the spot, while Joey Crazy Horse made it to hospital before he too was pronounced dead.

Boxer, Chopper, Crash, Beaver, Chief and a prospect named Max were able to make the trip west for the funeral. Weiner Kellestine was still behind bars, so his attendance wasn't an option. The trip was especially tough financially for Chopper, as he hadn't been out of jail for very long and was particularly short of funds. Big Paul Sinopoli wasn't yet a full-patch member, and didn't have the money for the flight anyway. Frank Lenti stayed behind as well, as his wife was ready to give birth any day to another son—or, as he indelicately put it, "the old lady is ready to drop any minute." It wasn't a full attendance at the funeral for the No Surrender Crew, but it was definitely a display of respect. Joey had been one of them, having joined up the previous summer, and now he was dead from the bullet of someone who still walked free. As a lasting tribute, Boxer and Big Paul tattooed "Crazy Horse" and "GFBD," for "God Forgives, Bandidos Don't," in gothic script on their right inner arms.

Boxer, Chopper and Lenti weren't impressed that no one from the probationary Winnipeg chapter had bothered to attend, even though they were far closer. The Winnipeggers hadn't shown much interest in other club events, but this was different. Club funerals were mandatory events for all one percenters, and this one was picked up by television news crews, which recorded the sparse turnout. With disgust, the No Surrender Crew members also noted that not one Bandido brother had travelled north from the mother chapter to pay his respects.

The television cameras also picked up something that infuriated local Hells Angels: a Bandido hugging someone who wore the patch of the tiny Pilgrims club from Saskatchewan. The Pilgrims were formed in the late 1990s in Saskatchewan as a non-criminal Christian-biker alternative to the Hells Angels. Several of their members were more biker than Christian, and all of them were resented by the Hells Angels. On one night, which the Pilgrims called "The First Last Supper," the Angels summoned them to their Saskatoon clubhouse. Once the doors were locked, the Angels told them they were about to be stripped of their colours: a patch with a golden cross outlined in red—the reverse of the Bandidos' colours. Angels with guns stood by, and the Pilgrims were told they would be shot if they persisted in wearing the red and gold.

There was no formal connection between the Bandidos and the Pilgrims, but there was a link nonetheless, as a result of Lenti's outgoing personality. The Christian bikers were brave enough to disregard the explicit threat from the Hells Angels, and soon there was word of a "foot fuck" order against their members, meaning they could be expected to be kicked to a pulp if they were caught. So when the western Angels saw the Pilgrim patch again at Joey Crazy Horse's funeral, they were livid. The fact that a Pilgrim was hugging a Bandido only made things worse.

There would be no arrests after Joey's murder—only

theories. The obvious one was that Crazy Horse had been the last holdout against his Rebels flipping over to the Hells Angels. Another was more personal: Joey was loved by his friends, but they knew he had trouble controlling his mouth. Shortly before his murder, he had gotten into a confrontation in a bar and dared another man to shoot him. Whatever the case, it was easy to think about how the American Bandidos hadn't done anything to help with the Edmonton tensions, despite repeated requests from Canada.

The bullets that dropped Joey Crazy Horse and Robert Simpson were sobering blasts of reality for Boxer and his crew. Joey was smart and likeable and tough enough to walk the streets of Edmonton as the city's only full-patch Bandido. His death hit the girlfriends and wives of the No Surrender Crew particularly hard. Joey Crazy Horse didn't have vices like booze or drugs, and the thirty-four-year-old was physically stronger than most, if not all, of them. The women couldn't help but worry. It was as if their men in the No Surrender Crew were just playing gangster, which seemed harmless enough, as long as no one else took them seriously. With Joey's death, it was clear this wasn't just a game and that biker violence wasn't just an issue in Quebec. Things could end permanently for any of them with the quarter-inch pull of a trigger. Were they all drifting towards disaster without even realizing it?

Soon, there was a place of honour for Joey Crazy Horse and Simpson on the Bandidos' Canadian website, with grand messages like "Rest in peace, my brothers. You will never be forgotten" and "This was a coward's way of doing things." The club's Canadian office praised the two dead bikers as men "who tried paving the road of brotherhood throughout Canada." The message continued with an old Bandidos saying that felt particularly appropriate for the time: "You cut one, we all bleed."

A few weeks later, the website boldly announced that more chapters were "coming soon" to Canada. No mention was made of Taz Sandham, but the Winnipegger was clearly part of the Bandidos' plans now. Boxer and his brothers weren't going to be deterred by the murders, although it went without saying that it was far harder to expand in the real world than in cyberspace.

Boxer was able to make a little money off a scheme he hatched in a restaurant on Danforth Avenue in Toronto's Greek district. He, Bam Bam and a couple of others were paid fifteen thousand dollars for scaring a businessman into paying off a seventy-thousand-dollar debt he owed to a restaurateur. None of Boxer's crew had big-time criminal businesses, like drug networks, and few of them besides Boxer had legitimate sources of income, so the opportunity to put some easy money into their jeans by acting tough was welcome indeed.

A feature of twenty-first-century outlaw bikers is that they patrol the Internet with a vigilance. Frank Lenti was troubled to find a message posted on March 10, 2004, by someone purporting to be the club's former *sargento de armas*, Eric (the Red) McMillan, who had faded away from the club since being stabbed in the stomach in the Oshawa parking lot by Hells Angels.

"Ya I got fucked up a bit in Oshawa and my bros did what?" the poster asked. "Fuck all. You hid like you always do. You talk about cowards. You don't even wear your colours out in Toronto at least I wore mine! I heard one of your brothers got his face kicked in the last time he wore his colours out a few months ago! You are so full of shit."

The poster went on to say that some former Ontario Bandidos were now begging the Hells Angels to let them join, to no avail. "The last of you are just wasting your time," he taunted.

The Internet tough guy said he would be glad to fight any of them in real life, if they had the courage to show their faces. He could regularly be found north of Highway 401, in a strip club frequented by Hells Angels where the featured dancer was a former Toronto Argonaut cheerleader. "The problem is you guys don't come out . . . fucking goofs," the emailer sneered.

It was troubling, but Lenti and the others couldn't think of anything to do, beyond grumbling vaguely about how someone should talk to an official with the poster's Internet service provider.

Whatever they did, or wherever they went, it was easy for Boxer's crew to imagine that the Hells Angels were nearby, watching and poised to strike. That April, a man walked into a Bandidos party in a Legion hall near Ripper's house in Toronto's South Riverdale district, wearing a Hells Angels support shirt. The man didn't appear to be too tough or aggressive, and said he thought it was a Hells Angels party. But the unsolved murder of Crazy Horse Morin had left the No Surrender Crew understandably jittery. Could the stranger's presence be just an honest mistake? Or was he really spying on them? Was this some kind of Hells Angels head game? Whatever the case, Boxer told the stranger to leave.

Big Paul Sinopoli was still a probationary member as the summer of 2004 began, meaning he had fallen behind Cameron Acorn, who had been fast-tracked by Boxer to full-patch status in just three months. Being a probationary member was not a lot more fun than volunteering to be a lackey, and Big Paul had to be on call to drive any full-patch member anywhere, at any time of day or night. One night that summer, Big Paul caught wind that he might finally get promoted to full status at a church meeting. Such a step required total approval of all chapter members, and just when it seemed time for Big Paul to get his reward, Chopper Raposo spoke up and dashed the idea.

While others wanted to boost the club's membership, Raposo remained a hard-liner. He valued quality more than numbers. He also couldn't forget how tough it had been for him to get his full-patch status with the Loners back in the late 1990s, when Ripper Fullager was a senior member of that club. Among other things, old-school one percenters like Ripper thought candidates for full membership should always have matches and toothpicks in their vests, just in case a full-patch member wanted to light a cigarette or pick his teeth. Many hopeful would-be members had been caught off guard by Ripper asking, "Do you have a toothpick?" or "Do you have a light?" It was a good way of checking on whether prospects paid attention to detail, and Chopper Raposo kept screwing up back then. Now Chopper saw himself as a guardian of high standards when evaluating prospects like Big Paul. So that summer evening, Big Paul went home to the basement apartment in his parents' home in Jacksons Point feeling deflated, still wondering when—if ever—he would be welcomed fully into the big club.

Minutes of the Hells Angels Ontario officers' meeting in July 2004 suggest that Boxer and the Bandidos remained cocky and kept on ignoring them, despite the Angels' efforts at initiating a dialogue.

If they couldn't compete with the Angels in terms of size or money, they could at least be rude. If they were becoming dangerously isolated, in the absence of their former Quebec leadership, no one seemed worried. Under "General," the Angels' minutes refer to the Bandidos by the negative nickname of "Bandits" and note: "Bandits did not want to have a meeting. Other issues on the 'topic' discussed."

By mid-summer, Nina was pregnant. If Boxer were to settle down with her now, no one could say he hadn't tried to make a go of the Bandidos. But Boxer wasn't one to walk away from his brothers, even when they sorely disappointed him. For the past six years, one percenter clubs had been his safe haven, his source of adrenalin and respect. It was through the club that he'd met her. And so he tattooed Nina's name on his left bicep, in big gothic letters, on one of his few patches of prime skin not already covered with Fat Mexicans or other biker totems. Then he decided to do something really big.

In July, Boxer hit the highway on his Harley with Chopper and Chief. The event was a national run in Edmonton. It had a grand name, it was intended as a public display of force and brotherhood and it was meant to celebrate a rare taste of glory for Boxer. The formidable Edmonton Rebels had finally agreed to patch over to the Bandidos. Unfortunately, the only other Bandidos in Canada were the No Surrender Crew in Toronto, which boasted few brothers who actually rode motorcycles. Wrongway Atkinson also had a working motorcycle, but he declined to make the trip because he didn't want to lose his job as a railworker. Boxer was enraged. Club rules said that members were supposed to have employment, but Boxer was the boss and he wanted the company. Besides, just three Harleys riding together doesn't look like much of a pack. Atkinson knew Boxer was upset, but didn't budge.

Bam Bam Salerno didn't risk Boxer's wrath, although he wasn't up to the rigours of getting his Harley on the road and riding it for days. Instead, he cadged some money from his wife and flew out to Edmonton to join his brothers there. Crash also dropped by from nearby Camrose, Alberta, where he had been working at a family dairy business. Crash had been particularly low-key since his beating by the Hells Angels in the Woodbridge restaurant the previous year. It was as if he wanted to fade away altogether, if only he could, but getting out wasn't so easy.

Snubbing the get-together would only draw more attention to himself.

Cisco Lenti hadn't been in shape for a long motorcycle haul since the bomb blast that almost killed him, so he drove west in a truck with a friend named Sam. When he learned that Taz Sandham and his Winnipeggers weren't bothering to make the run, he filled the air with salty language. It was a national run, and yet Taz couldn't put one bike on the road to support it? Taz Sandham liked to talk like a brother, but he didn't bother to ride like one.

Once in Edmonton, the Torontonians and Albertans all rode in a procession together, with the Death Hand support club out of Calgary bringing up the rear. Some new Alberta members celebrated by printing up shirts bearing the slogan BANDIDOS WORLDWIDE and flames running down the sleeves. They were fine T-shirts, but police surveillance officers couldn't help but wonder if they'd been printed because the No Surrender Crew couldn't afford real probationary patches for the Death Hand members. Whatever the case, it looked like Boxer and his brothers were finally moving ahead, towards the west coast. Rather than revel in the moment of victory and growth, however, the Bandidos' mother chapter in Texas sniped that the souvenir T-shirts shouldn't have been made without their official authorization. Things hit another sour note when Boxer announced that all No Surrender Crew members who missed the run without a valid excuse would be fined five hundred dollars. In the end, only Wrongway Atkinson actually paid the fine.

On July 24, 2004, Boxer was back in Toronto, and he sent out a mass email to fellow bikers rhapsodizing about his trip. It was as if he were living out a dream, no matter what the cost. The club was getting stronger and he was riding his Harley Fat Boy, partying with friends and sleeping under the stars. He had escaped from the factory, through a disability leave, and he was in love. His PBOL—proud Bandido old lady—was expecting their baby. Could life get much better? The message was classically Boxer—all capitals and no stops for punctuation:

> YA GOOD OLD TIME RIDING IN THE WIND FROM TOWN TO TOWN SLEEPING ON THE GROUND BEING REAL WITH OUR ONLY CONCERN IS OUR BROTHERS WELL BEING HAVING FUN PARTYING TURNING IT UP A NOTCH FLYING THE GREATEST COLOURS IN THE WORLD ROOSTER CHOPPER CHIEFERONE JOHNNY BIG PAUL GRUMPY JAY WHAT A RODE TRIP LOVED EVERY SECOND OF IT TO OUR BROTHERS IN EDMONTON AND CALGARY LOVE LOYALTY RESPECT BANDIDOBOXER

Two days later, Boxer was still on a high from the trip, telling Chief in an email how much he valued his friendship:

> CHIEF MY BROTHER WHAT DID I TELL YOU YEARS AGO ONE DAY WHAT LOVE LOYALTY RESPECT FOREVER MY BROTHER&† WHO LOVES YA YOU CAME THREW LIKE ALL BANDIDOS WILL IN A PINCH MUCH LOVE RESPECT BANDIDOBOXER NO SURRENDER CREW ALL OF CANADA AND WORLDWIDE ONLY THE BEGINNING WHAT A RIDE RED AND GOLD EVERYWHERE.

The next day, July 27, Boxer awoke at dawn, sending out an email to his Bandido brothers. It was a fresh day, and every breath was a celebration of Nina, his brotherhood and his Harley:

EVERYDAY IS A GREAT DAY GONNA START MY BIKE AND RIDE WITH MY PBOL WHAT A DAY JUST GOT BACK FROM CROSS CANADA RIDE IT WAS BREATH TAKING LOVE LOYALTY RESPECT TOO THOSE THAT COUNT

Four hours later, Boxer was back at the computer, sending off yet another email to his Bandido brothers. The spelling and grammar were as atrocious as usual, but his mood was still bubbly:

PEOPLE YOU KNOW AND TRUST SOMTIMES THIER FEW AND FAR BETWEEN BUT GOING THREW THE RIGHT MOTIONS GETTING TOO THE RIGHT PEOPLE IF YOU HAVE A HEARTBEAT AND BELEAVE IN BROTH-ERHOOD THERE ARE PEOPLE JUST DOWN THE RODE THAT CAN HELP . . .

The No Surrender Crew still didn't have a clubhouse, and that August, chapter members met at an entertainment complex with a hockey arena, laser tag, video arcade, bowling and other diversions. There were conference rooms for corporate team-building, and at the facility management couldn't have known that they also filled the bill for the club's church meetings. Individual members had more immediate concerns than finding a permanent clubhouse. Big Paul Sinopoli was so low on funds that he couldn't get his Harley on the road, and tried to talk a friend into fixing it for him. Bam Bam Salerno remained strapped for cash as well, since he and Stephanie had invested heavily in renovations to Stephanie's hair salon, which hadn't yet reopened.

It was at this August meeting that Weiner Kellestine reappeared on the Bandidos scene, having been released from yet another stretch behind bars for gun charges. Boxer couldn't help but be suspicious that he hadn't been locked up longer. Didn't informants sometimes get cozy deals for selling out their brothers? Boxer might have caught a whiff of betrayal, but he put such thoughts to the back of his mind when Kellestine got out of prison, phoned Boxer's parents' home and asked them for Boxer's new cellphone number, saying, "It's Crazy Wayne."

Kellestine organized a pig roast at his farm in his own honour, calling together his old cronies for his coming-out party. Tickets were priced at twenty dollars each, and proceeds were earmarked to helping get him back on his feet financially. Boxer deemed the pig roast a compulsory event for the No Surrender Crew, and about forty members and friends made the drive down to Weiner Kellestine's farm. The drive didn't just cost them time and money; it also meant they had to go through the inconvenience of being stopped, photographed and questioned by local police. It was hard to think how Kellestine's return made them a stronger club. Some members grumbled that they didn't really want Weiner back, but they did so out of earshot—and punching range—of Boxer.

Weiner constantly approached Bandidos friends and hangarounds with the greeting, "Hey brother." Somehow the words sounded vaguely threatening coming from him, as he pushed them to become full members of the club. "Have you decided to come our way? It's the place to be," he would say. If he sensed any reluctance, Weiner would scowl and add, in an ominous reference to the Hells Angels, "Unless you decide to be with the other guys."

Shortly after his release, Kellestine showed up at his old neighbourhood haunt, the Holland House Restaurant and Tavern, a homey little eatery that did double duty as a used bookstore and curiosity shop. The place was run by his neighbour, Marty Angenent, who had known Kellestine for some twenty years, since the days when the biker would bring his first-born baby daughter, Karley Davidson, by to play horsey with him, Angenent allowing her to ride his back. Angenent considered Kellestine to be a "good-guy biker," and was comfortable teasing him when he dropped in after his release, "Wayne, you gained some weight."

"Yeah, Marty, not enough exercise in jail."

Kellestine used to enjoy buying used books on World War II and leaving twenty-percent tips on his cheeseburgers and beer, but he was pinching his pennies hard now. "Marty, business is not like it used to be," Kellestine said. He didn't elaborate on the exact nature of his business and Angenent was too smart to ask.

As Kellestine settled back into his home, there were more parties, which, in addition to raising money for him, allowed him to play amateur movie-maker. In one of his home videos, Kellestine held the camera as a large, possibly drunken man climbed onto a woman. She clearly didn't want sex with him, and he clearly didn't care. The man slowly forced himself on her, as a worm might mount another worm, and Kellestine recorded the event, joking that it was turning him on. When the man was done with his assault, Kellestine filmed the woman sitting alone, looking upset and stunned. Kellestine asked her to lift up her top and bare her breasts to the camera. She balked, but he wouldn't stop asking. His tone was jovial but persistent, and he clearly wasn't about to let up or go away until he got his way. Finally, she obliged and hiked up her shirt, as Kellestine made a permanent record of her latest humiliation.

Despite filming the incident for his own amusement, Kellestine grandly considered himself a moral force and a staunch protector of innocence. He was still supporting probationary member Dave (Concrete) Weiche's group, called Bikers Against Pedophiles. They were the same bunch who had crashed the London gay pride parade, and they still sought to pressure the federal government to impose tougher sentences on anyone committing crimes against children. They also pushed for the government to create a publicly accessible directory of offenders who had committed sex crimes against children. Yet another stated goal was to raise the legal age of consent for sexual activity to eighteen. Weiner and his friends clearly loved the pose of being moral custodians. "We must surge together and show a wall of motorcycles as a wall of protection, a wall of support for our lost and wounded friends," the group's website grandly announced. "We act as a wall of protest, to our Government, demanding the rights of our children to have safety in their lives and security in their homes! . . . Once these things are achieved and our children, grandchildren, and great grandchildren are safe in their homes and neighborhoods, we will disband and fade into the shadows, always to be there in case we are needed again."

While Kellestine joked and acted crazy and posed as a moral guardian for the nation's children, it was clear that he still hadn't settled comfortably into his role in the club, as *sargento de armas* under his long-time follower, *Presidente* Boxer Muscedere. They may have been brothers, but a brother's envy can be the most dangerous of all, even if Kellestine tried to fight the feelings. It was also clear that Boxer had no intention of stepping aside, particularly now that he had tasted the success of expansion and the thrill of power. "The puppet has cut his strings," a Chatham-area friend said.

Also in August 2004, Wrongway Atkinson and Crash Kriarakis and their wives met quietly in Toronto's Greektown for the annual Taste of the Danforth food festival. They relaxed and joked, and then Atkinson got serious.

The club was clearly running on fumes now. Boxer seemed to be floating off into his own biker fantasy, a dreamland impervious to the insistent realities the No Surrender Crew lived with every day. Boxer was still glib about the threat of the Angels, blowing them off when he should have heeded their calls for a meeting. Club members were rankled by Boxer's favouritism towards Kellestine, while Boxer seemed blind to the fact that Kellestine was fully capable of stabbing him in the back. The pressures of being president, and the consumption of increasing amounts of cocaine, made Boxer increasingly short-tempered and myopic. And what about Taz Sandham from Winnipeg? At best, he seemed like an unlikely friend or saviour.

And then there were the Texans who ultimately ran the Bandidos. Atkinson was the Canadian Bandidos' *secretario,* yet Boxer chastised him for communicating with senior American members. The Bandidos were supposed to be a brotherhood, yet they were forbidden from talking with their European and American brothers. It was as though Boxer was jealous of Atkinson and Crash because they had biker contacts outside the country. It was hard not to feel a sense of doom, as power struggles replaced brotherhood and cocaine substituted for good sense. Weiner Kellestine's return from jail to the fold only made things worse. Atkinson told his good friend Crash that he was considering leaving the Bandidos for the Outlaws, a more established one percenter club in Canada. He wanted to take Crash with him. Crash was tempted: Outlaws actually rode motorcycles and they weren't as reckless and irritating to the Hells Angels. They were also survivors.

Crash wavered. Despite his fears that something bad was looming on the horizon, Crash didn't want to let down his brothers in the No Surrender Crew. The club was weak enough without his defection. There was also the matter of the five thousand dollars Sinopoli owed him for his used Harley-Davidson. If Crash quit the Bandidos before Big Paul paid up, Crash would clearly have to eat the debt. And what about Boxer? Could Crash expect to slip away from the club without feeling the crunch of his fists? For his part, Atkinson appeared ready to quit, whatever the risks.

"Those guys are going to get you killed one day," he warned.

CHAPTER 10

A Problem Here

I am not what I am.
OTHELLO, ACT 1, SCENE 1

Seems like we have a problem here.
BILL SARTELLE, TEXAS-BASED SECRETARIO OF THE
BANDIDOS

Wrongway Atkinson arrived for a church meeting at Weiner Kellestine's farm in October 2004 with all of his Bandidos paraphernalia, including his patch and vest, in a plastic bag. It was obvious what he was doing. Whether or not Crash was coming with him, Atkinson was leaving the club. A friend had warned him that quitting the club could bring on a beating, but he obviously wanted out. "If they've got a problem with me, then they'll have to confront me about it," Wrongway had replied to his friend.

Boxer was still on a high from the previous month, when the Bandidos opened up a new chapter in Calgary, taking in the former Rebels. Boxer was in the mood for praise and heady talk of further expansion, not quitting.

Atkinson could smell liquor as he was greeted inside Kellestine's barn with a collective cold shoulder. It was clear
that Boxer also had a nose full of cocaine. Weiner Kellestine, Crash Kriarakis, Frank Lenti, Bam Bam Salerno and
Chopper Raposo were all there, but Boxer was clearly the
man in charge.

"Could I talk to you outside?" Boxer asked.

Atkinson was on his way out the door when Boxer
sucker-punched him from behind. Boxer might have once
been a promising leader, but now he was no more than a
loose cannon. Sucker-punching a brother was worthy of
Weiner Kellestine, not the old Boxer. It was evidence that
Boxer had changed, and not for the better.

Kellestine quickly joined in, stuffing a pistol into
Atkinson's mouth and adding blows of his own. As he lay
on the ground, Atkinson caught a glimpse of Chopper
Raposo and Bam Bam Salerno looking away, while Crash
Kriarakis stared, horror-struck and frozen, directly at the
beating.

"Get up," someone eventually ordered, and Atkinson
was handed a rag to wipe off the blood.

He drove himself to a hospital, where his face was
stitched up and he was told his ribs were broken.

Within a few months, Atkinson had accepted a striker's
patch with the Outlaws, a probationary rank that put him
on track for full membership.

Atkinson had been respected by the top Bandidos in
Texas. Now, Boxer had lost a potential advisor and diplomat, and didn't even seem to know that he was listing
close to disaster.

Despite the warnings from Prairie bikers, who had ominously told Chopper to watch the papers for word about the former Alberta Rebels, who now wore Fat Mexican patches, the news still seemed to come like a bolt out of the blue, and it hit the club hard: just three months after Boxer's western tour, reports detailed how his Prairie expansion drive had crashed in flames. All it had taken was for the Hells Angels to dangle the promise of membership in front of the newly minted Alberta Bandidos, and they were gone. Suddenly, all of the Albertans' talk of Bandido brotherhood had been cast aside in favour of a better offer from the club's sworn enemies.

It shouldn't have been surprising, considering the increasing isolation of the Toronto Bandidos. But even dreading the worst does not take away its sting when it comes to pass. Some of the Alberta Rebels had only been Bandidos for a month, and it seemed as though the Fat Mexican patch had been nothing more than a bargaining chip to be leveraged into acceptance into the Hells Angels. The humiliation was difficult to ignore, especially for Boxer. It was easy to blame the *presidente* for the fiasco. He obviously hadn't impressed the Albertans. As a final indignity, when Boxer ordered the Albertans to give back their new Bandidos patches, they replied with words to the effect of "Come and get them."

Lenti quit in disgust soon after that, handing in a box

of souvenir support T-shirts and jewellery bearing the Fat Mexican logo. No one had the nerve to lift a hand against Cisco Lenti as he walked away, not as they had pummelled Wrongway Atkinson. No one could count on coming out on top in a fight with Lenti, not even Boxer, and guys who went toe to toe with the veteran biker sometimes came away with one less fully functioning eye. This time, it was the former Bandido who was looking for trouble on the way out the door. Lenti went after Boxer, and it took a crew of his former brothers to restrain him. It would be easy to later wonder if Boxer's fate might have played out differently, had 2004 not ended with the loss of two of his best and most experienced men: Atkinson the diplomat and Lenti the warrior.

In a face-saving move, the club executive maintained that they had kicked Lenti out of the chapter. Kellestine even managed to sound righteous as he sent out an email explaining that there were good reasons for stripping someone from full-patch status: "I'd like to mention something here about . . . old school and what I believe An MC [motorcycle club] is . . . : HEART AND LOYALTY. Have it or fuck off. Need I say more. Brother if someone should lose their patch and be demoted to Prospect, there is a reason for that. You fucked up.

"Everyone is part of the wheel that keeps the club going," continued Kellestine, who signed "Sergeant at Arms, Canada" after his name.[20]

The November 2004 minutes of the Ontario officers of the Hells Angels indicate that the big club was aware of the tensions within the Bandidos, and that some of them wanted to offer Lenti membership. A note under "General" states, "Vote on Frank issue was Yes 72 No 69 did not pass."

As the weather turned cold, the heady joy of Boxer's summer western tour was already a distant memory, and it was easy to wonder how many others in the No Surrender Crew would also like to quit, if they could only summon the nerve. The departure of Lenti should have been a wake-up call, but Boxer somehow seemed even cockier, like a nervous man whistling past a graveyard. He sometimes drank at a bar in the Queen and Broadview neighbourhood of Toronto, perhaps because it was a popular hangout with Para-Dice Riders members who hadn't patched over to the Hells Angels. Late one evening, when Boxer was staggeringly drunk, the bartender cut him off. Boxer hit back with a torrent of abuse.

"What's the problem?" a Para-Dice Rider asked.

"Mind your own fucking business," Boxer replied.

The lower the Toronto Bandidos sank, the greater their sensitivity over minor slights. Seconds later, the Para-Dice Rider lay crumpled on the floor, dropped by a sucker punch from Carlitto Aragon. Boxer joined in and gave the PDR member a few more hard shots.

Word of the dust-up spread quickly from the PDR to their friends in the Hells Angels, and in the days that followed, Boxer blew off an attempt at détente by the Angels. He seemed eager for any conflict that temporarily puffed up his importance, even if it jeopardized his future. He might not be able to beat the Hells Angels, but he could at least snub them.

Concerns from south of the border increased once Atkinson left. On November 24, 2004, Bill Sartelle, the Texas-based worldwide *secretario* of the Bandidos, emailed Chopper Raposo, with a troubling opening line: "Seems like we have a problem here." Like Sartelle, Bandidos in Texas take themselves seriously. Many have fought overseas in the military, and all of them treat their colours and their reputation with the same grave respect soldiers feel for their units. Moreover, the American Bandidos provide the leadership for a club that has more than two thousand members in 210 chapters spanning sixteen countries. Sartelle also had professional reasons to be proud, as he wasn't a gangster and made a legitimate six-figure income in the oil industry. So his tone was a little condescending as he continued: "You can't come here, we can't come there, but you do not want to answer any questions. There are issues that need to be resolved. I have made attempts to get these answers, but have not."

The Hells Angels may be slightly bigger internationally, but the Bandidos are a serious organization with a global reach and the muscle to carve up territory. When their leaders ask a member a question, they expect a quick answer, and it had better make sense. Since Wrongway Atkinson left the club, the No Surrender Crew had become even more isolated, and the Americans were growing more impatient by the moment. Sartelle wanted to know what had happened to sixty sets of Bandidos patches that had been sent to the Canadians. And when would the Americans get a current list of Canadian members and monthly donations?

Chopper Raposo emailed back to the Americans that "all is good but of course we have the odd problem [that could be]easily resolved." The exact nature of this problem, or the proposed resolution, remained a mystery, though not to Chopper. He knew there was a real problem—in fact, more than one. They had taken in members without the Americans' approval. They weren't up to date in their dues. They had been ignoring the Americans. They didn't even all have motorcycles. They had a lot of explaining to do.

Rather than work on mending their relationship with the Americans, the No Surrender Crew focused on easier topics, like Christmas cards and partying. This year, the Christmas cards were done by the end of November. They were nice enough, depicting a Fat Mexican holding a machete and firing a pistol over the Toronto skyline, against a red and gold background. At the No Surrender Crew's holiday party that December, a disc jockey from Keswick named Frankie cranked up the rap music at a restaurant on Queen Street East, east of Broadview. It was a small, pleasant place, and Frankie was a friend of the club, working for free and happy just to be there. He cheerfully soaked in the good feelings and teed up the tunes, until Weiner Kellestine approached him.

"Stop playing this nigger stuff," Kellestine ordered. "Play Lynyrd Skynyrd or something better than this shit or I'll blow your foot off."

The party lurched on, with more Lynyrd Skynyrd and no more rap music or pop. When Crash's wife, Diane, asked Frankie why there wasn't any more dance music, Kellestine shot him a dirty look and Frankie kept on with the classic rock.

It was the Nazi sympathizer in Kellestine, and not the man who preached brotherhood, that was at the surface now. It was a week before Christmas, and Weiner Kellestine emitted a palpable and toxic fusion of negativity, hatred and ambition. He was still under Boxer Muscedere in the club's pecking order, and he still craved control. There was nothing friendly about his eyes that night at the Christmas party. They were the eyes of a madman.

Back in Manitoba, Michael Sandham still schemed about gaining full membership in the Bandidos. He needed to attach himself to something strong and alive, like a tick to a host. Since his ouster from the police, he'd had limited success while operating two companies that provided training for police officers and by-law officers. His instruction style was enthusiastic, if bizarre. He once conducted a seminar for by-law officers on how to fend off a rampaging black bear with one arm, while shooting and reloading a shotgun with the other. "It was certainly more than we expected," said David Prud'Homme, who took the seminar. "I never seen anybody doing that. It was beyond what we required."

Prud'Homme was initially impressed, and he hired Sandham onto his staff at Prairie Bylaw Enforcement Services, a company that works under contract to Manitoba municipalities. Taz's new job was to teach self-defence to Prud'Homme's eight employees. He also worked some shifts as a by-law officer himself, driving a car marked "Peace Officer" and sometimes wearing a badge with a number, like a real cop. But after a few months, Sandham suddenly resigned in an email that said he was suffering from job stress and marital troubles. The complaints about job stress must have been puzzling for Prud'Homme, since Sandham was well paid and allowed to set his own hours. Six months after his departure, Sandham emailed to order Prud'Homme to return some belongings he'd left behind at the office or pay him four thousand dollars. Prud'Homme was instructed to heave the training manuals and martial arts equipment over Sandham's fence, and his wife would collect them from the other side. Prud'Homme complied, and the strange little man disappeared from his life.

CHAPTER 11

The Lounge

. . . full of sound and fury, signifying nothing.
MACBETH, ACT 5, SCENE 5

We can't meet on Valentine's Day. My wife will kill me.
FRANKIE (BAM BAM, BAMMER) SALERNO

Jamie (Goldberg) Flanz began 2005 with hopes of gaining membership in the No Surrender Crew. Perhaps he thought Kellestine was just play-acting in his Nazi fantasies, just as he, a businessman, was playing biker.

In time, Flanz was given a list of rules for prospective members by Ripper Fullager; one of them forbade him from discussing club business outside the club. "He understands that he is a Patchholder 24 hours a day whether or not he is wearing his colors," the club's guidelines state of any prospect. "Everything he says or does in public can affect the club or the brothers. He also understands that if he gets out of line, that he is subject to be counselled by his brothers for his own good and for that of the club." Joining a club is a lot like joining a cult—

the recruit learns to subordinate himself to the group. "It's committing yourself to a lifestyle in which you do not look for how your brothers can help you, but for ways that you can be of help to your brothers. You always look to give rather than to receive."

Goldberg Flanz was voluntarily joining a feudal world, and assuming the role of vassal. "Never let a Patchholder walk off alone in an unsecured area," the guidelines stated. "If he is going out to his car, his bike, or even just out to get some fresh air, go with him. Watch his back at all times." While bikers had sponsors, Flanz wasn't beholden only to Big Paul Sinopoli, who had vouched for him. As the guidelines continued, "Remember that you are every Patchholder's prospect, not just your sponsor's or just your chapter's."

They were proven guidelines for running a club, but the reality of Boxer's Toronto Bandidos was less impressive. The No Surrender Crew still had no clubhouse as 2005 began, when Little Mikey Trotta became a full-patch member and George (Pony) Jessome was admitted as a prospect member.

The next stop for the No Surrender Crew was a store-front on Jefferson Avenue in the west-end Liberty Village district, a once-industrial zone in the shadow of Lamport Stadium. The area had been home to the Central Prison between 1877 and 1912, but now there were yuppified condos, offices and coffee shops creeping onto the land where prisoners had once been housed, tortured and hanged. Boxer Muscedere instantly loved the area, and soon rented an apartment in a nearby high-rise for Nina and their daughter, Angelina. Little Mikey Trotta had a good enough credit rating to sign the lease on the Jefferson Street property in early February. Ripper Fullager and other members worked hard to install a bar in the basement, while an artist painted a mural on a wall for just fifty dollars and a case of beer. Much of the work had to be done at night, so that members with bail conditions that barred them from associating with known criminals could help out.

Upstairs was a place to crash and relax, furnished with a couch and big-screen TV, while downstairs was the meeting room, for church gatherings. None of it was fortified, and it was particularly vulnerable to attack because of the big, plate-glass front window, the same feature found in the restaurants and boutiques in the same strip mall.

It was a time of brotherhood and drugs, but not much business or expansion. The Quebec Bandidos had dried up, meaning the No Surrender Crew were on their own in Canada. They could turn to the Americans for advice, but that would leave them open to rebuke for not having sought advice about such important club matters as who should be admitted to the club.

Instead, they simply went to Jefferson Avenue and chilled. Members particularly enjoyed using percadine tablets, which were easy enough to obtain since several members claimed medical disabilities and had prescriptions to obtain the painkillers legally. They called them "groovies," for the relaxed, worry-free way they made them feel, and the Bandidos found them particularly comforting when Weiner Kellestine was around, cranking up the tension level. Since the Jefferson Avenue digs weren't really a clubhouse in the style of the fortified bunkers that housed the Hells Angels, members took to calling it "The Lounge." Boxer had plans of putting in a coin-operated pool table too, but a distributor thought twice and nixed the idea, saying he didn't want to lose his table in the event of a police raid.

For an outsider like Jamie Flanz, the No Surrender Crew might seem like an undisciplined but tough little army, or a secretive criminal enterprise. From the inside, however, Boxer's gang didn't really do much of anything. Crash and Pony often worked twelve-hour days, driving their tow trucks, but most club members didn't have jobs. Chopper Raposo, who had driven a truck for a mushroom-canning firm back in his Loner days, now smoked weed in his parents' upstairs apartment and watched a lot of daytime television. Bam Bam Salerno kept busy with his get-rich quick schemes and housework. Big Paul Sinopoli had worked for a few months in a sporting goods store in Aurora in the early 2000s, and had planned for little while to become a forklift operator before giving up. He settled in quickly on Jefferson Avenue, lying on the couch for days at a time like a massive cat in the sun. He still lived in his family's basement, had no girlfriend and privately fretted about his weight; The Lounge was a place where he could feel part of something exclusive and powerful just by walking in the door. One friend of the club liked the parties and souvenir T-shirts, but didn't see any point in actually getting his Fat Mexican patch. "I think it was a fantasy for them," the club friend later said. "I just didn't see a life in that life."

Weiner Kellestine still claimed to run a security firm, and at a club meeting in February 2005 he declared that he wanted everyone, including club friends and hangarounds, to write down their names, addresses and phone numbers. Apparently, he never bothered to check them out, just as he hadn't investigated Taz Sandham's past. At least one person present gave Kellestine phony personal information that was never challenged. Also that month, Bam Bam Salerno made it clear that the club couldn't hold a meeting on February 14. "We can't meet on Valentine's Day," Bam Bam informed the club. "My wife will kill me."

In March, less than two months after they moved into The Lounge, their new landlord refused to accept their rent cheque. Instead, he volunteered to refund their first and last month's rent if they would just leave immediately. Little Mikey Trotta, who had signed the lease, seemed relieved and didn't protest much. Boxer was sorely offended, but had no clue what they should do about it and so let it pass. Ripper said they would have to retrieve the downstairs bar, which he and Chopper had painstakingly built. "No way they're leaving that material out there," Ripper said. "It's all brand new shit."

The club then shuffled around from one meeting place to another. There was the Oriental Taste Restaurant on Dundas Street East, near Yonge Street and across the street from Filmore's strip club. The restaurant's owner would turn over the dining room on Saturday afternoons for a few hundred dollars, unaware of the nature of the meetings. There was also the banquet hall of a nearby hotel and a hotel near the airport.

By early April, the club was holding churches in a small farmhouse belonging to a club supporter in Stouffville, off Highway 404. To get there, Bandidos drove down a dirt road and up to the dishevelled building, which was surrounded by the skeletons of cars that had ceased to run years before. At one memorable meeting, Weiner Kellestine arrived with a carload of hangarounds, all of whom seemed terrified of him. He ordered them to speak in a clear voice when it was their turn, and they obeyed him like nervous schoolboys. It was as if Weiner was trying to bolster his region's strength, perhaps with an eye to setting up his own chapter. After just six weeks, the hangaround who owned the farmhouse simply bailed out, refusing to explain why the Bandidos couldn't use his property any longer. Again, Boxer Muscedere was bewildered and angry, and again, he really didn't know what to do about it.[21]

Weiner Kellestine arrived at Crash Kriarakis's wedding stag in April 2005 in a surly mood. Boxer had made it a compulsory event for No Surrender Crew members, friends and hangarounds, so Weiner was required to make the two-hour drive from his farm to the Speranza Banquet Hall in an industrial part of east Brampton, off Highway 407. The Speranza was a world away from Kellestine's hillbilly empire: its marble floors, chandeliers, skylit ceiling and water fountain made all the bikers look a little out of place. Family members of both the bride and groom were in attendance, nicely attired in suits. Bikers wore their colours, and Kellestine sported his standard outfit: his Fat Mexican vest and camouflage fatigue pants tucked into his black jackboots. It was easy that night to tell the bikers from the civilians.

Crash's fiancée, Diane, was a polished, upright woman who clearly loved him. Out of respect for her, Crash had booked no strippers for his stag. In their place, there were prizes, games and plenty of roast pig, red meat, seafood and pasta. Weiner Kellestine wasn't placated as he sat with Concrete Dave Weiche. When penne with tomato sauce was served as an opening course, Weiner sniffed, "Is this all there is? Where's the fucking food?"

Boxer was in far better spirits, smiling and puffing on an Old Port cigarillo in a corner of the front lobby with other chapter members. It was hard that night for Crash's Bandido brothers not to get philosophical. Crash was marrying a nice, forgiving woman and seemed to have so much more to live for than a leather vest with a Fat Mexican patch on the back. Bam Bam Salerno confided to a friend that he was thinking of moving on from Bandido life, saying, "One day when I have a baby and start another family, I'll be a retired member." He still had trouble settling his debts, but liked to offer special friends complimentary manicures and haircuts at his wife's salon, saying, "You'll feel 100 percent better. It's like buying a new pair of shoes."

Club members noted that Crash had stayed away from strippers, even though it would be fairly easy to hook up with one of Carlitto Aragon's lap dancers from a club on The Queensway in Etobicoke. Bam Bam claimed that he was also a faithful man. "I'm not the best-looking guy," Bam Bam confided to a friend. "I'm not Mr. Workaholic, bringing home a lot of money. But I'm not a womanizer. I don't cheat on her. I also don't abuse her. I do my best, within my abilities."

Big Paul talked that night about stepping away from the club for at least a few months. He wanted to get his stomach stapled to control his enormous weight; he was struggling with diabetes and seemed on a crash course with a heart attack if he didn't quickly turn his health around. There also seemed to be something sad about him, as if he was still lonely, even though he was surrounded by constant talk of brotherhood.

Boxer could be a frightening man, but he was gracious and supportive that night when Big Paul told him of his plans for the operation and hopes for a leave of absence from the club. "Well, hopefully things help you, brother," Boxer said.

"Well, thanks a lot," Big Paul replied. "I need the support. I'm a little nervous."

As the evening wound down, Boxer and the boys amused themselves by playing cards, while Weiner ordered someone he considered an inferior to find him a hotel room, as he was too important a man for such a menial chore.

A week later, on Saturday, May 7, several of the

Bandidos missed Crash's wedding. It wasn't meant as a snub; the problem was money. For all of their tough, swaggering, gangster personas, several of them didn't have the hundred dollars per head they would be expected to contribute towards the reception. It wasn't really shaping up to be a biker event anyway. Diane didn't want club colours worn at the wedding, telling Crash something to the effect of: "For one day, you don't have to be red and gold. For one day, you don't have to be a one percenter." When a Bandido named Beaver grumbled about not being allowed to wear club colours, Crash stuck up for Diane, saying, "Come on, bro. This is my wife's day."

CHAPTER 12

Tazman's Return

Love cools, friendship falls off, brothers divide . . .
KING LEAR, ACT 1, SCENE 2

*Canada has not been meeting the requirements
of belonging to this club . . .*
BILL SARTELLE, EL SECRETARIO OF
THE BANDIDOS WORLDWIDE

Taz Sandham looked as powerful as a bantam rooster on Saturday, June 25, 2005, as he rode up to Weiner Kellestine's farm. Sandham now considered himself president of the probationary Winnipeg chapter of the Bandidos, although that title had never been approved by the Torontonians or anyone else in power. It smelled more than a little bogus, but it was more real than his phony black belts, and if he played his cards right, he could soon be president of a full chapter. His three biker nicknames—"Taz," "The Tazman" and "Little Beaker"—suggested he hadn't yet established a strong identity within the Winnipeg group, and no one was sure exactly how many aliases he had. Sandham preferred the short, powerful and dangerous sounding moniker of Taz—an abbreviation for the Tasmanian Devil, the crazed, ravenous, stocky little Australian marsupial from the Looney Tunes cartoon series. Taz and Tazman projected toughness and wildness, while his other nickname, "Little Beaker," wasn't one he'd chosen himself or particularly liked to hear. It likened him to the squeaky-voiced laboratory assistant on *The Muppet Show*. The TV Beaker was a gawky, nervous character who was often a victim of circumstance—not a great image for anyone, let alone the would-be leader of an outlaw biker empire.

With Sandham that Saturday was Dwight (Big D, Dee) Mushey, a co-owner of a Winnipeg nightclub, second-degree black belt in tae kwon do, and likely the only Winnipeg biker with a pronounced liking for fine Italian leather shoes. While he liked finely tailored clothing, he had a reputation as someone who came up the hard way. He stood about six foot three and weighed at least 250 solid pounds, giving the impression of a 'roided-up version of the actor Jimmy Smits, and his clothing sometimes seemed like a flashback to the 1980s television series *Miami Vice*. Polite, even gracious, Mushey carried himself like a stone-cold killer who could spill blood without ever losing his temper or creasing his outfit. He was rumoured to have carried out hits for the mob in New York and Montreal. While Sandham and Kellestine spun tales about their exceptional fighting skills and sang-froid, in Mushey's case, the stories had a chilling ring of authenticity.

Also among the Winnipeggers was prospect member M.H., whose real name cannot be published because of a court order. M.H. was no stranger to the outlaw biker world: he had served as a personal bodyguard to notorious Hells Angels leader Maurice (Mom) Boucher and former Angels national president Walter Stadnick. By the time M.H. was moving into the Bandidos, Boucher was serving a life sentence for ordering the murders of two prison guards, while Stadnick was doing time for conspiracy to commit murder, heading a multimillion-dollar drug-trafficking network, and gangsterism—commiting a crime for the benefit of a criminal organization. M.H. said he personally never netted less than three thousand dollars a day while dealing drugs out of a Winnipeg hotel connected to the Angels, a sum he supplemented by collecting another thousand dollars a month in welfare benefits.

M.H. said he met Mushey at a nightclub in Winnipeg, where Mushey was co-owner and prospect member Marcelo (Fat Ass) Aravena worked part time as a bouncer. M.H. said he was recruited by members of the Winnipeg Bandidos, but initially declined because he was under strict house-arrest terms for possessing cocaine for the purposes of trafficking.

Once that two-year sentence expired in 2005, he and Mushey sat down with Michael Sandham, the self-appointed president of the Winnipeg Bandidos. Sandham seemed to have control over all aspects of the probationary chapter, holding the offices of both president and secretary-treasurer. He told the new prospects they would have their full-patch status soon, once the Toronto chapter, which sponsored the probationary Winnipeg branch, approved.

Sandham's high, squeaky voice made him sound as though he should be passing out colouring books or getting ready to lead a singsong, not leading an outlaw biker gang. But he coolly lied to the two underworld veterans about his biker past, spinning a saga in which he had been an Outlaw in Woodstock, Ontario, near London, and had been in charge of a puppet club called the Black Pistons. When most of the Outlaws were arrested in a police sweep, Sandham said, he turned his patch over to join the Bandidos. He said the Bandidos were so happy to get him they gave him full-patch status right off the bat. It was a remarkable claim, considering that even Lenti had had to serve a few months as a probationary member before getting his full patch.

Sandham handed Mushey and M.H. a list of club rules that promoted "The Bandido Way," including infractions that would result in expulsion from the club. These rules, which appear verbatim below, prohibited the following:

- coming between two brothers (members)
- needle use and smoking chemicals
  (if it doesn't grow, don't smoke it)
- lying to a brother
- talking about a member behind his back.

Sandham also forbade members of his chapter from communicating with their national president, Boxer. "We have a chain of command in our Chapter," Sandham told all new members in a printed handout. "USE IT! NO SIDE STEPPING." Sandham said he included this rule because chapter vice president Jamie Korn had been "going behind his back" and talking directly to Toronto.

Within a couple of months, Mushey was promoted to secretary-treasurer. Sandham had eliminated Korn's post of vice president, further consolidating his own power, then squeezed Korn out altogether by accusing him of using crack. What Sandham didn't say was that he resented Korn's constant communication with the Toronto Bandidos, which he saw as a threat to his own ambitions.

Though Sandham had botched many things in life, he had discovered a talent for ruthless politicking and manipulation. And now here he was, clattering along on his Harley, the ersatz president of a chapter of one of the world's most powerful motorcycle gangs, his two lieutenants with impressive underworld credentials at his side, ready to barge his way into the Bandidos fold whether they welcomed him or not.

While the June 2005 party at Kellestine's farm may have marked a significant moment for the Winnipeggers and their ambitions, several of the Toronto-area bikers were preoccupied with other matters. Big Paul fretted about how their shared cellphone plan with Telus might be cut off if they couldn't scrape up some money quickly. Big Paul owed $191.23, while Boxer's charge was $140.67;

another member, by the name of Wes (also known as Grumpy), owed $74.42; Mike Trotta, $88.77; Pony Jessome, $136.66; and Weiner Kellestine $88.33. Big Paul was now a member of an international outlaw biker club, yet they couldn't collectively figure out how to pay their phone bill. "They're screwing you somewhere," Big Paul fumed. Phones were a particularly sore point for the No Surrender Crew, as Boxer had already had his personal Telus and Fido accounts shut off in the first six months of 2005. Pony Jessome had the unsettling experience of having his account terminated in mid-conversation as he drove down Highway 400 in his tow truck, because of an outstanding $180 bill he couldn't cover.

But Pony had far more grave concerns than cellphones. His forty-four-year-old cousin had slipped into a coma and was in an intensive care unit at Sunnybrook Health Sciences Centre in Toronto with a brain hemorrhage. The cousin briefly opened his eyes after doctors drilled a hole into his head to relieve the pressure, but then he slipped back into a coma and hovered near death.

In happier times, Pony Jessome was laid-back and easy-going, letting life wash over him. He was no warrior, but had the gentle toughness of a survivor, as well as a no-bullshit kind of honesty that Boxer respected. Pony didn't complain that he didn't have a home beyond his truck and trailer, or any money beyond what was needed for basic expenses. If he was around friends and had a cold beer in his hand, that was generally good enough for him. But on that Friday, Pony let loose, in his high-pitched, screechy Maritime accent, about how his cousin had suffered repeated and severe beatings as a child and had been diagnosed with diabetes as an adult. "Cocksuckers that deserve to die in this life live to be a hundred and they prosper," Pony Jessome fumed to a friend. "This poor kid never did nothing to nobody." Pony chose not to go to the party that weekend. Instead, he went to his cousin's bedside, knowing that he would soon have to call his family around him and make the horrible decision to remove his cousin from life support.

Ripper Fullager had far more pleasant things on his mind. He had tickets to the Toronto Argonauts' home opener against the mighty British Columbia Lions. Season openers always held the promise of great things, but this one was especially exciting, since the Argos had beaten B.C. in the final game of the previous season to win the Grey Cup.

Little Mikey Trotta had plenty to think about too that weekend, besides beer and badly played rock music at Weiner Kellestine's farm. He was finally getting a chance to draw a steady paycheque at his trailer-rental job. Trotta was excited about the opportunity to manage the company's Canadian used-trailer department, and sounded like a corporate keener when he talked of how he worked for an organization with national scope. Life was looking good for him, as he and his wife and preschool son had moved into a comfortable house in a new subdivision in Milton, west of Toronto. He didn't say it, but he clearly didn't need the club any longer to feel like a somebody.

A video Kellestine made of the party showed how he redirected attention towards himself, even when aiming the camera at others. His guests were his audience, and even his six-year-old daughter, Kassie, was part of the act.

"Who's the bartender in the pink outfit?" he joked, pointing his video camera at Kassie, who sat in a roomful of bikers and their wives and female companions. "That better not be booze . . . Where's your age of majority card?"

He laughed heartily at his joke, a signal for others to join in. Then he panned the camera over a group of hairy men with protruding stomachs, including Bandidos supporter Eric Niessen. He had once been classified by the Outlaws Motorcycle Club as an "official supporter." Now, he held the same title with the Bandidos and was expected to pay dues of twenty-five dollars a month for the privilege. Long gone was Niessen's workaday life, where he had been expected to make a positive impression on strangers in order to sell them life insurance. Now, he collected nine hundred dollars a month in disability benefits for a degenerative back condition and looked as though he had crawled off the set of an old Cheech and Chong movie.

"Oh my fucking God," Kellestine said in mock horror. "I [feel] like I climbed out of a hillbilly fucking convention."

One of the revellers lifted up the back of his Bandidos vest to reveal a black T-shirt with a crest of a white-power fist. "Right on," Kellestine said approvingly as he panned the camera towards a live rock band, which was trying to pound out a song that might have been "Satisfaction" by the Rolling Stones or virtually anything from the Lynyrd Skynyrd catalogue. Or perhaps it was an original composition. Whatever the song, what the band lacked in talent, it made up for in volume.

Weiner's camera focused next on a Nazi flag, and he sang a few bars of the German national anthem, the first line of which translates to "Germany above all." Then he zoomed in on a Confederate flag behind the rough-and-not-ready band. Kellestine steadied the camera on the flag of the old South. He was an enthusiastic watcher of History Television, but tended to get his wars, allies and centuries garbled. "That's the most beautiful flag in the world," he proclaimed. It was as if he was recalling his own days as a great soldier, surrounded by men's men made of the same steely stuff and animated by a purity of purpose. "I love that fucking flag. My great-great-great-great-grandfather fought for the flag. The Confederates against the Yankees and French. Fucking Yankee bastards."

Weiner commanded someone to train the camera on himself, and he stood at attention, pretending a large spray can was a gun. "If this was a regiment, I'd be the regimental sergeant major," he said, before taking back the camera.

The camera soon settled on two women sipping beer.

"You want to make a porn?" one of the women asked Weiner.

"Oh, I died and went to heaven," he replied with a laugh.

As the bikers gathered that afternoon at Weiner Kellestine's farm, they sipped beer and exchanged stories outdoors under a canvas canopy set up in the miniature junkyard. Despite the beer and pleasantries, the Winnipeggers didn't lose sight of the business purpose of their visit. The chapter had been on probationary status for more than a year, and Sandham was irked that it still hadn't been promoted to full membership. Three years before, Sandham had been a full-time police officer, and now he couldn't understand why he wasn't a full-patch biker. The probationary status of his chapter meant that it couldn't begin sponsoring other chapters or support clubs or start a hard expansion push on the Prairies. It also meant that the Winnipeg Bandidos had just second-tier status in the biker world, and that even this could be yanked on a whim. If that happened, Taz Sandham would instantly evaporate from the outlaw biker world, just as he had disappeared from his first marriage, the military and the police, leaving barely a trace. If the Bandidos found out he had been a police officer, he could expect far worse.

When the party ended, Kellestine hugged members of Boxer's crew and called out "bro" and "brother" to them as they rode away in a cloud of dust down his driveway. When Boxer, Chopper and the rest of the No Surrender Crew were safely out of earshot and he didn't have to fake brotherhood any longer, Kellestine turned and grumbled to club friends Eric Niessen and Frank Mather: "You guys are worth more than all of the guys from Toronto put together. I'm proud of you guys."

During the same visit to Ontario, the Winnipeggers travelled north to Keswick, where they met with Cameron

Acorn, whose boyish appearance belied his status in the region's criminal underbelly, where crime tended to be more Hatfield-versus-McCoy than spy-versus-spy. With Acorn were Boxer Muscedere, Chopper Raposo, Crash Kriarakis, Goldberg Flanz, Big Paul Sinopoli, Pony Jessome and another Bandido prospect called "Stone," who got his nickname because he always looked stoned. Kriarakis wore a patch proclaiming "Our colours don't run" over his heart, but he still sometimes confided to friends that he wanted out of the Bandidos altogether, even though he had been promoted to become the club's national secretary to replace his departed friend Wrongway Atkinson.

Sandham and the Winnipeggers partied at a local nightclub where Flanz worked part time as a bouncer. Flanz didn't need the money, but found the club more exciting than his computer support business. The Winnipeggers never lost track of their purpose for the visit, even though they seemed to be under the impression that Toronto was led by Kellestine rather than Boxer, perhaps because Kellestine was more receptive than anyone else in the club to their arguments. "We were trying to push Wayne about getting a charter," M.H. later said. In Weiner's mind, London should get its own chapter too, and of course he was the natural choice for its president. As he saw things, that new London chapter would be in charge of all Canadian chapters to its west, which included Winnipeg. This would give Kellestine the necessary clout to be the de facto national *presidente*, even if his old friend Boxer Muscedere still officially held that title. Aside from the rush of power, it would also connect him with crystal meth networks on the Prairies.

Boxer didn't seem to sense that Weiner was planning something behind his back. Boxer would never plot against a brother, and couldn't imagine that a brother could plot against him, since real brothers just don't do that sort of thing. For other members of the No Surrender Crew, the idea of giving Kellestine his own London chapter wasn't all bad. It would keep the strange, talkative man out of their way, and spare them the two-hour drive to meetings in his barn. There was something creepy, even for an outlaw biker, about the trips west to his farm. Then there were the stories they heard about him—that, for instance, he'd played William Tell by shooting beer tins off the head of a First Nations youth or posed naked for photographs brandishing a rifle. Members besides Boxer had fallen into the habit of inviting Weiner to parties later and later, when they bothered to invite him at all.

It seemed to M.H. that the only Ontario Bandido who was really standing in the way of the Winnipeggers getting their full charter was Chopper Raposo, but Chopper wasn't someone to take lightly. The smile above that lean, triangle patch of a beard exuded more confidence than warmth, and it wasn't surprising that he was sometimes called upon by underworld elements to collect on debts. Nor was Raposo shy about saying what was on his mind, especially when he was cranked up on cocaine.

Chopper accused the Winnipeggers of not paying their dues, while the Winnipeggers replied that they had been faithfully sending the money to Toronto. The amounts in dispute seem small, with probationary chapters owing a one-time payment of a thousand dollars, plus twenty-five dollars per member by the first of each month. The issue should have been simple to resolve, but accusations came more easily to these men than reason. Taz Sandham returned to Winnipeg frustrated, with no commitment as to when, if ever, his chapter would get full Bandido status. The No Surrender Crew remained the only chapter in Canada.

The Toronto members were also getting on Boxer's nerves. He was trying to run a motorcycle club and yet his members were still dragging their feet about getting motorcycles. The club's July 29 minutes, recorded by Big Paul Sinopoli, who was the secretary now, noted that Boxer gave all members a deadline: "Everyone needs a bike or out of club by August 12, 05." It was a strong, clear order. But offending members simply ignored it. It was as if Boxer was a leader with no followers, of a club that had already died.

There was a party at a Legion hall in South Riverdale in the summer of 2005 that was attended by both Boxer Muscedere and Weiner Kellestine. Body language between the two men suggested they were no longer the tight friends they had been earlier in the decade, when they would ride together to the lakeside community of Port Dover for Friday the 13th biker get-togethers, back when Boxer was Weiner's trusted sidekick. Now, Boxer sat at a table, smoking a huge cigar, while Kellestine huddled with friends and hangarounds in another part of the hall, wheedling on the theme of brotherhood. Kellestine still resented Boxer's power. For his part, Boxer wasn't comfortable with Kellestine's enthusiasm for crystal meth. Even in the drug world, the substance, nicknamed "crank" or "speed," was associated with aggressive bottom-feeders. It was easily affordable to schoolchildren, and it rotted out the enamel of teeth as it attacked their nervous systems, making marijuana and cocaine seem almost innocuous by comparison.

The Legion party had been held in honour of Ripper Fullager. Ripper was a link to the old, brawling-and-brotherhood days of early one percenters, back when it was more about the guy beside you than business and expansion. There was always something comforting about sharing a beer in his kitchen or backyard, as Ripper had a gift for always making people smile and laugh and feel part of something big. Now he was dying of cancer before their eyes, and there was nothing doctors could do about it except wash away his pain with morphine.

Police had confiscated Ripper's Fat Mexican patch in a raid, and his friends in the No Surrender Crew felt they had to do something to make his final days more comfortable. That afternoon, tears welled in Bam Bam Salerno's eyes as the club gave Ripper a new commemorative patch—fit to be buried in.

During the summer of 2005, Weiner Kellestine quietly visited Winnipeg with another biker known as Grumpy. Weiner and Taz Sandham were pulling closer, and they often talked privately, behind Boxer Muscedere's back. Exactly what Weiner did in the west remained a mystery, since he didn't divulge it to his No Surrender brothers upon his return. Whatever happened, it certainly couldn't have been for the benefit of the rest of the No Surrender Crew.

Taz Sandham and M.H. flew to Toronto on September 9 to press their case for full-fledged chapter status and the right to expand. They met up with the others at Ripper Fullager's, where the unresolved issue of the Winnipeg dues still poisoned the mood. "You could hear them yelling through the door," M.H. later recalled. In a world in which so much depends on the ability to trust the guy beside you, this inability to settle a seemingly basic administrative dispute did not augur well for the brotherhood between the two chapters.

Still, M.H. and Mushey were finally given their patches as full Bandidos members later in the visit, though the promotions were bittersweet. When Sandham and M.H. flew back to Winnipeg two days later, their chapter remained on probation, still under the thumb of the No Surrender Crew.

Kellestine privately told the Winnipeggers that they had a supporter in him. Since Toronto wasn't speaking to the American Bandidos, Weiner advised, they should just get their own patches made up. To do so was an offence worthy of expulsion from the club, but Kellestine made it seem as though the Winnipeggers had somehow earned the right. Like Taz Sandham, his egotism and disregard for all rules allowed him to do just about anything in pursuit of expansion, no matter the consequences. "He wanted growth," M.H. later said. "He wanted to go coast to coast . . . He wanted chapters in every province . . . As many as we could get."

While Boxer smoked his cigars and weighed his options, his old chum Kellestine secretly went about building his own empire, plotting with Sandham to build the national network of chapters the Bandidos president dreamed of so ardently. Taz already had a spin-off group of eight supporters in Saskatchewan, a secret that would have cost him dearly had Boxer and the Torontonians caught wind of it. But Sandham, the ex-cop, had already hoodwinked the No Surrender Crew once, and figured he could do it at least once more, with Kellestine's help.

On October 10, 2005, an email from the Texans to Chopper Raposo and Bam Bam Salerno demanded that the No Surrender Crew account for itself. The spelling and grammar were poor, but the message was clear: "Well there is no easy way to put this, but I have been instructed to contact someone in Canada and find out why we have been getting no contact," Bill Sartelle, the club's world *secretario* began. He went on:

"Canada has not been meeting the requirements of belonging to this club, under the United States. I want to know how this can be remedied, imediately. If I am wrong then explain. There are many criterias invlved with Club Memebrship. One is monthly contact and mail sent to USA National Chapter. I believe this has been discussed over and over and as to my knowledge, nothing has been sent in a very long time.

This must be remedied imediately I would suggest the person in charge up there make plans to visit USA. Very soon.

We would like details with 48 hours.

Bill 1%er.

Chopper replied two days later, saying, with his own wretched spelling, that the Canadians were trying to make contact. "We are making arrangements to send a brother doun to se you," Chopper wrote. Privately, he knew that the Americans had reason to be angry. The No Surrender Crew had been sloppy about staying in touch with the mother chapter and hadn't been forwarding the required payments. Still, he offered excuses: "I have tried to call you but the 877 number I have it dos not work from Canada. as always the Canadian Brothers send are Love Loyalty and Respect BANDIDO Chopper 1%er."

Whatever his faults, Sandham could not be accused of giving up too easily. On November 26, he was back in Toronto with Mushey, knocking on the Bandidos' door, demanding his club's charter. But if his position hadn't changed at all, neither had the No Surrender Crew's. When Crash Kriarakis raised the touchy issue of the dues, he must have known an explosion would follow. The Winnipeggers remained insistent they had already paid the money, while Chopper Raposo was just as adamant as ever that they had not.

One obvious possibility was that someone was lying boldly in front of other senior members of the club. Another was that someone was quietly skimming funds and sabotaging the club in the process. Or perhaps more than one person was dipping into the club treasury. The club rotated its secretary-treasurer post around, and certainly Big Paul could use the money. There had been some money transferred from Winnipeg to Weiner Kellestine, but if Kellestine held the answer to the missing funds, he wasn't saying anything. He might have been trying to play the tension between the two clubs to his advantage. Or he may have simply wanted some extra cash. But although the strongest traces of the missing dues seemed to lead back to Iona Station, no one suspected that Kellestine was the source of the discord.

Taz then made things worse, handing Chopper an envelope stuffed with four thousand dollars' worth of receipts, anticipating that the Toronto crew would pick up the Winnipeggers' travel expenses. Boxer and Chopper had no intention of paying the bill, even if they had the money. But nor did they have the stomach to simply tell the Winnipeggers to go away. That would leave the Canadian Bandidos as a supposedly national club with only one chapter. The Hells Angels by now had three dozen chapters from coast to coast, including a half-dozen within an hour's drive of downtown Toronto, and were still growing. After the humiliating rejection by the former Alberta Rebels, the thought of the Bandidos remaining a one-chapter club was tough to contemplate. And so far, Taz and the Manitobans seemed just annoying, not threatening.

In any case, Toronto chapter president Bam Bam Salerno didn't seem to fear that Taz Sandham and his crew were tightening their grip on the No Surrender Crew like a giant snake slowly coiling itself around its prey. Nor did he have much interest in placating the Americans. He was busy wrapping his brain around a business scheme that put all his other brainwaves to shame. It would involve minimal work, but could net him some easy cash. The idea was to supply male and female strippers for stags and stagettes. His company was called Playboyz Productions, and his rate card read, "Bra and G string $175 / Topless $200 / Fully Nude $250." Customers could hire strippers dressed as nurses, schoolgirls, "slutty secretaries" and, in an interesting twist for an outlaw biker, police officers.

Club tensions could wait. Bam Bam was busy finding strippers to dress up as cops.

CHAPTER 13

A Place to Stay

An old black ram is tupping your white ewe.
OTHELLO, ACT 1, SCENE 1

"I'm fucking dead."
FINAL WORDS OF MURDER VICTIM SHAWN DOUSE

No Surrender Crew prospect Jamie (Goldberg) Flanz fell onto the police radar a few days after a party at his townhouse on Hattie Court in Keswick on the night of December 6, 2005. The weather that Tuesday evening was cold enough, a brisk minus-6 Celsius. Nobody particularly wanted to go outside, although there was only a centimetre of snow on the ground, and no more of it falling from the sky.

Twenty-year-old Mary Thompson was bracing herself for another bleary winter night of partying when her sometime boyfriend Bobby Quinn called someone on his cellphone and passed it over immediately to her, covering the receiver with his hand. Quinn was a close friend of Cameron Acorn, the former Killerbeez member Boxer had fast-tracked to full-patch status in the No Surrender

Crew. That night, Quinn told Mary to tell the person on the other end of the line to hurry up and drop by, and to bring along an eight-ball of cocaine, slang for about $250 worth of the drug.

Mary said her piece, but the man on the other end still didn't want to come. It was late. It was cold out. He didn't have money for a cab. There would be other parties. It was always party time at the townhouse on Hattie Court.

"Come on over," Mary urged him as Bobby stood nearby. "Come on over."

The man on the phone clearly didn't want to oblige, and Mary passed the phone back to Quinn, who began pressing him. Half an hour later, a white cab from Paul's Taxi pulled up in front of 45 Hattie Court, and a short, chubby black man in his thirties got out and walked towards the front door.

Mary was standing at the top of the steps leading to the main floor, and hers was the first face that the visitor saw when he came through the front door. Next in his line of vision were Cameron Acorn and Pierre (Carlitto) Aragon of the No Surrender Crew, then Quinn and an acquaintance of his named Randy Brown. Boxer and senior members of the chapter were down in Toronto, miles away from the party.

"You know my girlfriend?" Acorn asked, his words sounding more like an accusation than a question. "Yeah, my girlfriend."

Surprise and fear flashed across the small visitor's face. For an instant, it looked to Mary as if the man's face physically popped with shock, like a character in a cartoon. It was then that she realized that the little man at the front door was the one the Keswick Bandidos had been talking about so angrily for the past few days. They believed he was supplying crack cocaine to a teenaged relative of Acorn's girlfriend. There were rumours that he was sleeping with her as well. He was the man they wanted to hurt, or even kill. He was Shawn Douse.

No more words were spoken before Acorn threw a punch that caught Douse flush on the face. Something snapped with that blow, and in a moment they were all hitting him.

"Tell her to go upstairs," Acorn ordered Big Paul Sinopoli. As Big Paul ushered Mary upstairs, she could see Acorn, Quinn, Aragon and Brown dragging Douse down into the basement. "I'm sorry!" Douse yelled as he disappeared out of sight.

Mary filled her palm with sleeping pills and swallowed them fast. She felt no effect whatsoever as she looked out her window into the pitch-black sky. She saw nothing but what appeared to be a full moon, far off in the heavens. She could still hear Shawn Douse screaming from the basement.

A few moments later, there was the sound of vomiting in the upstairs bathroom. Her door opened and she saw Bobby Quinn. Blood was smeared onto his shirt and pants and he was shaking like a child.

"So what are you going to do?" she asked. "Are you going to have to kill him?"

The silence that followed was enough of an answer. She wondered again if she was going to be killed too, once they were done with Douse. She was a witness. Who would miss her if she vanished that night? Quinn left, and she could hear his retching as he walked down the stairs and back into the basement.

Not long after that, Mary heard Shawn Douse scream, "I'm fucking dead."

Finally, the shouting stopped.

Mary wasn't sure who it was that went upstairs to her room and announced, "It's over." She was led downstairs, past the blood on the front landing and basement stairway, into the furnace room. There, Acorn, Quinn, Aragon and Brown stood around something wrapped in coarse beige fabric that looked like burlap. It was in the shape of a short body, with a strap at its foot and chest area. There was no face visible, only fabric.

Blood was spattered over the men's bodies, and Aragon bled from a slash on his arm. They flipped Douse's motionless form over, so that he lay face down. Although he was apparently dead and wrapped in cloth, they still didn't want him looking at them. Mary stepped towards the canvas package and gave it a kick. Then she heard herself say a word she didn't normally use: "nigger." She felt horribly ashamed of the kick, and even worse about the racial epithet as it passed her lips, but she prayed that both would be enough to keep her alive through the night.

Mary had been living at the townhouse and didn't have anywhere else to go, even if she had been allowed to leave. The next few days for her were lost in a massive cleanup. It wasn't so hard to kill a man, but mopping up afterwards was a huge task. Everything had to go, even the washer/dryer and the carpet, until only a computer and desk remained. A fresh coat of paint was splashed onto the basement walls, and at some point, among all of the garbage, Shawn Douse's body was carried away.

Mary didn't wear a watch, so it was impossible for her to gauge when Goldberg Flanz first appeared back in his townhouse. Goldberg had every right to be angry at his biker brothers. It was bad enough that they had murdered someone, but to do it inside a residence connected to the club, and smear the place with DNA, was monumentally stupid. Still, Goldberg was only a prospect while Acorn, Aragon and Sinopoli were all full-patch members. He might be smarter than the others, but he still knew his place.

When Goldberg saw Mary scrubbing the mess, his words were gentle. He presented her with cleaning supplies—Comet cleanser, bleach, heavy-duty garbage bags and rubber gloves—and some money to pay her for the cleanup and some more cocaine.

"Thank you," he said.

The days after the murder ran together for Mary. They were a wash of cocaine and cleaning and fear. Mary suspected the bikers were debating whether to kill her too. Acorn decided to move Mary to his mother Sharon's house in Jacksons Point, a twenty-minute drive away.

Carlitto Aragon told Mary to relay a message to Sharon Acorn, who was known to the bikers as "Moma Bee." He wanted Mary to tell her the killing was somehow the fault of the dead man, Douse, and that the violence had erupted after Douse slashed his arm with a broken beer bottle. "Tell Moma that's why I had to do it," Aragon said.

A few days before Christmas, Mary pleaded to be allowed to visit her stepfather and sister for the holidays. The bikers' initial panic had passed, and they relented. There had been many sad Christmases in Mary's young life, but this was easily the worst. She didn't feel she could tell her family about the murder, while her stepfather felt free to take verbal jabs at her for what he considered her biker friends. Shortly after Boxing Day, Mary had had enough and was on the move again.

The bikers dumped Shawn Douse's body in a field in the north end of Pickering, in neighbouring Durham Region, covered it with gasoline and set it ablaze. When they returned the next day to turn it over and burn the remnants, they thought they saw a police car, and sped away.

Once the body was discovered by a man walking his dogs the next day, it fell to Dr. Michael Pollanen, the chief forensic pathologist for the Province of Ontario, to determine the exact cause of death. As he unzipped the body bag and considered the man's physical remains, his first question was whether the young man was alive at the time he was set on fire. One couldn't help but hope that he was already dead, as the pain of being burned alive was unimaginable.

Wedged deep into the dead man's mouth was a folded fabric gag, soaked in saliva and blood. It had been crammed in so tight that it had forced the man's tongue deep into his throat. Hemorrhages in the whites of the eyes were signs of possible blunt-force trauma. There were lacerations above the eyebrows, his nose had been broken, there was deep bruising to his rib cage and neck, and his jaw was broken and dislocated—all indisputable proof that he had suffered a hellish beating.

He had met an unthinkable death, but it could have been even worse. Mercifully, there were no traces of soot in his airways, suggesting to Pollanen that Douse was dead at the time his body was set afire. An examination of his neck and voice box yielded no evidence of strangulation. Elevated amounts of cocaine in his system indicated he was high when he died. Hopefully, that acted as a buffer against at least some of the pain.

On December 14, Douse's wife, Melanie, finally reported him missing to the York Regional Police. Soon after she spoke with them, an odontologist, or forensic dentist, compared the dead man's teeth to Douse's medical records and found that they matched. The murdered man was officially identified as Shawn Douse, a tool-and-die worker at Chrysler in Bramalea, northwest of Toronto, and a father of two. York police also knew him as a small-time crack cocaine dealer and user.

Those who were familiar with Douse's family knew there was much more to his life than a few pages of police files. Shawn had been the only one of Veronica and John Douse's five children who was born in Canada after their immigration from Jamaica. His parents were proud of how hard they had worked to give their children better opportunities in their chosen country. That work had paid off financially, in the form of a successful auto body shop and real estate investments that included shares in a golf course. However, their love of God, hard-earned money and physical fitness hadn't been enough to steer Shawn off the easy and dangerous course that took him to meet members of Boxer Muscedere's Bandidos at Hattie Court on the night of his death.

Mary was consumed with guilt and needed a refuge from Keswick. She wanted to talk to authorities about the murder, but also feared for her life. For his part, Goldberg Flanz wondered if he would be interrogated by police about the murder. How tough would it be for police to obtain taxi records that showed Douse had arrived at the townhouse he owned shortly before the murder? Flanz wasn't a hardcore biker and hadn't even been home the night of the killing. Still, Boxer and the others would expect him to be quiet about it—or else. Boxer wasn't a racist, and he wouldn't have approved of the murder, but he also wouldn't put up with anyone ratting on his biker brothers.

Mary Thompson and Goldberg Flanz each had good reasons to worry. It was easy to imagine that the killing had just begun.

CHAPTER 14

Living Dead

Have I no friend will rid me of this living fear?
RICHARD II, ACT 5, SCENE 5

Are we a dictatorship or a brotherhood?
What have we become?
GIOVANNI (JOHN, BOXER) MUSCEDERE

Neither the Winnipeg tensions nor concerns about the fallout from the Shawn Douse murder ruined Boxer Muscedere's holidays. He was clearly in a cheerful mood on Christmas morning, 2005, as he sent out a mass email greeting to others in the Bandido world, from himself, the club, Nina and baby Angelina:

MERRY CHRISTMAS AND HAPPY NEWYEAR TOO THE
BANDIDO NATION AND TOO THE NO SURRENDER
CREW WHO LOVES YA BABY FROM BOXER PBOL NINA
AND ANGELINA LOVE LOYALTY RESPECT IT JUST
DOESNT GET ANY BETTER.

A hangaround Bandido from Kuala Lumpur, Malaysia, named "Hafiz" sent the No Surrender Crew a greeting from halfway around the world, marking both the holiday and the crew's fifth anniversary: "We wish all the brothers & families A Merry X-Mas & A Glorious & Joyful Year 2006. Have a Safe & Happy Holiday Season. WITH MUCH LOVE, LOYALTY & RESPECT."

However festive the No Surrender Crew felt, there was no way of putting a bright face on the email Boxer Muscedere received from Texas on December 28. It was from Bill Sartelle, the Bandidos' world *secretario*, and it announced bluntly that Boxer's world had just collapsed. The mother chapter was disowning its Toronto brothers:

> For the past year or more we, BMC USA, have attempted to make connections with Canada . . . Up till now there has been no visit from the proper person. It has been decided that due to lack of participation, Canada's Charter is being pulled. Effective immediately: Return all Bandido patches and property . . . In approximately 30 days we will make notification to all that we no longer have a Chapter in Canada and that any person wearing our Patch, in Canada, is not sanctioned.
>
> Bill 1%er

Chopper Raposo was in the habit of sharing club business with his fiancée, Carrie Caldwell, a Harley-riding occupational health nurse at the Ford plant in St. Thomas.

It was against club rules to do so, but he trusted her and valued both her heart and mind. That meant she heard of a conversation in December in which Chopper asked Weiner Kellestine how he should deal with the Americans: "What am I supposed to do? We're breaking the rules."

Chopper had no way of knowing he was asking the wrong guy for advice. Faced with the apparently immovable force of Chopper, Kellestine's co-conspirator Taz Sandham had decided to do an end run around the Torontonians and complain directly to the Bandidos' mother chapter in Texas that the Winnipeggers were being overcharged for dues and patch money. He was toying with forces that could explode on him. It was one thing to try to manipulate the No Surrender Crew, and quite another to try to pull strings at the headquarters of the world's second-largest biker empire. The Americans were aghast. They were supposed to be consulted about expansion, and this was the first time anyone even told them that a Manitoba chapter of the Bandidos existed. They weren't interested in refereeing a squabble between one chapter they were growing tired of and another that didn't even exist as far as they were concerned. For the senior officials who ran the Bandido Nation, the best option was to shut down Canada altogether.

Somehow, things would get worse for Boxer's crew. Sandham would later tell police that Kellestine heard a rumour around this time that members of the No Surrender Crew were talking about trying to patch over en masse to the Outlaws, leaving him behind.[22] If this were true—and Taz Sandham was never a man to trust wholeheartedly—this represented not only abandonment but also death of a sort to Kellestine. He had already been rejected by the Outlaws once. Why would they want him back, especially with Wrongway Atkinson now wearing an Outlaws patch? Certainly, Wrongway couldn't be expected to welcome him after Weiner had stuffed a pistol in his mouth while others broke his ribs. There was an even slimmer chance of Weiner Kellestine getting into the Hells Angels. He was such a non-entity in their world that he was no longer considered worth murdering.[23]

The source of the rumour about the No Surrender Crew patching over to the Outlaws was never clear, although it obviously benefited Taz Sandham the most. He also had Weiner's ear. For all his blundering, it seemed Taz had finally done something truly Machiavellian by whispering rumours to manipulate the madman Kellestine.

Alone, nutty and hard-up for money, fifty-six-year-old Weiner Kellestine teetered on the brink of being exiled to the biker equivalent of the land of the living dead. His backwoods crazy Nazi act had apparently run its course, and his dream of becoming the Bandidos' de facto Canadian president would never be realized if the No Surrender Crew dissolved. Nor was there much room for him to start his own club, as there had been back in the 1980s, before the Hells Angels and the Bandidos moved into Ontario, gobbling up or squeezing out most of the independent gangs. In Weiner Kellestine's fevered mind, he was the victim of a deadly betrayal. He wouldn't go down alone. Now was the time to fight back.

As Taz Sandham later recalled, "Wayne Kellestine just blew up—like he just flipped out and he phoned me at home . . . just freaking out and swearing." Kellestine was particularly furious with Boxer Muscedere, the man he had considered his sidekick in the Annihilators, the Loners and the early stages of the Bandidos. Now, Kellestine fumed, Muscedere was talking of leaving him behind, after all he had done to bring him into the world of one percenter bikers.[24]

Sartelle's email stirred up a hornet's nest of activity on the Internet. It had been one thing to play fast and loose with the Bandidos' by-laws and protocols, and quite another to have to account for it to the mother chapter. Suddenly, what was at stake was no longer the grand dream of expansion; the Canadian Bandidos were pleading just to keep their patches.

On Wednesday, January 4, 2006, after stewing for a week about the American edict, Bam Bam Salerno sent Sartelle an email reply, under the subject heading "my life." Clearly, he had been thinking about the December 28 message long and hard.

> I'm sitting here feeling, confused, dejected, emotionally drained. I can't remember feeling as badly unless I count the times I was informed that Brother TOUT TOUT and the time Brother CrazyHorse JOEY were assassinated. You see Bill, I've been with this GREAT NATION since its inception in Ontario . . . At that time there was 7 of us here in Ontario. We were surrounded by no less than 6 H.A. chapters within a 50 mile radius. As you know, they tried EVERYTHING in their power to shut us down. We have been decimated with betrayal, defection to other clubs, law enforcement, but We stood tall and wear our colours proud . . . Bill, being a Bandido in good standing is my world. Quite frankly I resent have to go through this. I have always done the nation Proud.

A few hours later, Sartelle replied in an email to Salerno. He wasn't enjoying the process of kicking out the men who considered themselves his brothers, and he appeared to be softening, just a little. That said, he didn't have the power to reverse things—that was in the hands of *El Presidente* Jeff Pike. Sartelle wrote that the Americans felt let down that Boxer hadn't made a trip south or notified them that he had troubles crossing the border.

> I will pass this on to the proper people. It's not my decision alone. I do not know at this point what can

be done to reverse the decisions made as far as Boxer coming down or at least trying, I know about this because I am who asked him to come. He apparently had problems . . .

Not one call was made to me to let anyone know what was going on. We waited and waited because is that the proper way that should have been handled?? Anyway, I will see if someone can contact you?

Good Luck
Bill 1%er

What Bam Bam seems not to have considered is that one of the best ways to clear your own name is to blame someone else for whatever has gone wrong, and that is exactly what Taz Sandham had in mind as he made his case to Texas. The same day that Salerno was exchanging emails with Sartelle, Sandham went behind the backs of the Toronto chapter leadership again, making his own private plea to keep his membership. Now was the time to clearly separate himself and his ally Kellestine from Boxer Muscedere and the rest of the No Surrender Crew. "Probationary Bandido Taz here from Manitoba Canada," he emailed the Texans. "I am just hearing about a problem with Toronto. I hope that this not [*sic*] reflect on us we have worked very hard out here for almost a year and a half . . . The day I became part of this family was a great honour for me and my crew. I hope that we can work together to remedy this situation . . . Also Bandido

Wayne 'W' would like someone their [*sic*] to call him. He is in London, Ontario . . ." After distancing himself from his president, Boxer, and driving a wedge between his co-conspirator Kellestine and his own club, Sandham signed off with "Much loyalty, love and respect."

Boxer was also at his computer, pleading for the survival of the No Surrender Crew in an email to Keinard (Hawaiian Ken) Post of the Whatcom County Bandidos in Washington State, who had founded the Bandidos chapter in Oahu, Hawaii. Boxer considered Hawaiian Ken a friend, and someone he could trust. Boxer began, "My brother ken you will always be my brother," then quickly became emotional, saying, "There is no reason too [*sic*] take something the canadian brothers value more than there [*sic*] own lives when a brother is down you reach out your hand too [*sic*] help him up not kick them i feel like a knife has been driven in my heart would you beleave it my own brother has done what my enemys could never do without my death." He ended his message with "love loyalty respect bandidoboxer cut one we all bleed."

That same day, Boxer finally replied to the Texans. He and Chopper Raposo felt that Bam Bam Salerno's January 4 email to the Americans had been too soft—the Canadian Bandidos weren't about to grovel. Boxer's tone was defiant; if he had to go out at all, he would go out like a man. "MY NAME IS BANDIDOBOXER I SPEAK FOR THE NO SURRENDER CREW CANADA BANDIDOS MY PHONE NUMBER IS . . . REVERSE CHARGES I WILL PAY FOR IT MY ENEMY HAVE TREATED ALL OF US WITH RESPECT YOUR A PEACE OF WORK."

Sartelle got back to Boxer the same day, and his tone was unapologetic: "I find it interesting that it took my e-mail for you to decide to contact someone here in my Chapter. And yes, I am a piece of work. And proud of who I am."

Someone cleaned up Boxer's grammar and spelling as he quickly emailed back to Sartelle. He was still unrepentant, but no longer hostile:

> I'm glad you responded to my E-mail so then the communication problem has been taken care of. I also am proud of who I am and there is no doubt in my mind. The E-Mails have never stopped and we have tried endlessly to contact you. If there is anything you need to know you can reach me . . . anytime. Our club is our life and there is nothing worth living for without it.
>
> Bandido Boxer

Boxer wasn't done. On January 6, he wrote an open email to Bandidos around the world, relying again on the editorial skills of someone close to him. Still, the style was unmistakably Boxer: he blamed the current problems on "a miscommunication or lack of one," then noted that he tried no fewer than five times to cross into the U.S. to talk face to face with the Texans. That was true, although Boxer hadn't dispatched anyone else to try to make it past border security and down to Texas in his place. "We have always, will always, and hope to remain a part of this great Brotherhood," he continued. "As a whole we still wholeheartedly believe as the No Surrender Crew that it is better to die on our feet then [*sic*] live on our knees."

Then Boxer did something that amounted to nothing less than a mutiny in the Bandido world. He called on members from around the world to vote to determine the fate of the No Surrender Crew. He was directly and publicly challenging the power of *El Presidente* Pike: "We would like a worldwide vote from all of our brothers from around the world before we return our Bandido property."

Boxer must have known this move would obviously infuriate the Texans, but he didn't seem to worry, as he pointed out that the Americans hadn't bothered to come north for a visit once in the past five years. He was like a prizefighter in the final rounds of a losing bout, swinging wildly for a knockout blow and leaving himself exposed to a counterattack. "We have managed to not only visit our brothers across the border but also Europe as well," he wrote. Through the Internet, Boxer sent out a rallying cry for independence from Texan control to Bandidos from around the world: "CUT ONE WE ALL BLEED I AM MY BROTHERS KEEPER OUR COLORS DON'T RUN. Are we a dictatorship or a brotherhood? What have we become?"

The Bandidos were not a democracy, and had never pretended to be one. The world reaction to Boxer's rallying cry was one of stunned silence. Boxer regrouped, cooled things off a little and decided once again to try to get down to Texas to make his case face to face with the mother chapter. Yet again, he was turned back at the border because of his criminal connections. Desperate to do something, Boxer scrounged up the money to fly to Denmark and Germany, where security would be less strict. He and Nina spent a month abroad as the guests of club members in Copenhagen and Berlin and, in the words of Nina, "other places I couldn't even pronounce." There, Boxer appealed to his European brothers to stand up to the Texans and allow the No Surrender Crew to live on.

But it was not Boxer's attempt at international diplomacy that won the Torontonians a reprieve: it was Crash Kriarakis. Because he didn't have a criminal record, Crash was able to cross the American border and appeal directly to the mother chapter. His presence there seemed to have a calming effect, as it so often did. Crash was likeable and businesslike, and clearly no gangster or druggie. Ironically, Crash represented the Canadian Bandidos well because he didn't reflect much of its real leadership or membership. Unlike some of his clubmates, whose roiling ambition kept them at each others' throats, Crash didn't even want power; he just couldn't escape it. Before he returned home, the Texans summarily appointed Crash to the position of Canadian *presidente,* giving him the title that Boxer had enjoyed and Kellestine and Taz Sandham coveted. Somehow, the guy who had privately been hoping to get out of the club altogether had been promoted to the top position in Canada. Then Boxer returned from Germany and simply continued to act as if nothing had changed in his absence. True to form, Crash fell back into line, as if his promotion had just been a bizarre dream, or nightmare.

Dwight Mushey travelled alone from Winnipeg to Vancouver on January 14, and Taz Sandham covered the $401.62 tab with his Visa card. M.H. would later say that he accompanied Mushey to Vancouver in early 2006. The bikers were travelling on business—Mushey planned to buy a kilo of cocaine, and there were also plans to get some ephedrine, which was used in the production of methamphetamine. As M.H. later told things, they thought they could get a network going with Weiner Kellestine, who lived a short hop from Stratford, regarded as the meth-making capital of Ontario. In drug circles, rural areas were preferred by those who manufactured a form of the drug known as crystal meth, the production of which gives off a strong odour, like that of cat urine, and generates a lot of toxic waste. And one of the key ingredients in the manufacture of crystal meth is the agricultural fertilizer anhydrous ammonia, which is far more readily available in rural regions than in cities. Thus, the abundant countryside around the Ontario city known for its Shakespearean festival had become a centre of manufacture.

Even among drug dealers, crystal meth is considered an ugly thing. The drug is cheap—less than twenty dollars a dose—and highly addictive. It's also physically destructive, with side effects ranging from unsightly sores around the mouth to cardiovascular failure, strokes and death. Although Boxer had a partier's mentality about drugs, he was still a family man and shunned this particular drug, which he considered beyond the pale, even for a self-professed outlaw. Aware of this attitude, Weiner Kellestine knew better than to cut Boxer in on his plans.

Taz also certainly didn't share news of the trip with Boxer. He was currying favour with more powerful men now. Someone in the U.S. was clearly working with Taz, to make him so cocky. Forces he couldn't know of were aligning against Boxer, though he soldiered on in the faith that they were his brothers.

Bam Bam Salerno had sometimes privately grumbled that he wanted out of the club, but now that he was faced with the threat of expulsion, he became more of a Bandido than ever. He wanted respect now, as titular president of the No Surrender Crew, and protested to Carleton (Pervert) Bare, national *secretario* of the Bandidos in Texas, that Boxer had tried five times to enter the U.S. to visit fellow Bandidos. "He was turned down everytime [*sic*] and the last time detained until he was deemed an undesirable and escorted back to Canadian soil. The next time he is caught trying to enter he will face criminal charges . . .

"There must be another place in this world to meet," Salerno continued. "We have no problem getting into

Mexico, Europe . . . You know getting to the U.S. is virtually impossible."

With Salerno suddenly taking his responsibilities as Toronto *presidente* seriously, the Americans were in the position of having to decide whether they should treat Crash Kriarakis, Boxer Muscedere, Taz Sandham, Weiner Kellestine or Bam Bam Salerno as their point man in Canada. Meanwhile, Bam Bam took it upon himself to demote Kellestine's friend Concrete Dave Weiche, a full-patch member now living in B.C., to prospect status for refusing to keep a distance from Washington State members of the Bandidos. In an email dated February 25, Bam Bam reminded Concrete Dave that he still had to answer to the No Surrender Crew, even if he lived on the other side of the country. He was all business as he noted that all Canadian Bandidos were expected to attend a "mandatory party" on March 18. "We are Bandidos Canada," Salerno wrote. "Not Toronto or Winnipeg or Vancouver."

Bam Bam also ordered Weiche to start showing a little more respect to Chopper Raposo, the man who had continually blocked the Winnipeggers from gaining full chapter status and who was now acting as club secretary. "He is Toronto sec and better be respected as such." As with so many other things about the No Surrender Crew, and Bam Bam Salerno in particular, the message was boldly worded but ultimately doomed to failure. Not long after Bam Bam sent the email, it was returned to him as undeliverable.

Taz Sandham's Prairie bikers included a longtime biker from Kelvington, Saskatchewan, named J.B. for "Just Bob," who was in the habit of starting his day by scouring the Internet for fresh stories on the Bandidos. J.B.'s head snapped back when he saw an item that mentioned Taz, reporting that he was a former police officer. For a one percenter, that's about as shocking as news can get.

J.B. immediately phoned Dwight Mushey for answers. Mushey reassured him that he and M.H. had already checked out the stories and dismissed them. Everything was fine, Mushey repeated. Still, the subject was brought up at the next church meeting, where Taz shrugged it off as a bad joke. He said the story confused the facts of a temporary job he'd held in which he trained people in how to use Tasers and other law-enforcement gear. As Taz told it, the job had been his first out of the army, and certainly didn't involve working as a police officer or for a police force. By the time he was done explaining, Taz sounded quite proud of himself and his deadly skills. He also sounded a little like a great man who was naturally persecuted by lesser beings. Most other members had a good laugh at how the media had botched things once again when reporting on one percenters, but J.B. still felt a little uneasy. There were some things that just didn't seem right about the little biker leader. Most damningly, J.B.'s sources in the Outlaws were solid, and they were definite that, despite his claims to the contrary, Taz had never been a member of their club. It was easy to wonder whether there was a rat in their midst, and perhaps more than one of them. And yet the Bandidos did nothing.

Less than a year earlier, Taz Sandham had fawned on Chopper, Boxer and the rest of the No Surrender Crew, in hopes of his provisional chapter getting full Fat Mexican status. Now, alongside Weiner Kellestine, Taz silently declared war on them. Under the alias of John Smith, Taz sent out an email from Vancouver on March 4 to Manitoba members, with the subject line "hey bro." Taz had just promoted himself to full-patch status, just as he had once promoted himself to black-belt and grand-master status in various martial arts. "Things are going good," Taz wrote. "Do not answer Toronto at all!! W[einer] is coming out here to speak as well to the States. U.S. is behind us 100 % as well as Germany . . .

"Much Love, Loyalty, and Respect

"Bandido Tazman 1%er

"Bandidos Fuckn Canada!!!!"

Taz used his Visa card to cover Kellestine's air fare from Toronto to Vancouver to join him on March 7. He alluded to that upcoming meeting in an email sent that day to Dwight Mushey: "Just an update, all is going well, old man will be here today. All is good." Taz Sandham wasn't a rich man by any stretch, but it seemed like a good investment for him to pay the $635.88 for Kellestine's flight. If all went well over the next few weeks, Taz wouldn't be grovelling at the feet of the Toronto Bandidos any longer.

He could profit handsomely from the mess in Toronto.

If he could only pull the right strings in Texas, the No Surrender Crew would be ordered once and for all to disband, leaving just Weiner Kellestine, Taz Sandham and the rest of the Winnipeggers to control the destiny of the Bandidos Nation north of the 49th parallel. The thought of being national *presidente* in an internationally recognized biker gang was dizzying to the man who was still called "Little Beaker" behind his back, and who, just a few years before, had been little more than a dog catcher in rural Manitoba.

Curious police in British Columbia watched from a distance as Weiner Kellestine met in Peace Arch Park with Peter (Mongo) Price, the American Bandidos' national *sargento de armas*. It was the same meeting site straddling the Canada–U.S. border that had been used late in the winter of 2000 by Richard (Dick) Mayrand of the Hells Angels and George Wegers of the American Bandidos, back when the Angels had sought unsuccessfully to end the Bandidos' northern expansion. The intervening years had changed a few things. Wegers was in custody in the U.S. now, facing charges from a massive police operation that included kidnapping and organizing criminal activity. And the Bandidos' prospects in Canada were a lot less bullish. Back when Wegers was calling the shots, the question was whom they might let into the club. This time, the Bandidos were deciding whom to kick out. And how to go about it.

The police could only watch as the bikers sat down to talk, but they certainly had no problem spotting Mongo Price, who stood six foot four and weighed something in the neighbourhood of 350 pounds, and whose head was topped with a shock of hair dyed bright orange. Also in attendance with Kellestine and Sandham were Concrete Dave Weiche, fresh from his botched Internet demotion by Bam Bam Salerno; Keinard (Hawaiian Ken) Post of the Whatcom County Bandidos in Washington State and Brian Bentley, another Washington State Bandido.

M.H. would later say that Kellestine was appointed Canadian president at this B.C. meeting, while Taz Sandham was made national secretary. But neither of them would have authority over the No Surrender Crew which, once the meeting came to an end, ceased to exist. While Boxer was back at home, fretting about the fate of his beloved club, a handful of his brothers were sitting at a picnic table on the other side of the continent, taking it away from him.

Kellestine was given orders to start up his own chapter in London, while Taz Sandham remained in charge of Manitoba. The two men had finally got what they wanted. But one obstacle stood in the way of their dreams of expansion: someone would have to pull the patches of Boxer Muscedere and the rest of his No Surrender Crew. That meant Boxer and his friends would be, in biker terms, "out bad." In the one percenter world, bikers who are out bad are like lepers. Their friends are expected to shun them, and their enemies can freely attack them, without fear of club reprisals. According to M.H., the job of delivering Boxer to that fate fell to the man who had once been his best friend: Weiner Kellestine.

Chopper Raposo soon sensed that something was particularly wrong, even by No Surrender Crew standards.
He didn't know about the meeting in B.C., or that his
patch was as good as pulled. But he didn't have to know
the backstory to see that Weiner Kellestine seemed to
be spoiling for a confrontation. A friend of Raposo's had
left his bike on Kellestine's property before he was sent
off to prison. Chopper's friend was getting out of custody
soon, and he understandably wanted his motorcycle back.
Weiner simply said "No," although he offered no good reason for keeping it. To Chopper, this sounded a lot like a
direct challenge, and though he may not have been much
good at Internet diplomacy, he knew a thing or two about
responding to challenges. His first instinct was to just go
to Kellestine's to retrieve the bike. But getting anything
from the farm was easier said than done. Even if he navi-
gated past the inner barbed-wire fence, the German shepherd and Weiner himself, there was the final obstacle of
finding the bike amidst the clutter of debris strewn about
Kellestine's property.

Meanwhile, Chopper found that the Winnipeggers
had started treating him in much the same way Kellestine was. In an email sent March 8, Chopper told Taz that
a cellphone number Taz had given him wasn't working.
Chopper's tone was angry: "MY TIME IS BETTER SPENT
TAKING CARE OF OUR BROTHERS IN JAIL THEN [*sic*] TRY-
ING TO GET A HOLD OF OUR BROTHER OUT SIDE."

Thousands of kilometres away, and smug in the secret
knowledge that he would soon rank above Chopper in the
Bandido world, Taz Sandham didn't bother to call Chop-

per "bro" or kiss up to him any longer. "Chopper, there is a reason why I am not contacting you right now," Taz admonished on March 9. "I am not available, and I just talked with you last week. You have to stop calling the guys so many times a day and night. Some of the guys parents and families are getting very upset. Stop calling the brothers homes and families. If its money you need right away please say so, otherwise the 18th is coming up right away. Pass this message to the other brothers."

On March 13, Taz emailed Chopper again, still affecting his new-found tone of superiority. He could not seem to restrain himself from flouting the Torontonians' authority. "I received an email from Crash, who was obviously very angry and seems he is saying you all are not supporting Manitoba any longer," Sandham emailed the Torontonians. "Well not seems, he is telling me there is no Manitoba at all.

"He is also saying there is no support club. We told you, Boxer, W, and Bamer [sic] all about it in September. There was no problem then.

"They have grown now to 35 guys," Sandham continued. "We are not going to take that away from them now. Half of them have bought bikes already."

Taz wasn't about to tempt fate and push things too far, however, even with someone he was plotting to stab in the back. He signed off: "Love, Loyalty, and Respect, Probationary Bandido Taz."

Chopper had a queasy feeling about the national party planned for March 18 at the Legion hall in South Riverdale in Toronto. The affair was to honour the fortieth anniversary of the Bandidos, and it had been declared a mandatory event for everyone, including the Winnipeggers. Boxer, Chopper and the others in leadership had a business purpose for the party as well: the Winnipeggers were expected to finally settle up their back dues. Chopper had heard rumours that Weiner Kellestine had met recently with top Americans, behind the backs of his fellow No Surrender Crew members, a sure sign that his loyalty could no longer be counted on. Chopper would keep an eye on Kellestine, which meant he'd be carrying a pistol when he arrived at the party.

By 11 P.M., the mood at the party had turned sour, courtesy of yet another insult from the Winnipeggers, who not only didn't show up but didn't even bother to call with an excuse. Weiner Kellestine was mysteriously absent too.

Exactly what happened in Vancouver between March 20 and 22, 2006, remains unclear, although it was important enough for Taz Sandham to charge $1,162.76 for M.H. and Mushey to make the return trip from Winnipeg. Clearly, Taz wouldn't even try to forward this bill to Toronto for reimbursement. The Winnipeg Bandidos regrouped on the morning of Saturday, March 25, at Dwight Mushey's bungalow. There, Taz announced that the standoff with Toronto would soon be over. Marching orders had finally come from the United States: they were going to Weiner Kellestine's farm and telling him they would help him strip away the patches of the Toronto No Surrender chapter. Weiner wouldn't be told in advance, as he had been dithering for a couple of weeks about pulling the patches of Boxer and the rest of his old clubmates. It wasn't certain where his loyalties lay. But the time had come for him to act—or pay the price.

Accompanying Sandham and Mushey was thirty-year-old Marcelo (Fat Ass) Aravena, a six-foot, two-inch, 280-pound Bandidos wannabe and part-time professional boxer and mixed-martial-arts fighter. Aravena had lost far more bouts than he had won, but he could still throw a hard punch and absorb several more. The promise of a six-hundred-dollar purse was enough to press Aravena into the ring with pretty well anyone, with no notice required, since he had pretty much given up training for his fights anyway. He'd taken on a laundry list of forgettable opponents—though, to his credit, Aravena had displayed enough nerve to step into the ring with the likes of former world middleweight and super-middleweight boxing champion Iran (The Blade) Barkley and the round-but-fierce Eric (Butterbean) Esch, who had to diet to keep his fighting weight under four hundred pounds. "I put on a good show," Aravena said of his fighting career. "That's why people liked me. I kept getting up and fighting." In the ring,

Aravena traded on his Chilean descent, calling himself *El Condor*, for the bird of death. Others in the Winnipeg Bandidos had less flattering nicknames for him , such as "The Great White Chilean Ape," "The Mountain Gorilla" and, of course, "Fat Ass." Sometimes, they also dismissed him as "Beaker Two," a not-so-flattering comparison to Taz Sandham, who was Beaker One.

Also at Mushey's house that Saturday was Brett (Bull, Beau) Gardiner, a twenty-one-year-old former ironworker from Calgary who had moved in with Mushey and Aravena. Gardiner loved to read and write poetry, and could consume several books a week. Gardiner wasn't a coward, and he had once risked his life to retrieve the body of a friend's father, who had drowned in Alberta's Sheep River. He also seemed to be someone who was continually in search of guidance. Outwardly unassuming and polite, with a quick, easy smile, Gardiner struck others in the one percenter world as a follower, not a leader. Neither Aravena nor Gardiner actually owned motorcycles or had licences to ride one, but that didn't seem to matter as they met in Mushey's house. What Gardiner did have was a reputation for loyalty. His friends sincerely believed that if he could help them, he would, and any club can always use another loyal member.[25]

After the meeting, Taz Sandham telephoned down to Bandidos headquarters in Texas to Keinard (Hawaiian Ken) Post, the American whom Boxer considered a friend and confidante. Boxer had clearly misread him. Hawaiian Ken told Taz he was waiting for a call from someone named "Brian." Once he got that call, Hawaiian Ken said he would call Taz back.

Within hours, Hawaiian Ken was back on the phone, and he repeated the earlier plan. The Winnipeg chapter was to pull the Fat Mexican patches from all of the No Surrender Crew, including Boxer. Only Weiner Kellestine would be spared the indignity of expulsion. Weiner's reward for betraying his old crew was that he would finally take Boxer's title and become the new national *presidente*. His former clubmates, including his longtime supporter, Boxer, would be kicked out of the club, in bad standing.

M.H. went to his house and started to pack, with no idea how long they would be staying in Ontario. Mushey asked if they should bring weapons, and Taz told him not to bother. There were always plenty of guns at 32196 Aberdeen Line, no matter how many lifetime weapons bans the court had imposed on Kellestine. Sandham did pack his bulletproof vest, and a box of surgical gloves, which would allow him to handle a firearm and not leave any fingerprints or telltale DNA.

Aravena was scheduled to fight on a mixed-martial-arts card in Steinbach, about sixty-five kilometres northwest of Winnipeg, that weekend, so it was agreed that he would fly alone to Ontario. The rest of them decided they would drive the northern route, winding along Highway 11 through Longlac and Hearst. That was the extent of their planning. They hadn't yet figured out how they would pull the patches; all they knew was that it had to be done and that Boxer and his crew wouldn't give them up without a fight.

The prospect of a showdown with the No Surrender Crew must have weighed heavily on the Winnipeggers' minds, because all of them forgot they were supposed to

have dinner that night with J.B. and some of the Saskatchewan members who were in town. When the Winnipeg
chapter didn't show up, the visitors drove to Mushey's
house to find out what had happened, and the look on his
face seemed to say, "What the fuck are you doing here?"
Mushey, Gardiner and M.H. seemed unnaturally quiet, so
the Saskatchewan members just dropped off their vests so
that new patches could be sewn on, and left. Mushey gave
J.B. a decorative, hand-carved cane as a gift, but offered
no explanation about where the Manitobans were going,
and the Saskatchewan members couldn't help but feel that
something big was about to go down.

Taz and the Manitoba members had reached the northwest Ontario town of Dryden on the evening of Saturday,
March 25, when Taz got a troubling telephone call from
his new common-law wife, Kathleen. She told him that
men who sounded like Carlitto, Stone and J.C. were at his
in-laws' house, asking for him. She also told him that they
didn't seem particularly nice.

Sandham might have guessed at what Kathleen didn't.
The Toronto bikers weren't dropping by for a beer and a
chat. The reason they were at Taz's in-laws' wasn't surprising: that was the address he had given when he joined
the club, before he had a place of his own. Their rude-
ness wasn't surprising, either, as police would later hear
that Carlitto and Stone were in Winnipeg to kill Sandham. Bam Bam Salerno was finally flexing his muscles
as Toronto president, and was prepared to put an end to
Sandham's wheedling to the mother chapter. Under Bam
Bam's plan, Carlitto would be installed as the new Mani-

toba president, uniting Toronto and Winnipeg and doing away with the annoyance of Taz. Evidently, pulling patches and appointing new chapter presidents were expedients that had occurred to both sides.

There would later be speculation that Carlitto and Stone were coming and that Sandham knew it, which is why he rushed out of town. Perhaps the squads of Bandidos had even passed each other on the highway, both sides contemplating bloodshed.

CHAPTER 15

Fire in the Hold

Between the acting of a dreadful thing
And the first motion, all the interim is
Like a phantasma, or a hideous dream . . .
JULIUS CAESAR, ACT 2, SCENE 1

We'll do his ashes in a shotgun shell
and blast them down at the lake.
WAYNE (WEINER) KELLESTINE PLANS A FRIEND'S FUNERAL

A traffic camera captured a few images of the red GMC Blazer full of Winnipeg bikers that Sunday, as Sandham's crew headed west down Highway 401 near Cambridge, in southwestern Ontario. As they arrived at the iron gates of Weiner Kellestine's farm, Taz put in a call to Dave Weiche on the west coast. As M.H. later recalled, Concrete Dave told them that if Kellestine didn't cooperate, they should "pull his patch too." Concrete Dave didn't have any particular authority by himself, but he did have easy access to senior American Bandidos, which made him a powerful man.

There wasn't any lock on the inner fence to the compound that evening, and they were able to knock on the door of Weiner Kellestine's farmhouse. He was understandably surprised, but played along in the role of welcoming buddy. True to form, Sandham lied to his host, claiming not to know the purpose of his own visit. He said the Americans had told him to "show up there and that they'll elaborate more after," M.H. later recalled.

Kellestine had advertised himself as a proven killer, but yanking Boxer's patch would be no easy matter. He had wavered since the Americans made him part of the plan to pull patches. Boxer was his best friend, and that kind of loyalty was rare, even though they'd had their troubles. If Weiner could only get above him in the Bandidos' world, then everything would be fine again. Chopper Raposo was another matter; he wouldn't go down without a fight, and he wasn't nearly as trusting as Boxer.

Kellestine had to choose between betraying his brother and being betrayed by his brotherhood. For the time being, he would make both the Winnipeggers and the No Surrender Crew believe he was on their side.

The next day, another visitor arrived. Thirty-two-year-old Frank Mather, a perpetually down-on-his luck ex-con, had a pregnant girlfriend and no place to live. The red-headed Maritimer had been kicked out of a motel for not paying his bills; next, he'd crashed with a friend with a nasty crack cocaine habit. He and Weiner had met when they were together in Beaver Creek minimum security prison north of Toronto, and before they parted ways, Kellestine urged him to give him a call if he ever needed a place to stay. True to his word, Kellestine ushered Mather into the house to meet the Manitoba bikers. "That's one of my boys from London," Kellestine announced.

Mather had a swastika tattooed on his neck, but those who knew him didn't consider him particularly menacing. He certainly wasn't a leader or anyone particularly ambitious. He just didn't seem to learn much from past mistakes. His criminal record included eight break-and-enters and a three-year prison stretch in New Brunswick, but nothing that involved weapons or violence. At the time he showed up on the doorstep of Weiner Kellestine's farmhouse, Frank Mather was on parole for possession of breaking-and-entering tools; he'd been arrested while trying to steal a truck. He had worn a Bandidos support shirt at a Kellestine party, but it was hard to believe a serious one percenter gang would want him as a member. In his favour, Mather was known in criminal circles as a man who would stand by his friends. His reputation was so solid that there were stories that Mather had even copped guilty pleas to crimes he hadn't committed, to keep his buddies on the streets.

Marcelo Aravena arrived at the London airport at 1:25 P.M. the next day. Sandham and the other Winnipeggers drove to the airport to pick him up. Sandham wore dark glasses and a ball cap, as if he were a rock star trying to keep a low profile among a swarm of paparazzi. Mushey was as easy to spot as Sandham was discreet. A head taller than many of the travellers, his jet-black hair bounced off the shoulders of his gleaming, spotless, silverish track suit. Perhaps the Winnipeggers didn't notice, but their movements were being recorded again—this time on airport security cameras.

Recovering from yet another punchout in the octagon, Aravena was nursing a black eye, a possible broken hand and a concussion from his previous night's work. When he saw his friends, he didn't shake their hands in greeting, as his right hand was as sore as his face. None of his friends offered to carry his suitcase for him, however.

At suppertime on Saturday, April 1, Weiner brought his guests to the Holland House in Iona Station, where they hunkered down to a meal of bacon cheeseburgers, French fries, soup and beer. "These are the guys from Winnipeg," Kellestine announced to owner Marty Angenent, and his words didn't sound like anything particularly notable at the time. He explained that the men were in the area to work on the new bingo hall at the nearby Chippewa of the Thames First Nation.

There was nothing new about Weiner Kellestine bringing biker friends to Angenent's family restaurant, where a sign near the cash register read, "Friends and Family Gather Here." Over the years, Kellestine had occasionally taken members of the Outlaws, Annihilators, Loners and Bandidos to the eatery. During his visits, Kellestine seldom wore gang colours, and he always seemed to respect a rule laid down by Angenent, which forbade them from discussing biker business. Once, through a quirk of timing, Kellestine and a group of his biker friends happened to arrive at the restaurant shortly after about five dozen members of the Blue Knights, a motorcycle club made up of New York State cops. The stage was set for a nasty confrontation, but Kellestine and his biker buddies chose to socialize instead with the visiting police officers. Other times, Kellestine brought strippers from an East London club near the airport with him, and while they were on the premises, the pole dancers were fully clad and at their ladylike best. "They had a beer or they had two beers, or once in a blue moon they had three beer," Angenent later said. "They never did any wild things."

That night was no different. "He was fine," Angenent later said. "He was just like another farmer. He was just a regular guy. You'd never know he was anything else. I've never found him scary. I've never seen him misbehave."

That Saturday evening with the Winnipeggers, there was something about Frank Mather's twitchiness and mumbling that gave Angenent the creeps. There was also something threadbare about the entire group. They were clearly tight for funds on a tab that came to about ten dollars per head. Mushey seemed to have some level of responsibility in the group, as it was the tall black belt who scraped together the funds to pay for the meal, with not much left over for a tip. It hadn't been a particularly memorable evening, but within a few days, Angenent would be pressed for details about it from reporters from Chicago, Toronto and other faraway spots, who were hungry for any tidbits of information about Weiner Kellestine and his associates for publication in newspapers around the world.

Early the next week, Kellestine took the Winnipeggers with him to the reserve, after hearing that someone had stolen a trailer of cigarettes and driven it there. He dabbled in the illegal cigarette business and was on close terms with the reserve's gangster element, and now went to pick up the cigarettes for resale. Taz Sandham scraped his red Blazer on the trailer while pulling up to a gas station there. To make things worse, when they opened up the stolen trailer, there were no cigarettes inside, just two hundred or so frozen pizzas. It was a disappointment, but stolen frozen pizzas were better than nothing at all, so they took them back to Kellestine's farm, where Sandham worked, unsuccessfully, to fix the damage to his Blazer.

Sandham did most of the driving, and after a few days Kellestine gave him some Ontario licence plates to put on the red Blazer. By then, anyone who noticed the bright red SUV would likely be curious to know why it now bore Ontario plates. But it was Taz's idea to make the switch. He thought a lot about things like that, as if he were really a spy or a cop. He also chose to park the Blazer along a wooden fence behind the farmhouse, so that someone—say, a police officer on patrol—couldn't easily spot it from the road.

The surroundings at the Kellestine home were more conducive to business than pleasure. The toilet was wonky, the bloodsucking wood ticks seemed to be everywhere and there wasn't much to eat besides the stolen pizzas. As junior members of the club, Bull Gardiner and Aravena were expected to fetch water, cook pizzas, wash dishes and perform such general chores as chopping wood. At one point, Kellestine sent Gardiner out on a search for a pickle tree to bring him back a snack. It was good for a laugh at Bull's expense. As a junior member, however, Gardiner was powerless to tell Kellestine his request was absurd, even if he realized it. Far better to look like an idiot than be attacked for being disrespectful.

If the jokes fell a little flat, it was because the grim task of betraying their so-called brothers hung over everything they did. They would eventually have to get around to the business of pulling the patches of the No Surrender Crew, and no one relished the prospect of trying to get them, particularly Boxer, to give up their beloved Fat Mexicans. With Lenti now out of the club, the now-deposed president was clearly the most physically threatening member of the group. Indeed, someone floated the idea of enlisting Boxer to help out—if he fell in with his old friend Kellestine, the reasoning went, then the rest of the No Surrender Crew wouldn't prove much of a threat at all. But that was no more than wishful thinking. The problem with Boxer was his loyalty—there was no way he was going to betray his entire chapter in favour of the interlopers from Manitoba. Everything depended on how they handled the hard-nosed president, and Kellestine knew that nothing they came up with promised to be easy. "He was really worried about Boxer," M.H. later said.

Despite the seemingly explicit marching orders from the Texas chapter, Kellestine thought he could reinterpret the plan to suit himself. He definitely wanted Bam Bam Salerno, Mikey Trotta and Chopper Raposo out, but thought he might be able to spare Pony Jessome, Crash Kriarakis and Big Paul Sinopoli. He didn't particularly dislike Trotta, but considered him to be a close friend of Salerno. "Little Mikey, him and Bammer were kind of a package deal," M.H. later said.

The Winnipeggers weren't comfortable with that idea, and M.H. later recalled that Taz Sandham suggested they just shoot Boxer instead. As M.H. later described events, Sandham played the role of trained military sniper to the hilt, boasting that he could take Boxer out easily from a distance. He had visited Boxer's twelfth-floor apartment on Dufferin Street, and he and Kellestine knew that he would go out onto the balcony to smoke his cigars, so that baby Angelina wouldn't have to inhale the smoke. Though the Bandidos had dismissed Joey Crazy Horse's killers as cowards for shooting him in a face-to-face confrontation, Sandham argued that the way to deal with Boxer was to assassinate him while he had his guard down.

Ironically, as his murder was being discussed by his "brothers," Boxer was pulled away from the club, both by his love for his growing family and a rekindled passion for the gym. He had only been a one percenter for eight years, but that was long enough for him to realize that not everyone in clubs shared his love of motorcycles or understood that brotherhood was more than a word. Boxing clubs were a brotherhood too, and Boxer was feeling a pull back to the ring, for the training and the coaching. After sliding into drugs, he was now cleaning himself up with regular workouts that were growing tougher and more satisfying. Around this time, he wrote his little brother Joe an email that read: "Bro, I started working out at a boxing club. I'm 48 years old but I've always loved to box. It's like riding a Bike, you never forget. I train harder than most because I know the hard work it takes to fight. I enjoy it and its relaxing just like medicine."

While Boxer was hitting the gym, unaware that the Americans had already pulled the plug on his presidency, conspirators from inside the club in Canada were polishing off another frozen pizza and putting the finishing touches on their plan to carry out the club's dirty work. Eventually, the Winnipeggers settled on the idea of pulling the patches at a church meeting that Friday at Kellestine's farm. From that point on, whether Boxer would be shot or recruited depended entirely on his interpretation of the one percenter code. If Boxer meant what he had been saying all those years about loyalty and brotherhood, he would be heading to his doom.

The closest pay phone to Weiner Kellestine's farm was at a gas station in Dutton, a few minutes up the road from Iona Station. It was here, early in the Manitobans' second week in Ontario, that M.H. did something that could have gotten him killed: he placed a call to Winnipeg Police Constable Timothy Diack. M.H. had known him for several years, and it went without saying that if the other bikers learned of his call to the police, there would be deadly consequences. The Winnipeg police officer later wrote in his notes, "[M.H.] explained that the status of the Toronto chapter was to be pulled."

That sentence alone might have been enough to ruin

the Winnipeggers' plan. A phone call to the Ontario Provincial Police could be made. The 120-member Biker Enforcement Unit could be deployed. There could be surveillance, more phone taps and a roadblock outside the Weiner Kellestine farm. But none of those things happened, and the Manitobans' plan lurched forward.

For M.H., there would be plenty more chances to inform as the killers readied themselves. Once, he said, he got Diack's voice mail. A second time, he recalled, "[Diack's] voice mail was full. You weren't able to leave a message."

On Wednesday, April 5, 2006, a police wiretap intercepted a phone call from Weiner Kellestine to Cameron Acorn's mother, Sharon, shortly before two in the afternoon. He told her of an idea to dispose of the remains of John (J.J.) Vincent, the gun-loving former Annihilator and Loner who had recently died of cirrhosis of the liver. The idea was to do something respectful but distinctly bikerish.

"We'll do his ashes in a shotgun shell and blast them down at the lake," Weiner suggested.

Moma Bee preferred something a little more tasteful, like tossing his ashes to the winds from the back of a moving Harley-Davidson.

"Right on," Kellestine said.

The conversation shifted to her son, Cameron. Kellestine didn't know that he was in custody, awaiting trial on drug charges. One might have expected Kellestine to know such an important thing about someone he called a brother, but Kellestine was a self-absorbed man, and he hadn't needed Cameron Acorn until now. The real purpose of Kellestine's call is foggy, since he must have had more pressing things on his mind than a social call to the mother of a clubmate he didn't think about much. But the most obvious reason makes the call to Acorn's mother truly chilling: Acorn had been fast-tracked by Boxer to full-patch status. The two men were clearly close. Was Kellestine calling Acorn now to invite him to the church meeting, to ensure that the protege would share his mentor's fate?

Weiner's tone sounded almost nostalgic as he thought back to his days at the super-maximum-security lockup in Penetanguishene, where Cameron was now confined. He told Sharon not to worry about her boy, and passed on the message for him to stay cool. "I'm a warrior," Kellestine continued, veering into territory most people would be sure to avoid when talking to a friend's mother. "I'm into fist-fightin.' If I'm not fuckin,' I'm fist-fightin.'" Whether he was troubled by the enormity of the betrayal he was plotting, or buoyed by it, Kellestine was clearly staggering towards madness.

"If you talk to Cameron, just say one thing," he added.

"What's that?" the young biker's mother asked.

"Fire in the hold!" Weiner shouted, then burst out laughing, clearly amused by his own wit. "Fire in the hold" is an old naval alarm, warning of a fire below deck on a ship, where ammunition is stored. A ship with a fire in the hold is a floating bomb. In his leering, manic way, Kellestine couldn't help tipping off the mother of one of his potential victims: something big was about to explode.

CHAPTER 16

Baiting the Trap

Let not light see my black and deep desires.
MACBETH, ACT 1, SCENE 4

If we do one, we have to do them all.
WAYNE (WEINER) KELLESTINE

In a quiet moment on Wednesday, April 5, while the Bandido Nation was on the brink of violent convulsion, Brett (Bull) Gardiner signed onto the computer in an upstairs room of Weiner Kellestine's farmhouse and indulged a habit few of his biker buddies could ever condone: he typed out a poem to his common-law wife, "Baby Jessica," whom he clearly missed.

I choked back tears as I watched you leave
This was something I could not believe
I held back whimpers as I watched you go
An event that would lead to everlasting sorrow.

The poem continued its melancholy tone for a while, but ended on an upbeat note, with the lovers reunited:

> You met me by the sparkling lake
> And I immediately forgot my heartache
> We kissed and held each other very near
> The beating of our hearts was all we could hear
> Then we walked away, hand-in-hand
> We had just entered dreamland.

In closing, Gardiner typed, "YOU WILL ALWAYS BE IN MY HEART." Then he signed it, "PROSPECT BANDIDO BULL, MANITOBA."

There are many good reasons not to sign your name to the bottom of a poem like Gardiner's, but the young prospect probably didn't have them all in mind as he pined for his true love amidst the clutter of the Kellestine farmhouse. Poetry can wield unexpected power, and though it is impossible to know whether Baby Jessica was swept away by the tender-hearted verse, in the aftermath of the violence that was about to engulf Gardiner's life, these lines would be enough to threaten the lovelorn biker with serious trouble.

It was shortly after the crack of noon on Thursday, and Weiner was still in bed when Cameron Acorn phoned from his cell block in Penetanguishene. "I was just talking to your ma," Kellestine said, once he had shuffled to the phone. Soon, he was bragging about the good works he had done for prisoners. Not everyone in the No Surrender Crew was so noble about sending greetings to friends behind bars, he added darkly.

"I gave Chopper some envelopes," Weiner said.

"Yeah."

"With some cards and stuff in it."

"Yeah."

"And it never got to the guys."

That said, Weiner noted there was a rift between himself and others in the No Surrender Crew. "We're, uh, apparently we're not talking right now."

"Yeah, uh-oh."

"Nobody calls me," Kellestine continued with a laugh. "Yeah, oh yeah. But that's okay. It's okay."

Acorn had joined in the laughter when Kellestine suddenly shifted moods and got serious. Perhaps now he was going to reveal where he was leading the conversation.

"I'm gonna tell you this straight up, okay?" Kellestine said.

"Yeah."

"Okay, now, there's gonna be some major changes . . . The people in the States are super, super, super fucking choked."

"Yeah."

"Um, yeah, you know. I was out in Vancouver eh."

"Yeah."

"And I went to White Rock and, uh, they requested that I come there, so."

"Oh yeah."

"And don't say a word. Just leave it at that."

Acorn didn't press him, so Kellestine picked things up again, telling the young biker, "You're still okay."

"Yeah."

"I made sure," Kellestine said, implying that he had gone to the wall for Acorn, when in fact he cared so little about Acorn that he hadn't even known he was in prison until the phone call to his mother.

"Okay."

"Fuck, you know what I'm saying."

"Yeah."

"Okay, then. Uh, people have been lying to us."

"Okay."

"About everything being all right."

"Yeah."

"Everything ain't all right."

"Yeah, yeah."

"So I'm not gonna say another word," Kellestine said, a sure sign he was about to unburden himself of plenty more words, then continuing by alluding coyly to a rat in their midst who was stirring things up between Canada and the United States. What he didn't mention was that the rat was his new pal Taz Sandham, and no one stood to benefit more from the sabotage than Kellestine himself. "Someone is . . . in constant communication with the States . . . Someone in Toronto has stabbed, uh, Boxer and Bam Bam and, uh, Chopper and all them guys in the back, um, mentioning a bunch of fuckin' shit."

"Oh really?"

"I think I know who it is," hinted Kellestine. "I'm not gonna say."

Perhaps he was surprised by Acorn's call and was just babbling. Perhaps he was feeling pangs of guilt about plotting to murder his best friend. Perhaps he was sussing out Boxer's protege in anticipation of the inevitable fall-out. Or perhaps he was just gloating. In any case, Kellestine couldn't seem to stop himself from saying things the guy on the other end of the line would only understand months later.

Hinting again at wrenching changes in the club, the guy who stood to benefit most from them insisted both that he was not involved and that his motives were wholly altruistic.

"It's not my doing," he said. "I don't want no part of this. But I'm gonna try to salvage as many guys as possible."

Finally, Acorn figured out what Kellestine meant when he talked about "changes." This wasn't Weiner the bulls-hitter and braggart he was hearing. This was Weiner the killer.

"Oh fuck," Acorn said. "It's not what I think, is it?"

"What?"

"Hang on, hang on. I gotta turn the TV down, okay?"

"What?"

"What, what they were talking about before."

"Yeah."

"Are you fuckin' serious?" Acorn asked.

"Yep. You keep that to yourself."

"That's fuckin' bullshit, man."

Acorn was clearly upset at what he thought he was

hearing, and Kellestine played along, offering a credible approximation of sympathy and outrage over crimes he was about to commit himself. "I know it is," Kellestine replied. "I know it is."

An automated voice came on the line to say there was just another minute left in the call.

"That's fuckin' bullshit," Acorn repeated. The joking was long over.

There were only a few seconds left in the call now.

"Love you, buddy," Kellestine said.

Back at his farm, Kellestine decided against returning to bed. It was almost 1 P.M. now, and so he led the Winnipeggers to a shed behind his house and pulled out what he called his "wet work kit." He told them he used it for cleaning up after bloodshed. It included a clear jug of hydrochloric acid, which is commercially sold as muriatic acid and is used to etch concrete or stone surfaces, such as headstones. It was easily strong enough to remove traces of blood, and Kellestine had a supply of rubber gloves to be worn while handling it. He solemnly advised the Winnipeggers to be prepared for what he called "the worst-case scenario." M.H. later recalled that Kellestine cautioned that they should be prepared for more than a little violence. "If we do one, we have to do them all," Kellestine said.

He then telephoned Toronto to remind members of the No Surrender Crew that they were expected to drive down to his farm the next evening. As bait, he noted that Taz Sandham and some other Winnipeggers wanted to speak directly to Boxer and Chopper. He would have known that the No Surrender Crew had failed in their bid not only to kill Sandham in Winnipeg but to even locate him. The trap had been set. The hunters were now the hunted.

Friday, April 7, 2006, was marked by drizzle and a chilly fog as Kellestine and the Winnipeggers prepared for the church meeting. M.H. had heard strange stories that Kellestine had weapons squirrelled away under the shingles of his farmhouse. Apparently the tales were true, because around 4 P.M., Kellestine began carrying stocks, barrels and other pieces of guns into the house for reassembly. Kellestine may have been wrong-footed by the Winnipeggers' unannounced arrival, but it was clear by now that he was in charge and that Mushey and Sandham were his principle lieutenants. He made several trips down from the top floor of the farmhouse, sweaty and dusty, carrying gun parts by the handful.

Some outlaw bikers brag about their motorcycles; others like to boast of their prowess with women. For Kellestine, guns were the thing. They promised instant resolution to life's problems. Guns also attract something that might easily be mistaken for respect, if not examined too closely. Taz Sandham selected pieces of one of Kellestine's shotguns from a pile on his pool table, screwed them together and rubbed the weapon with an oily cloth. He also picked out a .303 Lee-Enfield rifle. The bolt-action weapon had been a standard army service rifle for Commonwealth infantrymen from the late nineteenth century until well into the twentieth. It may have been old and heavy, but it was more accurate and as lethal as just about anything carried by a modern soldier.

Mushey took a pump-action shotgun away with him to the garage to saw off its barrel so that it could be deadly in close quarters. Kellestine directed Sandham to retrieve a handgun that was hidden under his sink, but Taz couldn't find it. Kellestine looked for it himself, and moments later, he was cleaning it. It was a Hi-Point compact 9-millimetre (.380 calibre), a relatively cheap piece of killing technology that could be bought for $110 in the States. At 7.75 inches in length, it was almost small enough to be capable of being hidden in a man's hand. It was a little heavy, at thirty-one ounces, for true gun connoisseurs, and it certainly didn't have the smooth, sexy look of a Beretta or a Glock, but in a pinch, it could kill someone just as dead.

Kellestine also pulled together a Mossberg .22, another gun that cost well under two hundred dollars and which held a small ammunition clip. There was no serial number on it, as it was built before 1968, the year a regulation was introduced requiring serial numbers to be imprinted on guns. The company that built it, O.F. Mossberg and Sons, took a folksy approach to shooting and killing, and cheerfully advertised that the .22 model was ideal for family fun: "You and the kids will have a lot of fun shooting at varmints, critters and cans. If your kids are the sensitive type, explain they can always get new cans."

Bull Gardiner took a wire brush to clean off some shotgun shells. M.H. busied himself by cleaning a black pump-action shotgun. Now there was a sense of lethal anticipation and excitement, as they sat together and brushed and rubbed and screwed parts together, like participants in a big, deadly circle jerk.

As they readied their guns, Kellestine dispatched his common-law wife, Tina, their daughter, and Mather's pregnant girlfriend, Stefanie, to go stay at a friend's place. They were told that Boxer and Chopper were coming in a couple of hours, and it would be best if they weren't around. The women were told not to come back until Weiner said it was safe.

Taz Sandham took out a package of white surgical gloves and pulled on a pair. Others in the group followed his lead, although Gardiner seemed to keep tearing his gloves. Then Taz donned a second set of gloves, which were military green, just in case the first pair broke. No explanation for the gloves was given, M.H. later said. As an added precaution, Dwight Mushey pulled on a pair of tight leather gloves over the surgical latex, then duct-taped them around his wrists so they wouldn't come loose, even if things got rough.

Taz Sandham then took out his bulletproof vest, just like the ones worn by real police officers. Mushey was irritated at the sight of the body armour. "You should have told me you were bringing your vest," Mushey said to Sandham. "I would have brought mine."

Boxer looked forward to the church meeting with something like weary resignation. He was already thinking about the day after, when he and Nina planned a drive to Chatham. Boxer's disability leave was running out, and he planned to go back to work in Tilbury later that month. Nina was thinking about taking classes to upgrade her education. Boxer's mother was readying herself for the visit, and had prepared a bedroom in the old family townhouse for them and cooked several meals in advance. A chapter in the president's life as a one percenter was coming to a close. Boxer was growing tired of leadership in any case. The old pugilist was still enjoying his workouts at the Etobicoke Boxing Club, and was happy with his latest stab at fatherhood and being a grandparent, even when it came to changing diapers.

Boxer sounded sympathetic when Big Paul called him at 3:33 that Friday afternoon, saying he wasn't medically fit to attend the church meeting that night at Weiner's farm. As he asked Big Paul about his health, Boxer sounded like his old self. "Whaddya got? Ulcer, or what?"

"Yeah, my ulcer's bleeding a lot," Big Paul said. "There's

some lining in my stomach's thinning out, so I just gotta take this medication. Hopefully, it starts working. That's about it, bro."

Boxer wasn't angry, just a little frustrated, as he said, "Oh, okay brother."

"Awright."

"See, we gotta fuckin' try and straighten out some of this stuff, bro," Boxer continued. If he was primed for a showdown with the Winnipeggers, he didn't betray his agitation. Perhaps he expected fireworks, but thought Chopper was more than enough to handle little Taz Sandham. "Fuckin' I hate to talk to ya 'cuz you're not feeling well, but we gotta try and straighten some of this shit out there, bro."

"What's that, bro? My, my health."

"The club and everything—the club," said Boxer, his voice a mixture of concern and frustration.

Shortly after five that afternoon, Big Paul was back on the phone, this time with Bam Bam Salerno. Despite all his foreboding, Bam Bam didn't sense that anything major was in the works for that evening. The way he saw it, the absolute worst that might happen was that he could be kicked out of the club if he didn't quickly pay up some of the $550 in back dues he owed.

"Bro, uh, Boxer's freaking out," Bam Bam warned Big Paul. His words didn't echo Boxer's tone. If anything, Boxer seemed to want out of the meeting almost as much as Big Paul.

"Bro, you're on your last legs," Bam Bam continued. "You're almost out the door, so if I was you I'd get yourself to fuckin' church tonight and also, you got your fucking money for dues?"

Big Paul now sounded like his resolve had broken and he finally planned to attend. "Yeah, I have some money," he replied. "Yeah, I'm bringing it down."

"'Kay, you better bring it," Bam Bam continued. "Don't come there empty-handed, brother. And don't bother phonin' him and telling him you're sick and all this kinda shit. I'm telling you what to do. If you don't wanna listen to me, that's your problem. Don't come crying to me after, you know what I mean?"

"Yeah," Big Paul replied, sounding beaten. To stay in the club, Sinopoli had just fallen into a trap set by the men whose deadly purpose was to purge him from it.

Big Paul was on the phone all afternoon, chatting with Flanz and Kriarakis. Then, at 6:14 P.M., he was on the line with Kellestine.

"Howdy, doody," Weiner said, sounding threatening, despite the jovial words. "Whaddya doin,' Big Paulie?"

"How are you, brother?" Big Paul replied.

"Not too bad. How's yourself?"

"Uh, could be better."

"Well, yeah. Likewise. I'm stressing like a mother-fucker."

"Oh, I hear you, hear you," Big Paul continued.

"Uh, I haven't heard from you for a while. What's up, buds? You don't love me no more?"

Big Paul had no way of knowing that mutual love was no longer something Kellestine worried about a great deal. "Uh, I just been sick, bro."

"You've been sick," Weiner said. He appeared to be mocking Big Paul now, as he continued: "You're a sick man. Never mind. You're sick, but I still love ya."

"I know, I know."

Weiner was curious about what Chopper Raposo was up to. Kellestine might not fear Sinopoli, but he respected Raposo enough to do some scouting before the meeting. Chopper was a man who would bring a gun to a conflict, and wouldn't hesitate to use it. Perhaps Chopper had let something slip to Big Paul.

"Have you talked to, uh, Chopper?" Kellestine asked.

"Yeah, right now."

"Where is he?"

"Uh, at home."

Weiner hinted that there were some visitors to his farm that Chopper and the other Toronto members might want to meet. It didn't hurt to bait the trap again, just to make sure Chopper attended the meeting. A poor turnout could result in a protracted war, not a decisive ambush. "There's just some people passing through town right now," Kellestine said, hinting at Chopper's enemy, Taz Sandham. "They're not gonna be around for much longer. They're kind of . . . hurry to get going."

Weiner then had a sudden mood shift, veering from poisonous hints to jocular threats. "So we have two options," Weiner advised. "There's an old Roy Orbison song, 'It's Now or Never.'"

"Yeah," Big Paul said, sounding confused and sick.

"Hold me close," Weiner sang, borrowing words from the song, then improvising for his four-hundred-pound captive audience. "You homely little bastard. Be mine tonight!"

As the evening started, Boxer was reflective. Clearly, the move to Toronto to become a full-time biker leader hadn't been a success. What the future held for Boxer as a biker was unclear, but it was apparent that his priorities were shifting towards his wife, daughter and job, as he planned his move back to Chatham. Perhaps he was saddened by the fading of his one percenter dreams. Perhaps he was also wiser, a man feeling the pangs of growing up in the fifth decade of his life.

But he couldn't escape his old shadow, Kellestine. At least not that fateful night. Kellestine was on the phone, pushing hard to get Muscedere to church. True to form, Boxer couldn't say no to his old buddy, even if he hadn't been much of a friend recently. Boxer didn't relish the idea of driving to Kellestine's farm, returning to Toronto, and then turning around the next morning and driving west again. Hunting Taz Sandham down didn't excite him as it did Bam Bam and Chopper. What Boxer didn't know was that his last act as president would be to show up in order to be told he had already been deposed.

At 7:51 P.M., Bam Bam left a message on the voice mail of Carlitto Aragon's home in Oakville, to the west of Toronto. Salerno was livid that Carlitto and his Winnipeg contact "J.C." still hadn't met up with Taz Sandham. Clearly, Salerno had no clue that Taz Sandham and the Winnipeggers were down the road at Weiner Kellestine's farm, armed and waiting, when he left the following message on the answering machine:

> Yeah brother, I don't know what the agenda is out there, but, uh, it's not to have fuckin' dinner at fuckin' J.C.'s house, that's for sure. Ya know what I mean? Ya gotta fuckin' job to do out there—Taz fuckin' piece of shit and order him as a fuckin' Canadian Rocker to get his fuckin' ass to where you are. What is this? A fuckin' joke? . . . So bro, do the things you were sent to do . . . People are livid and freakin.'

In the background on the message, Bam Bam's month-old son, Mario, could be heard crying. A few minutes after he hung up, Bam Bam gave Mario a kiss, told him, "Take care of your mommy," and walked out of the house for the last time.

After dusk, M.H. and Mushey went behind Weiner Kellestine's barn with loaded shotguns, to a spot where they couldn't be seen but where they could easily peer out at any visitors. Kellestine dispatched Taz to the loft, where he was to stay perfectly still on his perch, like a real sniper, lest the old wooden beams betray his location by creaking.

Gardiner's job was to monitor Kellestine's police scanner and listen for any police cruisers in the area. If anyone from the No Surrender Crew asked them, Gardiner and Aravena were to say that they were from the nearby reserve. They were unknown to the Toronto Bandidos, and with their straight, black hair, they could pass for members of the First Nation.

Big Paul Sinopoli had originally told Kellestine that he was going to try to get Boxer and Chopper Raposo to the farm by about 7 P.M. Then he called back to say they would have to be a little later. Robert (Peterborough Bob) Pammett, Stone, Carlitto and another member named Irish weren't going to make the meeting at all. Neither would Ripper Fullager, whose cancer was far too advanced for him to travel. That said, there should still be a strong turnout from the No Surrender Crew.

Everything was set now. All Weiner, Taz and the rest of the Winnipeggers had to do was wait—and hope their guests didn't suddenly get wise.

CHAPTER 17

The Sound of Popcorn

'Tis the time's plague when madmen lead the blind.
KING LEAR, ACT 4, SCENE 1

I want to go out like a man.
GIOVANNI (JOHN, BOXER) MUSCEDERE

Guns are forbidden at church meetings, but Chopper Raposo had been carrying one with him for several weeks, suspicious that something nasty was in the offing. On this night he was particularly edgy and carried a sawed-off shotgun in a businessman's attaché case, which kept it close to hand but out of sight. As they gathered together in the large, central room of the old wooden barn, where dirty white plastic deck chairs had been arranged in a circle, and waited for the others to arrive, Weiner Kellestine, who had a pistol hidden in his combat jacket, made idle chit-chat with Boxer and Chopper about how chilly the weather had become.

M.H. later swore that he could hear from a hole in the barn as Weiner spoke conspiratorially about how he was about to go see their "little friend," Taz Sandham, knowing this would get an angry rise out of Chopper. Weiner lied that Sandham was holed up in a nearby hotel, and suggested the moment to deal with the mini-biker had come.

"I have a fucking surprise for Taz when he shows up," Chopper said. "I'm gonna put a fucking hole in him."

Chopper, Boxer and Weiner shared a laugh, though only Kellestine really knew the punchline to the joke: that Taz was perched in the rafters, listening to every word and peering down at the senior members of the New Surrender Crew through the sights of a rifle.

The sound of a vehicle in the laneway, crunching the gravel under its tires as it approached, broke the silence. It was hard to see anything in the glare of its headlights, as Mushey and M.H. crept towards the front of the barn. When they saw Pony Jessome puffing on a cigarette, they slipped silently back into the darkness. Goldberg Flanz joined Bam Bam Salerno, Little Mikey Trotta and Jessome at the barn entrance, smoking and making more small talk. By 10:30 that night, all eight Toronto members who were expected at the meeting were now in the barn, and whatever fears they felt in their drive to the farmhouse had apparently subsided.

Boxer seemed almost nonchalant as the assassins surrounded them in the darkness. He still trusted Weiner Kellestine too much to think that the current tensions were anything that wouldn't blow over once Chopper sorted out the problem of the irksome Taz. For all of his hard living, Boxer still had an adolescent faith that friendship and brotherhood were forever. It would have been impossible to warn him of the betrayal that awaited him; he simply could never have believed that such a fate was possible, particularly for a Bandido. And so Boxer smoked and chatted with Weiner and Chopper, not realizing that his brothers had already deposed him as *presidente*.

Taz Sandham tried not to twitch in his perch high in the rafters. A cough or a sneeze would be fatal now. Despite his posturing that he had once been a military sniper and was a martial arts master who had harmoniously melded his mind and body, Taz was prone to bouts of nerves. In that moment, hidden from his enemies, lethally armed, with his tormenters in his sights, the fate of the Canadian Bandidos rested on his trigger finger. For a man whose life had been marked only by failure and self-delusion, the scale of the triumph that lay only moments away must have been exhilarating and dizzyingly unfamiliar. The sheer weight of the enormity he could unleash by squeezing the trigger must have been crippling. Here he was, still on the outside looking in while others shared a joke, but this time *he*, ineffectual Taz Sandham, held the power, and the last laugh would be his. The strain was unbearable.

What happened next has never been determined. Did Sandham get impatient for the glory that awaited him as leader of his own chapter? Was he simply afraid? Or did Raposo detect his assassin up in the rafters and scramble for his gun? Was bloodshed inevitable, with two armed enemies in the same barn? Or could the violence have been averted at the last minute? All that can be known is that M.H. later said he heard a soft *pop, pop, pop* from inside the barn, just like popcorn, followed by a loud *bang! bang!* The sounds were so close together that they almost overlapped. A rifle and a shotgun. Two distinct sounds at nearly the same moment.

No one immediately knew who—if anyone—would be dropping dead. Weiner Kellestine rushed into the barn, as did Frank Mather, M.H and Mushey. For that instant, as they surveyed the aftermath of the shooting, Kellestine held absolute power in the Bandidos Nation within Canada. The Winnipeggers and the No Surrender Crew each thought Weiner was on their side as he stood in the middle of the barn, a loaded rifle in one hand and a pistol in the other. He and he alone would decide who else would live and who would die that night. Kellestine looked down to see Chopper Raposo lying on the floor, bleeding and nearly motionless. He was trying to say something, but couldn't form the words.

Taz Sandham was climbing down from the loft. It would be easy to wonder, in the months and years after that night, what Weiner Kellestine would have done if Chopper had won the shootout and Sandham had fallen dead from the loft. But the course of events was determined by the trajectories of those few rounds. As Chopper lay dead on the floor, Kellestine threw his lot in with the guy who was still standing. From that moment, the aging one percenter was irreversibly allied with Taz Sandham against the No Surrender Crew and his old friend Boxer Muscedere.

The moment of incredulous silence erupted into chaos. Boxer stayed cool, but Crash Kriarakis and Big Paul

Sinopoli bolted towards the door. It was a doomed effort, at least for Big Paul, as he couldn't run, now that his life literally depended upon it. Weiner raised his handgun and squeezed the trigger a couple times, hitting Big Paul in the thigh and Crash in the stomach.

Crash and Big Paul seemed more bewildered than angry, as if their wounding was all part of some sort of grotesque misunderstanding. Crash was sprawled near a freezer, close to Big Paul, who lay face down in a spreading pool of blood. In the melee, someone smashed Little Mikey with a gunstock, leaving his face purple and his eye swollen shut. Bam Bam sat stunned on the couch, bleeding from a hole left by a bullet that had found him during the brief, deadly exchange. Chopper still hadn't made a sound as he oozed blood from his neck and chest. A bullet had blown off his middle finger—the one he would use to playfully dis others—then penetrated his chest, filling the cavity around his heart with blood.

After years of talk, posturing and paranoia, the No Surrender Crew was finally involved in an actual shootout. But none of their avowed enemies, such as the Hells Angels or the police, were in sight—only the men they had always called "brother." Little Taz Sandham looked large as he stood over the bleeding men, his rifle in hand.

"Everybody get on the floor!" Weiner Kellestine shouted. "Nobody move! I'm here to pull your patches," he told fellow members of the No Surrender Crew, saying they were "done by orders of the States." He also spoke of two elite members of the Nomads chapter of the Bandidos who had come up from the U.S. to support him. M.H. couldn't help but think that he had never even heard of North Americans in a Bandidos chapter called the Nomads. It was easy to write off the shouting about Nomads as some kind of head game Kellestine might be playing.

Back in the farmhouse, Bull Gardiner listened for evidence of police cruisers on the scanner. He had no gun, just a two-way radio that allowed him to communicate with Kellestine in the barn. There was also a phone nearby—handy in case he decided to side with law and order and call 911. He would later claim that he didn't know anything bad was going on, and that his attention was focused on the television, not the scanners.

In the barn, Bam Bam was conscious and bleeding, but if he was afraid, he hid it behind a brave front. He pulled up his pant leg to show where he had been hit. Big Paul pulled down his sweatpants to show where he had been shot, near a tattoo of a griffin. They must have felt reassured when they were told by Kellestine, the man who had fired at them, that they would soon be taken for medical treatment.

The Torontonians were patted down for weapons, but none were found. Kellestine kept saying that he was sure the No Surrender Crew had brought three guns with them that night. He didn't explain how he arrived at that number, but he was positive he was right. Never one for self-doubt, he demanded, "Who brought guns?"

Nobody said a word.

Kellestine walked around the barn, looking about for guns, frisking Boxer like a cop handling a common criminal and telling Bam Bam to kick Chopper's sawed-off shotgun towards him, just like in the movies. Mather searched about and found a gym bag behind the couch. In it was another sawed-off lever-action rifle with black electrical tape over the handle. It remained unclear who had brought it to the meeting, and no one was confessing.

"Who shot first?" Weiner Kellestine demanded of Sandham. "Who shot? Was it fucking Chopper, or was it you?"

"Well, he shot me," Sandham replied, referring to the lifeless Raposo. His bulletproof vest had saved him, he said, shaking shotgun pellets from his hooded Adidas sweatshirt.

Kellestine shifted into another emotional gear as he collected the visitors' identification papers, money, pocket knives, cellphones and keys and put them on top of a freezer in the barn. He ordered Little Mikey Trotta to take down a list of the current addresses of members of the No Surrender Crew and to catalogue any Bandido property in their possession. Anyone kicked out of the club was required to return all club gear, which explained the need for the hasty inventory. Little Mikey's left eye was by now large, purple and even more swollen, as though he had a baseball under his skin, and it seemed to be growing, as he began to make his list on a piece of brown paper that looked like something torn from a lunch bag.

Weiner Kellestine called on Frank Mather, who was handed a gun. Then he ordered Mushey to keep an eye on Boxer.

"Shoot Boxer if he moves from that fucking spot," Kellestine ordered.

Any pretense of tenderness or brotherhood towards his longtime friend had evaporated as Kellestine ordered Mather and Aravena to start searching the visitors' vehicles. Aravena was the only Winnipegger without a gun. He later said that Kellestine handed him a pistol, but Sandham immediately grabbed it away before he could even close his hands on it, and said: "Give me that. You don't know how to use it." Aravena said that Sandham offered him his rifle but he refused, as the gun had just been used in a killing and he didn't want his fingerprints on it.

Instead, Aravena held just a baseball bat, although it looked intimidating enough in the hands of the 280-pounder. A few minutes later, the two men returned with the vehicle registrations, maps and spare change, and put them all on the freezer.

Kellestine kept asking about other guns the No Surrender Crew might have smuggled into the meeting, but his mood had shifted dramatically yet again. Now, he was dancing a crazy little jig and singing the opening lines of "Das Deutschlandlied," the German national anthem. This time, there could be no doubt: the madness that transformed his face wasn't an act.

Boxer ignored Kellestine's order not to move and bent over his motionless friend Chopper, checking for a pulse. Perhaps motivated by leadership, or perhaps brotherhood, Boxer wasn't about to be ordered about.

"We've got to get him to a hospital," Boxer said. "We've got to get him help."

"It's too late," Kellestine replied. "He's already dead."

"No, he's still bleeding," Boxer insisted. "He's still bleeding."

"No, he's already dead," Kellestine pronounced, showing no grief for his lost brother. "He's dead. He's going to shit himself and piss himself soon."

"He's still alive," Boxer protested, still not willing to give up on his brother.

Boxer wouldn't quit standing up, even though Mather was under orders to shoot him if he budged. Kellestine tried another tack to get him to sit still. Aravena later recalled that Kellestine now told the group, "'If anyone wants to smoke, then Boxer's got to sit down.' And then Boxer sat down and everybody got smokes."

Aravena noted that Little Mikey's eye was nearly shut now, like a boxer with a broken orbital bone. Then Kellestine ordered Little Mikey Trotta to roll Chopper's body into a rug by the couch. Goldberg Flanz moved to help out, but Kellestine slapped him across the head with an open hand.

The plan, in Weiner Kellestine's words, had been, "If we do one, we have to do them all." They had just killed one of their Bandido brothers, and seven more remained in the barn, alive. If Kellestine carried through with his plan, he was on the brink of committing the worst mass murder in Ontario history.

Everyone remained silent until Kellestine stopped singing and capering and turned to face Flanz with his manic leer, the one he had flashed at the Christmas party when he threatened to shoot the disc jockey for playing rap music. There were a dozen other men in the barn, and together they could have overpowered Kellestine. Instead, they all remained passive, like Sunday school students waiting for their teacher to tell them what to do next.

That was when Weiner Kellestine accused Flanz of being a rat for the police in the Shawn Douse murder investigation. "I'm going to do you last because you're a fucking Jew," he said, striking the prospect biker with an open hand. Flanz sat cross-legged on the floor with his hands on his head, like a prisoner of war.

Kellestine rammed his pistol up against Flanz's head, as if about to take his life, then yanked it away, saying, "Just kidding."

"He's not a police informant," Boxer Muscedere said.

A few minutes later, Kellestine rammed the pistol against Flanz's head again. "Just kidding," he taunted a second time.

If Boxer feared for his own life, he hid it well. He also didn't seem to think he had lost his authority as national *presidente*, even though Kellestine was treating him like a captive. Boxer asked Kellestine if they could speak confidentially for a moment, and they walked together towards the doorway.

"He's not a police informant," Boxer said again, perhaps feeling that the result of the argument would determine whether Flanz would live or die. Boxer must have realized that his own life was at stake, but he pressed on in defence of the club's lowest-ranked member nonetheless, standing between Wayne Kellestine, the would-be Nazi, and the Jew he had promised to torment.

"Something happened at his house," Boxer said. "He never ratted on them."

Kellestine didn't reply; he didn't have to. He was still holding his guns and Boxer was empty-handed. Guns trumped fists, even powerful ones. They also trumped logic, compassion and brotherhood that night in the barn. *Presidente* Boxer's authority over Weiner Kellestine had finally ended.

The combination of Big Paul's diabetes and nerves meant he kept having to get up to pee. He was allowed to walk to the front entranceway repeatedly to relieve himself until, finally, he was handed a bucket. Crash couldn't stop shivering, so Aravena passed him a blanket, and later recalled that M.H. seemed to shoot him a dirty look for the small act of kindness. Big Paul helped wrap Crash in the blanket as they waited for what would happen next.

Crash said a prayer in Greek, sensing he might have only a few more moments to make peace with his god. Bam Bam dropped to his knees and began reciting the Lord's Prayer. Kellestine knelt down on one knee beside Salerno and said a bit of the prayer too. It wasn't clear whether this was to mock the others, some sort of show of respect, or no more than a madman's passing whim. Whatever it was, it didn't last long.

One percenter bikers preach brotherhood over everything else, but now the Winnipeg Bandidos stood like robots with guns in their hands and did nothing as their unarmed brethren readied themselves for death.

Boxer Muscedere had been Weiner Kellestine's friend and defender for a decade and knew him as well as anyone. There was a time, not long before this, when Boxer talked of shooting Frank Lenti because Lenti had besmirched Kellestine's reputation. Now Boxer reached a grim, inescapable conclusion: his longtime friend was readying himself to execute him. His only scrap of hope was that he might still placate Kellestine if he agreed to join the gunmen and abandon the rest of his chapter to their grisly fate.

But that was something a guy like Boxer could never do. Instead, he gave his final order as Bandidos president to his old friend Weiner Kellestine: "Do me now. I want to go out like a man."

Weiner Kellestine gripped the black Hi-Point pistol in one hand and the .22 rifle in the other. He wasn't about to take an order from Boxer, not even one like that. Instead, he reassured Boxer that he wasn't going to be killed, saying, "John, come on, we're going to let you go." Then he walked towards the door with Taz Sandham and Dwight Mushey, while Frank Mather, Marcelo Aravena and M.H. stood guard. Before stepping outside, Kellestine again told Mather that if his old and loyal friend Boxer moved, he was to shoot him: Mather, whose long criminal record didn't include any violent crimes, stood by with his gun, wide-eyed and mute.

It seemed to M.H. that about ten minutes passed before Kellestine, Mushey and Taz finally returned to the barn. Crash still complained about his wounds. Bam Bam tried to calm things, as if it was all just a misunderstanding, some kind of huge mistake that could somehow be laughed off later, after a few beers or snorts of cocaine.

Crash talked about Diane, his wife of less than a year, and his love for his family, until Bam Bam finally told him to shut up. "You know how the game is played," he said. "We're not Boy Scouts."

Kellestine told Pony to get up off the floor and sit on a chair. Kellestine put a blanket over him, almost tenderly, and handed him a cigarette. Then he apologized for smashing him with the butt end of his rifle. Pony didn't reply.

Kellestine shifted his attentions to Big Paul. He chastised him for bolting towards the door when the shooting started, and said the huge man almost bowled him over. That was why he had to shoot him. "We're going to get you guys to the hospital, then you're going to go home," he promised.

First, however, they would have to hand over all their Bandido gear, including their vests and jewellery. Boxer said that Nina would never give away his vest, unless he personally told her it was all right. Kellestine said that even his best friend Boxer was going to have to be shackled, just to be safe. "It's not that I don't trust you," Kellestine said. Then he smiled and continued, "It's just that I don't trust you." But no one else was going to die, he pledged, unless they made a truly stupid move. "If you try anything or come back at me, I won't hesitate to kill you."

Moments later, for reasons known only to himself, Kellestine was again riding wild waves of fury, bellowing out the German anthem. There was some sort of grand plan in his feverish mind as he escorted Pony Jessome out, directing the tow truck driver to move Chopper Raposo's

Volkswagen. Little Taz Sandham was more animated now too. People would finally have to listen to him, now that he had a gun in his hand and a lifeless victim at his feet. He ranted in his squeaky little voice about membership dues, and suggested Chopper might not have been sending the money to the U.S. as he was supposed to. "We didn't know Chopper was doing that," Bammer protested.

"Ask fucking Paulie," Taz continued. "I've been sending the money orders."

Big Paul concurred, and Boxer was a little stunned. Perhaps Big Paul was agreeing out of fear, as Taz's rifle made his argument all the more convincing. Perhaps he actually had been cadging the money. Whatever the case, things were far past a mere money dispute now.

"Well, I didn't know," Boxer said. "Chopper didn't tell me."

Taz then shouted about Carlitto and Stone travelling to Winnipeg to hunt him down and kill him. Perhaps he was thinking that they knew his secret about having worked as a cop. If his life in policing became common knowledge, Taz would never rise up in the club—and instead, he might die a messy death.

Pony and Weiner Kellestine returned to the barn. It was too muddy to back the cars into the barn for whatever Kellestine and the Winnipeggers had planned to do next. So, instead, Kellestine ordered Goldberg and Little Mikey to carry Chopper's body, wrapped in the carpet, out to the Volkswagen. They kept dropping Chopper, as Flanz's hands were frozen, having held them over his head, prisoner-of-war style, for more than an hour. At one point,

Chopper's face became visible, and Crash gasped as he saw his dead friend. "Oh my God, he's stiff, he's stiff," Crash cried.

At thirty-seven minutes after midnight, Boxer Muscedere's cellphone began ringing from on top of the freezer in the barn. It had rung several times during the evening, and this time Kellestine told Boxer he could answer, but admonished him not to say "anything stupid." Most men would have seized the moment to beg the caller to dial 911 to save them. It would have just taken seconds for Boxer to blurt out, "Big trouble at Weiner's" and his life might be spared. It was likely that not even Weiner Kellestine was crazy enough to execute anyone if police were on the way. Only one man was dead so far. Taz could take the blame for that, and perhaps plead self-defence. Maybe they could just hide the body and try to go on with their lives, as if nothing had happened. Kellestine claimed to have done just that many times before.

Instead, Boxer sounded calm as he told Nina that he was in a meeting. Nina had just wanted to tell him that she had made a collage of photos of themselves and baby Angelina. "How's the baby?" Boxer asked. Assured that she was fine, Boxer ended the call, saying, "I'll see you in a couple hours. I love ya." He never talked to Nina again.

A quick glance at Constable Perry Graham of the Ontario Provincial Police and you could tell he wasn't a slacker. The eighteen-year police veteran with the shaved head looked like a pumped-up bodybuilder, even when wearing a jacket, and his attention to his beat in Elgin County was as diligent as his workout routine.

Graham made a point of passing Weiner Kellestine's farm at least once every shift. He had been working in the area for some sixteen years, and was well aware of the reputation of local outlaw bikers. Around midnight, Graham noticed two pickup trucks parked on a small ramp just off Highway 401. Nearby, there was also a minivan that appeared to be abandoned. Graham, who was working alone, pulled up behind the minivan and ran a quick check of its ownership. He learned only that it had been rented out of Toronto, which was no help at all in assessing potential danger.

Graham stepped out of his cruiser and walked towards it, alone in the dark. Approaching a strange car by yourself at midnight is a daunting experience, even when you are an experienced police officer who looks like he can bench-press a Harley-Davidson. Graham kept walking forward, and found two men in rumpled sports jackets sitting inside. They told him that they were part of a Durham Regional Police surveillance team, as were the officers in two tow trucks parked nearby. They were working together on a project relating to the Bandidos biker gang and a Toronto-area homicide.

At 12:05 A.M. on Saturday, April 8, Graham was on the move again, after he was called out to an accident on

Highway 401. At 12:13, he got a call from the Durham Region officers, saying they were about to leave the area. Two other traffic calls on the highway kept Graham busy for almost two hours. When that was cleared up, around 2 A.M., the energetic officer returned to Aberdeen Line, once again monitoring traffic near Kellestine's farm. He kept an eye on traffic until 2:55, when he was called back into action on Highway 401. Once his shift was over, Graham planned to pass along his observations to the OPP's Biker Enforcement Unit.

The Durham Regional Police surveillance unit huddled at 12:30 in the parking lot of a gas station just outside London. As usual, they compared notes. That done, they began their drive back to Oshawa, arriving there at 4 A.M., after sixteen straight hours on the job. The plan was to resume surveillance of Jamie Flanz later that Saturday. But they wouldn't have to wait that long before Flanz was on their radar again. By the time they had slept off their long shift, they would realize that their surveillance had failed to detect the biggest crime of their careers.

Certainly, Boxer was considered the most dangerous of the prisoners, and Kellestine wanted to get him out of the way quickly. Muscedere walked outside with his longtime friend with his head held high and his cherished one percenter beliefs untarnished by the venality and cowardice that surrounded him. Marcelo Aravena would later swear on a Bible that he was only carrying a flashlight as he fell in behind Boxer on the march outside.

"Don't get so close," Kellestine ordered Boxer.

"What are you talking about?" Boxer replied, still defiant. "I'm right behind you. I'm not doing nothing."

Then Kellestine ordered Boxer into the front seat of the Volkswagen, which was hooked up to the tow truck. In the back seat was the lifeless body of Chopper. Boxer refused to climb in, saying, "I'm going to get two bullets in the back of my head."

"You're going to sit there and look like a passenger," Kellestine ordered. "I'm not going to shoot you."

For some reason, Boxer sat down. Now, as Weiner stood before him, with his two loaded guns and lunatic's grimace, Boxer laughed. Did he laugh at his longtime friend for looking ridiculous, even when he had total power? Was he laughing at himself for ever trusting such a madman? Or was he somehow relieved to be going out with his dignity intact? Whatever the case, Boxer Muscedere, the consummate one percenter, literally looked death in the eye that morning and laughed.

When the first bullet hit Boxer, Aravena thought it had somehow missed, since Boxer looked calm and had a big smile on his face, as if enjoying some private, unspoken joke. The second bullet went in beneath Boxer's right eye. To Aravena, it now looked as though Boxer was sleeping.

It was at this point, Aravena later said, that Kellestine

jammed a gun against him. "Keep your mouth shut," Kellestine said to Aravena. "I ain't doing twenty-five years for you. If you say anything, I'm going to kill you and your family."

Aravena later recalled that he was paralyzed by fear as he replied: "I ain't saying shit. I ain't a rat."

Bull Gardiner, who had been walking into the barn as Muscedere was being led to his doom, heard the crackle of gunfire and, as M.H. later recalled events, worried that something might have happened to Kellestine. "Did you fucking hear that?" Gardiner asked. "I should go check on Wayne."

"Shut your fucking mouth," Mushey ordered. "Go back in the house."

Gardiner returned to the farmhouse. Left guarding the others were M.H., Mather and Aravena. Crash was still complaining that he needed to be taken to the hospital when the harmless-sounding *pop, pop, pop* signalled the end of Boxer's life.

At 1 A.M., Nina called back for Boxer. There was something she had forgotten to tell him, but now his phone was shut off forever.

After Boxer's death, there was a strange sense of calm, even relief. Boxer Muscedere had been the toughest of the

Toronto Bandidos; with him dead, what need was there to harm the others? It was as if he had sacrificed himself for his brothers. Perhaps they really were going home after all.

Weiner Kellestine tried to calm Crash Kriarakis, as if things could somehow be made all right again. "He kept saying, 'We're going to get you to the hospital. Pony's going to take you to the hospital,'" M.H. later recalled.

Mushey, Kellestine and Sandham stepped outside the barn into the darkness, while the other gunmen stood guard over the prisoners. Moments later, the three bikers returned, and Kellestine announced they were finally taking Crash to the hospital.

Little Mikey and Goldberg were given bleach, water and a push broom, and were ordered to clean up the blood from where Chopper's body had lain. There wasn't any conversation now inside the barn. Perhaps the remainder of the No Surrender Crew thought they might somehow be spared if they went along with the gunmen. Now would have been the time to try to overpower their guards, plead for their lives or flee into the darkness. Instead, Little Mikey and Goldberg silently mopped up the blood of their fallen brother, Chopper Raposo, as Kellestine and Frank Mather led Crash outside. Crash had thought long and hard about leaving the club, but never got around to doing it. Whether it was his love for his brothers, his fear of Boxer's reprisal or a natural attachment to the five thousand dollars Sinopoli owed him, Kriarakis must have spent the final minutes of his life thinking that leaving would have been immeasurably better than staying in the No Surrender Crew, no matter the consequences. The bikers in the barn waited for the sound of a car starting up to take Crash to the hospital, as Kellestine had promised. Instead, from the darkness outside came a now-familiar, hollow sound:

Pop, pop, pop, pop, pop, pop, pop.

Pony Jessome might have known what was coming next when he was summoned to follow the gunmen. A radio inside the barn cranked out loud music now, but it had still been possible for Pony to hear the staccato of bullets outside.

"Let's go," Kellestine said, then walked towards the door. Pony fell in behind, followed by M.H. It would have been easy for any of the conspirators to shoot Kellestine in the back and put an end to the slaughter, but somehow the hillbilly biker knew this wasn't going to happen as he turned his back on them yet again to lead Pony to the back seat of his own tow truck. Pony must have wondered how he had come to meet such a fate. In his time with the club, he hadn't raised his voice to anyone, or touched anything that wasn't his. He had worked hard at an honest job and hadn't ratted on anybody. All he seemed to want from life was a cold beer, a little coke and some friends around him as he lived out his final days before his cancer claimed him. As Pony climbed into his truck, Kellestine shot him point blank in the head. Then he slipped the barrel of the rifle under Pony's shirt and another shot tore into his chest as Kellestine made sure he was dead.

Since Ripper Fullager's cancer was discovered, Pony had spent at least an hour a day comforting his dying biker brother. Now Ripper had outlived him. In the past, Pony had shocked his family back in the Maritimes when he told them his stories of violence in Ontario. They never knew whether he was exaggerating when he talked about crime in the big city. Now Pony was himself a murder statistic.

Anything more than three murders at a time is considered by police to be a mass murder. Kellestine's crew had already killed four men they called brothers. Four members of the No Surrender Crew were still alive, and there were a few more hours of darkness before the sun came up again.

What happened next was bizarre, even by Weiner Kellestine's standards. He began to boast, to no one in particular, about his work ethic. The murders had already become more of a chore than a drama. His lifeless brothers were just a problem to clean up, a task he attacked with grim, heartless industriousness. And so Kellestine stood proudly in the midst of the slaughter of his biker brothers and bragged about how much effort he was putting into killing them. It was as if he expected praise for the job, like a little schoolchild who cleans the blackboards for his teacher. M.H. was no stranger to the rougher side of life, but he sounded stunned as he later recalled Kellestine's mood. "He was complaining about having to do all of the wet work," M.H. said. "[That] none of these other fucking guys do that."

At one point, after a huddle outside with Kellestine and Sandham, Mushey walked close to M.H. and whispered to him, "Be ready."

Goldberg Flanz was talking to Taz Sandham about his children and smoking a cigarette Taz had apparently handed him. Kellestine had been downing beer throughout the night and interrupted to order Flanz to put his cigarette into an empty.

Around this time, Kellestine turned to Bam Bam Salerno and called him a "fucking goof" and kicked him squarely in the head. Again, no one lifted a hand or uttered a word to stop him.

Salerno and Big Paul Sinopoli were sitting on the white plastic chairs inside the barn when Kellestine ordered Big Paul to follow him and Aravena outside. The massive biker obeyed meekly. His breathing was laboured at the best of times, and his fears of his impending death only made it worse. Aravena later recalled that Big Paul looked afraid, and he tried to comfort him, saying, "Don't worry, you're going home." Big Paul didn't react at all, as if he didn't hear the words. M.H. pulled Flanz's Infiniti closer to the barn and opened its rear hatch. Weiner ordered Sinopoli to lie down in the back, and he complied, perhaps having convinced himself that the madman was actually taking him to the hospital, as he had promised. Seconds after Big Paul had arranged his bulk in the back of the SUV, there was the sickeningly familiar soft sound.

Pop.

The hatchback was flapping and Big Paul was somehow still alive. Kellestine was enraged, since his rifle had jammed, slowing down his murder. "Piece-of-shit gun," he barked, then pulled a handgun out of his coat and levelled it on Big Paul.

"Shut up and die like a man," he commanded.

Pop, pop.

Aravena later said that Kellestine then ordered him into the front seat of the Infiniti, but he refused, saying, "Fuck no," before fleeing into the farmhouse.

Each trip back into the barn for a fresh victim seemed to excite Kellestine more, as though he was soaring on a second wind. He danced his strange little jig, brandishing his rifle and his pistol, carolling his own personal hymn to Nazism. When his musical interlude ended, Kellestine gestured for Salerno to follow him and Mushey outside. Before he did, Bam Bam did something shocking and totally unexpected, as if the final moments of his life called for a defining gesture to his biker brothers. "He tried to shake hands," M.H. later said, with what seemed like disbelief in his voice. "I never did. Dwight did. He asks Wayne to take care of his kid."

M.H. later said that he couldn't shake Bam Bam's hand because he liked him. Perhaps M.H. had to distance himself emotionally from the man who was about to become Kellestine's next victim. Perhaps a gesture of friendship was too much of a lie, even for that night.

Bam Bam also reached for Aravena's hand, but the Winnipegger refused, saying, "I'm not shaking your hand." Aravena would later claim that he didn't know Bam Bam was about to die when he balked at making contact with his bleeding, outstretched hand. "I didn't even know the guy," Aravena said. "I thought everyone was going to go home that night. Why would I want to ruin my clothes?"

"Make sure you guys tell my family where my body is," Bam Bam said as he was led out into the darkness.

Once again, from outside the barn, came the soft, horrible sound.

Pop, pop, pop, pop, pop.

Little Mikey Trotta and Goldberg Flanz remained inside the barn, still cleaning blood from the floor when Kellestine returned. Flanz talked quickly and nervously about his two preschool children, Hunter and Amanda, and asked for another cigarette. Taz Sandham handed him one, and listened to the young father talk about his love for his family.

Weiner Kellestine produced a jug of acid and interrupted Flanz as he ordered everyone not to touch it—it was too dangerous. Only he would handle the black jug, and when he did so, he would wear gloves and a special breathing mask. M.H. couldn't help thinking that it looked like the kind of bottle that genies pop out of in television cartoons.

Now, it was Little Mikey's turn to walk out into the darkness. True to his promise, Kellestine was making the Jew Flanz wait the longest, so that he would suffer the most. When they got to the Infiniti, Little Mikey would have had to contemplate the bodies of Big Paul Sinopoli and Bam Bam Salerno there before he joined them in death.

Pop, pop.

Finally, it was time for Goldberg Flanz. Kellestine

motioned for him to follow. There was no one left inside the barn to guard, so Frank Mather, Marcelo Aravena and M.H. wandered out into the starless night. Bull Gardiner pushed the scattered baby toys on the back seat of Trotta's Grand Prix out of the way, to make room for Flanz, who hadn't stopped talking about how much he loved his young children.

When Flanz had squeezed his imposing frame into the cramped back seat, Taz Sandham—who also had two young children—reached in, gripping the Hi-Point pistol. There was still time for Sandham to snatch something redeeming from that hellish night and his often-pathetic life. The little man who had always wanted to be a hero had the power to turn his gun on the killers and perhaps free Jamie Flanz. It would not have made up for the other seven killings that night, but with that one act, Sandham would finally have done something approaching the heroic. "You guys walk away," Sandham ordered his co-conspirators. M.H. later said he turned his head away an instant before the loud *bang* and the flash of a muzzle.

Somehow, as the silence and darkness closed back in, Flanz was still alive. Taz had shot him point blank in the cheek, but had only managed to wound his victim gruesomely. For the moment, at least, Flanz was still breathing.

Had Taz Sandham been a smarter—or braver—man, he would have kept quiet at this point. The others would surely have believed Flanz was dead. How could Sandham, who bragged he was a trained sniper, miss with an up-close shot to the head? But he was boiling with fear and remorse, and mumbled something about the pistol jamming as he lurched towards the farmhouse. The gun was in his right hand, and he seemed to be trying to unjam it with his left as he muttered to himself about Goldberg's young children.

Dwight Mushey took the gun from Taz's hand and walked into the farmhouse with him. Moments later, he returned and climbed into the Grand Prix, pressing the barrel hard between Flanz's eyes. Flanz's eyes bulged, and it looked as though he was trying to utter some last words, but he was interrupted by the morning's final muzzle flash.

CHAPTER 18

Clean-up Crew

As ignorant as dirt! Thou hast done a deed . . .
OTHELLO, ACT 5, SCENE 2

Dwight said that Head and Shoulders
was good for removing gunshot residue.
POLICE INFORMANT M.H., DESCRIBING A HAIR-CARE TIP
FROM BANDIDO DWIGHT (BIG D) MUSHEY

There's no way of measuring exactly how long the slaughter
took, except that Chopper Raposo was likely killed a little
before midnight and the darkness hadn't lifted when the
final shot was fired into the skull of Goldberg Flanz. Sun-
rise on Saturday, April 8, 2006, came at 5:55 A.M., and it
was wet and chilly as the crew of killers looked to dispose
of the limp bodies of their one-time biker brothers.

The killers' first plan was to drive the eight victims
about an hour east down Highway 401 and dump them
near the twin cities of Kitchener-Waterloo. Flanz's Infiniti, however, was proving a problem: Frank Mather and
Bull Gardiner couldn't close the hatch because Big Paul

Sinopoli's massive body was in the way. Even by joining forces, they couldn't shove him in, so Mather used his feet to push. Big Paul still wasn't all the way in, but it would have to do—the sun was starting to come up and Kellestine was looking frantic. The cover of darkness had almost lifted. "Come on," Kellestine urged. "Come on, guys. Gotta get going. Gotta get going."

Then Mather noticed that the Infiniti was almost out of gas. He produced a jerry can from the garage, but then noticed it contained oil, not gasoline. Kellestine sent him back for the right can, but ordered him not to use it all, because they would need the rest for other things. Finally, they were ready to leave, and Kellestine unlocked the chain that had sealed the inner fence shut. Frank Mather would lead the way, with Big Paul perilously close to falling out of the hatchback.

Behind the wheel of Pony Jessome's Chevrolet Silverado tow truck, M.H. followed, with Pony in the back seat wearing a black jacket, blue jeans and cowboy boots. Someone had placed a red and blue plaid jacket over Pony's face so they wouldn't have to look at their brother in death.

The Silverado hauled Chopper Raposo's silver Volkswagen Golf. Crash's body was slumped behind the steering wheel, blood hardening around a bullet wound behind his left ear. Blood was also caked on his face, and more of it was coming out of his nostrils. A green fleece shirt had been placed over his body, as if it could somehow comfort him. Beside his body was Boxer's, listing to his left, as if resting against his old friend. Chopper lay in the back hatch area, wrapped in a multicoloured carpet and curled in a fetal position, his eyes still open and registering what might be interpreted as shock.

Dwight Mushey drove Trotta's Pontiac Grand Prix, with Aravena beside him and the body of Goldberg Flanz slumped in the back. The Trottas had only been driving the car for three weeks, but already the back seat was cluttered with exactly the sort of things that accumulate in young families' cars: plastic children's toys, two backpacks, a car seat, games and tissues. There was also a letter from the Halton and District Catholic School Board and their veterinarian. Now, Flanz's blood stained the children's toys next to him. Someone had pulled a black nylon jacket over his head. Bringing up the rear of the convoy, Taz Sandham drove alone in his red Blazer. Weiner Kellestine remained back at the farm, plotting the next move.

The early-morning procession of vehicles emerging from 32196 Aberdeen Line was witnessed by several residents who were beginning farm chores or heading off to work. It was hard to miss, as the tow truck had its amber lights flashing.

The plan of driving to the Kitchener-Waterloo area was scuttled when Frank Mather noticed that the gas gauge on Goldberg Flanz's sport utility vehicle was still almost at empty. They hadn't put in nearly enough gas. It clearly wouldn't be a smart idea to drive the Infiniti up to a service station with the bodies of three murdered bikers in plain view inside. And running out of gas by the side of the road was even less appealing. Going back to the Kellestine farm with the bodies for more gas wasn't much of an option, either. So Mather made an executive decision. He pulled off Highway 401 about ten minutes west, at Union Road, and the rest of the vehicles followed him as he wound a short distance south on a gravel road, then up a side road called Stafford Line to the outer edges of the hamlet of Shedden. Finally, he stopped on a gravel lane by a farmer's field sheltered by trees. The No Surrender Crew's last road trip had taken them fourteen kilometres and lasted perhaps fifteen minutes.

By now, the sun was up. The Silverado was mired in the mud of a cornfield, but that didn't matter, since it wasn't going any farther. Taz was supposed to do a U-turn on the gravel road, so that he could pick up the others, but he appeared to drive far away down the road, before he finally turned and came back. "We were actually wondering where he was going, why he went so far," M.H. later said.

Considering the enormity of the crime, and Kellestine's already notorious reputation, investigators would later shake their heads at the decision to leave the bodies so close to his farm. Perhaps it was a jest of God that Goldberg Flanz had arrived at the meeting in a vehicle that was almost out of gas, even after meeting with his fellow Bandidos at a gas station en route to the farm. Perhaps there was something more psychologically complex involved. People who knew Weiner Kellestine couldn't help but wonder if, on some level, the hillbilly Nazi biker from Iona Station actually wanted to be caught so that he could become truly infamous. It was an intriguing thought, but a police officer who knew Weiner well dismissed it as the stuff of fiction. For all of his boasting and ranting about history, Weiner had always been a truly stupid man. Why should anyone be surprised that he behaved so stupidly on that defining morning of his life?

As the killers snaked through the countryside, Marcelo Aravena worried that he might be shot too, if it took so little for brother to justify killing brother in the Bandidos. He reasoned that the leaders of the slaughter would want to eliminate all witnesses, and he knew that Mushey, his sponsor into the club, was a man who relied on violence to get what he wanted. So he made a modest request as they rode together. If Aravena couldn't live, he at least wanted a funeral service with an open casket, so that his aging mother could see him one last time. "Don't shoot me in my face, my pretty face," he said, referencing every beat-up prizefighter's favourite joke as he pleaded his case.

The day-to-day routines of area residents help put things into a time frame. A woman who worked as a waitress at a local truck stop habitually left her house at 4:45 A.M. and made it a practice to drive slowly down Stafford Line, lest she hit any animals. She didn't see any vehicles abandoned by the side of the road that morning, so the caravan must have passed by after 5 A.M. A delivery woman for the *St. Thomas Times-Journal* did see the four vehicles as she began her route, a little after 6 A.M.

Kellestine was stunned by their quick return.

"How fucking far did you guys go?" he asked Mather. "I thought I told you to take them all the way to the Kitchener area."

"I was running out of gas in the car," Mather replied. "I had to leave them where they were."

Kellestine was annoyed and more than a little surprised, but still in control. He ordered Mather and the others to leave their clothes and shoes outside the farmhouse. They entered through his back door barefoot and in their underwear, as he stood in his blood-speckled combat jacket.

Guns were placed on the table, and Kellestine and Sandham made themselves busy, stripping them and packing them away. The weapons and shells were wrapped in cloth and placed in the same green duffle bag they had come out of a few hours earlier.

The dead men's coins, cellphones and identification documents were already on the coffee table. Kellestine scooped up the money and put it in a mayonnaise jar that held other loose change and sat on a shelf in the living room beside a hand grenade, an artillery shell and CDs by the Beatles, U2, Guns N' Roses and Vanilla Fudge. It was marked POTTY MOUTH JAR, and the rule in the Kellestine household was that if anyone said a bad word, they had to put a quarter in the jar. The money in the jar went to Kellestine's daughter, Kassie, who had turned seven that Thursday, the day before the killing started. The bloodied coins would be a posthumous birthday gift to her from the dead men.

Kellestine picked up Crash Kriarakis's black and orange Harley Davidson cap and admired it. He would keep it as a souvenir, a twenty-dollar trophy with just a dab of blood on it. He spotted a silver pocket knife he liked in the pile on the coffee table and took it for himself as well. Some of the paper money taken from the victims was also smeared with blood.

"Hey Taz, you need some money to get back with?" he offered.

Sandham declined, so Kellestine stuffed the cash in a garbage bag, along with the dead men's other possessions. Kellestine directed M.H. to drop the bag into a firepit close to the back door. Somebody had already dragged the couch out from the barn—it clearly had to go, since it was soaked in Chopper's blood. Also dropped into the pit were the killers' clothes and the blanket from the barn, which Goldberg Flanz and Mikey Trotta had used to mop up their friends' blood before they became victims themselves.

Sandham was having trouble lighting the fire, even with a can of gasoline to help him. He poured the remainder of the gas from the jerry can onto the pile; when he lit it, only one side of the pit ignited, though the flames leapt up at the little biker. "Taz, watch out—you're going to set yourself on fire!" M.H. shouted. It was apparent that the Winnipeggers' leader still hadn't gotten his jittery nerves under control. The realization that he had the moral turpitude to murder a friend and young father, but not the courage to cleanly carry out the deed, must have snuffed out much of the elation he had expected to feel in the wake of his defining, watershed moment.

The smell of smoke was heavy in the air when Kellestine's next-door neighbour, Patrick Timmermans, woke up at seven that morning. He could see that the smoke was coming from just in front of Kellestine's barn and thought it had an odd smell, like burning garbage. He quickly pulled his window shut to escape the stench.

By 7:45 A.M., it had been light for almost two hours when Mary and Russell Steele got a call from their friend Forbes Oldham. He was also a retired farmer who amused himself with "crop tours" of the area—early-morning inspections of his neighbours' fields. This morning, the old farmer was curious about the abandoned cars he had just seen on his friends' property. The Steeles left their breakfast table to walk up to the Grand Prix, and they tried to peer through the tinted window. They didn't see anything, but the mere presence of the car on their property was suspicious enough. The couple were viewers of the television crime series CSI and therefore were savvy enough not to touch anything, lest they damage the crime scene. Before most people had finished their morning coffee, the hastily stashed bodies had already been reported to the police.

An Ontario Provincial Police dispatcher cautioned a patrol officer that the grey Infiniti belonged to Jamie Flanz of Keswick, who was connected to a man named Robert (Bobby) Quinn. The dispatcher didn't have anything to say about Flanz, but warned that Quinn was described as a repeat criminal offender who sometimes carried a handgun. The officer peered inside the driver's window, which was already rolled down. There, he could see a man in the right rear passenger seat, with blood on his face. The man didn't appear to be breathing. Next, the officer noted that the rear hatch of the sport utility vehicle was ajar. He opened it to see a man lying on his right side, also motionless. The officer called the communications centre again, this time asking for a backup unit and an ambulance. From the roadside, Mary Steele could now see the outline of Big Paul Sinopoli, but his corpse was so large she thought it was two people. "I could hear the word 'body,'" she later recalled. "I thought, 'That's two bodies.'"

A paramedic arrived at 9:05, with lights flashing and sirens wailing, but it was clear there was no need to rush. The bodies remained inside the vehicles as they were towed back to London for further forensic testing, their second grisly caravan through Weiner Kellestine's neighbourhood in a matter of hours.

Nina waited up all night for Boxer to return home, and when he didn't, she called Weiner Kellestine's farmhouse at 8 A.M., asking if he knew her husband's whereabouts. Weiner said that Boxer had left the farm at 6:30—an answer that was true, as far as it went. He neglected to add that his friend had left the farm bloody and lifeless, or that he himself was the murderer.

After the phone call, the bikers quickly got down to

business. Aravena and Gardiner would be elevated from prospect to probationary status, M.H. later said. Frank Mather remained officially outside the club, despite his role in the carnage. Sandham asked Kellestine what he should do with Carlitto and Stone, who might still be looking for him in Winnipeg.

"Well, do them when you get back there," Kellestine said helpfully, as M.H. later recalled.

There was talk among the bikers that Bull Gardiner should stay back in Ontario to help Weiner set up his new London chapter of the Bandidos. The two men had travelled together with Boxer the previous summer to Sarnia, where they had tried unsuccessfully to set up a Killerbeez support club. It was suggested that Marcelo Aravena might stay behind too as Kellestine rebuilt the Bandidos in Ontario from the ground up. But Aravena balked at that idea; he was anxious to get back home to his family and there was no way he wasn't going to accompany Dwight Mushey, M.H. and Taz Sandham for the two-thousand-kilometre ride home. Gardiner, Mather and Kellestine watched them drive off from the kitchen window.

The Winnipeg crew were dead silent as they began the drive home, each of them newly wary of the men with whom their fates were now entangled. What was there to say, even if anyone had wanted to open up? M.H. pondered his options, and calculated what he might achieve by selling out his brothers. Aravena was still shattered by the thought that his friend and sponsor, Mushey, had almost killed him in cold blood. Mushey seethed with scorn for Sandham, who hadn't had the stomach to finish off Goldberg Flanz and had left that dirty job to him. Taz Sandham had to realize that the others in the car also felt he had wilted under pressure. He was now a mass murderer, and yet the men who knew him best considered him weaker than ever. And what could any of them say about Boxer, laughing in the face of death?

They hadn't been on the road long before they heard a radio news bulletin announcing that eight bodies had been discovered in vehicles near tiny Shedden. Not long after that, Taz Sandham pulled over at a Walmart in Barrie, north of Toronto, so they could buy some water, pop, chips, Cheezies, toothpaste and clothing. Marcelo and Taz didn't have any shoes, having tossed the ones they had into Kellestine's firepit. So they bought some plastic beach sandals. Mushey, who had luxuriant, shoulder-length black hair, also picked up some shampoo. One might have expected him to display an inner fury after his central role in something so huge and so awful. Instead, he seemed very cold and very calm as he studied the toiletries. Perhaps it was what American murderer Gary Gilmore once called a "calm rage."[26] Whatever the case, personal grooming, not remorse, seemed to be on the top of Big D's mind. "Dwight said that Head and Shoulders was good for removing gunshot residue," M.H. later recalled. Discreet in-store cameras captured Mushey and Aravena in the Walmart from 10:21 until 10:53 A.M., with Mushey always walking in front, and neither of them smiling.

The others took his advice, lathering up with the shampoo at a truck stop on Highway 11, where four dollars would get you a shower and a clean towel. Taz also shaved off his bushy beard, and Mushey removed his goatee. They hadn't slept for a day, as the killing and body disposal had taken the entire night. They were drained of adrenalin, but tidy and clean as they climbed back into the Blazer.

In St. Thomas, it didn't take long for police to realize they had a biker massacre on their hands. In Chopper Raposo's Volkswagen they found a printout of the tense email exchange between him and Sandham, dated March 6, 2006. Tucked under the seat was Raposo's black leather vest, with its Fat Mexican crest and Canada rocker on the back. It was in particularly rough shape, with one shoulder held together with a giant bobby pin and several patches so brittle they appeared ready to crack. There were two strips of what appeared to be reddish snakeskin sewn onto its lapel area. On one front pocket was a crest of a bulldog, and on the other were the words "OUR COLOURS DON'T RUN."

That afternoon, the Ontario Provincial Police applied for a warrant to search the Kellestine property. Since Weiner Kellestine wasn't one of the victims, it was only natural to wonder if he might be one of the killers. In London, an OPP identification officer completed a preliminary check of the bodies of the eight murdered men. They were all Caucasian, and all except Chopper

Raposo had apparently died from gunshots to the head. The faces of Chopper, Crash, Boxer and Goldberg had all been covered, as if the killers either couldn't bear to view their handiwork or thought they were showing some form of respect.

The person with the most bullets in his body was Bam Bam Salerno, who had bloody patches on the bridge of his nose, right cheek, left ear, right thigh, lower right leg and right hand. The only victim who was seated behind a steering wheel was Crash Kriarakis, so it was only natural to wonder if he somehow thought he was going to be allowed to drive the Volkswagen to safety, until the bark of the gun that killed him. For someone who was considered non-violent, Crash had attracted a particularly heavy amount of firepower, with seven bullet wounds, including two shots under his left ear, two other shots to the face and single shots to each of his shoulder, chest and abdomen.

At 7:04 A.M., officers pulled the remains of Boxer Muscedere from the front passenger seat of the Volkswagen. Boxer hadn't yet been identified, and police could only describe him as appearing to be in his fifties, with a bullet wound under his right eye and another in his torso.

On the road back to Manitoba, the Winnipeg killers stopped somewhere by a small lake north of Lake Superior for ice cream. Next was an overnight stop at a gas station in the hamlet of Jellicoe, about eighty kilometres west of Longlac, a former Northwest Company trading post. They pulled over near the pumps and slept in the Blazer. When the sun came up a few hours later, Taz Sandham knocked on the door of the gas station's owner, who came out and filled up the tank.

By the time they reached an Esso station just inside the Manitoba border, Taz and Mushey were nervous that the Blazer might somehow be bugged with a police recording device. Everyone got out of it for a few minutes while they calmed themselves down. But an absence of listening devices didn't mean the police weren't wondering what the Winnipeggers were doing. The Royal Canadian Mounted Police would soon be asking about Mushey's whereabouts; he'd been charged with conspiracy to produce methamphetamine, and one of the conditions of his bail was that he notify police whenever he left Manitoba. Before he made the drive to Weiner Kellestine's farm, Mushey had told the RCMP that he was going to Ontario, and he had phoned them again the day before the murders. The Mounties in Manitoba knew Mushey was the secretary-treasurer of Taz Sandham's Bandido chapter and their point man in drug trafficking. It would be natural for them to wonder what he knew about the massacre of his clubmates.

The best strategy for Mushey was to say that he had left the province on Friday, before the shooting started.

The press quickly called the Shedden slaughter the worst biker massacre in the history of the world, even though there wasn't a Harley-Davidson in sight. Naturally, the Hells Angels were blamed, and just as naturally they scoffed at the suggestion. Donny Petersen, the Hells Angels' Central Canada Region secretary and Ontario spokesperson, was asked by the *Toronto Star* that Saturday morning about the murders. He said he wasn't surprised that many people were quickly jumping to the conclusion that the killing must somehow be the Angels' doing. "Any society needs a bogeyman," he said.

Petersen, a former boxer who ran a successful Toronto-area motorcycle shop and had no criminal record, sloughed off the suggestion that the Hells Angels might have slaughtered the Bandidos as part of a drug turf skirmish. "One of the reasons we [Hells Angels and Bandidos] don't travel in the same social circles is that they don't have two nickels to rub together," Petersen said. "We're not taking anything. There's nothing to take." Petersen also dismissed media speculation that the killers might have been attempting to curry favour with the Hells Angels to become members themselves. "None of them had any prospect of being a Hells Angel," Petersen said. "Certainly, there were no overtures from this side . . . We never approached people to become members. People approach us."

The massacre was big news around the world, from

People's Daily Online, the official Internet voice of the government of Communist China, to *The Sydney Morning Herald* in Australia, the *Irish Examiner, The Times* of London, *Newsday* on Long Island and major American television networks, including Fox and CNN. Small airplanes buzzed low over the Infiniti so that news photographers could catch photos of Big Paul, his mammoth gut hanging out and his body curled up like that of a giant baby.

Mary Thompson learned of the deaths of Goldberg Flanz and Big Paul Sinopoli from a newspaper story. She had been afraid of the Bandidos as a gang, but Big Paul and Goldberg were always nice and even protective towards her. Just a few days before his murder, Big Paul seemed apologetic that he had borrowed a little money from her, and promised to pay it back soon.

Sergeant Gordon McDowell of the Durham Regional Police surveillance team woke up that Saturday morning to news that the massacre had happened, almost under their noses. "I was shocked," he later said. Disbelief, not fear, was the reaction of Kellestine's neighbours. Before the carnage, tiny Shedden had been best known for its annual rhubarb festival. None of the eight victims was from the area, but now, newspapers and broadcasters were referring to the slaughter as the "Shedden Massacre," which seemed a little unfair. As Marty Angenent, owner of the Holland House restaurant, said, "They were all strangers to us."

When Ripper Fullager heard the names of the victims, he quickly noted that Boxer Muscedere had been murdered, but not his longtime friend Weiner Kellestine. The two men had been together for decades, and it was suspicious that Kellestine was still alive.

"I bet you he fucking did it," Ripper said to Glenn Atkinson.

PART III

HUNTERS TO HUNTED

CHAPTER 19

A Time to Remember

No, no, no life!
Why should a dog, a horse, a rat, have life,
And thou no breath at all? Thou'lt come no more,
Never, never, never, never, never!
KING LEAR, ACT 5, SCENE 3

Why? Why? Why? Why didn't he just leave?
WIDOW OF GEORGE (CRASH) KRIARAKIS

Ripper Fullager's health went downhill fast after the Shedden Massacre. His head was bald, his beard had disappeared and he was gaunt from chemotherapy. The tapestry of his tattoos was too big for his shrinking frame. He told a visitor that he had just been visited by his old friends Boxer Muscedere and Chopper Raposo. The visitor gently suggested that he must have been dreaming.

"No, no, no," Ripper replied. "They were in the room, talking to me."

Glenn (Wrongway) Atkinson visited him not long after that, and it was hard to connect the lethargic, emaciated old man lying in the bed with the longtime one percenter who used to revel in ripping about the streets of Toronto on his Harley.

"It's okay," Atkinson said, holding the old biker's hand. "You can let go."

Not long after that, Ripper's grip loosened, and he was gone.

There was not much for a guy like Ripper to hold on to. He would hardly have recognized the wasteland his world, and his club, had become. Gone were his best friends, snuffed out by the cynicism and myopic ambition that had overwhelmed one percenter society. Gone was the world he had grown up in and helped create, where rugged misfits could ride shoulder to shoulder and challenge the mainstream on terms they chose. Like Boxer, Ripper may not have been a perfect man, or even a particularly good man by some people's standards, but a world in which brother killed brother for a patch of cloth was not one he would have wanted to call his own.

Out of respect, Donny Petersen attended Ripper's wake with another full-patch member of the Hells Angels. Also at the funeral were Frank Lenti and his massive friend Big Gus. No American Bandidos went to the trouble of showing up, and Texas had refused to send up a new Fat Mexican patch for the burial to replace the one that had been confiscated by police. The once-optimistic No Surrender Crew was down to one authentic Fat Mexican crest. Members would take turns wearing it that summer, when they wanted to try to make their presence felt on the streets.

Somehow, the dreaming and plotting, the ambitious

plans and earnest avowals of brotherhood, had come to this. Boxer had already written that he would not want to live without the Bandidos, and perhaps there had been a time when that was true. But the unexpected horror that became so public in a field near Shedden had the unsettling effect of putting the biker ethos into perspective. The dead men thought of their killers as brothers, only to find themselves at the wrong end of their clubmates' guns. They thought of themselves as outsiders who could rely only on each other, but if they could have seen the outpouring of grief that marked their passing, they would have known how dearly they were loved, and how little they really needed the Fat Mexican.

The first funeral for the murdered men was that of Jamie (Goldberg) Flanz, since Jewish tradition calls for an avoidance of embalming and for burial as soon as possible after death. No one wearing biker colours attended the dignified, simple service on Tuesday, April 11, at the Paperman & Sons funeral home in Montreal. It was here that send-offs for literary greats Mordecai Richler and Irving Layton had been held, and the two hundred mourners at Flanz's funeral included Liberal Senator Yoine Goldstein, a family friend. It had been nine years since Flanz left Montreal for Ontario, and those who remembered him from the middle-class neighbourhood of Côte St-Luc recalled a rough-and-tumble hockey defenceman, a caring volunteer ambulance medic who had saved lives, a volunteer coach of children's hockey and baseball teams, a Harley-Davidson motorcycle aficionado and an exuberant spirit. It was impossible to also see their Jamie as an outlaw biker with the nickname Goldberg who had died a lurid death. He had been connected to the Bandidos for only half a year, and that association had ended his life at the age of thirty-seven. Abandoned now by his false brothers, Jamie Flanz was sent off from the world by those who truly loved him.

"Jamie stood out and stood up," his younger brother Robbie said in his eulogy. "We were different planets in the same solar system."

Robbie Flanz then addressed his brother directly: "I leaned toward the conventional. You preferred the beat of your own drum. I will never forget that roguish smile." Robbie asked others not to accept simplistic media portrayals of his brother as nothing more than an outlaw biker. "I challenge everyone to see who you were and not what you are presented to be."

Rabbi Chaim Steinmetz read an address that had been written by Flanz's sister Jennifer, which gently hinted at his motorcycle club associations. "I take comfort in the fact that before his death, he spoke of turning his life around and moving forward. My brother was a wonderful person—a supportive son, brother and father. That is how I want him to be remembered."

There were plenty of people in black suits—including a half-dozen or so police officers—at the funeral home for the visitation of George (Crash) Kriarakis, where his old friend Glenn (Wrongway) Atkinson appeared in a black Outlaws T-shirt to pay his respects, accompanied by two Outlaws in club colours.

"Glenn!" called Crash's widow, Diane, from the receiving line, and dozens of necks craned to see Atkinson.

The two hugged each other and thought back to how Crash had considered leaving the No Surrender Crew and joining Atkinson in the Outlaws, just six months before. He had stayed with the club out of loyalty and fear, and now, aside from Pierre (Carlitto) Aragon and a member named Luke, no Bandidos could be seen at the funeral for the man who had briefly been their Canadian president. There were also no floral tributes, messages or anything else from any of the two thousand American, South American, European, Australian or Asian members of the international club on display. But there was real pain, which made all of the biker bravado seem like so much dangerous play-acting.

"Why? Why? Why?" Diane cried. "Why didn't he just leave?"

At the funeral, Carlitto Aragon wore his black Bandidos vest over a black leather coat. With him was a member named Luke (also known as Rooster), who had faded in and out of the club. He wore an official black club dress shirt. Father Paul Drakos told the packed congregation that George Kriarakis now belonged to the "King of Kings" and that Jesus Christ would grant his salvation. When his words were completed, black-clad mourners said goodbye at his open casket. Bruises to his face were clearly visible, despite thick makeup.

Carlitto and Luke formed an honour guard of sorts as Crash was buried at the Elgin Mills cemetery in York Region. Over Carlitto's heart was a patch with the now-discredited words "Our colours don't run." It was an effort at support and strength, but they were almost lost in the crowd of men, women and children of Greek descent, who had little understanding for the biker subculture that had taken the life of their loved one.

The only biker colours on display at the funeral of Big Paul Sinopoli at St. Charles Borromeo Church, at Dufferin Street and Lawrence Avenue in Toronto, were inside the casket. Father Fre Mazzarella told the hundred mourners that it was not their role to judge Paul Sinopoli, who never married or had children. "Many questions we would like answered, and I don't have them," the priest said. "We are not here to judge, we are here to pray. None of us are perfect."

Sinopoli's family could not have learned of his death in a more horrifying manner: they recognized the corpse of the man they loved in a front-page aerial photo that depicted him lying in the back of Jamie Flanz's Infiniti. They had been eager to help Detective Tom Dingwall with the investigation, and pulled together everything they thought was related to his biker life and put it in a bin for him: Christmas cards from Bandidos chapters from around the world, three pages of Bandidos by-laws, a price list for Bandido memorabilia, and some jewellery, including a necklace inscribed with the words BANDI-DOS FOREVER. But forever can be a short time, and there were no Fat Mexicans in attendance. Before the ceremony, however, Durham Regional Police had returned Big Paul's massive vest to his family so that he could be buried in it, according to his wishes.

Cesidio (Joe) Muscedere told about a hundred mourners in Chatham that his big brother John died "next to some of his best friends." He didn't know yet that his killer was also his friend, Weiner Kellestine, the man who sponsored him into one percenter clubs years before. The only sign of a biker presence was a lone member of the old Black Diamond Riders club, one of Ontario's first biker clubs, and Robert (Peterborough Bob) Pammett, wearing his distinctive yellow leather vest with the Fat Mexican on the back. Peterborough Bob had a particularly poor attendance record at club meetings, and his failure to attend the Friday night church at Kellestine's farm explained why he was alive to attend Boxer's funeral.

Boxer was remembered as a solid son, brother, friend, father of five and grandfather of three. Joe Muscedere told mourners at St. Joseph's Roman Catholic Church that he was "our superman. John was truly a free man. How many of us here today can say that? He had no fear and no limitations. He lived his life to the fullest.

"Through his whole life, John's love for his father, mother and grandparents was undeniable," Joe Muscedere continued, as his grief-stricken parents stared at the floor. "They in turn loved him more than anything. They wanted him to be happy, safe and healthy. In our family, this bond lasts forever, no matter what."

Boxer had talked of turning his life around in the final months of his life, and forensic testing supported the claim. No traces of drugs or alcohol were found in his system; the same was true of the bodies of Crash Kriarakis and Big Paul Sinopoli. Testing of the blood and urine of Salerno revealed morphine, methadone and heroin, as well as a small amount of alcohol. Trotta had a small amount of marijuana in his system, while the blood of Raposo and Flanz contained a by-product of cocaine. Jessome's body held therapeutic levels of oxycodone, a painkiller.

Priest Dennis Wilhelm told the assembly that God loves everyone, even those who make disappointing life choices. "I have no right, as a human being, to judge John Muscedere. We only have one judge. That is Jesus Christ."

Carlitto Aragon and two other surviving No Surrender Crew members agreed to meet with *Toronto Star* reporter Betsy Powell in a Toronto roadhouse late on the night of Tuesday, April 11, and provided her with a two-page hand-written note to the victims' families, friends and the world. They wore black T-shirts decorated with the Fat Mexican logo, and as they played pool they spoke of their pain, anger and numbness. Their letter read: "No words will ever be able to accurately describe our emotions at this time. The loss of eight brothers is a shock to us all. We all will maintain and carry on like the way we know they would have wanted us to. Times are tough and we who are left standing are fuelled with rage and sorrow. Nobody knew our brothers as we did, and to depict them in the media as anything other than the victims of a senseless and brutal crime is insensitive and inhumane.

"These men were fathers, sons, and most of all brothers, who, contrary to media reports, were truly motor cycle enthusiasts who paid the ultimate price for their passion to ride free side by each.

"Rest in peace brothers. You truly are free to ride on in the forever chapter in the sky. You will always be loved and never forgotten." It was signed, "Your brothers, No Surrender Crew Canada. Love. Loyalty. Respect."

In Texas, the Bandidos of the mother chapter were rather less melancholy than Carlitto Aragon. Police noted with interest that messages of condolence for the eight slain Bandidos and associates were deleted from the Bandidos' American website. Taz Sandham had explained to the Winnipeggers that the No Surrender Crew didn't merit online tributes, since they had been killed during removal of their patches. In the eyes of Sandham and the Bandido Nation, they were dead before anyone pulled the trigger on them.

CHAPTER 20

Tazman on Top

A little water clears us of this deed.
MACBETH, ACT 2, SCENE 2

"Boxer, I loved him with all my
heart and soul. . . . I loved all them guys."
WAYNE (WEINER) KELLESTINE TALKS ABOUT
THE MEN HE MURDERED

It had taken more sucking up, betrayals and even murders
than Taz Sandham could ever have imagined, but finally
the little ex-cop was free of Boxer, Chopper and the rest
of the No Surrender Crew. Weiner Kellestine might disagree, as might any American Bandido who gave the matter much thought, but Sandham now considered himself
the top Bandido in all of Canada. Surely, he could outma-
noeuvre Weiner Kellestine, who was both unstable and
isolated. Taz gave himself the title of Manitoba chapter
president—which, he figured, made him national *presidente* as well. Never mind that the Americans had given
that title to Kellestine just a month before; in Taz's mind,

that simply didn't matter. Compared to what they had already done, this was just a minor detail to be corrected. The Tazman was drunk on what he considered his new powers. He could now deal directly with the most powerful Americans, Europeans and Australians in the mighty Bandido Nation as a force in his own right.

Almost immediately, Sandham had to ponder a hard truth that countless leaders from all walks of life had learned before him: the sharp joy of holding power can be considerably blunted when you're surrounded by idiots. It's even less fun when you realize that those idiots often talk too much, bragging about things that should remain unspoken, or when you realize that they don't really love you at all, even though they so readily pledge their love, loyalty and respect. Taz knew better than anyone that, given the right circumstances, they would kill him, just as he had set up the murders of Boxer and Chopper and all the rest of the No Surrender Crew. It was relatively easy to plot destruction with the likes of Weiner Kellestine, but far harder to work with him to rebuild and thrive.

There is an underlying irony to membership in any motorcycle gang—the world of one percenters is a society for guys who reject society, a club for men who don't join clubs, a fraternity of outliers. Seen this way, it can't be particularly surprising that bikers kill their clubmates so readily. Groucho Marx's quip that he wouldn't belong to any club that would have someone like him for a member needs only minor amendment to express the perilous irony of biker brotherhood. A guy like Sandham *shouldn't* belong to a club that would have someone like him as a member, let alone president. Because, almost by definition, the guys wearing the same patch as you may very well also share the same unimaginative remorselessness about killing in pursuit of their own fantasies of power.

But the problem for the fledgling Winnipeg Bandidos was more acute than the difficulty of getting a band of violent sociopaths to get along. After all, gangs of all kinds somehow manage to go about their daily business. But the Hells Angels and the Mafia can rely on something Sandham destroyed at the moment he reached for it: authority. Ripper's photocopied codes of biker conduct and Raposo's punctilious obsession with matches and toothpicks must have seemed absurd to many prospects, just as new recruits in any army around the world shake their heads at the rigorous attention they are expected to devote to making their beds and shining their boots. But these are the small details that make clear to new members that the group they are joining is much bigger than they are, and that they will have to submit to the claims it makes on them. In the Bandidos, those claims culminate in the office of the president. To be feared and obeyed, to be able to compel grown men covered in tattoos to listen to what you say—these are the privileges Sandham tried to snatch from Boxer. Instead, he snuffed them out along with the man he had pledged to follow.

If the life of the club's president is something members can tamper with to suit their whims, then everything else is up for grabs, too. Rules, traditions, procedures—all are merely provisional when the president is little more than an inconvenience for others. It is one thing to recruit new members into a well-established hierarchy. It is something totally different to try to impose that pecking order or expect others to play by the rules when you have violently toppled the old system and broken every rule.

That was the problem the man called Little Beaker faced as his club of plotters and murderers arrived back in Winnipeg late Sunday night. The men parted ways silently and sullenly, and each holed up in isolation to nurse their guilt, their ambition and their fear. Aravena didn't move back in with Mushey; instead, he chose to stay with his girlfriend as he slid into depression and paranoia. He couldn't stop wondering how close he'd come to being the ninth victim that night, as the gunmen discussed whether it would be smart to eliminate witnesses. For the next few weeks, *El Condor* Aravena barely ventured outside.

M.H. was a lot more active. The day after he got back, he sat down with Timothy Diack, his contact in the Winnipeg police department. It was their first conversation since Thursday, April 6, the day before the murders. The cop knew all about the harvest of bodies in the field near Shedden, and he knew that M.H. had been in the neighbourhood. Naturally, he wanted to know what his snitch had been doing.

"Did you hear what happened out there?" Diack asked when they met early in the evening.

"Yeah," M.H. replied.

"Were you there when it happened?"

"No, we left on the Friday."

Not long afterwards, Winnipeg police went to Sandham's home to warn him that they had learned of a "credible threat" to his safety. He wasn't at home, so they told his common-law wife that they had heard that people associated with the Shedden Massacre were in Winnipeg to kill him. Whether the police were genuinely still in the dark about the farmyard massacre or they were just looking for a reaction, Little Beaker had hardly been home long enough to check his email before the police were at his door.

Not surprisingly, Weiner Kellestine was being watched carefully as well. Just hours after the bodies had turned up, officers from the Ontario Provincial Police's emergency response team began low-profile surveillance of Kellestine's farm. At 3:05 P.M., an officer noted the arrival of a blue 1989 Ford LTD sedan. A check of its registration revealed it belonged to Kerry Morris, the forty-six-year-old common-law wife of Weiner Kellestine's friend Eric Niessen.

Kellestine still needed help removing incriminating evidence from his farm, and from his barn in particular. Just as importantly, he also needed an alibi for the past night. The OPP surveillance team watched with binoculars from a distance as several people carried buckets between the house and the barn. The buckets appeared to be filled in a trough. Unusually dark smoke was now coming out of the chimney of the Kellestine farmhouse.

As Niessen drove with Morris up to the Aberdeen Line farmhouse, he could see police surrounding the property. Inside the Kellestine farmhouse, the phone rang constantly. A shared point of view was that Weiner must either be a killer or a victim, so when he answered the phone, people were naturally suspicious. One of the calls was from Sarah McGrath, an enterprising reporter with the A-Channel television station (formerly known as CFPL) in London.

"That shooting down in Shedden involved a Wayne Kellestine," McGrath said.

"Involved me?" Kellestine asked.

"Yeah."

"In Shedden?"

"Yeah."

"When was that?"

"Last night there were eight people killed."

"Whoa . . . whoa, really? . . . Whoa."

"Yeah."

"Holy . . . No, I'm still alive, thank God."

Kellestine was clearly enjoying himself as McGrath told him that there was a rumour that he was one of the eight victims. If he had felt remorse about slaughtering his best friend Boxer and the rest of his crew, those feelings had quickly passed.

"You know what? I hear different rumours," Kellestine replied.

McGrath soldiered on, asking, "Are you the Wayne Kellestine that's been involved in some of the shootings over the years?"

"No, hell no."

"No?"

"No, hell no."

"All righty . . ."

"It's all conjecture."

"Someone down in that area said maybe one of them was you."

"One of them was me?"

"So I just thought that, well, we don't really go on rumour, on speculation, we like to check and find out, so I just thought I'd call you."

"Hang on for a sec. Am I alive? Geez, I've been with a house full of people in here for the last two days. I think I'm alive. I've drank a few beers but . . . okay, thanks, I'll have to check that out."

"All right," McGrath continued.

"Thank you, I don't talk to reporters," Kellestine jeered, hamming it up for the benefit of his guests, thoroughly enjoying himself. With that, he hung up the phone and got back to the business of the cover-up.

Later, Niessen would say, "Wayne and me looked at each other Saturday afternoon soon as we got the phone calls about Chopper . . . and Boxer. We looked at each other and, basically at the same time, said, 'You're gonna get fucking nailed for this.'"

The crime Kellestine was going to get nailed for was all over the evening news that night. Whether the manic biker was thrilled or terrified by the spectacle of seeing his handiwork on television, it somehow reminded him that he would need an alibi, and he wanted Niessen to provide it: Niessen should say that he'd been at Kellestine's house and nothing much happened there that night. A little while later, Kellestine ordered guests at his farmhouse to give the same story to police: they were partying together at the time of the murders. Not the most sophisticated alibi in the history of crime, perhaps, but it was certainly credible.

But the police weren't the people demanding answers right away. Just before midnight, Boxer's younger brother Joe telephoned Kellestine's farmhouse. The two men barely knew each other, but Joe Muscedere had found Weiner's number in his brother's papers and thought he must have some answers. Niessen answered the call and told Joe that he thought two of the bodies found near Kellestine's farm were those of Boxer and Chopper. Then he backed Kellestine's lie and said he had been at the farmhouse for a two- or three-day drinking party and didn't know about the murders.

Joe Muscedere wasn't about to be sloughed off. He and Boxer grew up to be very different men in many ways; Joe was an executive in the auto industry, not a biker, but he was still Boxer's brother and he needed the truth. So he phoned back the next day, after he and his father visited the rural road in Shedden where the bodies had been found. That Sunday morning, he had identified Boxer for police from a photograph, and now he wanted answers from the man Boxer visited on the last day of his life.

"It's Boxer's brother Joe," he said when he called.

"Oh shit," Kellestine replied.

"My brother's dead," Joe Muscedere said.

Kellestine's answer to that was an odd one for someone who supposedly had just lost a close friend: "Have you been to the police?"

Joe pressed on, saying he needed to know anything that the last people who saw Boxer alive could offer. The younger Muscedere clearly shared his late brother's determination and fearlessness. Kellestine's tone struck him as surprised, evasive and somewhat nervous.

"My condolences, you know," Kellestine said. "You know what your brother meant to me . . . I can't talk over the phone."

Joe said he wanted to come over to talk, but was told he couldn't. He suggested that they meet for coffee, but Kellestine blew off that idea as well.

Then Kellestine complained that he had just been phoned by a reporter, asking if he was dead. There was laughter now in the background, and Joe Muscedere could hear Kellestine yukking it up with someone in the background, saying, "Do I look dead?"

Seconds later, Boxer's old friend Weiner Kellestine hung up.

That Sunday, Chopper's fiancée, Carrie Caldwell, called Kellestine on his cellphone. She had seen Chopper's

Volkswagen on the news, as one of the vehicles that held the bodies of murdered men near Shedden. She asked where Chopper was and if it was true that the man she loved, along with most of the rest of the Toronto chapter, had been killed.

"He didn't answer me straight out," she later recalled. Kellestine's mood was hard for her to gauge. There was clearly something suspicious going on with him. At points he sounded "offhand, blasé," in Caldwell's opinion. At other points in the conversation, he sounded full of grief, saying, "I got fucked up and I fucked up." His voice was soft, as if he was crying.

The OPP's plan was to move in on Kellestine's farmhouse that evening, once it became dark. It wasn't too difficult to sketch a floor plan of the dirty white farmhouse, since it had been built to a fairly standard design for homes in the area. Perhaps more importantly, numerous members of the paramilitary Tactics and Rescue Unit had been inside it in the past, in various operations against Weiner Kellestine.

Around 7 P.M., they began to move onto the farm site, dressed in fatigues and helmets and carrying submachine guns. Detective Constable David Dowell, an OPP negotiator, called Kellestine at the same time. Kellestine talked simultaneously with the police officer on his home phone and his lawyer, Ken McMillan, on his cellphone.

"Okay, now do you have a search warrant, sir?" Kellestine asked.

"Yes, we do," Dowell replied.

"Okay, I got no problem, I'm not gonna interfere with that."

But a few moments later, Kellestine was on the offensive with the negotiator.

"Okay now, let's you and I get one thing straight," Kellestine said, trying to exercise something like authority.

"Sure."

"Right fucking now."

"Sure."

"I will leave the door unlocked," Kellestine continued. "You pieces of shit don't have to kick my fuckin' door in like you did the last fuckin' time."

Dowell gave his word that Kellestine's door would be respected.

"Yeah, your word," Kellestine said, sounding genuinely offended now. The consummate liar loved to accuse others of not being trustworthy, especially police. "You're a cop. I don't trust you . . . You're likely gonna fuckin' shoot me, motherfucker."

Several minutes later, Kellestine still hadn't come out the front door, and the negotiator wanted to know why he was delaying. Kellestine explained that he had put his German shepherd into its pen, and now he was getting dressed.

Whether he was scrambling to hide evidence or simply

enjoying the drama, Kellestine was still inside the farm-house several minutes later, and Dowell called again.

"I'll just, ah, change my socks, my underwear," Kellestine explained. "Tried having a shit. I'm not stallin'." These were the biker's last words as a free man.

A police aircraft circled overhead and undercover offic-ers hid in a field as Kellestine finally walked up his lane-way, his arms in the air. Behind him were Brett Gardiner, Frank Mather, Eric Niessen and Kerry Morris.

"Don't point your fucking guns at me," Kellestine demanded. "My hands are up."

He was thoroughly patted down for hidden weap-ons, and his leather belt, with "1%er" painted on it, was seized. The search completed, Kellestine was handed over to Detective Constable Mark Loader and Detective Constable Jeff Gateman of the Biker Enforcement Unit, who were to drive him to the London OPP detachment for questioning. Kellestine was placed in the back seat of their unmarked Nissan Altima and Loader sat beside him.

Loader would later say that Kellestine appeared som-bre as he said he had no fears for his own personal safety, despite the slaughter of his clubmates. "I don't give a fuck about myself," Kellestine said. "I am invincible. I am ten feet tall and invincible."

He admitted, however, that he feared for the safety of his wife and school-age daughter in the wake of the mur-ders.

"From who?" Loader asked.

Kellestine burst into laughter and replied, "You don't know who?"

The outlaw biker veered from mirth to drama, making an unconvincing display of crying. "I wish that they would have put a gun to my head and killed me too," he sobbed.

A second later, he must have remembered he wasn't supposed to know the victims' cause of death. All of the victims had been shot in the head, but police had been careful not to release such details to the media. So Kellestine corrected himself and said he wished he'd been stabbed, or killed in whatever way his friends were killed.

Loader still couldn't see any tears, although Kellestine kept up the pretense of weeping. "Why me? Why me?" he demanded melodramatically.

Loader asked why Kellestine felt he had been spared.

"I'm lucky, I guess."

Kellestine's interview with Detective Gateman began at 9:07 P.M., and Kellestine quickly insisted he was in rough shape and needed some sleep.

"Look at me," Kellestine said. "Do I look like shit to you?"

"I think you actually look good," Gateman said.

Kellestine was wearing a ball cap pulled low on his head and a baggy black T-shirt with the design of a white-supremacist fist on the back. He had been awake for nearly a day and a half and had spent the previous hours washing away his friends' blood. He can't have looked all that good.

But he was still up for a fight, and he came out on the offensive. The way he figured it, the police themselves might be his alibi. He said he assumed that he was under police surveillance, since he had been warned a few weeks before that there was a threat on his life. "If I had twenty-four-hour surveillance," he asked, "what am I? Houdini? I'm magic?"

Though Kellestine hadn't shed any tears, he began to take credit for his emotional vulnerability: "I actually broke down in front of you . . . which I'm embarrassed about . . . I'm trying to keep my composure . . . The last thing I want is this on film in court, seeing me bawling my fucking eyes out—"

"I haven't seen you cry, Wayne," Gateman said. "I've never seen you cry."

"Thank you," Kellestine replied. "Thank you, thank you. I appreciate that."

Kellestine ordered a triple-triple coffee and resumed playing the victim. He said he worried that police were making a mess of his house, searching for evidence. Then he made a great show of embarrassment over the fact that he couldn't remember exactly what he'd done on Friday, which was unusual for him. "I can ramble off regimental serial numbers, social insurance numbers, old OHIP numbers, driver's licence numbers, fingerprint identification numbers, stuff like that."

"Tell me what you did on Friday, Wayne," Gateman said. "How hard is that?"

"Oh fuck," Kellestine replied. "I thought Friday was yesterday . . . Don't tell me I was up for three fucking days drinking and partying. Oh, Sunday. That's why I feel so goddamn shitty." Then Kellestine, a drug dealer, said he felt like a hypocrite to tell the officer he'd gotten high as well as drunk over the past few days. "I don't like people that do drugs . . . I'm always putting down people that are fucking drug addicts."

Gateman pressed on, asking, "Did you murder these eight people? How's that for a question?"

"That's a dumb fucking question," Kellestine countered. "How could you say that to me?"

He suggested the real killer or killers were going free while he was being subjected to pointless questions. "You get tunnel vision. You get tunnel vision and you focus on me. And this is an old commercial. Pity."

Detective Staff Sergeant David Quigley entered the room and warned Kellestine that officers had checked out each of the victims, lasering their vehicles for clues and testing for DNA samples. Kellestine continued to deny he was still with the club. "I haven't been invited to the last two parties," he insisted. "I did go to a funeral. You know that. You had pictures of me there."

The officer asked Kellestine if they could take his shoes, to make forensic comparisons to footprints at the crime scene.

"I know I don't have to," Kellestine replied. Then he doffed the shoes anyway, grandly saying, "Keep them."

"You're a gentleman," Quigley said. "So much appreciated."

A few minutes later, Kellestine was shoeless and alone in the interview room, his movements and words recorded by hidden cameras.

"I can't believe it," Kellestine said to himself and the cameras. "I gave them my shoes. I can't believe it. Why the fuck would I do that for? . . . Now, what about my buddies? I'm not leaving without my friends."

He wasn't leaving at all. Shortly before midnight, Kellestine was arrested on eight counts of first-degree murder.

Late that night, police released Eric Niessen and Kerry Morris and drove them home to the town of Mitchell, close to their farm. Sometime before midnight, Morris saw a car parked outside their isolated farmhouse. Its parking lights were on, as if whoever was inside was staring at their home. "We had no idea who it was," she later said. "Every hair on the back on my neck went up. I thought, 'My God. We're going to die.' I thought it was the Hells Angels." More cars appeared, and they advanced en masse down their laneway. "I thought, 'This is the end,'" Morris later recalled. "My heart was in my throat."[27]

The phone rang and the person on the end of the line said he was a police officer. He asked Niessen to come outside, and he obeyed. The phone rang again. This time the caller said, "We're arresting Eric for murder."

"What?" Morris screamed.

"We want you to come out."

"Okay. I'm just going to make a couple of calls and then I'll be out."

She phoned her work, where she was an office manager, to leave a message on the answering machine that she wouldn't be in that day. She didn't explain why. Even if she'd wanted to, what could she say? How do you gently tell your boss that you have been picked up by police in a mass-murder investigation? Then she left a message with a lawyer to say that she and Eric needed help.

Shortly before noon on Monday, Kellestine was back in the interview room with Detectives Gateman and Quigley. He was now wearing a prison-issue jumpsuit with white plastic boots, which made him look a little like a shaggy astronaut enjoying some downtime. His voice was weary but arrogant, like that of a great man who was being sorely tested, as he repeated his earlier assertion that police must have known he was innocent because they were constantly watching him. "I know I had police watching me. I listen to them on the scanner. You know I've got three scanners."

He said he imagined he was now in danger from both the Hells Angels *and* the Bandidos. "You just charged me with murdering eight Bandidos, who were my close brothers . . . If the real perpetrators of this crime are Hells Angels, then they're still out there laughing."

The police weren't the only people he tried to deceive. He borrowed an officer's phone to call his common-law wife, Tina, and assure her she was safe. "You've got nothing to worry about. You're only guilty of being my old lady." Seconds later, he added, "I want to apologize to all the neighbours for the inconvenience." He also suggested that the police might be able to give their daughter a ride to school, since they had unmarked police cars. And he reminded Tina again that she didn't have to worry about anything from the men who killed Boxer and his friends. "It's a code of honour of the society we live in that old ladies and children aren't to be molested or bothered."

He told her that he suspected the Hells Angels were the real killers. "I hate them cocksuckers . . . I hate them more than I hate the cops." Then he talked of Boxer: "Boxer, I loved him with all my heart and soul. And fucking, I loved all them guys."

He repeatedly told Tina that he had nothing to do with the murders. "Don't you worry. They've got nothing on me. I haven't done anything . . . I love you baby, with all my heart and soul."

He also reassured Tina that he was not saying anything stupid to police, although he had been playing stupid. "Just played a little. I played the fucking bumpkin. You know, the fucking country bumpkin idiot that I am, you know."

A few minutes later, Quigley asked Kellestine what he thought Bandidos *presidente* Jeff Pike would think about the slaughter.

"Who's Jeff Pike?" Kellestine replied gamely.

CHAPTER 21

Police Microscope

When shall we three meet again?
In thunder, lightning, or in rain?
MACBETH, ACT 1, SCENE 1

Snitches are a dying breed
SLOGAN ON A POPULAR OUTLAW BIKER T-SHIRT

On Friday, April 14, M.H. met again with Timothy Diack, who had a yes-or-no question that would change his life forever. "Would you like to put on a jacket?" he asked, using police slang for a hidden recording device. M.H. knew he didn't have a lot of options. Diack had already relayed a blunt message from Ontario Provincial Police investigators: they knew M.H. was somehow involved in the murders. He could either assist the police investigation or go down eventually with the rest of the killers. "He [Diack] said something to the effect of 'either you're on the bus or you're under the bus,'" M.H. later recalled. So when Diack asked him to wear a wire, he wasn't exactly asking for a favour. He was offering a deal.

"Would I testify and stuff?" M.H. replied.

"Yes."

M.H. did not immediately commit to siding with the police against his brothers. But neither did he refuse. If he could betray the No Surrender Crew and the man he called president, why not Taz Sandham and the rest of the killers? He had already accepted a thousand-dollar payment from the police just a few days earlier (which he had wheedled out of them by complaining that he couldn't afford bicycles for his children), and he seemed to be getting cosier with his sworn enemies in law enforcement all the time. Whatever M.H.'s answer that day, the Winnipeg Bandidos were on the verge of being betrayed.

Meanwhile, the police weren't sitting idly by, waiting for their snitch to see things their way. They were already all over Sandham's group. Undercover police officers were following at a discreet distance when Marcelo Aravena and Dwight Mushey dropped by to visit M.H., who was in hospital for tests on his gall bladder. The bikers were in a small room in the emergency ward, cordoned off by a curtain, when Mushey started talking about the last moments of Goldberg Flanz's life. Mushey still resented having to do the dirty work of finishing off the prospect Bandido with the very pistol Sandham claimed had jammed. How could Mushey respect a man who would cower like that and hand off the gun? M.H. later recalled Mushey describing how Flanz "looked at him just before he shot him. About his eyes being wide. It was almost as if he wanted to say something."

Aravena said at the hospital that he was afraid he might also be murdered that night, as the killers pared down the list of potential witnesses. "You guys came pretty close at one point," Mushey confirmed, sounding now as if he were describing nothing more serious than dropping a player from a beer-league hockey team.

Taz Sandham wasn't answering his cellphone or his door.

He was consumed by the wrenching certainty that the police were dogging his every step. The snare that caught him, though, was one he stepped in quite by chance. An off-duty Winnipeg police officer named Grant Goulet, from the organized crime unit, was in the waiting room of the city's Chamois Car Wash late on the morning of Monday, April 10, when Sandham drove up in his red SUV. Goulet recognized Sandham, who signed in under the name "Shane Stevenson," but Sandham didn't recognize the cop. Goulet noted with interest as Sandham had the interior of the Blazer detailed, in hopes of shampooing away any potential clues.

The following Saturday, a police surveillance team that included Goulet started tailing Sandham. The paranoid biker wasn't an easy target. He would reverse direction without warning, or meander in a circular route, looping blocks entirely. There were also stops at fast-food restaurants. But as spooked as he clearly was, he didn't seem to notice the police team when he finally came to a stop at the Walmart in Selkirk, about forty kilometres northeast of Winnipeg. This time, he signed his name "Jon Sandam" on a work order and claimed to be from the nearby town of St. Clements.

Officers watched as Sandham's tires were replaced and the used ones were returned to him, wrapped in plastic. Police followed him and looked on as he heaved the old tires into a ravine outside town. Once Sandham was comfortably out of sight, police climbed down the ravine and retrieved the tires, which they noted were actually much better than the ones he had just had installed. Then they replaced the tires with others, in case Sandham should come back to check on them. Two days later he did, and apparently didn't suspect a thing. Meanwhile, forensic testing found that the tire treads and mud from the discarded tires were an exact match for tire tracks and soil from Kellestine's farm and the field where the bodies had been dumped.[28]

The noose around Sandham and his co-conspirators tightened still further on Sunday, April 16, when Diack drove M.H. to the Fairmont Hotel in downtown Winnipeg, where Detective Constable Mark Loader and Detective Constable Jeff Gateman of the Ontario Provincial Police were waiting. M.H. later claimed that Diack told him en route to the meeting, "I made sure you'll get a large sum of money so you can live comfortable." A figure they discussed, he said, was $750,000.

There was a time, back when Ripper Fullager was a young man, when bikers boasted about not being materialistic, wanting little more than the vests on their backs and the Harleys under them. But the lucrative drug trade had changed all that, as had the often-related vocation of snitching to the police. For bikers who chose to betray their brothers, an informant's payoff was like a lottery jackpot. M.H. may have been dreaming of ways to spend his blood money as he and his police handler sped through the dark streets.

Once he began talking with the Ontario officers, however, M.H. was cautioned that he shouldn't expect to get rich from his testimony. They could make their case without him; it would just be more difficult. If M.H. was accepted into any witness protection arrangement, he would be expected to eventually get a job to support himself, under an assumed identity, once he was moved somewhere far from his underworld contacts. He would have to agree to settle for free rent, medical care and $1,300 for living expenses, plus $350 or so monthly for prescription drugs—not much more than he made on welfare back in his drug-dealing days.

But that didn't mean the police weren't offering a sweet deal. There was still much for M.H. to gain by cooperating with the police. He could gain immunity from prosecution for the eight murders, each of which carried the potential of a life prison term. The possibility of dodging a lengthy stretch in jail proved enough to turn M.H. against his biker brothers. Whatever money they offered only sweetened the deal.

First, however, he would have to convince the police he was a credible witness. That was by no means a slam dunk. He had already churned out an impressive array of lies to cover his own tracks, and was in a poor position to start telling the truth now. M.H. had originally told Diack that the Manitoba Bandidos had gone to Ontario to be officially promoted to full-patch status. Then he changed his tune and suggested that the massacre was part of a larger war between the Bandidos and their rivals in the Hells Angels. According to the story he told, the Winnipeg Bandidos had received instructions from the mother chapter in Texas to begin a war with the Angels as part of mounting continent-wide tensions between the clubs. Anthony Benesh III of Travis County, Texas, had ended up with a sniper's bullet between his eyes as he walked out of a fast food outlet store after ignoring warnings from Texas Bandidos to stop wearing the Hells Angels' colours and to abandon his plans to set up a chapter of the Angels in Austin. Shortly afterwards, Hells Angels leader Roger Mariani of Stratford, Connecticut, was gunned down as he rode on Interstate 95 in West Haven with other bikers. There wasn't any connection between these murders and the Shedden massacre, but they made M.H.'s lie a lot more credible.

Even when he vowed to come clean, the snitch offered up a fanciful patchwork of lies, truth and speculation. He began by telling the Ontario investigators about the dispute between the Toronto and Winnipeg chapters of the Bandidos over dues money. The sums must have seemed absurdly small to the investigators, when put up against the magnitude of the slaughter. Among the points of contention in the dispute was Toronto's efforts to charge the Winnipeggers a $750-per-member initiation fee, half again as much as the $500 the Winnipeggers expected to pay.

As M.H. talked, Loader appeared to already know what had happened. Clearly, someone else had been telling the club's secrets. M.H. should have known he would have to stick to the truth. But that was more than he could manage.

The initial purpose of inviting the No Surrender Crew to the barn, he said, was to expel them from the club, not to murder them—despite the hard-to-explain stratagem of positioning a sniper in the rafters. "We were just trying to get them together . . . We were just there to pull patches." As M.H. told the story, Boxer Muscedere refused to give up his patch, even though he had no gun and the Winnipeggers were armed. "The next thing you know, [Kellestine is] taking them out, one at a time, and they're not coming back."

For some reason, the informant told the investigators that Kellestine and the Winnipeggers had been expecting two members of the club's elite Nomads chapter from the U.S. to arrive and help out, but they never arrived. Still, everything depended on the split second that took Chopper Raposo's life. As M.H. told the story, the bikers agreed that Sandham was not to blame for the exchange of gunfire that started the carnage. "Even Bam Bam agreed Chopper did shoot first," M.H. said, invoking the word of a man he had helped kill. "So, like, he had no choice . . . because if he would have got the other barrel off, he probably would have killed Taz."

M.H. sounded a little dazed as he told the police investigators: "But, I mean, the others . . . I don't know what the hell happened there . . . It just went downhill after that. So for the longest time he [Kellestine] kept saying everyone's going home."

It all sounded unreal, as M.H. recalled things. "I wasn't even sure we were going to get out of there that night . . . The only time I felt safe was when I was actually in the vehicle, going home."

The police officers stressed that any potential witness deal would fall apart if they ever discovered that he was lying, and M.H. swore that he was telling the truth. Then he went home to his wife and lied to her that he had just cut a deal with police for seventy thousand dollars a year. He had to keep lying when he got home because he was afraid he would lose custody rights to his children if she refused to move with him to a new location, under a new name. "I just told her that to appease her," he explained later. "I basically said that to her to get her to come with me."

Near Shedden, police officers walked side by side along the ditches that run parallel to Highway 401, searching for any physical evidence to help make sense of the slaughter. Perry McMillan was in the area too, as foreman of a road crew that cleaned road kill and litter from the roadway. Close to Kellestine's farmhouse, at the CNR overpass near Union Road, McMillan picked up a set of car keys with a tab bearing the licence plate number AWHN 276. McMillan delivered the keys to the Ontario Provincial Police, who determined that they belonged to a Pontiac Grand Prix that had been rented by the common-law wife of Little Mikey Trotta, one of the Shedden victims. It was the same Pontiac that had been discovered on the Stafford Line two days before, holding the body of Jamie (Goldberg) Flanz beside the child seat.

An OPP officer dressed in a sterile white jumpsuit was combing through the basement of the Kellestine farmhouse on April 21, almost two weeks after Kellestine was arrested. Such work can become tedious, even when it's done at the scene of the largest massacre in the province's history. The officer lifted a small flap in the ceiling, shone his light inside and spotted something curious squirrelled away. He reached in, pulled out the object and saw that it was the butt end of a rifle. That brought to three the number of rifles in the farmhouse so far, but none of them had been used on the night of April 7–8.

Either the killers had secreted the murder weapons off Kellestine's property immediately after the slaughter, or they had hidden them extremely well.

Fours days later, the police were still combing through the detritus of the Kellestine property. An OPP officer poked behind a panel in the house and found a piece of towel wrapped around what felt like a firearm. Inside was an oily cloth, and inside that was a Mauser model 1943 pistol. It was in poor condition, its metal pockmarked by corrosion. It also wasn't a murder weapon, at least not in the past decade or so. In the west wall of Kellestine's garage, in the centre shelving, police found a shotgun. It was also an illegal weapon, since its barrel was sawed-off to a pistol-sized 12¾ inches, but it wasn't one of the murder weapons from the massacre either.

As they continued their search of Kellestine's workshop, police found themselves drawn to a blue vise attached to a workbench. There were hacksaws and iron filings nearby, signs that a gun barrel had been cut down there. The tools were seized for further study. It was all interesting, but also extremely frustrating: police had been intensely searching the property for more than two weeks, and though plenty of the bloodsucking wood ticks that infested the house found *them*, they still hadn't found any of the weapons actually used in the massacre. It would be nice to have at least one murder weapon. Meanwhile, public scrutiny of the case was enormous. The thought of being outsmarted by Weiner Kellestine was almost too embarrassing to contemplate.

Fate had offered a bit of black comedy the day before,

when an agitated Kellestine appeared in court for a vide-
otaped appearance from the Elgin-Middlesex Detention
Centre in St. Thomas. Some out-of-town news reports
had confused him with a hapless local bank robber by
the same name who, in the words of one misinformed
reporter, "was known to police as a former bank robber identifiable by his incompetence" and who quickly
earned "a reputation for being caught within minutes of
the crimes."

It was an easy mistake to make. Both Wayne Kelles-
tines lived on the outskirts of London, both were in their
late fifties and both had troubled relationships with the
law. The local bank robber, however, was Wayne Forest
Kellestine, and he was more Forrest Gump than Charles
Manson. At one particularly low point in his criminal
career, he was apprehended by police as he tried to flee
from a heist on public transit. Weiner's full name was
Wayne Earl Kellestine, and he clearly wanted the public
record set straight that Monday morning. He was a one
percenter biker accused of mass murder, not some bum-
bling bank robber.

"Your name?" Justice of the Peace Isaac Condo asked
through the video hookup with the detention centre.

"Wayne *Earl* Kellestine," he barked, emphasizing his
middle name with more than a little pride. After all, it had
taken the police hours to catch him, not mere minutes.

Constable Timothy Diack's notes for May 7 indicate that M.H. had decided to become an official police agent and to wear a wire. He was henceforth an official police agent. Agents work with police as an active part of investigations and are the police equivalent of spies. They take orders from police handlers and testify in court, in this case, before their former clubmates. For one percenter bikers, "agent," "snitch" and "informant" all translate as "rat." A popular T-shirt sold at one percenter events shows two pistols being fired and a hospital monitor recording a flat line. The slogan on the T-shirt reads, SNITCHES ARE A DYING BREED.

In early May, M.H. was back in the hospital for tests on his gall bladder. His heart must have begun beating a little faster when Dwight Mushey and Marcelo Aravena dropped by to visit. His police recording device was covered only by his flimsy hospital gown.

Mushey had a suggestion for the gall bladder, should it have to be removed: "Fucking keep it," he said.

"Pickle it and put it in a jar," Aravena chimed in, trying to join in the fun but still sounding a bit melancholy.

Mushey was upbeat, teasing Aravena, who had been promoted to prospect Bandido status since his return from Shedden. That was the first official step to full-patch status and gave him the right to wear a Bandidos leather vest. He still didn't have the stature to wear a Fat Mexican crest on his back, but the promotion was significant nonetheless. Aravena's mother had thought of making his vest from a pair of leather pants, but they decided to buy one instead. Some bikers spend five hundred dollars for their club vests, but Aravena settled for a twenty-nine-dollar number. It had little straps on the back, which M.H. said made him look like a waiter. Whatever the case, Aravena was clearly happy.

"Marcelo's prancing around like a princess right now, with his new vest on," Mushey said.

M.H. was wearing a vest of a very different kind, and it was funnelling a whole new source of lies to the police. Presumably to keep his club in order, Sandham had invented some good news, which Mushey duly delivered to M.H. and his police handlers: Winnipeg had been granted a full charter in the Bandidos Nation. They believed they were now real bikers. They could all enjoy the privilege of sewing "Canada" patches on their vests, and could begin to recruit new members to serve under them.

The reality wasn't quite as glamorous. The patches were made by Aravena's mother in Winnipeg, even though club rules required that all Fat Mexican patches must be supplied by a mother of a different sort: the Texas mother chapter. In effect, the Winnipeggers had ended eight lives of men they called "brother" so that they could occasionally wear counterfeit crests of a cartoon character on their backs. The Texans would be livid if they were to hear of the latest Canadian breach of club rules. Meanwhile, Aravena's mother sewed away dutifully, presumably as they spoke. "Yours should be finished today," Mushey told M.H. in an attempt to lift his mood.

After skulking and waiting for the worst for a couple of weeks, Taz Sandham eventually emerged from hiding. His first venture as the president of a biker gang was to set up a tattoo parlour, a popular sideline for outlaw bikers. It allows them to easily launder money, since it's impossible to prove how many tattoos they did or did not ink. They can also count on their clubmates and friends to keep them busy with work. The trouble for Sandham was that he didn't have any money to launder even if he'd wanted to. And he didn't really have any friends, either.

In a May 10 email exchange, a biker named John told Sandham he was eager to join the Bandidos. Apparently, Taz was letting him sign on as a probationary member, skipping the prospect stage altogether. In the meantime, John wanted to arrange a tattoo for his girlfriend: "Michelle wants some ink very soon to go with her new tittys," was how he framed the matter.

"Of course I would give your old lady a tat for free," Taz offered.

In the meantime, however, Taz volunteered that he was "in a pickle." He was willing to let John buy into his tattoo parlour, as a "silent partner," for just two thousand dollars. It would also be nice if John could expedite some club dues. And perhaps he would like to purchase a fresh tattoo for himself. A new probationary member like John was eligible to have BFFB, for "Bandidos Forever, Forever Bandidos," and GFBD, for "God Forgives, Bandidos Don't," inked onto his body. He would have to wait until he had full-patch status before Taz could also provide him with a likeness of the Fat Mexican, but there were plenty of other tattoo possibilities in the meantime. Taz knew it was a little embarrassing for a big-time biker leader like him to be hustling for money like a midway barker. But slaughtering his brothers didn't free him from such mundane things as having to pay the bills.

"It's just because of all these club commitments these past few months have fucked things up a little," Taz explained. "Haven't had time to do enough tats to make some real money."

John sounded sympathetic as Taz volunteered that he had just two days to come up with five hundred for rent. He could help Taz out soon, once he got his tax refund. There was also a wistful discussion about ten thousand dollars he said his wife was owed by her ex.

It's tough to maintain the aura of an all-powerful organized criminal while having to mooch money, but Taz was willing to try. He talked tough now, as befitted a big-time biker boss. "Sounds like I need to pay Michelle's ex a visit and discuss this matter with him."

John was hundreds of miles away, somewhere in northwestern Ontario. He mentioned that he sure would like his probationary patch—could Taz somehow Xpresspost it to him? Ripper would have been mortified by the breathtaking breach of biker etiquette. In his day, anyone asking for a patch—or even asking when he might receive a patch—could expect a beating, followed by banishment from the club.

It was impossible for Taz to turn back now, but he also wasn't moving forward. The harder he pushed, and the more power he gained, the farther he fell from Ripper's one percenter ideals of brotherhood. Ripper's Bandidos were about almost childlike honesty among brothers, while Sandham's club was built on a foundation of lies and betrayal. It was as though Taz truly believed that if he lied long enough and strongly enough, the fabrications might someday become truth. On this day, however, Taz wasn't in a philosophical mood to think about such things. He clearly wasn't getting any money in the near future from John and wasn't in the mood to bend the rules any further for him. "Unfortunately that is not the way we do things, I kind of bent tradition by even telling you, LOL. We have to present it to you in person, its kind of a initiation thing."

CHAPTER 22

Create This Brotherhood

Is this the promised end?
KING LEAR, ACT 5, SCENE 3

I thought there would be a helluva lot more . . .
There was nothing.
BANDIDO PIERRE (CARLITTO) ARAGON COMMENTS ON
THE LACK OF SUPPORT HE FEELS AFTER MURDERS

On Wednesday, May 3, a police wiretap picked up yet another phone call between Carlitto Aragon and a guy called Mick the Nomad in England. Both the Hells Angels and Bandidos have elite chapters called Nomads, which are made up of senior members who don't take day-to-day direction from others in the club, largely travelling where they want, doing what they want. Perhaps because he was what he might have called a 110 percent one per-center, Mick had been troubled that no Bandido from outside Canada had bothered to attend any of the funerals of the eight murdered men. "There's, like, two thousand of us in the world," Mick the Nomad said. "I'm sure

someone, somewhere could have gotten to the funerals."
Mick didn't, of course, but he stayed in regular contact
with Aragon at a time when the latter biker was pretty
much the only guy in Toronto wearing a Fat Mexican.

Carlitto complained that just seven hundred dollars
had been donated to the families of the victims through
the online PayPal network. That came to less than a hundred dollars per murder victim from the international
brotherhood. Members had an excuse for not coming to
Canada to pay their last respects, because of tightened
border security after the 9/11 terrorist attacks, but there
was no nice way to explain this cheapness. It was as if they
belonged to a tiny club that only dreamed it was part of
something great. "I thought there would be a helluva lot
more," Carlitto said. "There was nothing."

Carlitto hinted that his safety might be at risk if he
were to go to a top Bandidos meeting in the U.S. Clearly,
he felt that Taz might have poisoned the waters, setting up
an ambush. "Just to be on the safe side, I thought I'd rather
go to a world meeting," he said. He noted that the Ontario
Provincial Police had warned him that all of the Bandidos
in Ontario were still considered to be in danger. His voice
sounded drained of emotion as he continued, "There's so
much I'm dealing with and this is just another thing . . . It's
pretty much 'Don't trust anybody' right now."

"You can trust everyone in Europe," Mick the Nomad
said grandly. He added that perhaps things weren't as
bad as they seemed with Pervert Bare, the club secretary
in Texas. "That could be Pervert's bad English. His English is not perfect." Then Mick the Nomad pressed again

for Carlitto to meet with his Bandido brothers overseas. "Once you're here, you'll pay for nothing and you'll see true brotherhood."

"It's like I have to create this brotherhood," Carlitto said, sounding thoroughly depressed and alone. But it is a lot easier to destroy something than it is to create it.

In the wake of the slaughter that decimated the Bandidos in Canada, it slowly dawned on those who remained, both in Toronto and in Winnipeg, that they might have more to fear from the mother chapter than from each other. A few days after he was on the phone with England's only Bandido, Carlitto got the first of many emails from Pervert Bare. Sandham was cc'd under one of his code names, John Smith. Perhaps Bare didn't know that the two Canadians hated each other; maybe he just didn't care. From his vantage point, everyone north of the border wearing a Fat Mexican patch looked alike: like an idiot.

The idea of a mother chapter may seem reassuring when times are good, but when most of your friends have just been killed and a guy you've never met would rather lecture you about trivial-seeming rules from thousands of miles away—and charge you an annual fee for the privilege—it is to be expected that a chapter might prefer to think of autonomy. But rules in the one percenter world are not meant to be open to interpretation. And neither is the question of who answers to whom. So Pervert Bare wasn't just refereeing a family squabble, he was stamping out insurrection.

Pervert's tone was peremptory and hinted at the trouble to come. "Send me a picture of your self so I know who I am talking to," Pervert ordered. "I have dealt with a few people from Canada in the past and I have never gotten the CORRECT story ever. I never understand why this is. When I was in Canada I met a lot and many did not even know how to ride a motorcycle. I hope you take the time to read the by-laws I sent you. That is the real understanding of who we are. Who we are not is CRIMINALS. There may be a few scattered here and there like every org. but we are a motorcycle club with riding principals [sic] first. Being a criminal street gang and thug will only end with troubles . . ."

Sandham was first off the mark with his reply, bubbling with Fat Mexican fervour the next day. He didn't seem chastened at all by Pervert's scathing email, which ordered the Canadians not to act like criminals; rather, he sounded like a keener on the first day of school. Taz Sandham was at his most animated when he was sucking up, and he was doing that now for all he was worth. He welcomed the Texan's tough words, just as he had once fawned over Boxer and Chopper. The subject line on his email read, "Canada run right way now," and his opening gambit was "Right on my brother!! Thanks for letting me know what is up."

Then he told Pervert that the troubles lay with Carlitto and they should be immediately addressed. "He is not adhering to our protocol," Taz continued. "'THE BANDIDO WAY' You are exactly right, this is our way, and all of us here in Manitoba ride and live by the by-laws ... He sounds like he is trying to grab anybody and get them to join. Fuck that shit ... I have an idea who two of them probably are and they are NOT Bandido material and do NOT meet the criteria. 'THE MAN MAKES THE PATCH. THE PATCH DOES NOT MAKE THE MAN' exactly my brother, words to live by.

"In two years he has always come to runs in Toronto on four wheels. Like you said so very well, No bike, Your not a Bandido. From now on Canada will be run the TRUE BANDIDO WAY!! ...

"MUCH LOVE, LOYALTY, and RESPECT."

Taz sent another email to Bandido Pervert later that day, and gushed on further: "This Brotherhood means everything to me, and to wear the best colours is [*sic*] the world is a great honour for me."

Carlitto Aragon didn't bother currying favour with the Americans. Why should he need an American's permission to conduct his business? Instead, he telephoned Australia in hope of support from Bandido leader Jason Addison. With virtually everyone else from his chapter either murdered, in jail or on the run, Carlitto might be considered the No Surrender Crew president now. But he had next to no members to command. He didn't even have a patch to wear on his back, as his had been confiscated by the police during a raid, and the Americans wouldn't condescend to send up any more patches. If he was going to find brotherhood, he had to look to the other side of the world.

Without hearing a lot of details, Addison blamed the mess on the American secretary. "Fucking Pervert," Addison said. "I just want to bash him on the head."

"We have a chance here to build now, despite the unfortunate circumstances," Carlitto said.

"They're too busy sitting down in Texas with their head stuck up their ass," Addison replied. Addison had just been appointed Australia's national president for a new four-year term, but he was quick to tell Aragon that he didn't have much fondness for Jeff Pike, the Texas-based worldwide president of the Bandidos. Pike had never been elected by members, but he hadn't gotten into trouble with the law, either. He had been appointed to the post by George Wegers just before Wegers began a prison stretch.

Bandidos like to have their leaders on the streets and not in jail, and so Pike got the job on an interim basis. Wegers was freed from prison a month before the Shedden Massacre, but Pike still hadn't given up his caretaker role, much like Boxer had refused to step aside for Weiner Kellestine a few years earlier. Wegers, who was a backer of the No Surrender Crew, didn't yet have the clout to assert himself, leaving Pike as the only person in the Bandido Nation allowed to wear a patch with *El Presidente* on his back. They might be one percenter bikers, but Bandido politics were as convoluted and poisonous as anything found in a mainstream parliament or corporate boardroom. "It's the same fucking shit," Addison said. "It makes me absolutely wild."

Carlitto noted that Sandham's Manitoba chapter had been having talks with the Texans. Hopefully, he could parlay Addison's anger against the Americans into some kind of support against Taz. "When they started talking to Texas, they got on their high horse," Carlitto said. After that, the Americans cut off their support to the Toronto chapter, while the Winnipeggers began sending their dues directly to the Texas headquarters.

"America will be looking at making some extra money," Addison said. Then he guessed that the problem might not be Winnipeg. The Australian president suspected that the Texans were wheeling and dealing over territory with the Hells Angels, and that they had sold out the No Surrender Crew in the process. The way Addison saw things, the Americans figured the Torontonians were no more than pawns they could trade to suit their owns needs.

"It's a world club, man," Carlitto said.

"America actually hasn't got that much power," Addison said. He alluded to the famous statement by Theodore Roosevelt, the U.S. president in the early years of the twentieth century—"Speak softly and carry a big stick and you will go far"—saying, "Their big stick isn't a big stick."

However, their stick was big enough to intimidate Carlitto Aragon twelve hours later when he spoke on the phone with Pervert Bare. Pervert told Carlitto bluntly that the Canadian Bandidos fell under the authority of the United States, even if they were originally sponsored into the club by Danish Bandidos. The rules establishing the hierarchy within the Bandido Nation may be as complex and as iron-clad as the Treaty of Paris, but no one is going to go to the Supreme Court or the UN to adjudicate between rival interpretations. In the one percenter world, making your argument often means making it loudly and without a great deal of introspection. Bare was going to tell Canada what to do, and Canada was invited to shut up and comply.

Pervert tore into Aragon the way an army drill sergeant might speak to a dim-witted private, repeating the familiar litany of complaints against the No Surrender Crew, including what to Aragon seemed the trivial question of where the patches were manufactured.

But Carlitto wasn't interested in discussing the finer points of the Bandido by-laws, no doubt because he knew he was in grievous violation of many of them. Instead, he wanted to talk about the big picture—life and death, or peace and war, not little pieces of cloth bearing the likeness of a cartoon character. He said that he had been recently in Manitoba, trying to make contact with members there. He put a different spin on his westward trip than M.H. or Taz Sandham. As he described it, they weren't a hit team trying to seize control of territory; they were reaching out for brotherhood. "These guys avoided me at all costs . . . ignoring the boys over here," Carlitto protested, sounding a little offended.

Pervert softened, just a little, as he said that he had gotten along well with Crash Kriarakis and Bam Bam Salerno. But he was not to be distracted from the central point: that Canada fell under the authority of the United States. It was not debatable, no matter what anyone else in the Bandidos Nation might say. "You guys are directly under the United States, under North America . . . Not Jason [Addison] . . . You're not independent."

"We had eight funerals and I haven't seen one American brother," Carlitto replied heatedly.

Pervert wasn't backing off. He wasn't apologizing. This was a time for order. He wasn't in the mood for dishing out sympathy. In Texas, prospects for the Bandidos signed their Harleys over to the club as a surety of sorts. In Canada, men somehow became full members without even knowing how to start up a motorcycle. Pervert said he was particularly unimpressed by Eric (The Red) McMillan, who had once served as the Canadian national *sargento de armas*. "He didn't even know how to ride a motorcycle. No clue . . . Do you see where we get our views from?"

He seemed to gasp in horror for a second at the memory of another Canadian biker who asked to ride on the back of an American Bandido's Harley. Bikers call that the "bitch seat," because that's where their "old ladies" ride. "This is what we're getting out of Canada," Pervert said.

The only way anything was going to get sorted out, beginning with the Canadians' reputation, was a face-to-face explanation in Texas. Until then, the remnants of the No Surrender Crew could expect nothing from the mother chapter. They could also forget about going around the Americans' backs and appealing to international members for support. "There is no world meeting," Pervert said. "Somebody needs to come to Texas."

By May 23, Taz was far more blunt in his emails to Pervert, openly lobbying against his old enemy. Carlitto, he said, was a problem they needed to address. He didn't even own a motorcycle; he was a gangster, not a real biker like themselves, Taz claimed. "Brother, he emailed me, pissed off that I said anything about him not having a bike, and he said he was in the process of buying a bike soon, possibly Chopper's . . ." Sandham went on to say that Carlitto joined the club—or "patched up"—so that he could further his criminal career. "He (Bandido Carlitto) was patched up for reasons other than riding and Brotherhood and he is NOT an original member," Sandham wrote the Texan. "He also has threatened me once again for talking to my BROTHERS (that's his style)."

As Sandham told things, he had to take threats from Aragon pretty seriously, and he hinted that the Toronto biker had already shown up on his doorstep once before with what Taz believed was the intention of shortening his life. Sounding like a grade-school snitch, Taz continued that his rival Carlitto "was sent hear [sic] along with a non member by vehicle for other reasons . . . (I have to talk to you in person about that . . .) some of us were away so he harrassed [sic] our families instead . . . Because of this my Brother, I cannot be in the presence of Carlitto."

In other words, Taz claimed it was too dangerous to be in the presence of his Toronto biker brother.

The Hells Angels held a Central Canada officers' meeting in Toronto in June 2006, where members were given copies of an intercepted email sent out by Carlitto Aragon. No explanation was offered as to how the email was obtained. It spoke of hopes of rebirth, drawing upon former members of the Loners:

... I am going to start of [*sic*] by saying that I am proud to be a member of the best motorcycle club in the world. God rest my brothers souls who have passed away on to the forever chapter. We are having talk with 30 ex-members of the defunct Loners Motorcycle Club and also a Dirty Pack Nomad from Germany. We are resuming where we left off. Everyone of them has a harley and is interested to become members of BANDIDOS MC CANADA. Our goal is to have a new clubhouse by next year. This year "On the Road" will be postponed but will continue once a date is set. I have managed to recover some of our past brothers information and club wear. Unfortunately the cops are having a field day and have seize 9 patches, 50 club member shirts, 1 motorcycle, 2 computers so far to my knowledge. BANDIDOS MC CANADA has the name NO SURRENDER CREW for a reason cause we don't give up and fall down. We were also in the process of setting up a

Manitoba Probationary Charter. Since our brothers passing, communication has not been reestablished . . . Thank you for all the support worldwide. THE BANDIDO NATION WILL BE PROUD.[29]

Soon, rival versions of the truth were popping up in in-boxes around the world. On May 26, Taz was on the computer to Carlitto's Australian contact, Jason Addison, drawing him into the Canadian squabble by telling him that Manitoba now ran the Bandidos for all of Canada. "We are the only existing chapter with 13 guys for which I am president, as well as a 35 member support club," Taz wrote, inviting the Australian to take sides. "Basically we are all of Canada right now."

As an act of diplomacy, Sandham's email could hardly have been a bigger blunder. The Texas Bandidos weren't amused to hear that the Winnipeggers were calling themselves a full chapter. It meant nothing that Sandham claimed they had the backing of the Washington State arm of the club. At first it had seemed that the Americans had become embroiled in a squabble between two Canadian chapters. Now the Canadians were caught up in a spat between American chapters. Wegers might say one thing, and Pike another, but it was no use invoking one Bandido's authority to the other, since neither one acknowledged the other's power. "Texas basically said, 'We don't care what Washington State says,'" M.H. later recalled. "'We run Bandidos worldwide.'"

The Texans emailed that they wanted to meet the Winnipeggers face to face. Taz wanted M.H. and Dwight Mushey to travel with him, but they both declined. Taz liked to do every-thing else by himself, so why shouldn't he face the heat alone too? At first, Taz thought of flying or driving his wife's car, but he ultimately decided to do the bikerly thing. By the time he rolled up on his black Harley to the border crossing at Neche, South Dakota, on May 30, authorities were waiting for him—M.H.'s steady stream of information meant that the police were always up to speed. Border agents at all Canada–U.S. border crossings had been issued bulletins telling them to be on the lookout for Michael Sandham, who was described as the "president of the Bandidos motorcycle gang in Winnipeg." The Texans might not have acknowledged the little biker's authority, but the cops did.

When Sandham appeared at his station, ninety minutes from Winnipeg, border guard Tim Vetter typed his name into the computer and found there was a "possible situation." Sandham said he was en route to Sturgis, saying he wanted to take a look at the town before its August biker rally. Vetter checked out Sandham's backpack and saddlebags, which contained nothing to indicate he was connected to the Bandidos, and couldn't help but note how calm the little biker appeared. "He was not agitated whatsoever," he later said.

Once across the border, Sandham rode immediately

towards Texas, and when he arrived on the outskirts of Houston, he phoned Bandido Pervert and was told he would have to wait a couple of hours before they could get together that evening. He checked into Room 309 of the Comfort Inn in North Houston. If things went as planned, his status would be far different by the time he checked out. He was nothing if not ambitious, and if his direct appeal to the mother chapter went smoothly, his rise to power would be official: he could ride home as the bona fide president of the Bandidos for all of Canada, from coast to coast to coast.

Later that afternoon, Sandham rode off looking for an Exxon station where they were supposed to meet. At first, Taz struggled to find his way, and when he stopped people for directions, they couldn't speak English.

Eventually, he found his way to the gas station, where he met Pervert and a greying biker. They directed him to a bar, which they said was their place. He was introduced at the bar to someone named "Jeff," and Sandham later said he didn't realize the man was wearing a leather vest with an *El Presidente* patch or that he was the top Bandido in the world, Jeff Pike.

Before they could talk, Pike and a biker named Scarey Larry, the North Houston *sargento de armas*, led Sandham into the washroom. Scarey Larry stood watch at the door, barring entry to patrons who needed to use the facilities, as Sandham was ordered to strip.

The bikers checked him for hidden recording devices, then rifled through his wallet, checking his identification. Sandham later said that they apologized, but he wasn't offended, and in fact he respected their regard for security.

Then it was out to the bar, where the topic of Shedden naturally arose quickly, and Sandham said he had lied to them when he said that he had left Kellestine's farm by the time the slaughter started. Pervert Bare would later tell police that he asked Sandham what he knew about the Ontario killings. As Bare later recalled, Sandham gave a strange and vague answer: he probably did know about the murders. Asked to clarify what this meant, Sandham then called Kellestine a "crazy motherfucker."

As Sandham later recalled, he complained to the Texans that Carlitto had been dispatched by Boxer to kill him. Pike apparently wasn't shocked, as Sandham said Pike gestured towards *El Secretario* Bill Sartelle and said: "Well, orders are orders. If I order him [Sartelle] to go take a piss in that corner, he'd better be getting up and taking a piss in that corner."

Sandham sipped a little on his Coca-Cola and then was dispatched back to his hotel as the bikers hunkered down to transact confidential club business.

On June 1, while Taz was still in Texas, Pervert Bare telephoned Carlitto Aragon. He still wasn't offering sympathy; instead, he demanded an explanation for what he had been hearing from Taz. Pervert had heard that the Toronto chapter was bragging about recruiting new members, despite specific orders against this from the mother chapter. "You don't run Canada," Pervert said. "That's a fact."

Pervert noted that the Toronto chapter's Internet guest book made it sound as though they were free to recruit new members. That wasn't about to happen. "I'm not stupid," Pervert said. "Crash was cleaning the club up. We were sick and tired of the fucking gangster mentality in Canada . . . All it was, was 'Fuck the Hells Angels, fuck the Hells Angels, fuck the Hells Angels.' Down here, we don't have that. That's why we don't have any problems."

Pervert was in high gear now, too angry to stop. Canada was a small country with a history of presenting huge problems. "We don't want Canada to get any bigger at all because of all the bullshit . . . Canada has not done what all of the countries have done to be Bandidos . . . It's all about being bigger than the Hells Angels . . . It's not about the first priority. It's about other bullshit . . ."

When Carlitto finally got a word in, he complained about Sandham and his direct approaches to the mother chapter. Unaware that Little Beaker was just around the corner from Pervert, he grumbled, "It's just a bunch of backdoor bullshit."

Pervert shot back that the Texans weren't impressed with what they had seen from the north. Clearly, Taz Sandham hadn't impressed him much, either. "We don't know that you have a clue on what it takes to run a normal chapter, to be part of a normal chapter. It hasn't been normal up there for years."

Sandham later said he waited all day and night for a call from the Texans. Finally, he spoke to Pervert on Saturday, June 3, and was asked: "They said you were a police officer or received police officer training. Is that true?"

Sandham said he gave his standard lie, about only being an auxiliary officer. He asked Pervert if they could get together for a coffee, but Pervert was busy with club business. The Texans had some more investigating to do. Sandham said he got a queasy feeling that he would soon meet an unwelcome visitor if he didn't get out of town quickly. "I thought it was a set-up. I thought there was going to be somebody coming to kill me."

As Sandham began his ride home that day, Pike sent out an email to all Bandidos chapters around the world, advising them that Sandham had been kicked out of the club and that all Canadian memberships were suspended. Short of being murdered or beaten, things couldn't have gone worse for Taz in his attempt at biker diplomacy. It was as if the eight murders and all of his lies and schemes were for naught, and Taz was lucky to get out of Texas with his own skin intact.

Pervert Bare was on the phone on Tuesday, June 6, to Carlitto Aragon, making sure he knew that all of the Canadian Bandidos' memberships were now suspended. There would be no more Bandidos anywhere north of the border—not in Quebec, Ontario, Alberta or anywhere else in Canada. Everyone was barred from the club until further notice. "Carlitto, if you ever want to get anything going up there, you'd better shut the fuck up and just listen," Pervert said.

"I guess it's just been a waste of time for the past few years," Carlitto said. His voice had a weary, dreamy tone.

Pervert wasn't about to let up on his lecture. Taz Sandham's smears on Carlitto's reputation had clearly had an effect on him. "I tell you ten times not to bring in new guys and you do it right away . . . Fuck, that was horrible . . . Everybody up there is so fucked . . . The name is fucked. The reputation is fucked." The lecture shifted to the massacre. There was no mention that it was the Americans who had enlisted Weiner Kellestine to pull the patches of the No Surrender Crew. Instead, Pervert said he couldn't believe reports that Kellestine participated in the murders. Whatever the American secretary's strong points were, he was clearly no long-distance judge of character.

Perhaps, sometime in the far-off future, the Torontonians might be able to redeem themselves, mused Pervert. There was an enormous amount of work to do in the meantime. "You guys build another club up from scratch." That new chapter, if it was ever created, would have to learn to listen. "We live by guidelines," he said.

Jeff Pike put the same sentiments in writing the next

day in an email to bikers throughout the Bandido Nation, under the heading "Canadian solution."

"Ever since the very first patches were issued to the original Rock Machine members there has been nothing but lies and deceit running rampant through your country. They totally mis-represented themselves. Claiming to be a Motorcycle Club. When in fact Motorcycles were the last thing on their agenda." Then he zeroed in on the Canadians who would read his message:

> You people change Patches like you change your underwear! Carlitto has told us several times that all membership has been frozen . . .
>
> Carlitto! If you ever want to get anything going up there you better shut the fuck up and start listening!!
>
> Taz was here in Houston last week. Within 10 hours of meeting him, The OPP and Biker Enforcement Unit from Canada was at my door.
>
> As it turns out, Taz is or was a police officer in Winnipeg when asked about it, he said everybody in Toronto knew about it and didn't have a problem with it.
>
> WE DO NOT HAVE OR NEVER WILL HAD COPS OR EX-COPS IN OUR CLUB!!!! . . .
>
> Nobody in Canada has ever been around anybody in the Club long enough to learn a Goddamn thing about us.
>
> It is also a requirement that you own a Motorcycle. I know this sounds strange to some of you, But it's true . . .

You have 2 supposed chapters in Canada. But you don't speak to each other.

You talk Shit about each other, snitch on each other, then want to call me brother?

Your kind of Brotherhood and mine are two completely different things.

And one more thing. Bandidos don't vote. They do what the fuck they're told.

I wish you the best of luck, I hope you can pull it together.

True to his nature, Sandham fought back with a lie. The same day Pike issued his missive, Taz emailed Pervert again, protesting the decision. He just didn't protest as himself. Unlike Boxer, who called out Bill Sartelle of the mother chapter when the senior Bandido started giving him a hard time, Sandham pretended to be Dwight Mushey in a phony hotmail account he had created. "What just happened?" Sandham wrote, posing as Mushey, " Taz is not a cop nor was he ever a real one, VERY FAR FROM IT."

Then he sent an email to Carlitto Aragon, again pretending to be Mushey. It was bizarre that Sandham would reach out to his enemy, even while impersonating someone else. Perhaps he felt they were somehow closer, since they now shared the Texans as enemies. Or perhaps Taz was truly losing his mind. "Things are really fucked up," he wrote. "For one thing Taz is not a cop nor has he ever been a real one . . . We have all worked very hard, including Taz, you know that. He is not dropping anything and neither are we. I guess Canada will never get endorsement from the states. At this point I don't think they ever planned too [*sic*]. True Bandidos DO NOT let their patches hit the ground." What Sandham didn't know was that Aragon didn't even have a patch to let fall.

He also didn't know that a new tattoo appeared on Frank Lenti's left forearm in the spring of 2006, a month after the massacre. Even arms as beefy as Lenti's didn't have much room left on them for fresh artwork. Much prime real estate was taken up by the tattoo of a sombrero and the dates "2002–2004," indicating that he joined the club in 2002 and then left in 2004. But the veteran one percenter found room for one more: another sombrero, inked onto his skin after he agreed on May 24 to help reorganize the Bandidos north of the border, so that they might some day be allowed back inside the club. Exactly who he made the deal with was a mystery, but Cisco Lenti was now a man on a mission.

He finally had control and could do things his way. He would rebuild the No Surrender Crew from the ashes up. If Little Beaker didn't like it, that was his problem.

CHAPTER 23

Mother's Day

. . . bear welcome in your eye,
Your hand, your tongue: look like th' innocent flower,
But be the serpent under't.
MACBETH, ACT 1, SCENE 5

It's not about riding anymore.
BRETT (BULL) GARDINER TALKS ABOUT
CHANGES IN OUTLAW BIKER WORLD

Sunday, May 14, was Mother's Day, and when Eric Niessen spoke with his mother by telephone from jail, it wasn't long before she started to cry. She couldn't bring herself say "jail" when she talked to her boy about his current situation—the very word repelled her. The reality it represented was far too much to comprehend, especially on this day. "Oh God, I can't even say the word, Eric," she said, then started to cry again.

"Anyway, anyway, whatever," Niessen said, trying to sound laid-back and philosophical, but it didn't help. Everything was tainted now, even the relationship between a bit player like Niessen and his mother.

"What do you get for breakfast?" she asked, sounding very much like a mother.

"Depends."

"Porridge?"

"No, eggs . . . It's not that bad."

His mother sounded close to tears again. The more she tried to sound maternal, the uglier the current situation seemed. She really couldn't protect her boy now. "They have to let you out because it doesn't mean anything," she said bravely, unable to stay on the less painful topic of food.

"It doesn't mean shit," Niessen said. His voice was rising now as his cool faded. "It doesn't mean shit."

"When they get the right people . . . ," his mother said, her voice trailing off and sounding almost dreamy as she contemplated a world in which her innocent son walked free—and could enjoy a wholesome breakfast.

But of course, Niessen wasn't innocent at all. He may not have been a particularly bad man, and he was no murderer, but he was far from innocent. Niessen had stumbled into the kind of trap every mother worries about. He was rudderless and credulous and had the poor fortune of falling in with a guy like Wayne Kellestine. The world may need followers, but biker gangs seem to need them more than just about any other kind of organization. They need patsies and hangarounds and friends with working credit cards. They need guys like Niessen to take the fall for them when it comes time to lie to the police. Niessen may have believed that he was simply in the wrong place at the wrong time, but the fact is that he was in the wrong place *all* the time.

Still, Niessen's mother wasn't the only woman in Canada who spent that Mother's Day wishing her son hadn't kept better company, and Niessen wasn't the only follower who had ended up in an Ontario prison after believing a little too naively the myth of biker freedom. Bikers love to tell themselves that they are fearless non-conformists, rebels who live outside the mainstream because they can't bear to be told what to do. But anyone who is willing to trudge through the woods in search of a pickle tree is someone who doesn't mind being told what to do.

Not only did Brett Gardiner comb the Kellestine farm for fresh pickles, he also submitted when called upon to stay behind in Ontario while his "brothers" headed back to Winnipeg, even though he was pining to see Jessica McDowell, his common-law wife, and their child. Gardiner was no outlaw or rebel; he just didn't know any better than to follow the loudest voice in the room. Only hours after meekly agreeing to be left behind, he was in police custody.

At 6:01 on the evening of Saturday, June 17, 2006, Gardiner made a collect phone call from jail to Jessica. Their toddler, Shane, was watching a cartoon in the background as they chatted.

"How was your day?" she asked, as though one day in jail might be very different from another.

Gardiner replied that someone was making "an eight-hour video." That was his way of saying that he now knew that M.H. had turned against the group and had made a lengthy video statement for police in return for immunity from prosecution.

Jessica needed reassurance that the other bikers knew that he was keeping his mouth shut. "Do they know that you haven't said anything?" she asked.

He grunted something that she took as an affirmative statement, and then she asked again, just to make sure, "So are you still safe?"

"Yeah. Yeah."

Then he paused before adding, "I love you."

"I love you too."

Their conversation was a lattice of trivia and long silences. It was too painful to talk about the legal problems ahead. It was too difficult to pretend that they both weren't worried. It would be too lonely for them to cut the line of communication by hanging up the phone, sending him back to a block full of convicts and her back to their toddler. This was his muse, the woman who figured in his melancholy poetry, and now he had nothing to say to her. So they chose to be silent together for a few long seconds, until Gardiner finally asked, "So, anything to talk about?"

"I'm so tired," she replied.

Gardiner began calling for his boy, so that the toddler could hear his voice.

"He's just going to end up hanging up on you," she said.

Gardiner gave up on the idea of talking with Shane. Instead, they started talking about their car, a less emotional point of contact. "Car still a piece of shit?"

"Yeah."

Another long pause, as they were once again stumped for something fresh to say.

"I love you," she said.

"Love you too."

Finally, she asked, "Excited about your birthday on Monday?"

His tone turned sarcastic. "Yeah, a whole lot excited."

"I wish I could spend it with you," she said.

"Wish you could spend it with me here in jail?"

All other topics seemed poisoned, and so Gardiner turned back to what was on their mind: the threat from his "brothers" in the Bandidos. He sounded weary as he mentioned the club. But then, Gardiner's thoughts on the one percenter world shifted according to his mood and his audience. Just a few days earlier, he had been holding forth to Jessica's mother on the topic of the decay of biker morality, as though it was something he still believed in. He had been voicing his disapproval of Winnipeg Hells Angels president Ernie Dew, who had recently made the news after being charged in the wake of a year-long undercover sting operation against a methamphetamine and cocaine network. "It's not about riding anymore," Gardiner complained, despite the fact that he didn't even have a motorcycle or a licence to ride one.

But now his mood had shifted, and he didn't feel like defending the purity of the biker code. "I don't want to hear about that shit ever again," he said. "What's Shane watching?"

"I don't know."

"What's he wearing?"

"His Hawaiian shorts."

The pauses were painfully long now.

"When you get out, are you going to keep in contact with these people?" she finally asked.

"No."

Baby Shane's gentle crying could be heard in the background now. Then he began to coo.

"Sooooo," Jessica said, the word hanging in the air, somehow both an accusation and a concession of defeat.

"Talk about something," he said.

"What do you want to talk about?"

There was always Shane to brighten the conversation, though Gardiner sounded more depressed still when he thought about their child. "Miss him so much . . . Tell me some new stuff."

She noted that Shane was on a laxative now, while she was on a three-day fast. She held their baby up to the phone.

"High-five," Gardiner said. "I love you."

Baby Shane was silent now, neither crying nor cooing.

"What are you thinking about?" she asked.

"Everything."

"I love you," she said.

"I love you," he replied.

"Talk to me," she said.

"You got your truck back?"

"Nope."

"You driving your mom's car?"

"Yup."

He told her that the hamlet of Hartley Bay, British Columbia, was where he planned to settle once he was finally released from custody. It was an isolated First

Nations community of two hundred souls, 650 kilometres north of Vancouver and accessible only by water and air. There was almost nowhere in Hartley Bay to ride a Harley, even if someone wanted to.

"Not 'we' anymore?" she asked. "Just 'me'?"[30]

Gardiner was talking to his mother from jail on June 18, when she wished him a happy Father's Day. She was making a brave effort to talk about hope. For her, that seemed to come in the form of opening up to police and telling the truth.

"They want you to talk," his mother said.

"What's there to talk about?" he replied. " . . . I was sitting down watching TV. Whatever happened was none of my business . . . I'm not telling them anything."

He likely knew that police were recording his conversation. He was a suspected mass murderer, after all. Why wouldn't they be listening? He also knew that police would like to move him into a witness protection program in return for his testimony. At twenty-one, he was the youngest of the group, and theoretically the one with the greatest chance of rehabilitation. He hung tough that he wasn't about to budge. "The only thing I'm going to say is, 'Here's my lawyer's number,'" he told her.

He said that he had been offered a full patch in the

Bandidos, but didn't sound eager to go deeper into the group. "When I'm out, I'm leaving," he said, " . . . I want people to know that I'm done with this shit."

"It's finished?" his mother asked, hopefully. "Right? Right?"

But it was far from over for Gardiner and the Bandidos. Complicating matters for the club was the fact that some of the Shedden victims would themselves be suspects in another murder if they were still alive. Jamie Flanz might have been dead, but the investigation of the murder that took place in his Keswick townhouse was not.

Mary Thompson had always planned to tell police her deadly story about the Shawn Douse murder. That spring, a homicide investigator paid Mary a visit, and by early June she had given police two detailed statements that dispelled whatever mystery still surrounded the drug dealer's grisly end.

Finding Cameron Acorn and Randy Brown wasn't a challenge for investigators, as they were already in custody on unrelated charges in the Penetanguishene and Lindsay jails respectively. Carlitto Aragon was arrested without incident near Kipling Avenue and The Queensway in Etobicoke. Five days later, on June 26, Bobby Quinn surrendered to police. He had fled to Nelson, British Columbia, a former haven for Vietnam War draft dodgers in southern British Columbia, fifty-five kilometres from the border with Washington State. The four men now faced second-degree murder charges for the beating death of Shawn Douse. With the arrests, the Ontario Provincial Police pronounced the Bandidos biker gang officially dead in the province of Ontario.

Police offered to move Mary Thompson into a witness protection program. She chose instead to try moving back in with her mother, who once again had promised to stop drinking. This sojourn lasted two weeks, until her mother was evicted from her home. The next stop for Mary was a women's shelter, and then she was back on her own again, a day before her twenty-first birthday.

Finally, in September, Mary agreed it would be best if she finally went into the witness protection program. The goal was for her to disappear into the safety of anonymity until the trial. Once she was given a new name and relocated, she emailed her mother to reassure her that she was okay. Shortly afterwards, her mother was in a bar, talking about the email. Word got back to police, and Mary was told to pack her few belongings and move, quickly, yet again.

CHAPTER 24

Claiming Glory

With Cain go wander through shades of night,
And never show thy head by day nor light.
RICHARD II, ACT 5, SCENE 6

This guy, he went out like a man.
DWIGHT MUSHEY DESCRIBES THE FINAL SECONDS
OF JOHN (BOXER) MUSCEDERE

The Ontario Provincial Police secured a court order authorizing to plant recording devices in Weiner Kellestine's house after police forensics crews had left, presumably to catch his wife or fellow bikers discussing the mass murders. Already, police had sifted through his farmhouse, cluttered barn and shed and collected plenty of guns, as well as several other items of interest, including a confidential OPP intelligence report on Ontario bike gangs, dated May 7, 2002, and photos of local officers in the provincial Biker Enforcement Unit and of bikers in other clubs, including the Hells Angels. Ashes in the firepit on the Kellestine property had been searched by a forensic archaeology team, which discovered keys to houses and apartments of the murder victims, as well as coins and buckles and zippers from at least two pairs of pants. There were also parts for half a dozen cellphones, two money clips, a wad of burned twenty-dollar bills, a lighter with a Harley-Davidson logo, two steel toes from a pair of work boots, an imitation pistol stuffed into a box of frozen hamburger patties, some jewellery with a peace symbol on it and a piece of paper with the letters ONICO, the name of the computer company owned by Jamie Flanz. An underwater search team had checked the well and pond, an emergency response team had conducted a grid search of the property and a septic team had completed its decidedly ugly task. Certainly, the police had gathered up many interesting things, but they still had not gotten their hands on even one of the weapons used for the massacre.

Constable Al Dubro thought the kitchen would be a good place to hide the bug, in a little enclosure in the pine wall built to hold the microwave oven. On May 24, he lifted out the microwave to install the recording device, and he discovered what he thought might be a secret door. He gave it a tug and it came open. When he shone his flashlight into the darkness, he saw what appeared to be a stack of disassembled guns.

Dubro immediately called Detective Inspector P.A. (Paul) Beesley of the homicide squad. Once Beesley returned to the farmhouse, investigators reached into the secret compartment and pulled out eighteen firearms, including a .22 with no serial number, a .380-calibre automatic pistol and a Savage 930 rifle with a sawed-off handle and barrel, which made it look like a pistol. Mixed in with these weapons was an assortment of other gun pieces, bullets and shotgun shells, including a banana-shaped clip to hold bullets for an automatic rifle and eight rounds of ammunition for a German Luger 9-millimetre pistol, of the sort that Nazis carried in World War II.

The guns that were of prime interest were the .380 automatic pistol, a .22-calibre Mossberg, a .22-calibre Cooey and a sawed-off double-barrelled shotgun. They matched the types of guns forensic experts had determined were used in the massacre. When they were dusted for fingerprints, they came up clean.

A gun without fingerprints may obscure the identity of the person who last used it, but it is also a pretty strong clue that it was last used for something unsavoury. After all, there is no need to hide your identity if you haven't been firing the gun for some illegal purpose. Sure enough, when a weapons expert from the Centre of Forensic Sciences in Toronto tested the black Hi-Point .380 semiautomatic pistol, he concluded it was the gun used to fire shots into Goldberg Flanz, Little Mikey Trotta, Big Paul Sinopoli and Bam Bam Salerno. Big Paul had also been shot in the head with the .22-calibre Mossberg. The Hi-Point also matched a shell that had been found in the driver's-side rear seat of the Pontiac Grand Prix, close to Flanz's body and a child's car seat.

It wasn't clear which weapon had been used to kill Chopper Raposo, since the projectiles that were removed from his body were severely damaged and fragmented.

Bullets from the Mossberg rifle had been removed from Boxer, Bam Bam and Crash. Testing of the Mossberg revealed DNA from Pony Jessome, Big Paul Sinopoli, Goldberg Flanz, Crash Kriarakis and Bam Bam Salerno. The Hi-Point .380 pistol had traces of DNA from Big Paul Sinopoli and Little Mikey Trotta. Clearly, they had all been shot at close range. When the evening of April 7 began, Weiner Kellestine held both the Mossberg and the Hi-Point. How long they remained in his hands was known only to the killers. Why he didn't just throw them away was a question only he could answer.

Cartridge cases from the Mossberg and Hi-Point had been found on the floor of the barn and in the vehicles that carried the dead bikers' bodies. Testing of the barn floor itself found that its dark rust colour was a result of being washed with hydrochloric acid, the same chemical Kellestine had in his "wet work" kit for cleaning up after executions.

Ontario Provincial Police locksmiths concluded that the keys found in Kellestine's firepit were matches for the locks for Trotta's home; Boxer's apartment; Raposo's front door, outside gate, backyard shed, and motorcycle; Sinopoli's front door and mailbox; and the BMW registered to Bam Bam Salerno's wife, Stephanie. DNA from Crash Kriarakis was also found on an inside tag of a black Harley-Davidson motorcycle cap, while Flanz's DNA was detected on a silver ring. The cap and the ring were each picked up by police investigators inside Kellestine's farmhouse.

Was the manic old biker so sure of himself that he thought the police would never stumble on the mountain of evidence on his property? Did some nagging, unacknowledged tug of guilt keep him from completing the task of effacing the clues that would identify him as his best friend's murderer? Or was he simply sloppy? No matter what the explanation, he had plenty of time in the detention centre to contemplate all the things he should have done the day after the slaughter, instead of taunting and playing coy on the phone.

While Kellestine's farm was surrendering its secrets to the police, the Winnipeg Bandidos had a leak of their own. On Friday, June 9, M.H. was prepared to formalize his status as an agent for the Ontario Provincial Police and the Ontario Attorney General's office. The province had agonized over the deal, fearing the kind of backlash that followed the "deal with the devil" reached back in 1993 with schoolgirl killer Karla Homolka. That agreement allowed Homolka to serve only twelve years in prison, and plead down to two counts of manslaughter, in return for her testimony against her former husband Paul Bernardo, who was convicted of two counts of murder and was later declared a dangerous offender. In the end, the province decided, correctly, that the public is far more upset with people who murder innocent teens than those who execute outlaw bikers, and M.H. was handed a witness agreement. It called for him to promise to answer all relevant police questions honestly. In return, the Crown agreed not to prosecute him for his role in the largest massacre in the province's history. One paragraph on the third page of the deal stated that the signed agreement could be torn up by authorities if it was ever proven that M.H. had any knowledge of plans to harm any of the eight murdered men. He didn't get a large lump-sum payment, but there was free housing and $1,300 a month for expenses, plus prescription medicines. Most importantly, he received a guarantee he wouldn't be prosecuted for his role in the mass murders, as long as he told the truth.

A stroke of a pen made it official. The rats in the Canadian Bandidos fold had started to jump ship.

M.H.'s wire didn't just record evidence related to the investigation swirling around the Winnipeg bikers. It painted a picture of the rancour, resentment and poisonous ambition they exhibited. M.H. and Dwight Mushey had been in the club less than two years, but it was clear they were both thoroughly disillusioned with their ambitious and secretive little leader, Taz Sandham. Mushey suspected Sandham was going to pull rank and scoop up the back dues owed by a former member of Los Montaneros, even though the money should have been collected by Mushey, the secretary-treasurer, and placed in club coffers.

"The Little Beaker is gonna pull a presidential inter-
vention," Mushey told M.H.

"Oh yeah," M.H. replied, laughing.

"Go himself there," Mushey continued, in his sometimes fractured English. "If he does that, that's just some
sneaky ass-fuckin'. . ."

"Yeah," M.H. agreed.

"Shitty," Mushey concluded. He was clearly the most
dangerous of the group, and it didn't take him long to realize that he was the smartest and most capable as well. The
thought of remaining subordinate to Sandham was too
much to stomach, especially when he thought about the
way the self-appointed president had buckled when given
the job of executing Jamie Flanz.

Mushey told Aravena that he wasn't allowed to go
anywhere without clearing it with him first. Perhaps the
killers were still nervous that Aravena might talk, but it
was also clear that Mushey was stepping up now to assert
control. In the one percenter pecking order, Mushey had
sponsored Aravena into the Bandidos, and now Aravena
had to do his bidding, as a vassal once served a knight,
until he too achieved full-patch status. He might be useful
as Mushey moved to consolidate his power. Mushey wasn't
the type of man to sit back and grumble forever without
taking action.

"Probably claiming all of the glory, the fucker," M.H. said
of Sandham, as though killing his clubmates was something
glorious.

M.H. was at Mushey's Winnipeg bungalow on Monday, June 12, when Mushey called up the No Surrender Crew's website, which still displayed their motto defiantly: "We are the people your parents warned you about." He then clicked on the ENTER WITH RESPECT button and a husky bandit wearing a sombrero appeared on screen, laughing, firing a pistol and revving up his Harley. Once into the site, Mushey could see no mention at all of the Canadian Bandidos' banishment from the club. In cyberspace, Boxer's crew and Taz's ambitious probationary chapter lived on, defiant and untouchable as memory. M.H. threw out a comment about Taz Sandham, their supposed boss. "He made it sound . . . like he's got more heat than anybody, you know?"

"Yeah," Mushey agreed.

"'Cuz, 'I did three.' I'm sure he said that."

M.H. and Detective Sergeants Mark Loader and Jeff Gateman thought that Mushey might have killed three men at the farm, and guessed it would infuriate him if told that Sandham had claimed to kill the same number.

"See, what I notice is, like I say, he takes a lot of our stories and all of a sudden it becomes his, you know what I mean?" Mushey said. "Like the perfect saying: 'The man makes the patch, not the patch makes the man.' That's my fuckin' sayin'."

Mushey was now using hand signals instead of words,

as he was worried that police had bugged his house and car—not realizing they'd bugged his friend. M.H. was trying to get Mushey to verbalize as much as possible so that he would have an electronic record for police. When they did talk, it was customary now to use code, with "out there" referring to Kellestine's farm.

Mushey was guarded but trying to make a point: they were all guilty.

"We talked about this," Mushey said, flashing eight fingers. "After this, united." He made a gesture across his throat, then one of someone standing guard with a rifle, as he continued, "Whoever did this or this, it's the same shit, really, if you think about it."

The plan was to go to the gym with Aravena, but it wasn't yet noon, so the fighter was asleep, as was his habit. As M.H. and Mushey drove together to the weight room, Mushey recalled how Sandham didn't say a word to protect his fellow bikers when Kellestine seemed geared up to kill some of the Winnipeggers to eliminate witnesses. To Mushey it was one more sign of weakness and Sandham's lack of fitness to be a leader. Taz the betrayer was becoming Taz the betrayed, as Mushey was clearly becoming agitated. "He didn't say nothing," Mushey continued. "He was just like with a cock in his ass."

The defiant Shakira tune "Whenever, Wherever" played on their radio as they discussed their lack of faith in their leader. Once they got inside the tiny Freight House gym, on the second floor of a community centre, the quality of the police recording went downhill, their voices sometimes lost in the sound of grunting patrons and clanking exercise equipment. Mushey's voice could be heard at one point, saying he was impressed by how Boxer Muscedere had faced his death with his head held high, like a true one percenter.

"This guy," Mushey said, then held up his fists in a boxer's pose, "he went out like a man." Then Mushey noted that Boxer had, with his final breaths, laughed at Kellestine. "Supposedly, the first one he got, he laughed. Went like a man."

"I didn't . . . ," M.H. said. He would later say this referred to murdering someone that night. "You did."

"Oh yeah, of course," Mushey laughed.

Their workout done, they drove to Sandham's house, where they were ushered down to his basement. They would pretend they respected Taz now, for the time being, just as Taz had once pretended to respect Boxer and Chopper until he set them up for the kill. Mushey wanted to know how the Texas trip had gone. Taz still hadn't told them that it was an absolute disaster and that they had all been kicked out of the club—that they had murdered eight of their brothers for a greater share of nothing.

"They're going to appoint you this—at least for now?" Mushey said, forming a *P* with his hand to indicate "president for Canada."

Taz ducked the question. Instead, he said the club would be putting out the information that the Toronto chapter had been expelled from the Bandidos.

"So T.O.'s done now?" Mushey asked.

"Everything's done," Sandham replied, then corrected himself slightly. "They're all ex-members."

"Well, Manitoba's intact, right?" Mushey asked.

"Yeah, it's intact," Taz lied.

Taz said that Carlitto had been causing trouble with the Americans, claiming to be the Canadian leader even though "the meat and potatoes is here," meaning Manitoba had most of the active members.

"All of a sudden, he is fuckin' dictating to us," Taz said.

"Yeah," Mushey replied.

"Well, it is a dictatorship . . . ," Taz continued.

Mushey held up eight fingers and said he didn't want Taz talking about the murders, either. His bragging had to stop. He was talking to Sandham as if he, Dwight Mushey, was already the new boss. "I just don't want this fucking going around."

There was a long pause, as Mushey and Taz wrote on a piece of paper, and passed it back and forth, out of M.H.'s line of sight. If they were beginning to suspect M.H. and his questions, he could soon be the ninth murder victim.

The next day, M.H. was back at Mushey's house, once again wearing a hidden recording device. Soulless electronic music from a boxing video game played in the background as they discussed their worst fear: whether Taz Sandham would break ranks and ruin their alibi when questioned by police. Might he have already betrayed them?

"He might have said, 'I came back myself," M.H. said.

"If he did that, he's an idiot," Mushey said. "The three of us should go talk to him."

But someone else got to Sandham that Monday, with a message that spelled the end for Taz's fantasy that he was the Canadian *presidente* of the Bandidos. Sandham's dream was shattered not by a bomb or a bullet but the click of a mouse, to open an email from Frank Lenti's massive friend, Big Gus.

Apparently, Big Gus planned to attend a Bandidos world meeting, where he would lobby hard to get Canada reinstated into the club's fold. Big Gus was feeling magnanimous, and he promised to put in a good word for Taz. But for now, the hulking biker suggested, it was best for everyone concerned if Taz just got out of the way. In his words, it was time for Taz and the rest of the would-be Bandidos "to stop looking like assholes in front of the USA and get along." It went without saying that Big Gus had the backing of Frank Lenti, and Taz knew that it wasn't wise to toy with Lenti, unless you wanted to have your eyes gouged, or worse. "Are you going to step aside and let someone else take over, or what?" Big Gus asked.

The "or what" option was never very enticing for anyone dealing with Lenti and Big Gus. Taz buckled, but was snippy as he slinked away from power: "You are asking me to throw down my patch," he typed. "Over bullshit!!" He suggested that Big Gus could learn things from a man like him, and he didn't mean the art of Sando. Big Gus had worn a one percenter patch for a quarter-century, since joining the Satan's Choice in his late teens. Now

Sandham, who had never legitimately been promoted to full-patch status, felt justified in lecturing him. "Between you and me, do you not stop and think for a minute that there is a chance your brotherhood might be being tested?" Taz asked. "Just wondering what your answer is. So you go to the world meeting and have fun, share brotherhood and learn the Bandido way."

And that was the end of Sandham's reign as self-appointed president. As it turned out, all anyone really had to do was tell him to get lost in an unfriendly tone of voice, and he would have disappeared. No doubt Boxer had felt tempted many times to do the very same thing, but chose instead to bite his tongue in the hopes of expanding the club westward.

Taz Sandham would later say that he didn't get home until a little after midnight on June 16. His tattoo parlour wasn't doing so well, so he had just started a second job as a labourer at a factory. His wife waited up for him with fried chicken from Chicken Delight, and Sandham said they enjoyed modest domestic bliss, watching television together until 3:30 A.M.

A crashing sound on a front window ended his sleep two and a half hours later. "I thought it was a pipe bomb," he later said in a particularly squeaky voice, describing how he ran over smashed glass to retrieve his son and pull him to safety, before realizing it was a police raid. The officers had thrown a hammer through his window, followed by a telephone so they could negotiate his arrest.

Within a few minutes, Taz was outside his house. His white shirt was marked by red dots as tactical police officers trained their laser scopes on him. A police dog strained on its leash, trying to lunge at him. The former officer who had once taught effective use of Tasers saw that police were now ready to use the weapons on him, should he resist.

He lay face down on the front yard, where he was handcuffed and then lifted up and placed in a police cruiser. Seven times in the cruiser, he denied being at Wayne Kellestine's at the time of the murders. Sandham also acted exasperated that the police felt the need to send in a tactical unit and break a window during the arrests. "I was one of you guys, for crying out loud," he protested. "You think I'm going to give you guys a hassle?" Sounding like a biker Judas, he continued: "I'm not even a fucking member, for fuck's sakes . . . Holy fuck, I wasn't even there."

He didn't know that, the previous evening, Mushey had been scooped up without incident. That morning, Aravena was also taken into custody in a pre-dawn raid. When the tactical officers came to arrest him, Aravena pulled on some shorts and a T-shirt and kissed his dog, Harley, on the nose before being led out to a police cruiser.

By the time workers were in their offices for the start of another business day, the three bikers were in custody, each facing eight counts of first-degree murder. Police also

towed away Taz Sandham's red Blazer for forensic testing and picked up an odd diagram from inside the house
shared by Mushey and Aravena. It showed, in precise
detail, where patches and crests should be sewn on Bandidos' vests.

Later that day, Sandham was questioned for the first
time by OPP Detective Sergeant Mick Bickerton. He
denied 223 times during that interrogation that he was
at Kellestine's farm at the time of the murders. Later, he
would say that he only did this because he felt that police
might otherwise arrest his wife and authorities might strip
them of custody of their children. "I was just looking out
for them," Sandham said.

The operation was wrapped up quickly because police
had caught wind of information that Mushey might be
playing a role in three more murders. They couldn't stop
the murders without compromising their sources, and so
they decided it was time to pull the plug on M.H.'s undercover operation and bring the case to trial.

The project was code-named Operation Octagon, to
reflect the fact that there had been eight victims.[31] A cloud
had hung over the operation for the past two months, ever
since confidential police documents had been discovered
by a passerby in the mud outside the Winnipeg police station. The passerby noted that the papers listed the names
and addresses of the Winnipeg bikers who were under
surveillance, and handed them over to the city's CBC
News bureau. The public broadcaster reported that sensitive documents had been found, but didn't divulge the
contents of the muddy, lost papers. And so Taz and the

Bandidos carried on as if everything was all right, while police tightened their net around them.

Now in custody, true to form, Taz Sandham lied to police. As he told the story, he wasn't even a member of the Bandidos, although he had been one once, and so he did know Wayne Kellestine and Dwight Mushey. Taz said that he had no idea why tire tracks from his Blazer had been found in the mud at Kellestine's farm. Taz swore that he didn't shoot anybody and hadn't even seen Chopper Raposo since the fall of 2005. He told police he wasn't in Ontario at the time of the murders, but was raking leaves that day, ignoring the fact that his front yard was no more than a patch of mud with no leaves to rake.

A couple of days after the arrests, a new Harley-Davidson that Mushey had ordered finally arrived. If not for the arrests, it would have meant that two of the Winnipeg Bandidos—Mushey and Taz—actually had working motorcycles.

The question was, would they ever ride them?

CHAPTER 25

Preliminaries

Now, gods, stand up for bastards!
KING LEAR, ACT 1, SCENE 2

. . . the first thing that comes to my mind is,
"Holy shit, I'm surrounded by a bunch of killers."
MICHAEL (TAZ) SANDHAM

At 12:31 P.M. on December 29, 2006, Taz Sandham crossed a
new threshold in his life. He was ushered into an interview
room to speak with police, and his words were recorded
by two video cameras as he announced that he was finally
willing to come clean about everything that happened on
the night of April 7–8, when Boxer and his crew were mas-
sacred. Taz had just closed the door on his biker life forever. It was one thing to be a killer, quite another to be
a rat. Killers could be tolerated, even respected, but rats
were the lowest of the low, who merited death for both
ethical and practical reasons. Taz fully understood that he
was shifting gears from being a biker leader to a target as
he sat down in the interview room and began to talk.

In return for his testimony, Sandham said he wanted to be reinstated into the military to fight for Canada overseas, or to be enlisted by police as a special agent to do deep undercover work. Under his plan, he wouldn't just be a pretend commando or spy any longer. He wanted to leverage the most damning act of an often-pathetic life into something heroic. The police didn't commit to anything, however. He would have to tell his story first.

Sandham gave his version of the meeting with American Bandidos he and Kellestine attended at the Peace Arch Park in British Columbia weeks before the slaughter. If Sandham's claims could be belived, the plan then was to take out—or murder—only the two leaders, Chopper Raposo and Boxer Muscedere. Sandham told Detective Sergeant Mick Bickerton of the Ontario Provincial Police that he was against killing anyone, but Kellestine, Mushey and M.H. all favoured a bloodletting.

As Taz told things, he had been a lone agent of peace throughout the entire sordid operation. In an often-squeaky voice that called to mind his Little Beaker nickname, he said that Kellestine told the men at the Peace Arch Park meeting, "The only way I'm going to get Boxer's patch is to kill him." Sandham told the police he had been a voice of moderation: "'You don't wanna do that,' I said. 'You've known this guy forever. You don't wanna do that.'" He said that one of Kellestine's friends jumped in at this point. (This friend wopuld not be present at Kellestine's barn on the night of April 6, 2009.) "He says, 'Well yeah, you're gonna have to kill him and that's that.' And they start arguing about it. They argue to the point where they were arguing over who's going to do it.

"And then Wayne got so upset with him that they actually were forehead to forehead and Wayne was screaming in his face, 'I'm the only fuckin' assassin,' he says, 'in this club. Any killing has to be done I'll fucking do it,' he says." Even by Weiner Kellestine's psychopathic standards, he was way out of line here, as Sandham told the story, noting that even Kellestine was shocked. "And I'm talking to Wayne later on . . . he's saying to me, 'Please tell me I didn't say that out loud.'"

Taz said that the Peace Arch Park meeting ended with the Americans ordering the murders of Boxer and Bam Bam. Why they now decided to kill Bam Bam and not Chopper was not explained. Perhaps they thought Bam Bam's title of Toronto president made him a worthy target. Or perhaps Sandham was lying, as he was wont to do when under stress. SInce there was no police recording of the meeting and no one else from the meeting was talking to police, all investigators had was his version of events, which was woefully short of the standard required to charge anyone. If they chose to believe Sandham, which was always a dangerous course to follow, then the idea was clear: lop off the leadership of the Toronto and Canadian chapters, so that the rest of the No Surrender Crew would fall into line.

If you're willing to kill a guy, why not frame him too? Taz continued that it was Boxer who ordered the hit on Keswick drug dealer Shawn Douse, and that Weiner Kellestine also wanted that murder carried out. "Boxer decided to kill this guy in Keswick and . . . ah, they went and did it . . ."

His facts didn't come close to matching up with the evidence from the Douse murder investigation, which had determined that Muscedere and Kellestine played no role. But Bickerton didn't interrupt as Sandham spun his story. In his meeting in Texas after the murders, Sandham said, he met face to face with Bandido Pervert in North Houston. With Pervert was the chapter's *sargento de armas*, Scarey Larry, a frightening slab of humanity who lived in the back of a biker bar. They talked about Weiner Kellestine being an exterminator, and then the Americans asked about Carlitto Aragon. According to Sandham, Carlitto was a big problem in the eyes of the Texans. It was all a little vague and a lot menacing.

"A lot of people would tell you you're either nuts or you've got a big set of cahoonies because you go down there by yourself," Bickerton said.

"Uh-huh," Sandham agreed.

"Down there, you could disappear in a big hurry. Nobody would ever know."

"Oh yeah, and I almost did," Sandham agreed again, warming to the praise and relaxing enough to ask for a coffee and to complain about the quality of the decaf in jail.

Between sips of coffee, Sandham rambled on and on, welcoming the opportunity to portray himself as a hero. He said that he had argued with Mushey and M.H. in Ontario after the Peace Arch Park meeting because they were bent on murdering Boxer and Chopper. Sandham said that he boldly replied: "I tell you right now that no one is dying. I'll talk to Wayne myself."

By Taz Sandham's account, there was no one more

bloodthirsty than the prosecution's star witness M.H., who was ready to kill women and children if it came to that. Sandham said it was M.H. who shot Big Paul Sinopoli and Crash Kriarakis with a shotgun. This didn't appear to be supported by the forensic evidence, which had found that the .22-calibre Mossberg had been used to kill Kriarakis and that Sinopoli had been shot in the head with both the Hi-Point pistol and the Mossberg—not a shotgun like the one M.H. held.

"I didn't expect anybody to get hurt," Sandham said. He didn't stop to explain how a midnight confrontation between heavily armed and violent men could end amicably, or why he would be lurking in the rafters with a rifle and a shotgun and wearing surgical gloves if his intentions were brotherly.

Sandham sounded like an ex-cop now, as he told the investigator that he was trying hard to "disengage" himself from the operation. He admitted he had been hidden in the shadows above the No Surrender Crew, but he made no mention now about how he had supposedly once been a sniper, trained to hide in the shadows and pick off his targets. From his hidden perch, Taz said, he could hear Chopper Raposo say that it was ironic that Carlitto and Stone were in Manitoba, trying to kill him, when Taz was actually in Ontario. It was at this instant, Taz told the interrogator, that he realized he was marked for death. "Here we are," Chopper allegedly said. "We're going to have to fucking do it."

He said he was able to see Chopper's shotgun, and heard Jamie Flanz remark, "That'll put a big hole in somebody."

"I was very scared," Sandham told Bickerton, his voice rising. "Very, very scared."

Sandham said he crouched uncomfortably high above the gunman Chopper Raposo, terrified he might cause the old wooden beams to creak. "I'm trying to peek through there," Sandham said, his voice still high. "I'm trying to see what's going on and they're talking about this stuff and the first thing that comes to my mind is, 'Holy shit, I'm surrounded by a bunch of killers.' All I can think of is, 'How am I gonna get home to my family?'" Sandham said he hadn't chambered a round in his rifle as he hid in the attic, fearing for his life. "I'm thinking to myself, 'I'm a dead man.'"

At that point in the interview, Sandham pulled out a sheet of paper and handed it to Bickerton. He had drafted a list of sixty-five questions that he would like to answer. Perhaps the investigator would like to read them out for him.

It was an absurd situation, but Bickerton played along and read out the first question: "Were you so in shock that you could barely speak?"

"Yes," Sandham replied.

"Were you shaking to the point that your jaw was rattling to the point that everybody noticed?"

"Yes."

The next question was whether Sandham feared for himself and the lives of members of his family.

"Yes, very much." Taz paused for a second, then added that he was too afraid to go to police because he thought his family would be killed.

"Did you walk in on a conversation where Wayne

Kellestine, Mushey and [M.H.] were planning to murder Boxer and Chopper?"

"Yes."

Bickerton continued to read: "In this plan, did they say Mushey and Kellestine would kill them and then [M.H.] would help Mushey remove their heads, hands, feet and then they would . . . throw all the parts in the river?"

"Yes."

Bickerton declined to point out that there wasn't a river running through the farm to throw the body parts into, even if they did chop them off. Instead, he continued to read: "Did hearing this make you sick to your stomach?"

"Very much."

Sandham rubbed his eyes, as if to fight back tears. It was as though he was hearing the question for the first time, rather than having written it himself. Then Taz managed to add, "They're a bunch of cold-hearted people . . . Wayne swore to me that nothing was going to happen. He said nobody was going to get killed." He was rubbing his eyes even harder now, as if tears were ready to explode. "I don't care what these guys [Toronto chapter members] have done. Nobody deserves that, and their families are suffering."

Sandham's voice was cracking when Bickerton broke the mood. "Just be careful rubbing your eyes there," the police officer counselled. "You might hurt yourself. You be putting your fingers in there pretty hard. You wanna couple of minutes? We'll see if the food's arrived."

"Yeah, okay," Sandham replied. The thought of a warm meal distracted him from his eye-rubbing and almost-crying. Once Bickerton had checked into the progress of the food, Sandham soldiered on with his tale. M.H. had said he wanted to also kill Carlitto and Stone, or, in his words, "I want to float them both."

Again, Sandham portrayed himself as a lone brave voice for good sense. "I said, 'No, we're not pissing in my own backyard.'"

In a break from the scripted questions, Bickerton sounded self-effacing. He said he wasn't smart enough to be a lawyer himself, but that it was his job to help the Crown build a case that would weather the questioning of bright defence lawyers in court. However, as he broke from Sandham's script, Bickerton posed a question that would do any defence lawyer proud.

"Okay, and then you subsequently provided them with latex gloves, right?"

"Not for that," Sandham replied limply. He didn't explain what other reason there might be for bringing the surgical gloves with him from Manitoba. He also declined to mention the bulletproof vest that he had packed.

That said, Bickerton returned to the questions Sandham had dreamed up in his cell.

"Did [M.H.] grab Wayne's baseball bat and say that he would kill Chopper when he came into the living room [of the barn]?"

"Yes."

Six and a half hours after the interview began, Bickerton finally wound things down. "I appreciate you coming forward," the investigator said. "We talked about the 'credibility' word before." There was a slight pause, and Sandham must have felt a drop in his stomach as he anticipated what he must have known would be coming next. "I'm having a hard time believing you," Bickerton continued. The police investigator's words weren't angry or sharp, but merely a blunt, honest statement of fact, which made them all the more powerful.

"I'm sorry to hear that," Sandham replied.

"There's no way to corroborate what you have said," Bickerton went on, adding that forensic science didn't back Sandham's story.

"I know it proves otherwise," Sandham admitted. His tone now was that of a man whose high hopes had been beaten down once again. Sandham would have known that his statement was passed on to the other defendants, as is the customary practice in pre-trial disclosure of evidence. Soon, other prisoners would want him dead. Boxer, for all of his faults, was looking good as a Bandidos leader now. No one ever called Boxer a rat, while the Tazman had just sold out his entire crew. For nothing.

Taz wouldn't be getting immunity from prosecution, a new identity, reinstatement in the Canadian military or an assignment deep in some undercover police operation, as he had hoped. It just kept getting worse and worse for him—it seemed that the harder he tried, the lower he tumbled. Sandham had enjoyed flickers of respect and glory in the military, the police and the world of outlaw bikers, but they had never lasted for long. Now he was totally alone, and he had seemingly run out of macho groups to join or brothers to betray.

Bickerton continued: "As a cop and as a soldier, ah, it's quite miraculous that, you know, you're scared, you get startled and you just happen to pop a round off and that happens to go right through the chest of a guy that's shooting at you totally by accident. What a fluke. It's a miracle . . ." Bickerton then compared Sandham's theory to some of the far-fetched scenarios offered for the assassination of John F. Kennedy.

"Okay," Sandham replied, tired after a full day of lying. His words that afternoon filled more than four hundred pages and seemed to have come close to to a dim-witted confession. A series of questions for the prosecutors would naturally flow from his statement. If he truly wanted to save lives, why didn't Taz go to police after the Peace Arch Park meeting? Why did he instead drive to Ontario with his surgical gloves and bulletproof vest to hook up with a man with a stash of guns?

The man who boasted he was a trained sniper had just shot himself in the foot.

The preliminary hearing began at the courthouse in downtown London on Monday, January 9, 2007. Weiner Kellestine had a defiant bounce to his step that day as he was led into the court, even though he was shackled in leg irons and handcuffs. He wore wire-rimmed glasses, and his shoulder-length salt-and-pepper hair was pulled back in a ponytail, making him look as respectable as a man of his ilk possibly could. He cast his eyes over at half a dozen reporters and a couple of sketch artists, paused, made sure most of them were looking in his direction, stuck out his tongue lewdly and then gave the artists the finger.

It was a bleak reunion for the Shedden conspirators. Beside the leering Kellestine, Mushey, Aravena, Gardiner, Mather and Sandham sat in adjoining Plexiglas cubicles. Taz was closest to the judge. He didn't look like a soldier, police officer, martial arts grand master or outlaw biker now. A court officer handed him a tissue as he slumped forward, his head hidden in his hands, and sobbed like a bullied schoolboy.

The purpose of a preliminary inquiry is to determine whether the prosecution's evidence is strong enough to send an accused to trial. It doesn't have to be an iron-clad case, just strong enough that it might sway a jury. The hearing also gives the accused a chance to see how much evidence police have gathered against him or her. In the case of the preliminary inquiry for the Bandidos massacre, there were statements from witnesses, the accused, biker gang experts and informant M.H. There were also photographs, videos, audio files, diagrams and forensics reports dealing with biology, chemistry, locks, archaeology, bloodstain patterns, firearms and DNA—enough data to fill some 120 gigabytes of space on a computer hard drive. That's enough memory to hold two dozen comprehensive encyclopedia sets, or more than 1,660 times the computer memory required to land *Apollo 11* astronauts Neil

Armstrong and Edwin (Buzz) Aldrin on the moon back in 1969. Prosecutors in the Shedden Massacre seemed comfortable that it was also enough to land Weiner Kellestine, Dwight (Big D) Mushey, Taz Sandham, Marcelo (Fat Ass) Aravena, Brett (Bull) Gardiner and Frank Mather in prison for a long, long time.

Managing the file for the Crown was Kevin Gowdey, Crown attorney for the County of Elgin. Nicknamed "Rowdy Gowdy" when he was a basketball star at London South Collegiate Institute, he now looked like the type of earnest lawyer you'd expect to see played by James Stewart in old movies. With him were assistant Crown attorneys Tim Zuber, Fraser Kelly, David D'Iorio and Meredith Gardiner, as well as David Arntfield, special counsel for the Office of the Director of Crown Operations, West Region. To make sure there were no embarrassments for the Crown in the ultra-high-profile case, they were cleared from handling any other files for the duration of the case.

The public was also paying for the lawyers on the defence side of the courtroom via Legal Aid, as all of the accused bikers pled the need for financial assistance. Before they went the Legal Aid route, at least three of the accused had been turned down by their first choice of lawyers because they couldn't afford the retainers.

Sandham's lawyer, Don Crawford, was a courtly, platinum-haired man given to three-piece suits, watch chains and the occasional outburst of righteous indignation. He was well acquainted with criminal law clients who were little more than ambitious dimwits: in one of his previous cases, a crew of would-be Mafiosi who unsuspectingly administered the secret initiation ceremony of the Calabrian *'Ndrangheta*, or Mafia, to an undercover RCMP officer.

On Kellestine's defence team were local courtroom veteran Ken McMillan and Clay Powell, a likeable and clever septuagenarian who looked a little like he had been carved out of a potato. It would likely be the last big case for Powell, whose resumé included defending Keith Richards of the Rolling Stones on heroin-possession charges in the late 1970s. That case had ended with Richards being sentenced to perform benefit concerts in Oshawa for the Canadian National Institute for the Blind. Also for the defence was Tony Bryant of Toronto, whose former clients included serial sex killer and rapist Paul Bernardo. His client was Marcelo Aravena, the ultimate fighter who had stood guard over the No Surrender Crew so that none could escape before their execution. Bryant was a human version of a Jack Russell terrier in that he always seemed eager to jump into a scrap.

Early on in the proceedings, police took defence lawyers and prosecutors for a tour of the Kellestine property. In the winter of 2007, Weiner's common-law wife, Tina, still lived in the dirty white farmhouse; the lawyers found her chain-smoking alone when they arrived. During their afternoon visit, a yellow bus pulled down the potholed driveway. A pretty little blonde schoolgirl stepped out and skipped past the German shepherd and dachshund into the farmhouse, where the main floor was still decorated with Weiner Kellestine's Nazi memorabilia. School was out for the day, and Kassie Kellestine was happy to be home with her mom. The legal tour passed an outdoor sauna that was now used to store various pieces of junk, and then stopped briefly inside the workshed behind the house. There, they found Kassie's pet rabbits in their cages.

CHAPTER 26

Devil's Tour Guide

Where is that viper? bring the villain forth.
OTHELLO, ACT 5, SCENE 2

*I informed him that the Hells Angels had
put out a hit on him.*
INFORMER M.H. SAYS HE SAVED A POLICE OFFICER'S LIFE

The prosecution team quickly got to the core of its case, calling M.H. to the witness box to act as a tour guide of sorts through the world of outlaw bikers. As M.H. was escorted into the courtroom by a pair of plainclothes police officers, it was clear he had been cleaned up nicely for his appearance. The man in the well-tailored, conservative blue suit resembled nothing more than an insurance agent, stockbroker or accountant.

There weren't many observers in the courtroom, since a publication ban prevented the news media from saying much about the pre-trial proceeding. One of the reporters in attendance, upon seeing M.H., whispered, "Mr. Potato Head."

"Dead man walking," said another.

M.H. was asked to relate the events from the time he left Winnipeg until his return more than a week later. His former clubmate glowered at him, but could do nothing from the prisoner's box, where they were chained to the floor. The killers might never testify, as this would expose them to the prospect of a withering cross-examination, so it fell to M.H. to represent the face of evil, and it became his role to explain how brothers could slaughter their brothers, one by one, over patches of cloth. M.H. didn't present himself as a passionate one percenter, nor did he display the swagger one might expect of a career criminal. Instead, he displayed the sort of professional detachment one might associate with an expert police witness who had submerged himself in countless facts about a criminal culture without ever actually joining it. Though he described a world of crime and violence, the banality of his expression suggested that, to him, such a lifestyle was not more noteworthy than selling used cars.

In any case, he apparently felt he had nothing to feel remorseful about. As M.H. narrated things, he didn't pull a trigger once; he simply stood guard while Kellestine, Mushey and Sandham took care of the slaughter.

The court heard that M.H. left school at age sixteen, after Grade 10. After that, he said, "I worked a lot of different jobs." His abilities were, in the opinion of experts who tested him, "very, very scattered." He read at the Grade 5 level, and his scores in other disciplines ranged from the second percentile, which is only slightly superior to that of a corpse, to the seventy-fifth, which is well above average.

Former theology student, soldier, cop, outlaw biker and wannabe informer, Michael (Taz) Sandham. CROWN EXHIBIT

Happier times: Weiner Kellestine (left), Concrete Dave Weiche and Boxer Muscedere. CROWN EXHIBIT

Boxer Muscedere was one of the few Canadian Bandidos who actually knew how to ride a motorcycle, and he loved the feeling of riding with rain and sleet on his face. BETSY POWELL PHOTO

Boxer Muscedere had been an outlaw biker for only five years when he was appointed *presidente* of the Canadian Bandidos. CROWN EXHIBIT

Chopper Raposo took a hard line on admitting prospective members; he didn't think the club should let just anybody in.
CROWN EXHIBIT

Crash Kriarakis had a strong marriage and no criminal record, and thought he could clean up the club from within.
CROWN EXHIBIT

Bam Bam Salerno, the Toronto chapter president, talked of quitting the club after the birth of his son.

Bam Bam Salerno seemed capable of talking himself out of any tough situation. JULIAN CARSINI PHOTO

Big Paul Sinopoli was a massive man, but not as huge as he appears in this photo. He stood on a milk carton so he would tower over a visiting biker from Thailand.

JULIAN CARSINI PHOTO

Michael (Little Mikey) Trotta was accepted into the club only months before his murder.

CROWN EXHIBIT

When he wasn't running his successful computer consulting firm, prospective member Jamie (Goldberg) Flanz seemed to be only playing biker.

George (Pony) Jessome went through life without making enemies, but that didn't spare him from being murdered.

Friends and murder victims passed through the iron gate leading to Weiner Kellestine's farm. PETER EDWARDS PHOTO

Fellow bikers were led one by one from Weiner Kellestine's weather-beaten barn to their deaths. PETER EDWARDS PHOTO

Caged and defiant, Weiner Kellestine makes a rude gesture at the press on the opening day of his court case in January 2007, while red-haired Frank Mather (left) and Brett (Bull) Gardiner look on.

Taz Sandham, sitting by Marcelo (Fat Ass) Aravena (middle) and Dwight (Dee) Mushey (right), went through plenty of tissues on the opening day of court.

He told the court that he had been diagnosed as having a learning impairment, but he couldn't remember its precise nature.

Although he had been connected to a number of outlaw biker gangs, M.H. said he had no particular interest in motorcycles. He didn't own a Harley-Davidson or have a licence to ride even a moped. He did have muscle, having provided personal security for Walter (Nurget) Stadnick, the former national president of the Hells Angels, as well as the infamous Maurice (Mom) Boucher.[32] He had also been deeply involved in a biker-connected cocaine operation run out of a motel in Winnipeg. It was in this line of work that he met a man who forever changed his life, Winnipeg police Constable Timothy Diack. Some days, Diack would barge into the motel's bar four separate times in one shift in an attempt to catch the bikers in the act of selling drugs. Because of his raids, the bikers installed a camera system and silent, vibrating alarms so that they'd have time to stash the cocaine in magnetized containers secured under a deep fryer. "He just liked booting doors in," M.H. recalled.

M.H. was charged during one of the police raids and later said he began to question his life. In time, M.H. said he wanted to go straight. "I said, 'I want to get out of the life' . . . Me being charged, I said at one point, was a good thing. You just don't go up to the club and say, 'I'm quitting.'"

But a strange thing happened on the road to become a law-abiding citizen, M.H. said: "I was actually talking of quitting everything and going the straight route, but he convinced me to stay there . . . He said that they had a major investigation going on, that they needed more information."

The Crown had sought a three-year term for his drug dealing. Instead, M.H. said, he was sentenced to house arrest. M.H. shrugged off Powell's suggestion that this gentle treatment left him feeling that he owed Diack anything. "Indebted to him? No. He said that we were even. I informed him that the Hells Angels had put out a hit on him."

As M.H. told things, brothers Donny and Ron (Sawed-off) Burling pulled him into the orbit of the Bandidos gang in the early 2000s, when the Fat Mexican crest first arrived on Winnipeg streets. While M.H. claimed he wasn't a violent man, no one wasted breath making the same claims for Ron Burling, who had since run afoul of the law for kidnapping and torturing a drug rival, crushing his fingers with a sledgehammer and slicing off a tattoo with a knife.[33]

As M.H.'s testimony wound down, Don Crawford cleared his throat to announce dramatically that there had been a third shooter in Weiner Kellestine's barn, during the exchange of fire between his client, Taz Sandham, and Chopper Raposo. "And that was you," Crawford declared, pointing a finger towards the witness box and sounding a lot like the old television lawyer Perry Mason.

"I was outside," M.H. replied calmly, as if he had been waiting for the accusation.

Bam Bam Salerno's mother listened to M.H.'s testimony because she needed to know what was on her boy's mind when he died. She needed to know if her Frankie suffered. She particularly needed to know if Frankie made his peace with God. For her answers, she made the two-and-a-half-hour drive through the snow from her home in Maple, north of Toronto, to the courthouse in London, where she passed through the two security checks to sit in the same small courtroom as her son's killers. As she walked in, she came within a few feet of the six men charged with murdering her son and his friends. She avoided eye contact with anyone in the prisoners' box as she sat on a wooden bench, much as she would in church. A box of tissues had already been placed nearby by courtroom staff.

She sat quietly as she heard her boy Frankie described by a police biker expert as a full member of the Bandidos biker gang. This was no surprise, as she already knew her boy wasn't an angel, and that he had made what she called "bad choices." However, she also knew that Frankie had plenty of good qualities. She was there to hear about the man who, for at least a year before his murder, had tearfully talked with his wife, Stephanie, about quitting the Bandidos.

Frankie's mother felt she had to hear M.H. describe her son's death, even though it was unspeakably painful. Some people in the court that day thought she fainted briefly when she heard how her boy had dropped to his knees and begun reciting the Lord's Prayer moments before his execution, as Weiner Kellestine improvised his Nazi dance. She was still looking weak when she heard that her son had tried to shake the hands of his executioners before limping off to his death. More tears flowed as M.H. talked in a flat voice about how her Frankie pleaded with his biker brothers with his last few breaths to take care of his newborn son, Mario. As she sobbed at the back of the courtroom, a few of the prisoners seemed to cringe and turn away from the raw emotion of the tiny, elderly, well-dressed mother.

A couple of hours later, when court was over for the day, Frankie's mother was by no means satisfied, and there was no way she could begin to understand why the men in the Plexiglas cubicles felt they had the need, or right, to kill her boy. But she had finally stopped crying. In place of the overpowering need to weep, she now felt a strange sense of peace and calm. Her boy, for all of his flaws, had chosen to talk to God in the final seconds of his earthly life. He had begged for the killers to think of his baby boy, Mario. For all of his troubles, Frankie had finally made his peace with God. Frankie should be waiting for her in heaven, when her time also came.

"I was looking for a sign," she said softly, then stepped out into the blowing snow for the long drive home.

The preliminary hearing on the Shedden Massacre concluded on April 5, 2007, with Judge Ross Webster concluding that all six accused men should answer to eight first-degree murder charges. "There is certainly evidence upon which a jury could conclude that the murders of all eight victims were in furtherance of the plan to pull patches by detaining at gunpoint," the judge concluded. "As a result, the eight murders become the acts of all of Kellestine, Sandham, Mushey, Mather, Aravena and Gardiner regardless of which of those individuals actually pulled the trigger each time."

There seemed little doubt that, barring something totally out of the blue, Kellestine, Mushey and Sandham were damned in the upcoming trial. The fate of the lesser defendants, Mather, Gardiner and Aravena, seemed to promise more interesting legal arguments. What would a jury think about Frank Mather? No one claimed that he shot anyone that night, but he still stood guard as the victims were marched to their deaths. There was also video, taken by Kellestine, of Mather wearing a Bandido support shirt, and a probationary vest had been found in his room at Kellestine's farm. Gardiner and Aravena hadn't pulled a trigger, either, but had also played their own roles in the slaughter. They were clearly guilty of something, but would a jury call them murderers, eight times over?

The court proceeding held on Monday, October 15, 2007, was hush-hush, even by the tight standards that govern preliminary hearings. Reporters could not disclose any of the arguments made by prosecutors or defence lawyers, or any rulings by the judge, for fear that publication might prejudice the upcoming murder trial. Journalists were even barred from reporting that a hearing was being held that day.

Eric Niessen wore a blue sports jacket and yellow striped dress shirt as he appeared in the prisoners' box, calling to mind the days when he was a junior insurance sales manager. His long black hair was tied back, and his full moustache was trimmed, but still covered his upper lip. Mr. Justice D.R. McDermid of the Superior Court of Justice asked him for his plea on a charge of obstructing justice, laid for his helping to clean up at the Kellestine farm after the murders.

"Guilty," Niessen replied in a soft, flat voice.

Crown and defence lawyers agreed that a two-year prison term was appropriate, in addition to the eighteen months he had already spent in custody. Lawyer Jonathan Bliss suggested that his forty-six-year-old client had learned a hard life lesson about associating with outlaw motorcycle clubs. "This has been a rather illuminating experience for Mr. Niessen," Bliss told the court, saying Niessen had learned the hazards of "association even on a friendship basis."

Among those sitting at the back of the courtroom that morning was Kerry Morris, who had been released on bail after being held in custody for forty-five days. She and Niessen had shared torrid telephone calls and letters, either unaware or not caring that these communications were monitored by police and jail staff. A police officer had joked that the officer whose duty it was to monitor the steamy communications should be given a leave, like those afforded officers suffering the effects of post-traumatic stress. Now, Morris and Niessen didn't dare look at each other as she sat stiffly beside her lawyer, David Barenberg.

After her lover, Niessen, was led away to prison, it was Morris's turn to stand up before the judge. Gowdey agreed to drop charges against her for obstructing justice, and she was free to resume her life. With these details out of the way, the Crown could get to the core of its case.

But connection to a mass murder, no matter how tangential, is not something that can be blithely assigned to the past just because a lawyer decides not to pursue charges. To simply pick up where one left off would be impossible for anyone, and Morris was perhaps more affected than most, since her lover remained behind bars. "It's been horrible," she explained. "Absolutely horrible. My life's been destroyed . . . Friends, they've just turned their backs."

Since the arrests, she said, her life was "lonely, very lonely. I'm out in the middle of nowhere." The farmhouse she had shared with Niessen was now home only to her cats and herself. She kept taking in more stray cats to cope with her loneliness, and she had trouble feeding them all, since no one would give her a job. She began to cry as she talked of the kindness shown by a worker from the Society for the Prevention of Cruelty to Animals who gave her free cat food when her cash dried up.

But her eyes lit up as the conversation finally shifted

to Niessen, whom she met at a Walmart when he worked as a greeter. She considered him a saviour of sorts—someone who rescued her from an abusive relationship. She described him as an admirable dancer, a fine Christmas cook and the best man she and her children had ever had in their lives. When she talked of Niessen, the middle-aged mother looked like a dreamy schoolgirl. To hear her describe it, they had lived a sort of fairy-tale romance, if you didn't include the part about the Saturday-afternoon drive to Weiner Kellestine's farm after the worst biker slaughter in memory.

CHAPTER 27

A Hug

How far that little candle throws its beams!
THE MERCHANT OF VENICE, ACT 4, SCENE 1

Even in the darkest of tunnels, there is a light.
VERONICA DOUSE, MOTHER OF MURDER VICTIM

The preliminary inquiry into the second-degree murder charges against Cameron Acorn, Bobby Quinn, Carlitto Aragon and Randy Brown in the beating death of Shawn Douse was held in Oshawa during the first week of July 2007, in a grim courthouse in a one-storey strip mall, flanked by a funeral home and a cemetery. Twenty members of the Durham Regional Police stood guard inside the courtroom, and a dozen or so more watched outside, when Mary Thompson took the witness box to tell about the late-night killing in the townhouse on Hattie Court in Keswick. In Mary's soft voice there was a fusion of disbelief and horror. Everyone in the courtroom had to strain to hear as she told how she had also feared for her life the night of December 6–7, 2005, when she kicked the dead

431

Shawn Douse's body and said that hateful word, "nigger."

The dead man's mother and sister, Veronica and Mary, looked like they were dressed for church that day, with skirts that fell past their knees and hats with broad brims. They cried during Mary's testimony, and were particularly demonstrative of their grief when they heard how their Shawn had screamed out "I'm sorry" in the last moments of his life. When they heard snickering from the prisoners' box, Veronica and Mary Douse stared across the room at the young bikers, who showed not a trace of fear. If they were troubled by the angry mother and sister, they didn't show it, as their barely stifled laughter continued. It was easy to think that Boxer Muscedere and Ripper Fullager would have been mortified by how the accused men were representing their club. For all of their faults, Boxer and Ripper weren't racists, nor were they bullies towards women. They had fast-tracked Acorn to full-patch status in the hope that he would be part of the future of the No Surrender Crew, and it would have pained them to see him acting like a racist thug.

The word "nigger" seemed to hang in the courtroom on July 6, as Mary Thompson's three days in the witness box wound down. That morning, Crown attorney Gregory O'Driscoll took John Douse aside in the courtroom hallway to relay a message from Mary. She needed to tell the Douse family something. Would the family agree to meet with her once her testimony was done?

Once the witnesses were led out of court in chains, the victim's father, John, Veronica and Mary Douse were escorted into a small room in the courthouse. Already inside were several police officers and Mary Thompson.

John Douse saw that Mary was terrified as she looked in his direction. The officers were ready to jump in, in case things turned violent.

"I'm not a racist," she said softly.

"If you were a racist you wouldn't be here as a star witness," said John Douse in his Caribbean lilt. "You don't have a streak of such a thing. This is my privilege."

Then they were hugging, as a loving father hugs his child. John Douse later said he could feel her shake mightily as she sobbed in his arms, like a forgiven little girl. When they finally pulled themselves apart, he could see there were also tears in the eyes of several of the police officers.

"I'm sorry," Mary said, once she could put words together again.

"Why are you sorry?" John Douse asked. "You helped us. You are the star witness. Without you, there would be no case."

He gave her fatherly advice, much the same sort of words his son Shawn had ignored for so many painful years. "Let's hope that you use this opportunity to turn your life around."

"For sure," she promised. "I'll never look back."

Mary Thompson and Veronica Douse were now looking at each other. Veronica was very much her own person. She wouldn't accept Mary's apology just because her husband had done so, especially for something as enormous as the violent death of her son. She was face to face in a small room with the woman who had admitted kicking her son's lifeless body and defiling it with a sickening epithet. Still, she was not there for vengeance.

"Can I give you a hug?" Veronica Douse asked softly.

Mary melted into the mother's arms, sobbing again, all attempts at self-control long abandoned. Mary Douse joined in the embrace. When they finally separated, Veronica told Mary Thompson that she had done something wonderful and courageous for the Douse family that week. Finally, they had some hope of justice and some understanding of how their boy had died. "Even in the darkest of tunnels, there is a light," Veronica said. "You were that light."

Though the horrors of Shawn Douse's death might have been expected to drive them apart, something as fleeting as a hug was enough to show that, although thugs and misanthropes can damage a great deal, it is not within their power to snuff out what is most decent in even those who endure the most.

Mr. Justice Edwin Minden sentenced Shawn Douse's attackers six months later, on Monday, January 7, 2008. He did not mince words, calling the attack "a vicious, senseless, callous and cowardly killing."

Thirty-six-year-old Randy Brown of Jacksons Point admitted that he stuffed a T-shirt into Shawn Douse's throat to finish him off after Shawn was beaten unconscious. For this, Brown pleaded guilty to second-degree murder and was given life in prison, with the opportunity to seek parole in June 2016.

Twenty-seven-year-old Cameron Acorn, the full-patch No Surrender Crew member whom the Crown called the architect of the murder plot, was sentenced to nine years for manslaughter, while twenty-eight-year-old Bobby Quinn, also of Keswick, received five years and eleven months on the same charge. Full-patch Bandido Carlitto Aragon pleaded guilty to aggravated assault, and the twenty-four-year-old was sentenced to three years and eleven months.

Whitby court heard that Big Paul Sinopoli of the No Surrender Crew was one of the men who beat Shawn Douse on the night of his death, but that Bandido prospect Jamie (Goldberg) Flanz of the No Surrender Crew played no part in the killing. Flanz also had not been a police informant, as Weiner Kellestine had alleged on the night he was murdered. Boxer was right when he stood up for Flanz that night at Kellestine's barn.

Mary Thompson cried uncontrollably when she heard that the court case was finally over. She was far away, and the news came to her by telephone that those involved had chosen to accept plea bargains rather than go to trial. Finally, there was something in her life that felt like justice. Asked the reason for her crying, Mary replied, "They're happy tears."

CHAPTER 28

Cut-throat Defence

Thou art the best o' th' cut-throats . . .
MACBETH, ACT 2, SCENE 4

SLOW DOWN! AND LISTEN TO THE RHUBARB GROW
SIGN ON THE ROAD INTO SHEDDEN, ONTARIO

Jury selection for the trial of the biggest mass murder in Ontario's history was a painfully slow process. On one day alone, 114 potential jurors were rejected. Out of the first 875 candidates to be queried, only eight jurors were chosen. Finally, on March 31, 2009, five weeks after jury selection began, a shaggy-haired retired postal worker—who bore more than a passing resemblance to Wayne Kellestine—was deemed suitable by both the Crown and the six defence teams to fill the twelfth and final seat in the jury box. He was the 1,513th person to be questioned, after a parade of schoolteachers, custodians, homemakers, salespeople, farmers and a cake decorator. It was perhaps fitting that a trial of this magnitude had required the largest jury pool in memory anywhere in the country. For someone who faced the prospect of spending at least half a year of his life listening to details of mass slaughter, juror number twelve seemed perhaps a little too enthusiastic. Asked how he felt about sitting in judgment of the gang of accused killers, he straightened his back and replied, "I'd be honoured."

Meanwhile, in Shedden, locals shuddered at the press accounts the trial generated. They preferred to talk about almost anything else, like layoffs in the local auto industry or, preferably, the annual rhubarb festival in June—while the gears of justice ground on in London, a local resident was dressing up in a fuzzy costume as Rosy Rhubarb to entertain children and tourists. If cornered and pressed—hard—to talk about the massacre, locals would invariably note that none of the victims or accused was from their community. Something seemed dishonest and unfair about the press continually calling the killings the "Shedden Massacre." As eighteen-year-old university student Helen Slee put it, "A rhubarb festival isn't that big of a deal, but it's a lot better than a mass-murder dumping ground."

There's a courtroom truism that if you can't beat the evidence, you try to beat the trial. That means pushing for a mistrial, and hoping that the Crown's case somehow crumbles the next time around. Perhaps it was a sign of the Shedden defendants' confidence in the arguments they could muster in support of their innocence that calls for a mistrial began almost immediately. Long gone were any hopes the defence might entertain of showing that the accused weren't at the barn that night. Clearly, the killers were in the courtroom as the trial began. What remained to be determined was exactly who was guilty of what. So, rather than mustering their resources to plead their clients' innocence, defence teams protested that lead Crown attorney Kevin Gowdey had taken things too far in his opening address. Ironically, those calls came at the same time that some members of the Toronto press were griping that Gowdey should have gone further and been more entertaining, instead of plowing ahead in his earnest, straightforward style. If one side thinks you're too provocative, and the other thinks you're too tepid, you're probably not far off the mark.

So detailed was the Crown's case that the megatrial had reached its third month before it was time for the star prosecution witness, M.H., to finally be called to the witness box. Then a severe medical condition suffered by the wife of Dwight Mushey's senior lawyer, Ted Royle, caused both a delay in the trial and a scramble to find replacement counsel to work with junior lawyer Christian Angelini. Finally, on July 14, Michael Moon arrived in his burnt-orange Porsche from Toronto, fresh from a terrorism case involving defendants known as the "Toronto 18," and the trial was ready to resume.

By this time, the jury had already heard from forensic experts, a police biker expert and relatives of the victims. They had seen volumes of email correspondence between the killers and the killed, as well as members of the Bandido Nation from around the world. They had cringed as they listened to the searing, raw sobs of the victims' families as pictures of their dead and bloodied loved ones were shown. While the eight dead men may have made imperfect decisions in life, it was painfully clear to the jury that they were well loved nonetheless. No one was stronger in the witness box than Boxer's common-law wife, Nina Lee, who came across as a proud and still-grieving widow. "I loved him very much," she said, as her voice cracked with emotion.

The jury wouldn't have been able to see the design on the right calf of Boxer Muscedere's stunning daughter Tereasa, now in her early twenties, as she accompanied Nina to the courthouse. It was a tattoo of a rosary; from it dangled a pair of boxing gloves. They also couldn't see the tattoo of a cross on the right arm of Pony Jessome's son Richard, with the initials GPJ and RIP.

Boxes of tissues left on wooden benches marked the part of the gallery set aside for family members of the victims. Many of those sitting in these seats hadn't met before, but they soon formed a makeshift community of sorts. Jamie Flanz's sister Jennifer, a soft-spoken, extremely dignified woman, hugged the sister of Bam Bam Salerno, who sobbed uncontrollably as she heard details of his walk to his death. She also held Boxer's daughter Tereasa as they learned about how Boxer had stuck up for Flanz in the final hours of their lives. That the dead men, who at first glance were outsiders, were so dearly loved by quality people made it all the more mysterious that they were drawn into the vortex of Weiner Kellestine, Taz Sandham and their followers.

Each day of the trial, Sandham was the first to be led into the courtroom. He had been isolated from the other prisoners since they learned that he had offered himself up as a government witness, only to be rejected. His steel handcuffs were removed and his legs shackled to the floor, out of sight of the jury. His beard was shaved clean, his hair was thinning and he had clearly gotten fatter and softer. Despite the added girth and the puffiness of his cheeks, he still looked tiny. Sometimes he tried to chat with his police guards, as if they still shared some sort of brotherhood of the badge. Brown paper was taped to the Plexiglas of his cubicle, so that other prisoners couldn't glare at him. Most of the time, the would-be biker leader slumped low in his prisoner's chair, making himself barely visible to the body of the court.

Next to him was Marcelo Aravena. His prizefighter's body was pudgy now and his face a mask of depression. Word sifted into the courtroom that he had been severely beaten by a group of prisoners in their early twenties, which explained a black eye he sported. He often didn't bother to shave, not seeming to care that the stubble made him appear all the more menacing.

To Aravena's left was Frank Mather, who seemed to have thrived in jail. Gone was the threadbare waif who had surfed couches in a downward spiral all the way to Kellestine's farm. He was neatly dressed in a black sports jacket that nicely covered his tattoos. He had bulked up considerably—in particular, his arms were bigger now. Three square meals a day clearly agreed with him, at least physically. True to form, Mather was solid in his support of the other accused, even though his association with them threatened to end his freedom forever. Police once listened in on his jailhouse phone calls to hear him wishing Kellestine a happy birthday. On another occasion, he told his father he was depositing funds into the canteen accounts of his co-accused from Winnipeg.

In the next cubicle was Brett Gardiner, the youngest of the accused. He looked like a middle-aged man now, though he had turned only twenty-five in June. Even so, the gravity of his situation seemed to be lost on him. One day, Gardiner appeared deep in thought as he wrote a note for his lawyers, Christopher Hicks and Bella Petrouchinova, to pass on to *London Free Press* reporter Jane Sims. In it, Gardiner lamented how the *Free Press* had recently revamped its comic section and dropped the cartoon strip *DeFlocked*, which chronicled the adventures of Mamet, billed by fans on the Internet as "comedy's most lovably derelict sheep." "I love that little sheep," Gardiner wrote the reporter.

But few gestures of callousness could be more damning than making a pass at a woman who is emotionally moved by the death of a man you have helped kill. On one particularly tearful day, Gardiner gazed across the courtroom at sketch artist Karlene Ryan. The attractive twentysomething Ryan appeared sombre as the widow of Bam Bam Salerno testified tearfully about how her Frankie loved taking her and their newborn son, Mario, out to restaurants and reading bedtime stories to his niece. "He became a much better man towards the end," she testified in a trembling voice. "He was a wonderful man . . . He was liked by the neighbours. He was a terrific father." During a break in Stephanie's testimony, while the court caught its breath after a troubling glimpse into the human side of one of the victims of Gardiner's group, Gardiner slipped a note to Ryan that read, "Why aren't you smiling?"

Gardiner's lawyers kept him well supplied with pulpy paperbacks. But if he had a literary bent of his own, he was embarrassed by it when it was revealed to the court. On the same day that Stephanie Salerno spoke of her lost husband, Gardiner's love poem "Love Not Lost" was displayed on screen. What was important to the prosecution case was not its sentimentality, but rather the way he signed off: "Prospect Bandido Bull Manitoba." For someone who was denying membership in the club, the evidence appeared damning. Gardiner's lawyers gamely suggested it could have been written by someone else, but the prospect of a burglar/poet breaking into Kellestine's inner compound and sneaking past the assembled bikers and two dogs to send a sugary love poem to Gardiner's girlfriend seemed remote. The odds of another aspiring poet in the gang of visitors to Kellestine's farm seemed even more unlikely.

Gardiner's squeamishness that day brought welcome comic relief to Dwight Mushey, who sat in the cubicle next to him. Mushey and Gardiner often whispered back and forth to each other during testimony and joked during breaks. Of all of the prisoners, Mushey was clearly the best preserved, and prisoners from his detention centre noted that the black belt was staying fit by having an inmate sit on his back as he did push-ups in his cell block.

Feelings of brotherhood between Mushey and Kellestine, however, had clearly long since evaporated. The two killers didn't look at each other anymore, a quantum departure from their preliminary hearing two and a half years earlier, when they often shared a laugh in the prisoners' box. Now, there were stories that Mushey was upset with Kellestine for yapping to police immediately after his arrest. Word floated out of jail that Mushey had had Kellestine beaten a couple of times as punishment for the rambling statements he had given to police. Others speculated that the beatings were carried out by someone hoping to gain favour with the Hells Angels. Whatever the case, Kellestine didn't look any the worse for wear in the courtroom. Three months into the trial, the biker submitted to a dramatic makeover, giving up his ponytail in favour of a short haircut and shaving his moustache. His face was now that of an earnest professional as he studied those of potential jurors. Now the postal worker juror with the flowing locks looked more like Weiner Kellestine the outlaw biker than did the old man sitting in the far end of the prisoners' box.

For all of the changes, Kellestine didn't appear embarrassed or depressed or worried. If anything, he seemed as righteous and cocky as ever. At one point, during a break, he asked reporter Jane Sims for a complimentary subscription to *The London Free Press*. If his story was selling papers, he reasoned, he was entitled to a free copy at least.

In a twist of fate that no one could have anticipated when Kellestine's buddy Concrete Dave Weiche founded Bikers Against Pedophiles, accused child-killer Michael Thomas Rafferty was placed in Kellestine's wing of the Elgin-Middlesex Detention Centre that summer. In a hugely publicized case, Rafferty stood accused of abducting and killing eight-year-old Woodstock girl Victoria (Tori) Stafford. Kellestine was outraged at having to share a cell block with such a man. "You'd look good on my resumé," Kellestine screamed through his bars at Rafferty. "I'm charged with killing eight people." There aren't many places in the world where that kind of track record would offer anyone the moral high ground.

Kellestine was certainly conscious of the fact that he was now known beyond his neighbourhood and biker circles. One intercepted conversation with his common-law wife caught him comparing himself in jail to a goldfish in a bowl, watched by everyone. "I'm the most famous person this place ever had," he said.

As the six accused killers spent each day in court in their separate Plexiglas cubicles in the prisoners' box, their legs chained to the floor, it was easy to think of Woody, the Loners' mascot, pacing his tiny cage north of Toronto. As they sat there, looking tired and banal, it was a challenge to remember that they were ever dangerous predators. Some members of the public poked their heads briefly into the courtroom for a peek at them, but only a few diehards returned each day once the novelty of seeing accused mass murderers in person wore off.

The crime that might have bound the killers together tore them apart instead. By the time M.H. was finally called to the witness box on July 16, all semblance of a united defence strategy was long gone. If the bikers who definitely didn't open fire that night—Gardiner, Mather and Aravena—could have their charges reduced to second-degree murder or manslaughter, they had the hope of walking free in the foreseeable future. If the first-degree murder charges stuck, they would receive automatic life terms. In order to have their charges reduced, they would have to pin the blame on Kellestine, Mushey, Sandham and the Crown witness, M.H. They may have all gotten into this mess together, but they were going to try to get out their own separate ways.

Such a defence required that the lawyers for the bikers who stood guard that night in the barn portray their clients as virtual hostages themselves. The jury needed to be convinced that, had the three of them broken ranks with the rest of the hit team, they would surely have put their own lives at risk. There was more than a little irony to this—guards arguing they were prisoners—but it had a chance nonetheless. The gambit couldn't be further from the biker ideal of brotherhood. So much for "cut one, we all bleed"; instead, Gardner, Mather and Aravena would pursue what is known as a "cut-throat defence."

But it's hard to be more cut-throat than to snitch on the guys you call "brother" in exchange for immunity from prosecution for crimes you committed shoulder to shoulder with them. When M.H. took the witness box, he had already proven himself to be the most cut-throat of all the Bandidos.

For his first day in the witness box, he again wore a neatly tailored blue business suit and tie. His hair was cut short and his face was shaved clean, a sharp departure from his appearance during his biker and drug-dealing days. "Looks more like a banker than a biker," a reporter observed.

M.H. didn't flinch when Aravena made a pistol shape with his fingers and pretended to shoot him. He also remained stoic as Aravena twice gave him the finger. The other defendants were more restrained, although Mushey glowered at the man he had once sponsored into the club. But if M.H. were the flinching type, he probably wouldn't be making enemies of guys like Dwight Mushey anyway.

As M.H. recounted his story of joining Sandham's Winnipeg crew, he made the little biker seem like a megalomaniac who felt he had some sort of divine right to be the national president of the world's second-largest outlaw motorcycle club, even though he had been a police officer just a few years before. M.H. told of being made an executive officer in the chapter just a few months after joining, and said Taz had effectively cut off communications between Winnipeg and Toronto to consolidate his power. It all sounded like a corporate raid, in an odd sort of way. For guys who would tell each other they can't tolerate the mainstream, the bikers seemed to do a pretty earnest job of emulating the institutions they said they despised. But banks and Kiwanis clubs don't kill people.

Frankie Salerno's sister was comforted by the sister of Jamie Flanz, but she sobbed nonetheless as M.H. described how Salerno was led out to his death. That was when the informant's voice cracked. "He [Frankie Salerno] wants me to shake his hand," M.H. said. His voice quavered and he dropped his head as he continued: "I don't do anything. I don't shake his hand or anything." Then he put his head down and sobbed for more than a minute before he was able to proceed.

When it came time for cross-examination, Aravena's lawyer, Tony Bryant, chose a full-frontal assault. He showed M.H. a photo of each of the eight victims alive. Then he showed them photos of each of the eight bikers as they had been found on the outskirts of Shedden, bloodied and dead. He drove home the point that M.H. and Aravena could easily have died that night too.

"Marcelo wasn't singing that night?" Bryant asked, pointing out that the sullen Aravena was moved by feelings very different from those that animated Wayne Kellestine.

"No," M.H. replied.

"Marcelo wasn't dancing that night, was he?" Bryant continued. "He was sweating like a pig, or how about like a deer caught in the headlights?"

"Yeah, that's a better way to put it," M.H. replied.

At this point, Aravena appeared to be fighting back tears in the prisoners' box as his lawyer pushed for details of that evening.

M.H.'s voice cracked and he began to cry himself as he was asked whether he killed any of the victims.

"No," he replied.

The spectacle of the outlaw biker tearing up passed, for the moment, and M.H. returned to his story. He said the original idea was just to pull patches, and it was a confused one. He dabbed his eyes with a tissue and then continued: "There was no plan."

Bryant was due to continue his cross-examination the next day, Friday, July 24. After the jury settled into their seats, Mr. Justice Thomas Heeney told them, "Unfortunately, our witness has taken ill and for that reason, we're not able to continue today."

With that, the jury was sent home for the weekend, and several of them were smiling at the early break. They weren't told that M.H. had been rushed to hospital that morning, after suffering chest pains and sweating profusely. His skin was pale and it was hard not to fear the worst: that he had suffered a heart attack. If so, the defence might finally be handed what they had sought for the past four months: a mistrial.

CHAPTER 29

"The Perfect Patsy"

My offence is rank, it smells to heaven;
It hath the primal eldest curse upon't,
A brother's murder.
HAMLET, ACT 3, SCENE 3

It'll be tried some day in a higher court than this.
BANDIDO INFORMER M.H. TESTIFIES IN MEGA-TRIAL

M.H. managed to pull himself together after a four-day weekend, although he looked a little drawn and pale as he sat back in the witness chair on Tuesday, August 4, for another round of grilling. He was testifying only to serve his own purposes, but the defence lawyers had their own uses for him: they wanted to coax him into fingering any of the accused other than their own clients. Bryant noted cynically that the witness was extremely well prepared, and M.H. acknowledged that he had studied hundreds of hours of exhibits. He had even been allowed to sit in the witness chair before the trial actually began, so that it wouldn't be too much of a shock when he finally took the witness box.

When Bryant compared him to an actor who had studied hard to learn a role, M.H. appeared ready for the question. "Can I get something straight?" M.H. replied, his voice cracking once again. "I relive this every day of my life. Sometimes things take me back—a smell, a sound. I was there and the accused were there."

M.H. dismissed a suggestion by Bryant that his client, Marcelo Aravena, "came within a whisker" of being the ninth murder victim that night.

"I didn't see anybody put a gun to his head," M.H. said of Aravena. "I didn't see anybody threaten him, if that's what you mean."

"But *you* were scared?" Bryant pressed, forcing M.H. to acknowledge that Aravena had at least as much reason to fear for his life as he did.

"I was scared," M.H. agreed.

Bryant asked M.H. if he could recall a walk through the woods behind the Kellestine farm in the days before the murders. As Bryant recounted, the bikers were in a cheerful mood as they tramped through the woods. Then Kellestine reached into a tree and pulled out a black substance that he stuffed into his mouth. Between chews, he announced that he had just taken a mouthful of raccoon shit. M.H. couldn't recall the incident, but agreed with Bryant that this was just the type of thing you'd expect during a walk in the woods with Weiner Kellestine, the crazy old biker with the perpetual shit-eating grin.

"That's pretty much Wayne Kellestine," M.H. told the court. It was easy to think that a guy who would eat raccoon droppings would be capable of anything.

But lawyers for the accused weren't inclined to let the Crown's witness blame others without accepting his fair share of culpability. Though the police had already dismissed Sandham's claim that M.H. killed Chopper Raposo and Pony Jessome, the defence had a go at that line of argument. But the evidence from the ballistics experts was against them. M.H. held a shotgun that night, yet forensic pathologist Dr. Toby Rose told the court that Raposo and Pony were both killed by bullets, not shotgun pellets. Whatever else he had done that night, the accusation that M.H. had killed Chopper and Pony quickly ran out of momentum.

The lawyers also challenged the witness's credibility, noting that M.H. now seemed to recall details that had somehow eluded him just weeks after the murders. How could it be, they asked, that immediately after the massacre the informer didn't seem to know what type of gloves the Winnipeggers had worn that night—yet now he did? M.H. said that he couldn't understand how his memory worked, but that he was telling the truth. Throughout his testimony, it was clear that he was trying hard to make the prosecution's case.

"I'm suggesting you're pedalling as fast as you can to avoid eight counts of murder," said Michael Moon, one of Dwight Mushey's lawyers.

"It'll be tried some day in a higher court than this," M.H. replied softly, while appearing once again to tear up. Perhaps he wanted to make sure his witness protection deal didn't fall through. Or maybe he genuinely felt guilty. Only he knew whether his weeping was authentic.

Whatever the case, M.H. seemed uncomfortable as he spoke of his role in the murders, but he was absolutely unapologetic for his betrayal of his one-time biker brothers who were now in the prisoners' box.

The longer the trial went on, the more the other accused bikers pointed fingers at Kellestine to explain the night of madness. These men, who loved their boastful "Our colours don't run" emblems, now hid behind a legal defence that hinged on just how cowed they were by Kellestine. It was as if everyone in the barn was his hostage that night. By August, the court heard Moon suggest that even Mushey, the coolest of the accused, slipped out of the barn to take heart medication to combat extreme stress. It is impossible to know how ice-cold Dwight Mushey, biker, assassin, martial artist and drug dealer, felt about portraying himself as a victim, but it cannot have been a role he was familiar with.

It was clear that Kellestine wasn't going to take the heat by himself when one of his lawyers, Ken McMillan, began to question M.H. In fact, the old biker was willing to try on the victim's mantle himself. Kellestine hadn't invited the bikers to his home, McMillan noted. Left alone in Ontario, he hadn't done anything against the No Surrender Crew since receiving the order to pull their patches. The dishevelled Nazi sympathizer had been minding his own business until the Manitobans showed up unannounced. The clear implication was that Kellestine might have been a murder victim as well if he hadn't gone along with Taz Sandham's crew. McMillan asked M.H. why the Winnipeggers felt the need "to sneak up on him."

"You'd have to ask the States," M.H. replied. "Orders are orders."

While M.H. and Sandham had provided lurid accounts of Kellestine's bloodthirsty eagerness to assassinate his so-called brothers, McMillan argued that Kellestine had always hoped to do things peacefully—to pull the patches of the No Surrender Crew without violence, and perhaps even keep a couple of the men in the club. After all, Boxer and the rest of them were his friends. He had little motive to get rid of them, McMillan argued, then noted that Sandham's crew, on the other hand, had plenty to gain by pulling Kellestine into their plan to rub out the No Surrender Crew.

"You guys were set up as the only chapter in Canada and you had the perfect patsy back here in Ontario," McMillan continued.

"I disagree," M.H. replied.

McMillan wasn't going to let up. The other bikers could talk now about Weiner Kellestine's craziness, and how he ate raccoon shit and danced and sang between murders, but didn't they seek Kellestine out *because* of his madness? And why hadn't any of them turned a gun on Kellestine as he turned his back on them seven times that night to lead victims from his barn to their executions?

How could these burly, well-armed, younger bikers have been so intimidated by Kellestine that they would act so heinously against their own consciences?

"You guys didn't have to do anything you didn't want to do," McMillan continued. "You could say, 'I don't think so,' and you could have blown Wayne's head off. I suggest you were doing the killing."

"You can suggest all you want," M.H. replied.

George Kriarakis's mother sat at the back of the courtroom, dressed in black, for some of M.H.'s testimony. She listened as lawyers grilled M.H. on whether Aravena and Gardiner were friends of the club, prospects or just prospective members. M.H. said the distinctions really didn't matter in the end.

"We all were bikers that night. Everybody stuck to the biker code that night," he told the court, without a trace of irony, "We were all Bandidos that night."

She also listened as the court was told the gruesome details of the shooting's immediate aftermath as lawyers tried to ascertain whether her son's body had been dragged from one vehicle to another. What to her was a nightmare that would scar the rest of her life was just another piece of confusing evidence in a massive legal proceeding. She couldn't control her tears that day, and on her way out of court she banged her fist against the Plexiglas where Kellestine sat.

"Don't look at them," a court services worker advised when she re-entered court later in the day.

During a break in testimony, Crash's mother said that her son had briefly considered a career as a lawyer but abandoned that because he didn't think lawyers were always fair with people. Somehow, instead, he became a tow truck driver. She shuddered at the memory. It was this job that led to his friendship with members of biker clubs. She wished she knew more about the Bandidos at the time her George joined the club, but also realized it didn't really matter anymore. Her boy George had always been loyal to his friends, and somehow this had become a dangerous thing when he joined the Bandidos. Though bikers make more noise about loyalty than any other group, in no other group is it more dangerous to actually believe it.

Pony Jessome's twenty-year-old son Richard also attended court to hear M.H. testify. He shares his father's thin build, reddish hair and quiet demeanour, and Kellestine appeared startled at first when their eyes met as he walked into the room. Perhaps it was like seeing a ghost. Kellestine quickly recovered, smirking, laughing and making a threatening face, as if it was all a joke that only he understood. "I felt like I was disrespected and that he wanted to harm me," Pony's son said. "And I felt very angry and sad all at the same time."

None of the victims' families was in court the day the jury heard that Kellestine had sent Brett Gardiner out to search for the fruit of a pickle tree. At first, Gardiner cringed to hear the story recounted in open court, but a conversation with his lawyers seemed to soothe him. The more stupid he looked, the more plausible his defence. Just as Gardiner had been so easily led by his biker brothers, he was now as pliable as a choirboy in the hands of his lawyers.

Like the rest of the accused, Gardiner had far better reason to trust his legal counsel than he ever had trusted his
biker clubmates. Better to be led out of prison than into it.
But the bikers' lawyers were leading their clients in another,
more troubling way. Their defence rested on a humiliating
repudiation of all the club had stood for. While once the
accused had worn the Fat Mexican to hide their weakness,
they were now eager to flaunt that deficiency. Their lawyers
were now competing to prove their clients were dumber,
weaker and crazier than their old Bandidos brothers.

For his part, Pony's son Richard left court with a feeling
of disgust about the brotherhood that ended his father's
life. He asked a reporter to print some of an open letter to
the men who had called his dad their brother. "Don't play
stupid," he wrote in his letter to the bikers. "All of you were
in it together."

The lawyer who can address the jury last, immediately
before deliberations begin, enjoys a distinct advantage.
He or she is in a position to counter all of the arguments
raised by opposing counsel and have his or her views
fresh in the minds of jurors as they prepare to deliberate.
In this trial, the lawyer who addressed the jury last could
end up with the rare opportunity to mount a counterattack amidst five other consecutive closing statements by

defence lawyers also attacking the Crown's case—all of which would follow the prosecution's closing statement. But there was one proviso: all of the defence lawyers would be allowed to speak after the prosecution *only* if they all decided to keep their clients out of the witness box. If even one defence team called on its client to testify, the Crown would get the all-important final address to the jury. If ever it made sense for the remnants of the Canadian Bandidos to mount a show of unity, it was now, as the trial reached its final chapter.

Despite the risks, and the advisability of a final display of brotherhood, Taz Sandham had been toying throughout the trial with the idea of testifying. In order to test his skills as a witness, his legal team had prepared a mock cross-examination, held during downtime in the case. To some observers, the exercise was an utter disaster, but the only view that counted was that of the Tazman.

Sandham ended speculation as to what he might do as court resumed on Wednesday, September 9, 2009. He wore a conservative business suit and shirt and tie, and walked across the courtroom to the witness box. Along the way, he looked directly at the twelve strangers who would decide his fate and mouthed "Good morning."

What followed was a prolonged betrayal of all of the biker principles Sandham had once said he embraced. His voice was high and squeaky, calling to mind his Little Beaker nickname, as he swore on the Bible, then recapped his life story, which was a lie-filled fusion of self-pity and selfless heroism, to defence lawyer Donald Crawford. He told the jury that he had once attended Bible school and was married, with two children, "but technically I have four."

He testified that he used to write up parking tickets in his days as a bylaw officer, but didn't mention that he had once falsely advertised himself as a one-man army, pretending to have black belts in a dizzying number of martial arts—or that he'd once claimed to be the founder of his own martial art, Sando. He did claim that his skills as a bodyguard had been sought out by generals and assorted world leaders, including Princess Patricia. When defence lawyer Michael Moon noted that Princess Patricia had died in 1974, when he was just four years old, Sandham was temporarily puzzled, until he vaguely said that he had guarded a different, non-British Princess Patricia. He also claimed he'd served in Bosnia with the now-disbanded Canadian Airborne Regiment, but admitted under cross-examination that he never actually enlisted, due to illness. He hinted that he hadn't been kicked out of the East St. Paul police force because of his involvement with biker gangs, and suggested obliquely that there were ongoing investigations into the force that he didn't wish to jeopardize. "There were a lot of issues I had, sir, with the East St. Paul police," he cryptically told Moon.

"I suggest you were going to eliminate Boxer and Chopper because they were your chief antagonists," Moon said.

"No, sir. That's not true," Sandham replied.

"I think you suggested you should be bait for Boxer and Chopper. And you convinced Wayne," Moon continued.

"No, there's no convincing Wayne," Sandham replied.

The past three years, Sandham said, had been "emotionally and psychologically draining." "I'm under psychiatric care," he said, between tears. "I take medication . . . I suffer flashbacks. I relive these events every day."

Tears came fast and hard as the Tazman insisted his motives for testifying were nothing if not pure. "I wanted to make sure everyone paid for what they did," he said. Apparently there wasn't much blame for himself, but plenty for the others in the barn that night, as well as down at the Bandidos' mother chapter in Texas—according to him, the order to murder Boxer Muscedere and Bam Bam Salerno had come straight from the top level of the Bandidos in Texas. A month before the murders, Sandham said that the club's top *sargento de armas*, Mongo Price, told him and Kellestine that *El Presidente* Jeff Pike wanted Boxer and Bam Bam dead. Sandham testified that Mongo said to them at the Peace Arch Park meeting: "We don't want to tell you what to do, but this is what you're going to do. We want you to kill Boxer and Bam Bam."

Sandham told the jurors that it was "important everyone in the case came to justice," as if he were an officer of the court reminding them of their civic duty. One might be forgiven for forgetting that he was the one who rounded up and delivered the Winnipeggers to Kellestine's farm as he continued, "I wanted to make sure the families knew the order came from the U.S. and the Americans wanted to murder two of their loved ones."

He said that Concrete Dave Weiche played a troubling role in turning the Americans on the No Surrender Crew, and repeatedly spoke of a *coup d'état* to purge the club of its Canadian leaders. "I didn't know what that meant," Sandham testified. "It was making me uncomfortable." Often, his testimony was diametrically opposed to that of M.H., who portrayed Sandham as a little megalomaniac and habitual liar. Faced with the choice of believing Sandham or M.H., it was easier to believe M.H. than the sweaty ex-cop, who seemed driven to portray himself as a hero. Sandham said in his little squeaky voice that he had never sought power in the club, nor had he even really held any. As he told things, Concrete Dave Weiche cooked up a story that Sandham was Manitoba president, then "basically threatened me to back up his story."

Sandham repeatedly said that he thought the trip to Kellestine's farm would end in nothing more than the pulling of the Toronto members' patches. He got nervous, however, after arriving at Kellestine's, when a neighbour contacted the aging biker and said he wanted a gun to murder his cheating wife. Sandham said he was further troubled when they all went for a walk through the woods behind Kellestine's farm. A rabbit ran out, and the others urged him to shoot it, but Sandham said he just couldn't bring himself to harm the helpless bunny.

There were plenty of pauses for more tears as he continued with his story. He told jurors that Kellestine promised him that they wouldn't harm any visitors to his farm, saying, "No blood will be spilled on my property." Sandham swore he still couldn't help but worry about the intentions of the others, especially M.H., Mushey and Kellestine. Once, after he left the farmhouse, where he had been playing Battleship on Kellestine's old computer, he overheard the others talking about killing Chopper and Boxer and cutting them into little pieces. Mushey seemed to particularly enjoy talk of murder. "He actually had goosebumps on his arm," Sandham said, recalling that Mushey told the others, "Look at my arm, I've fantasized all my life about this."

Sandham acknowledged he wore a bulletproof vest on the night of the murders, but dismissed this detail as insignificant. It was "ratty," he said, and something that he wore whenever he felt threatened, making it sound more like a child's security blanket than a sniper's body armour.

Sandham said he was hiding in the loft that night when he saw Chopper brandish a sawed-off shotgun and overheard him tell Boxer and Kellestine, "That's for Taz when he comes through the door. That fucking pig. I'm going to put a hole in him."

"I thought, 'I'm surrounded by a bunch of killers,'" Sandham said, teary-eyed at the memory. "I started to think about what I'm going to do. I just started to think about my daughter. I started to think I'm never going to see her again."

Not long after that, as Sandham recalled, Mushey, M.H. and Kellestine "drew down" and pointed their weapons at the Toronto visitors, each of whom carried guns. That was too much for the man of peace perched in the rafters, as he told the story: "I popped up. I was concerned for people's safety. As soon as Chopper saw me, he pulls out his shotgun. I put out my hand and said stop. We are here to talk. But he starts grinning and shoots at me."

According to Sandham, what happened next was a mystery and a miracle. He must have chambered a round in his rifle, because Chopper was now lying on the concrete floor. "I flinched, and *boom!*" he said. " . . . I did not mean to pull the trigger. It just happened. I didn't take aim. I was just trying to get Chopper to stop from shooting me.

"I actually felt the warmth from the gases when he shot the gun."

For the man who couldn't even shoot a bunny, the sight was altogether too much. "Chopper laying on the floor there is starting to make me feel sick to my stomach," he said, "so I step outside for some air."

The Bandidos in the prisoners' box rolled their eyes as Sandham's face reddened yet again. In his squeaky little voice, he chastised himself for not shooting Kellestine, but said this was hard for a pacifist such as himself. "I should have shot him when I had the gun, but I didn't. I couldn't bring myself to. Targets are one thing, murder is another."

Sandham claimed he did his best to comfort the wounded and the terrified. Crash Kriarakis seemed to be slipping into shock, so Sandham said he "snugged" a blanket around him. As he escorted Crash outside to what, he testified, he thought would be a ride to the hospital, the doomed biker "thanked me for helping him." He said he declined to shake Bam Bam Salerno's hand as he was led from the barn, since it was covered in blood. The sight left him sickened and he walked out of the barn himself again for fresh air, only to see Kellestine murder Bam Bam.

Throughout the night, Sandham said he wanted to run but felt trapped and couldn't reach a phone to call for help. "I didn't do anything. I just sucked it up and just stood there and just pretended I was going along with everything." He took a long pause, as if fighting back another bout of tears or waiting for a hug. Then he took a breath and said he played no part in the shooting of Flanz, and that Mushey fired both shots at Flanz's head. After the first shot, Sandham said, Mushey's pistol jammed, and he fumbled with it before getting off the second shot. He added that he was capable of easily unjamming the pistol, if he'd so desired.

As Sandham recalled things, he deliberately didn't tell Mather where to find gas for the Infiniti, as he wanted them all to get caught. He also refused to get into a vehicle with the victims' bodies. "I said, 'I am not getting in one of those cars with them.'" Instead, he drove his Blazer alone, and at one point on the drive to Shedden, he said he pulled over, sobbed and pounded on the steering wheel as a passing motorist honked at him and gave him the finger. Several times throughout the night, he said, he thought of racing off to the OPP detachment in Dutton to tell of the murders, but he didn't want the bikers to hurt his family. As Sandham spoke tearfully about wanting to protect his family, Kriarakis's father could take it no longer. From the back of the courtroom, he shouted out, "You didn't think about mine."

Sandham testified that he wasn't trying to destroy evidence when he had his Blazer shampooed after his return to Winnipeg. He just liked to keep things clean. "Imagine four large men going on a long trip and back. The car needed to be cleaned. There was mayo on the seats."

The other accused looked disgusted, but not particularly surprised, as Sandham told his story. On his second day in the witness box, however, all heads in the courtroom seemed to turn in unison as Sandham said something that was truly bizarre, even by his standards.

Sandham testified that he had never really been an outlaw biker at all, but instead was working deep undercover against one percenter bikers. His actions, he claimed, were inspired by author Yves Lavigne's book *Into the Abyss*, about FBI agent Anthony Tait, who infiltrated the Hells Angels in the U.S. "I got an idea in my head to infiltrate outlaw motorcycle clubs." Before he was overcome by that brainwave, he said, he didn't know much about one percenter bikers, but he was soon avidly reading about them on the Internet. "There's a lot of information there."

His story fizzled badly when he got into details of his life deep undercover. He could provide no names of police officers who were involved in his alleged ruse. He also couldn't explain why there was a need to go undercover on the Bandidos, since they didn't really exist in Winnipeg until he helped bring them there. He was able to assure the jury, however, that he didn't make an illegal penny from the club.

It was yet another utter betrayal of his former biker brothers, delivered in a squeaky Sunday-school teacher's voice. It's possible to argue that, of the accused, Taz Sandham was the one most responsible, since the eight murders would have never taken place if he hadn't stirred things up within the club and delivered the Winnipeggers to Kellestine's farm. Now, somehow, he was portraying himself as the only innocent amongst the group.

The bikers on the dock already knew that the little man could lie, but the content of his testimony was breathtaking. Mather looked agitated and Gardiner appeared deeply depressed. Aravena alternated between glowering at reporters and laughing to himself. Mushey smiled painfully and took several shots from his inhaler to steady his heart. Kellestine smiled and winked at a reporter. His fate had already been determined long before, but now Sandham's train wreck of a performance in the witness box meant that he likely wasn't the only one whose fate was sealed.

The advantage of being able to address the jury last was all but forgotten by the time the shackles were removed from the ankles of Marcelo Aravena so that he could lumber up to the witness box on Tuesday, September 22. Lawyer Kathryn Wells smiled as she turned a lectern so that she could face the jurors directly before she began her questioning of Aravena. The senior member of Aravena's defence team, Tony Bryant, was a sharp and seasoned courtroom brawler, but they'd decided the situation called for Wells's softer approach. She was as likeable as Bryant was combative, and they needed to play every card in their hand to save their client from spending the next quarter century in prison. Wells's voice was confident, but not overly aggressive, and she had a pleasant, girl-next-door demeanour as she asked the jury to dismiss the eight days of testimony from Sandham, even though he told a good story. "Mr Sandham is nevertheless a murderer . . . a murderer who refuses to accept responsibility."

Wells sounded genuinely concerned for the families of the eight murdered men as she repeated a phrase from Gowdey's opening address for the prosecution more than six months earlier. "Good or bad," he said of the men, "they never deserved that."

What followed was a twenty-minute précis of the life of a loser, but not a murderer. Often pausing to look out at the jury, Wells mapped out the fusion of failure and dreams that led Aravena to be sitting before them as an accused killer. Jurors appeared to be genuinely moved as Wells told of how Aravena's father had left his Chilean seamstress mother when he was just a toddler, and how Aravena had failed grades seven, eight and nine. Not surprisingly, he never did complete high school. Next was work as a pizza delivery man, pizza shop manager and flashes of what passed for glory on the bottom rungs of the mixed-martial-arts and boxing circuits in the Prairies. He seemed to always be searching for the guidance and validation that a father might have provided, even if it was brief applause from a fight crowd as he absorbed punches to the head. Even the coldest-hearted juror must have been moved as Wells described how Aravena had been awakened at four in the morning in June 2005, to be told that his cousin, who was also his roommate and best friend, had been murdered outside a bar.

It seemed sadly understandable that Aravena would be impressed that summer by nightclub owner Dwight

Mushey, whom he soon considered his new best friend. It was Mushey who helped out Aravena as he pulled out of cocaine addiction in early 2006, making living space in his basement available for $100 a month, when Aravena could pay it. Mushey was a successful businessman, a great cook, a nice guy with children, an accomplished martial artist and someone who always seemed in command of situations. Aravena initially lacked the commitment to join Mushey in the Bandidos, but was eventually "drawn in by the promise of camaraderie and brotherhood." "I trusted Mushey, that's why I wanted to join," Wells quoted her client as saying, then added, "Mr. Aravena kept his mouth shut and didn't ask questions."

Aravena then picked up the narrative as Wells began questioning him before the jury. He recalled how his life changed forever one morning in late March 2006, when he was awakened in Mushey's basement by fellow Bandido wannabe Bull Gardiner. That was when he was told they were leaving immediately for Ontario, "and if things go good, we can become prospects." At first, Aravena volunteered to drop out of an MMA fight card that weekend in Steinbach, but Mushey said that Taz Sandham's SUV was already too crowded, and that he should use some of the six hundred dollars he'd earn from the fight to pay for a flight. It was impossible not to feel a bit sorry for Aravena as he described how he put up a strong fight in Steinbach, despite losing in about ninety seconds. "I was doing good at first," he offered gamely, until he was caught with "five or six really good shots in the head."

It didn't take Aravena long after he arrived in Ontario

to conclude that Kellestine was "a wild man" who provided experiences that went from "mundane, bizarre to absolutely terrifying." Weiner Kellestine was so nutty that he didn't just eat raccoon feces; he also smiled and said, "mm-mm good" before swallowing them. At first, in Aravena's words, the man they called Weiner appeared not much more than a "little bit of a weirdo. He made me laugh a bit."

As Aravena described things to the jury, the visit to Kellestine's farm started off more like a boys' week out than a hit squad on the loose. Dizzy and aching from his quick but harsh pummelling in the ring, Aravena lay around for a few days, but eventually went out with the others. At one point, he visited London with Kellestine and Mather, and they stopped in to see Mather's father, a goldsmith, so that Mather could get Kassie Kellestine a gold necklace for her seventh birthday. Another visit that day was to Mervyn Breaton, an octogenarian whose voluminous criminal career included bank robbing and gun-running. Aravena didn't seem to realize that Breaton was a man with many stories to tell; he had once been Inmate No. 1254 in the U.S. federal penitentiary on Alcatraz Island, where his friends included Richard Stroud, the famed "Birdman of Alcatraz." While visiting Breaton, Aravena was far more impressed with Breaton's dogs and cats than with whatever the old ex-con might have to say about life as a creer criminal. "He breathes louder than he talks," Aravena recalled. "It's hard to talk with the guy." Before they left, Breaton presented Kellestine with a bandana full of musty shotgun shells.

Aravena testified that he and Gardiner were stuck with the dog work at Kellestine's farm, which included heating up pizzas, chopping wood, fetching water and picking up dog feces to spread over the vegetable patch. "It would make his vegetables fresh," Aravena said, unintentionally setting off a ripple of laughter through the courtroom.

Aravena quickly saw that guns were everywhere in the Kellestine home, and every night, the strange little man would patrol his property with a rifle on a green strap over his shoulder, like a soldier in some private little army. Aravena had the responsibility of keeping the inner compound locked, but he didn't know where the key to the rusty old lock was, so he just pretended to secure it.

On the night of the murders, Kellestine left a shotgun by a couch and ordered Aravena and Gardiner to monitor a police scanner in the farmhouse. Towards the end of that horrible night, Aravena said that he was sure Kellestine wanted to kill him too when he ordered him into the front seat of the Infiniti. Aravena said he refused to get into the vehicle, and instead approached M.H. and said, "If you guys are going to kill me, please don't shoot me in the face." He recalled that there was something unsettling about M.H.'s eyes and cold laugh, as if he was enjoying his terror, so Aravena sought out his old friend and mentor, Mushey. He climbed into the Grand Prix with him, and then repeated the plea, this time to his best friend, not to shoot him in the face.

"What the fuck are you talking about?" Mushey replied, according to Aravena. "This shit was not supposed to happen."

"Someone went nuts," Mushey continued. "This wasn't supposed to happen."

As Aravena sat with Mushey in the Grand Prix, fearing for his life, he smelled something odd behind them, and turned to see the lifeless body of Jamie Flanz. He said he covered Flanz with a jacket. Next, he said he and Mushey shared a bonding moment, of the sort one might have with a real brother. "Right there, we made a pact to watch over each other." As Mushey sat in court and heard Aravena solemnly recall their vow, he appeared to be overcome by emotion for the first time in the trial. He lowered his head and rubbed his temples. About ten minutes later, Mushey stared directly up at the ceiling, again hiding his face, and making observers in the courtroom wonder if the man police considered a stone-cold killer had somehow been moved to tears.

Aravena testified that the night of the murders was the first time he had seen Mushey when the black belt didn't seem totally in control. "I'd never seen him scared before. He looked something, maybe afraid." He painted Gardiner as so clued out he couldn't possibly be part of any plot; he spent much of his time on the night of the killings "sitting there in his own little world," bug-eyed, as if he was going to break out in tears. "The guy would sit there like he was catching flies." Neither he, Gardiner nor Mushey had a clue that the night would end in slaughter, he told the jury. "If I knew what was going to happen I would not have shown up, and I'm sure Mushey and Brett wouldn't have, either."

He described Kellestine, Sandham and the Crown's star

witness, M.H., as being made of much nastier stuff. On their drive home, Aravena claimed M.H. turned to him in the back seat of the SUV and asked, "How are you doing?" to which Aravena replied, "How do you think? What about you?" At this point, M.H. made a buzzing sound with his lips, pointed to his chest and then made a slashing motion across his neck. Then he mouthed "Pony" and moved his arms as if riding a horse. The implication was clear: M.H. was claiming credit for murdering Pony Jessome.

Once they had returned home, Aravena admitted to the jury to feeling something like pride when Mushey offered him a Bandidos prospect patch. "I knew there was no way out now. After what I just witnessed, I was glad I was friends with these guys . . . Because we got out of there alive. I was really happy not to be dead." He described how he and Mushey went out to buy a black biker vest so that he could sew on his new prospect patch. First, they went to see an elderly woman who had taken out an ad to sell her dead husband's clothing, including a fleece-lined brown vest. It was cheap, but clearly couldn't pass for a true one percenter vest. Finally, they found something for twenty-nine dollars at a downtown store—Mushey loaned him twenty dollars towards the purchase. Then Aravena bought some matching thread and delivered the items to his mother to sew, like a proud Cub scout with a merit badge. His mother dutifully sewed on the patch, then repaid the twenty-dollar loan from Mushey by reducing a bill he owed. "She was a nice woman like that," Aravena recalled to the jurors with a dreamy, little-boy tone.

There was no ceremony on the day he finally became a Bandido prospect, beyond a hug from Mushey. Mushey just said, "You're in the club," and that was it. "I thought it was a little bit embarrassing," Aravena said. "No one had bikes and we didn't even have a clubhouse."

Aravena's woeful fight career made him used to mismatches, but none of his ring losses matched the two-day peppering he took in cross-examination from assistant Crown attorney Fraser Kelly. Before Kelly began his questioning, another assistant Crown attorney placed a large board, to which pictures of the eight dead men had been attached, immediately before the jury. Then, on computer screens in front of them, each juror was shown pictures of the No Surrender Crew in death. The message was clear: the killers from the barn were in the courtroom now, and Kelly wasn't about to let anyone forget that.

Kelly noted that Aravena somehow couldn't remember who had killed Crash, Pony, Salerno or Trotta. Aravena's version of the Flanz murder suggested it was all the work of Sandham, and not that of his old mentor, Mushey. In a dramatic gesture, Kelley pulled on a pair of blue rubber gloves and held the Hi-Point pistol that had been used to kill Flanz. It was hard not to imagine the terror felt by the victims as Kelly got Aravena to describe how Kellestine kept ramming his pistol up against Flanz's skull, and how he kept taunting him by saying, "Just kidding." Kelly asked Aravena why he didn't do anything to stop it.

"So I can get smacked around?" the prizefighter replied. Kelly next showed the court a video of Kellestine, shirtless and looking plucked, like a broiled chicken. It was taken less than a week before the murders.

"How many of your opponents looked like that?" Kelly asked.

"One was old, but he wasn't that old," Aravena replied. The jurors and others in the courtroom laughed, although it wasn't really meant as a joke.

Throughout the cross-examination, Aravena kept saying that he genuinely believed the Toronto men were all going home alive that morning. He appeared stunned when Kelly asked how he could reconcile this with his comments that he was afraid for his own life. And Aravena gamely admitted that, while he didn't see Raposo getting murdered, he was eager to see the body as it lay on the barn floor. "I wanted to see. I'd never seen a dead body before."

Aravena swore that he thought they were only going to confine Boxer, Big Paul and the others, so they could drive them back to Toronto and collect their club vests and memorabilia. The injured men would be driven to a Toronto hospital, where staff would be told they were victims of a drive-by shooting.

"It didn't cross your mind there was no way a tow truck with two bodies in it would go to a hospital?" Kelly asked.

Aravena merely absorbed the question, like a stiff punch to the head. He insisted he didn't feel the need for a gun that night, and bragged he wasn't afraid of either Boxer or Big Paul as he walked them outside. "I'm a little conceited as to who I can beat up and who I can't." He did seem to marvel at Boxer's mental toughness. At the moment of Boxer's death, Aravena said the old fighter had "a big smile on his face," one so powerful that Aravena thought Kellestine had somehow missed him with a point-blank shot to the head.

Mushey's mood lightened as Aravena told the court that he chatted in the jailhouse yard with Kellestine, when both were in the Elgin-Middlesex Detention Centre, awaiting trial. "He wanted me to lie for him," Aravena said. "He said, 'Be nice to your Uncle Wayne.'" Aravena told the jury of how Kellestine caught his attention on another occasion in the yard and mouthed "Mushey" and, holding up four fingers, "four." Next, he mouthed "me" and "two" and held up two fingers. He did the same for M.H., mouthing "one," the same number of murders he attributed to Sandham.

As Aravena told of the jailyard conversations, Mushey gestured to Kellestine, whom he had been studiously ignoring throughout the trial. Kellestine leaned forward in the prisoners' dock and smiled at the apparent gesture of goodwill. Then Mushey made a motion with his fingers like a mouth speaking and mouthed the words "rat, rat, rat." Kellestine was horror-stricken, as he had just been publicly tricked into letting down his guard. Kellestine jutted out his jaw, and his rage made Mushey and Gardiner laugh all the harder.

Once, when the jury was not in the courtroom, Aravena asked the judge if he could hold a small Bible as he continued his testifying, and was granted permission. He was gripping the Bible as he admitted that he and Gardiner were supposed to patrol the Kellestine property every night, and that it was pitch black once he got a few feet from the farmhouse.

"In the dark, is not twenty yards like twenty miles?" Kelly asked.

"Yeah," Aravena agreed.

The suggestion was clear: if Aravena, Gardiner and the other Winnipeggers were truly afraid for their lives, they could have quickly fled into the dark. If they had freed just one hostage, that person would have easily been able to hide in the darkness.

Aravena was still clutching the Bible when he swore he heard only the shooting of Chopper, even though there were at least twenty-four shots fired that night. And the holy book was still in his hands as he admitted that Kellestine and all of the Winnipeggers had been moved up within the club after the murders.

"Everyone got promoted?" Kelly asked.

"Yes."

CHAPTER 30

Last Breath

*If ever I were traitor, My name be blotted from
the book of life.*
RICHARD II, ACT 1, SCENE 3

Where did all of this start?
DEFENCE LAWYER CLAY POWELL

Gordon Cudmore, the veteran lawyer from London, got his chance
to shine in his closing address for Michael Sandham, and he
made the most of it.[34] Cudmore was reasoned and witty and
seemed to genuinely mean it as he talked of the importance
to a free society of the presumption of innocence, which
British writer John Mortimer called "the golden thread of
British justice." Cudmore also sounded like a wise old uncle
as he evoked childhood readings of Aesop's fable about the
little boy who cried wolf and who kept on lying, only to find
out he wasn't believed when it really mattered, when he
was telling the truth. Michael Sandham was that little boy
grown up. "He has damaged his own credibility, but on the
things that matter, he is telling the truth," Cudmore said.

"Did he have a motive to lie?" Cudmore asked the jury. "Yes. His freedom is at stake . . . He has become his own worst enemy. He has painted himself into a box."

Sandham stared sadly out at the jury, looking particularly tiny in the dock, as Cudmore noted that his client had admitted fatally shooting Chopper Raposo. This was justified, however, by the fact that Raposo had a shotgun and was attempting to kill him. "Simply put, you are allowed to use reasonable force to defend yourself," Cudmore explained.

Cudmore also brushed off suggestions that the murders had been planned: "Horrible events? Yes. But not planned events." In the end, as Cudmore described things, it was Raposo himself who set off the horrible chain of events that wiped out the Toronto chapter. "It was a blast from that shotgun—not a plan—that set off a night of chaotic madness."

One doesn't expect the lawyer of an alleged mass murderer to sound soothing, but that's the effect Cudmore had on the courtroom. Once the warm glow of his speech cooled, however, little Taz Sandham reverted to looking like someone who belonged in prison for a long, long time. The effect of Cudmore's fine words was about the same as splashing fine perfume on an open sewer.

Next up was Greg Leslie, who reminded the jury that his client, Frank Mather, had neither a motorcycle licence nor a motorcycle and certainly wasn't a dangerous outlaw biker. Indeed, his name didn't appear in any of the fifty thousand biker-related emails investigators had pored over while preparing the prosecution's case. "He's not a Bandido. He's not even associated with the Bandidos . . . Why would Frank Mather be associated with a mass execution? What's in it for him?" What Mather did have was poor taste in friends. "Frank Mather made a mistake. He became friends with Wayne Kellestine. That's it," Leslie said.

Mather didn't go to Kellestine's farm to carry out any grand biker plot. He simply stumbled in, looking for a place to stay with his pregnant girlfriend. "Wrong place, wrong time," Leslie said. Mather's defence made a game effort to salvage all of the non-shooters from that night. "Mr. Gardiner didn't have a clue what was going on that night. Nor Mr. Aravena. Nor Mr. Mather," Leslie argued. As Leslie spoke the words, it was hard to reconcile the sad, lost man in the prisoners' box with the image of him holding a gun that night in a barn, while the No Surrender Crew waited to die, one by one.

Marcelo Aravena's lawyer, Tony Bryant, began his closing remarks to the jury by opening an envelope, pulling out a letter and reading: "Dear Dad, I wish I knew where to begin. I have so much to tell you . . . I need to tell you about stuff that really happened at the farm." What followed, for the next seventy-five minutes, read like a letter from a homesick boy at summer camp to his father, but the topic was mass murder, not arts and crafts.

"Dad, I've been a number of things in my life, but I'm not a murderer," Bryant read. "I don't want anybody to think that." Aravena looked sad and soft, staring up at the ceiling and appearing to fight off tears—a far cry from the day he mimed a pistol with his fingers and pointed them at M.H. on the witness stand.

The letter was remarkable, considering Aravena had flunked three straight years of school and spent the past dozen years stopping punches and kicks with his head. There was a certain homespun clarity in the way the letter spoke of his fear and confusion regarding Wayne Kellestine that night: "People who are threatened are just like robots."

"What a jerk," Bryant sniffed of Kellestine, reading from the letter. "Killing these guys. And what for?

"I didn't know any of these guys were going to be killed, Dad," Bryant continued. "And I didn't hear any gunshots."

The letter writer apparently wasn't bitter for his treatment by the courts, only sad. He explained that "the boss of the law" was "that nice Justice Heeney," and he reassured his father that his lawyers had told him that juries were made up of smart people. He was altogether comfortable that his own legal team would face the jury with "no smoke and mirrors, no light show, no video. Just straight-up stuff" and "knock them dead." Despite the bold words, there was also a little melancholy in his comments, as he recalled how his mother had died while he was in custody, awaiting trial. "It's pretty sad when you think of all of the hard work Mom did to raise me . . . I just wish Mom was still alive, so I could tell her too." His mother would likely have been proud that her boy even had gentle words for M.H., the turncoat: "It was hard not to feel sorry for him. He just seemed to have his priorities wrong, like worrying if his pet guinea pig was going to go with him and his family [into the witness-protection program]."

Brett Gardiner looked like he was blinking away tears too as the reading finally concluded. Bryant appeared a little emotionally drained himself as he put the letter back in the envelope, walked across the room to shake his client's hand, then sat down without saying a word.

The next morning, before the jury came in, Mr. Justice Heeney agreed with Kellestine's lawyer, Clay Powell, that he couldn't believe the letter had been written by Aravena. "Unless Mr. Aravena's gone to law school, I highly doubt he wrote the letter," the judge told the lawyers. Powell wanted a mistrial, but the judge wasn't biting. Brant had never actually said that the letter was written by his client. When the jury took their seats, Heeney suggested they look at the letter as a literary device, not an actual missive from the accused. Jurors could be forgiven if they looked a little stunned as the judge continued: "It has been conceded that this was not a letter from Mr. Aravena to his father."

Things had been ugly for quite some time between the Gardiner and Kellestine legal camps, and Gardiner's lawyer, Chris Hicks, certainly didn't hold back when he began his final address to the jury. "Kellestine is a psychopath, a psychotic killer," Hicks said. "There are no kinder or gentler words which you can use.

"There are monsters among us and Kellestine is one," Hicks continued.

Then, in case anyone missed the point that his defence was founded on a vilification of Kellestine, Hicks said: "It was Kellestine's plan and Kellestine's plan alone.

"Kellestine's actions were completely unexpected and

unexplained," Hicks said, adding that even the lowly M.H. "was shocked and stunned to be in the centre of a human abattoir."

Hicks then shifted his focus to the credibility of the man he painted as Kellestine's sidekick: Michael Sandham. "Kellestine was driving this train," Hicks said. "Mr. Sandham was right behind."

Then Hicks switched metaphors as he described his client, Gardiner, as "the lowest man on the totem pole, the last to know anything on the Bandido hierarchy." In case anyone had forgotten the story of how Gardiner once hunted for a pickle tree, Hicks told the jury that his client was far too stupid and had been deemed not important enough to be included in any talk of club business, let alone serious planning. "It was the opinion of all observers that he [Gardiner] simply wasn't very bright," Hicks said. As his lawyer spoke those words, Gardiner stared at the jury, looking suitably stunned.

The reputations of Sandham and Kellestine had already been thoroughly trashed by defence teams by the time Dwight Mushey's lawyer, Michael Moon, addressed the jury. He homed in on the credibility of Sandham nonetheless, several times describing his testimony as "lies, lies, lies" and asking the jurors, "How stupid does he think we are?"

He told the court that Sandham had strong reasons for joining Kellestine in the night of slaughter. The Toronto Bandidos knew he had once been a police officer, and this dirty little secret could easily cost him his life. "At the end of the night, everyone who knew that he was a cop was dead," Moon said.

Moon also made it clear that Mushey was proud to be a Bandido, while at the same time he denied he took part in the barnyard murders. "Being a member of the Bandidos was not something that he was ashamed of . . . He took it as a brotherhood."

There was a buzz in the packed courtroom on the morning of Wednesday, October 21, and it wasn't just because local legal notable Clay Powell was ready to deliver his closing address to the jury on behalf of Wayne Kellestine. Soon, the court heard that Gardiner and Mushey had each just fired their lead lawyers, Hicks and Moon.

"The reasons are what?" the judge asked.

"Sorry, Your Honour," Mushey replied earnestly. "They're personal reasons."

With that, the lawyers were discharged. While the firings sounded dramatic, there wasn't much left for them to do anyway. If Mushey or Gardiner were found guilty of first-degree murder, a twenty-five-year sentence was automatic.

The most likely explanation for the firing of the lawyers may lie in the outlaw biker code. It is a point of honour among true one percenters that they don't testify against anyone, even their enemies. Men like Mario Parente and Frank Lenti live strictly by that dictate, even when doing so means hard prison time. Hicks and Moon had ripped into Kellestine and Sandham in their closing statements, and that act might be viewed harshly by the true one percenters Gardiner and Mushey could soon be meeting in prison. Firing the lawyers could provide hope of saving face, in a manner of speaking.

It seemed fitting that Kellestine's legal team got the last word, and every seat in the courtroom was filled for what many believed would be the final major case for local legal personality Clay Powell. He was a popular man, despite his often unsavoury clients. Two decades earlier, Powell had been counsel in the inquiry into sexual abuse for three hundred boys at the Mount Cashel orphanage school in St. John's, Newfoundland. It was a harrowing story of betrayal and suicide, and when Powell returned to his practice, it was common knowledge that he wouldn't take on cases of anyone who might have done bad things to children. Defending outlaw bikers might not be uplifting work, but it was mentally stimulating and necessary, and compared with the emotional toll of delving into the suffering of children, relatively mild.

Powell smiled and fiddled with his microphone, and the jury seemed to take an instant liking to him. "I'm Nick Paparella," he joked, imitating a local television news reporter, who laughed from the body of the courtroom. Powell laughed heartily at his own joke, as if surprised by it. Then he took a deep breath. "Where did all of this start?" he asked. He was speaking without notes, in a heart-to-heart, personal way. "Kellestine's at home on his farm with his little kid when the boys from Winnipeg arrive unannounced." He suggested the answer to his question about the origin of the bloodletting lay in the feverish, ambitious mind of little Taz Sandham, whom he mocked as "the genius" and "a cutie boy and ex-cop."

"He had everything to gain," Powell said. " . . . He's smart and he's cunning and he's ruthless."

Powell told the jurors he had seen plenty of strange things in his career as a lawyer. But he appeared dumbfounded that Sandham could serve up his story about being a secret agent for police. "It's incredible that he thinks you people would believe it," Powell said with what sounded like wonder.

He also bluntly dismissed Sandham's tale that he had killed Chopper by accident.

"Hogwash," Powell said, seeming almost to rise off the floor with the word. He did have kind words, however, for his colleague Cudmore: "There wasn't much he could do for Mr. Sandham, but he sounded good."

Powell urged the jury to dismiss both the credibility of M.H.—"a liar . . . a game player"—and Sandham. "If Sandham stuck a parking ticket on your windshield in Winnipeg, it would likely be forged." Then he turned to Aravena, "the letter writer," and his team's "slick letter trick." "I've been around a lot, and I've never heard of that." He mimicked the sturdily built mixed martial artist's claim that he was afraid of Kellestine. Aravena laughed along with everyone else, until Powell interrupted his impersonation by saying, "Give me a break."

"If I had to decide the case on the evidence of [M.H.], Sandham and Aravena, I'd worry about that," Powell said.

There was something calming and reassuring when Kevin Gowdey finally took the stand to make the Crown's final remarks to the jury. Gowdey sounded like a good neighbour, not a showman, and he urged the jury to agree with him that the facts of the case pointed to only one conclusion: eight convictions of first-degree murder for each of the accused. "Feel free to take as much time as you need in the jury room," he reassured them.

Men might have joined the Bandidos looking for brotherhood, but on the night of April 7–8, 2006, they were driven by far baser motivations. "It's about politics and it's about power," Gowdey said of the murders.

He didn't attempt to defend M.H. as a person, but noted the Crown witness's account was supported by forensic evidence. Sometimes tough decisions have to be made in life, and giving M.H. a witness deal was apparently one of those choices. "He clearly is guilty of murder. He confined the No Surrender Crew until they could be walked out to their deaths. He walked Pony out to his death."

Gowdey explained that the law stipulates a couple of key prerequisites for a first-degree murder conviction. One is confinement, and another is the presence of a plan. Either confinement or planning was enough for a first-degree murder conviction, and Gowdet argued convincingly that they were both present. It was absurd to think there wasn't confinement in the barn that night, as the victims' car keys and cell phones had taken away and they were forced at gunpoint to lie on the cold concrete floor in a room with only one exit door. "Why would they want to stay where their friend had just been killed and was lying there dead on the floor?" Gowdey asked.

Planning also seemed undeniable. "Think about the deliberateness of it all. Think about the time that it took . . . Think about the wide selection of weapons they had at their disposal . . . Think of the time and complexity of this undertaking: killing eight men."

At the end of the night, all of the No Surrender Crew members, except for Chopper Raposo, were shot in the head while sitting inside vehicles; each member of what Gowdey called "the farm team" was alive and uninjured. "If this wasn't a plan, this is amazing luck . . . It has plan and ambush written all over it."

Gowdey conceded that not all of the accused men pulled triggers that night, but argued that they should all be found guilty of first-degree murder if the jury agreed they were "aiding and abetting—if they helped or encouraged the killings.

"People who intentionally help or encourage others to kill are as guilty as those who pull the trigger," he said. " . . . This was a concerted effort by shooters and their helpers; executioners and their henchmen."

It would be too simple and incomplete to simply lay the blame on Kellestine, as defence lawyers would have liked. "Kellestine was out of the barn repeatedly, with his back turned to the others."

After the fractious, cut-throat defence, Gowdey now put what was left of the Canadian Bandidos back into a unified group for the jury: "Together, they advanced their Bandidos ambitions. Together, they face trial . . . Everybody was a Bandido that night."

Down in Texas, Bandidos and others monitored *The London Free Press*'s Twitter reports on the trial. They seemed more amused than threatened, and were far from brimming with guilt. One of the Americans wondered what was worse: the fact the Weiner Kellestine ate raccoon feces, or that the trial revealed that he plodded through cyberspace on a dial-up Internet connection?

It took the jury just fourteen hours to reach its verdict. Taz Sandham was the first of the accused to stand on October 29, 2009, to face his judgment; he sat back down and stared straight ahead as the jury foreperson said "guilty of first-degree murder" for each of the eight charges. A first-degree murder conviction brings with it an automatic life sentence, with no chance of parole for twenty-five years, and now Michael Sandham, the man of many identities, would be known by a federal inmate's number.

Frank Mather and Marcelo Aravena looked stunned as the foreperson said "guilty of first-degree murder" for all of their charges except for the killing of Chopper Raposo, which brought manslaughter convictions. Next was Brett Gardiner, and the emotion was clear on his face, but he made no sound as he was told he had been found guilty of manslaughter for the slayings of Chopper and Boxer, and guilty of first-degree murder for the rest. Dwight Mushey kept his composure and bowed his head politely towards the jury, as befitted a black belt, as he heard that he was found guilty of first-degree murder on all eight charges. Kellestine was the last to hear his verdict, and it was anticlimatic when he received the same damning judgment.

He shrugged his shoulders and smiled slightly, as if to say, "What are you going to do?"

The judge was midway through praising jury members for representing the best of the jury system when Aravena suddenly stood up and interrupted. "Fucking goofs!" he called out, glaring at the jury and making obscene gestures with both hands. "You're pieces of fucking shit. You know that some of us are innocent." When Tony Bryant moved to calm him, Aravena responded with a loud "Fuck you, Tony! Fuck you!" Moments later, Aravena spat over the Plexiglas wall of his cubicle at Bryant, and police escorted him from the courtroom.

The next day, the families of the No Surrender Crew had their chance to tell the court what the massacre meant to them. Tony Bryant was now sitting far from his client, Aravena, well out of spitting range.

George Kriarakis's mother, Vickie, sounded like she was transported back twenty-nine years as she spoke of the sense of wonder and joy she felt the day George was born, and how when she looked into her first-born's bright, tiny eyes, it felt like she was looking at nothing less than life and the future. "I saw the world in his eyes," she told the court. Then, she said, on April 8, 2006, "my heart stopped . . . My special gift was taken away." More than three years later, she still held out hope that someday, somehow, her George might walk through the door and make her smile and laugh again. "Our house was full of love, life and fun, and now it's all gone," she said. She was crying now and clearly in intense pain, but she carried on: "I feel like one of the living dead. I miss George ... I wake up in the middle of the night and I feel the terror in his eyes."

Boxer's twenty-four-year-old daughter Tereasa told the court how badly she missed her father, and how she wished he was there to be grandfather to her five-year-old daughter. Her little girl was almost killed by a car a year after the massacre, and Tereasa cried as she talked of how dearly she had longed for her dad to comfort her in those dark days and nights as her daughter fought her way back from a coma. That horror had passed, but Tereasa still missed her father more than she could say "My daughter will never feel the tickle of his moustache," Tereasa said, standing tall but crying. "He will always be remembered by his picture, but not his touch."

Frankie Salerno's mother, Marilyn, told of how she wanted to be a good Christian, but kept feeling anger trising up inside her. The court heard how deeply grateful she was to police, the Crown, victims' services workers, the judge and the jury. She was also able to find a way to forgive M.H., even though he had held a gun the night her boy was murdered. "I would like to thank M.H. for stepping forward, at great risk to his safety and the safety of his family, to do the right thing," she told the court. As she spoke, her surviving son, Paul, stood by her, his hand on her shoulder and his eyes on the killers. "I can forgive him for any involvement he had that night," she continued. "I will pray for him and his family."

Both Gardiner and Mushey dropped their heads and stared at the floor as the tiny woman spoke of the aftermath of that horrific night at Kellestine's farm. The other prisoners stared off into space but showed no tears as she continued, "Your Honour, I know that when this tragedy occurred that many ignorant individuals expressed the opinion that the world would be a better place with eight less bikers. This deeply saddened me, because Frank was my son."

Like the rest of the family members who spoke that day, Frankie Salerno's mother said she wasn't able to stop imagining how her son and the other murdered men felt that night: "What constantly tortures me is imagining the horror and betrayal Frank must have felt when he realized that his friends were being murdered one by one and that those he had once trusted were now about to take his life." She also told the court how foreign the outlaw biker culture was to Frank's real family. "During the evidence of the wire-tap conversations I continually heard the expression 'Love, loyalty and respect,' apparently a mantra of the Bandidos club. Each time I heard those words I cringed. Where was the love, loyalty and respect ... when our loved ones were ambushed and murdered by their so-called brothers?"

Many in the courtroom were crying as she ended her address to the jury by reading from the poem In Memoriam A.H.H. by Alfred, Lord Tennyson, which she learned as a schoolgirl and which, she said, "speaks to a yearning beyond death and retribution, a yearning that in my rare and few optimistic moments is my only solace":

Oh yet we trust that somehow good
Will be the final goal of ill,
To pangs of nature, sins of will,
Defects of doubt, and taints of blood;

That nothing walks with aimless feet;
That not one life shall be destroy'd,
Or cast as rubbish to the void,
When God hath made the pile complete....

In Keswick, Ontario, the site of the pointless and cowardly murder of Shawn Douse, there's still talk of a glorious day when the Bandidos will ride again in Canada. There's a belief that there really was once a golden era of love, loyalty and respect, and that those values can someday be revived. Certainly, men like Ripper Fullager and Boxer Muscedere thought those words were more than a catchy slogan, or a way of getting a rival to lower his guard. Ripper and Boxer each grasped the old one percenter ideal of bikes and brotherhood, although they alternately lacked the vigour or the political skills needed to make a club work in the twenty-first century.

Taz Sandham sorely wanted to be the club's leader, and had plenty of energy and political skills. But he had no inkling of the meaning of brotherhood, beyond the Cain-and-Abel variety. The harder the little ex-cop chased his dream of running a biker gang, the further behind he fell, until he was all but invisible, like a speck of dust on a Texas highway. His co-accused Weiner Kellestine also had a vision for the club, but his version of brotherhood only made sense in his own mind, deep within the crazy confines of his padlocked inner compound on Aberdeen Line. A potential future leader of the group, Cameron Acorn, will likely be out of prison in a few years, but there will always be questions about his grasp of brotherhood. Faced with the chance to alert Boxer and Chopper as they drove to Kellestine's farm, Acorn said nothing, betraying his president with his silence on the night of his murder.

In Texas, at the mother chapter, the true Bandidos are far more realistic. Only when the likes of Taz and Weiner are sufficiently forgotten, and worthy candidates appear who don't make a virtue of stupidity or betrayal, can they even start to think about expanding to Canada, yet again.

There likely was a time, when Ripper Fullager was alive and vibrant, when a one percenter could boast that he was part of something great that stood for freedom and brotherhood. Boxer caught a whiff of that sentiment, and it was intoxicating enough to keep him in the club, even though he was surrounded by enemies who constantly professed their love and respect for him. Perhaps the utter ridiculousness of his killers' version of brotherhood was what made Boxer laugh with his final breath.

Last Lap Dance

Every third thought shall be my grave.
THE TEMPEST, ACT 5, SCENE 1

*It was proposed that the agent kill Lenti and leave him in
the middle of the highway in his [Bandidos] colours. Lenti
couldn't just disappear; he had to be found to prove a point.*
COURT DOCUMENT ON AN ALLEGED
HELLS ANGELS MURDER PLOT

Everyone in Cisco Lenti's world knew exactly where to find
him on Friday nights. His "office" was the small games
room in the north end of the Club Pro Adult Entertainment Lounge in Vaughan, a marble-and-brushed-steel
attempt at upscale decadence on a suburban street
crowded with auto body shops and building supply stores.
From his chair close to the emergency exit, Lenti could
survey much of the lobby and the main room, with its bar
and strippers, but it was hard to see him as he sat in the
dark. It was also one of the few spots in the Pro that wasn't
covered by the sixteen motion-sensing cameras Lenti had

carefully helped to install. It was here, in the dark, where Frank Lenti surveyed the chaos and plotted the return of the No Surrender Crew. Boxer had had his chance. Now it was Frank Lenti's turn.

Lenti wasn't a bouncer or a manager or an owner at the Club Pro, but he was clearly one of the most important men in the building. His business cards described his position simply as "Security." When he was first hired to his nine-hundred-dollar-a-week job, back in the early 1990s, he didn't submit a resumé or fill out an application. Club owner Domenic (Mimmo) Marciano vaguely defined his job one day in court as that of a "cooler" or "buffer." Questioned further about Lenti's specific qualifications for the job, Marciano replied, "He has been around." Pressed to explain what that meant, Marciano continued: "He has been involved. In that underworld. That world . . . He was part of a gang, I would say." In a further attempt to explain Lenti's job, Marciano said, "He's there so that I can run my business."

Lenti kept going to the Club Pro on Friday nights, even after he was warned by police in June 2006 that the Hells Angels had taken out a murder contract on his life. That September, two Hells Angels—Remond (Ray) Akleh of the Ontario Nomads and Mark Cephes Stephenson, president of the Oshawa chapter—were charged with conspiracy to commit murder and counselling to commit murder. The reason for the contract, police said, was to shut down Lenti's recruitment drive for the Bandidos. The case against Akleh and Stephenson was based on evidence gathered through the services of Oshawa Hells Angel Steven Gault, whose lengthy criminal record included bilking seniors in home-renovation scams and biting off a chunk of a man's ear in a bar fight. Neither the police nor the Angels particularly liked Gault, who once threatened to tie his former common-law wife to a tree in the woods and cover her with honey so that she would be eaten alive by wild animals. But bikers and cops often have to do business with people they don't like.

Police often have to make deals with the devil to fight groups like the Hells Angels, but this was an exceptionally expensive pact, both in terms of money and morality. For his services against the Hells Angels, Gault received more than a million dollars from the government. High-priced rats-for-hire like Gault were proving to be the flipside to the Hells Angels' successful expansion through Ontario.

Officers from York Regional Police tried to sit down with Lenti to discuss Gault's story about the contract on his life, but Lenti brushed them off like a true one percenter. Privately, Lenti found the reports particularly troubling. He didn't know Stephenson, but he had considered Akleh a friend from their days together in the old Satan's Choice club back in the 1990s. If the police story was true, the plot didn't just endanger his life; it also hurt his feelings a little.

York Regional Police officers kept calling Lenti to talk about the alleged plot, and in early October he finally called them back. He bluntly refused to change his routine or consider entering a witness protection program. He simply told a police investigator that he knew the Ontario Hells Angels weren't happy with him, as he was trying to get the Bandidos "off the ground" after the Shedden Massacre. His term with the Bandidos would be short, and he would retire again once he had completed his organizational task. In the meantime, he was watching his back and keeping a low profile, while continuing to man his chair in the darkened games room of the Club Pro. "Everyone in the world knows that I work there," he said. "They'll leave me alone." Police interpreted his demeanour and comments to mean, "Yeah, they're not happy, but that's too bad. I'm Frank Lenti."

Despite his public show of bravado, Lenti's son Jessi thought that his father looked preoccupied now. "He didn't say anything," Jessi later said. "He was concerned . . . You could tell [he was worried] by his expression." His father never betrayed his fear in so many words, but it came across in other ways. "[It was] just the way he would react. His expression. How he would move." Frankie Lenti Jr., another of Lenti's sons, put on a cool front when police talked with him about the murder contract. "Somebody's always threatening him," Frankie Jr. responded.

On Friday, December 1, 2006, the hidden cameras at the Club Pro picked up Dana (Boomer) Carnegie and another man entering the circular front lobby of the club at 9:26 P.M. Carnegie was easy enough to spot on the monitor, with his spiky blond hair, six-foot, three-inch, 225-pound frame and confident strut. He wasn't exactly a celebrity at the club—like grim-faced action-movie hero Steven Seagal, who had dropped by when filming in Toronto—but nor was Carnegie anonymous. And he was certainly no stranger to Lenti. Many regulars at the

Pro knew that Carnegie had recently retired from playing semi-professional hockey, although few could name his teams, or even their leagues—like the Verdun Dragons of the Ligue Nord-Américaine de Hockey, where he was a fighting goalie in what is unofficially known as the world's roughest, toughest hockey loop, or the now-defunct Toronto Torpedoes of Major League Roller Hockey. Now thirty-three, Carnegie had been out of hockey for a couple of years, ever since being knocked into a coma when he rolled his Harley.

That Friday, Boomer Carnegie seemed in a particularly good mood as he left the Pro at 10:03 P.M., shaking hands with a doorman on his way out. He returned at forty minutes after midnight in a white 1998 Cadillac driven by West Toronto Hells Angels prospect Carlo Verrelli. Sitting beside Carnegie in the back seat was Scott Desroche, a full-patch member of the West Toronto chapter, while David (Dred) Buchanan, the chapter's sergeant-at-arms, rode up front.

Frank Lenti would later say he had a "gut feeling" that something was going to go wrong that night, but he showed up for work at the Pro anyway. As insurance that night, he'd tucked a 9-millimetre pistol against the small of his back, under his shirt and well out of sight. It was a semi-automatic, the same kind used by police.

Jessi Lenti was working that night as a "bar back," making sure the bar was well stocked with cold beer. He noticed his father was in the games room shortly before 1 A.M., with his back to the wall, as was his habit. Talking with him was Buchanan, who was accompanied by Carnegie, Verrelli and about four others who hadn't been seen in the Pro before.

As Frank Lenti later recalled things, Buchanan was livid at him about his efforts to recruit for the Bandidos after the Shedden Massacre. "You know what?" Buchanan barked. "You should know better than to be a Bandido." Lenti said another Hells Angel in the games room pulled open his coat and flashed the butt of a pistol as Buchanan told him, "We talked to your guys in the States. They don't recognize you guys."

Lenti later recalled replying, "It's no concern of yours. You do your thing, we do our thing." Lenti's movements were recorded by his hidden cameras now as he shuffled out of the dark and into the light of the front lobby.

Buchanan was still in Lenti's face, glaring at him and repeatedly asking, "Who's staring at who? Who's staring at who?" Doorman Derek Delicata said that he asked the Hells Angels to leave but they ignored him as Buchanan bore in verbally on Lenti. Getting no response from Lenti, the Hells Angels shifted their attention to Delicata. About eight men surrounded him, including Buchanan, Carnegie and Verrelli. Bouncer Juan Moises Rodriguez-Castillo could hear the Hells Angels repeatedly ordering Delicata to "Go outside, motherfucker!" It seemed to Rodriguez-Castillo that Buchanan was the Angels' leader. "He was like crazy, he was angry . . . He was like the commander, like the boss. He was giving order to take out . . . I grabbed Mr. Derek by the arm and bring him back inside."

Rodriguez-Castillo stood six foot six and weighed about three hundred powerful pounds, and was able to quickly retrieve the bouncer from the angry Angels. As he did, Lenti removed his heavy gold necklace, with its Bandidos pendant, and shuffled across the lobby towards them. Rodriguez-Castillo later recalled Lenti saying, "Please, go home." The Colombian military veteran remembered that Buchanan reacted with renewed fury against Lenti, saying words to the effect of "You shut up, motherfucker, old guy," before punching Lenti with a looping right hand to the face. The other Hells Angels rallied around their sergeant-at-arms. "As soon as Mr. Frank spoke to [Buchanan], they came like wasps," Rodriguez-Castillo later recalled.

Lenti lifted an arm in a defensive posture as he was quickly surrounded by the younger, more agile men. Within seconds, he had run out of space to retreat as Buchanan pushed up close to him yet again. That was when Lenti's right arm slipped behind his back, in a smooth, almost imperceptible movement. When his hand reappeared, he was pointing the pistol.

Buchanan immediately dropped to the floor as Lenti squeezed off a round. Lenti kept panning the pistol to his left, hitting Verrelli and slightly wounding Carnegie in one fluid motion. Desroche bolted to the safety of a nearby closet, while Carnegie was gone like a flash through the front door.

Buchanan lay on his left side, his mouth open, as if trying to speak, but no words came. His right arm reached up towards Lenti, who now stood over him. Lenti pumped another shot into Buchanan from point-blank range, and the Angel's body went limp. Buchanan's body was covered with tattoos of guns, including one of a ghost holding pistols, but the hidden cameras in the lobby recorded no definitive pictures of Buchanan holding a real gun himself.

Lenti leaned over Verrelli and squeezed off another round. In just six seconds, he had fired seven shots. The shooting had started at 1:05 A.M., and by 1:06, Lenti was hustling as quickly as his damaged leg would carry him out the front door. Verrelli dragged himself across the floor to Buchanan's motionless body. Desroche emerged from the broom closest and ran his hands over Buchanan's torso. It might look like he was performing cardiopulmonary resuscitation, but to Delicata's mind, he appeared to be searching for a hidden gun.

There were 250 people in the club that night, but few reliable witnesses. Doorman Maurizio Graziano also told a prosecutor that he didn't see much, even though the lobby was small and he was facing the gunfire: "I probably had my eyes closed." Roma Derfel, the Pro's coat-check girl, also reported that she had seen precious little. She added that she considered Lenti "just a customer" and swore that she didn't even know his last name. "I remember hearing firecrackers," Derfel later said in a court proceeding.

"Do you have any memory of Frank Lenti going up four feet in front of you with a gun?" Crown attorney Peter Westgate later asked her.

"No, I don't. I'm sorry," she replied.

A couple of hours after the shooting, Frank Lenti telephoned his son Jessi and asked how bad things were. "It's pretty bad," Jessi Lenti replied.

At 2:44 P.M. on Saturday, December 2, Detective Angelo DeLorenzi of York Regional Police called Mimmo Marciano and said he would like to speak with Frank Lenti. DeLorenzi and Marciano had known each other for nearly two decades, since meeting in 1987 or '88, when DeLorenzi had infiltrated the East Toronto Satan's Choice and Lenti was a member of that club. Lenti was never a drug dealer and wasn't charged in the undercover operation. After DeLorenzi's true identity was known, he and Lenti remained on polite, professional terms.

Seventeen minutes after DeLorenzi placed his call to Marciano, Lenti was on the phone, promising to turn himself in to York Regional Police at six that evening. DeLorenzi was in the police station on Rutherford Road at 5:23 P.M., when he got a call from the front desk announcing, "Mr. Lenti has arrived."

Flanked by his lawyer, Frank Piccin, Lenti immediately told DeLorenzi that he was innocent and that he was only acting in self-defence. "Angelo, if I knew that I was guilty of something I would have taken the first fucking plane out."

The veteran cop and the biker chatted a little about old times. DeLorenzi had been on the scene back in 1995, when the bomb wrecked Lenti's Explorer and almost ended his life. He reminded Lenti that he had found a hidden 9-millimetre pistol and a machine gun in the bombed-out sport utility vehicle, close to Lenti's mangled, bleeding body. The conversation shifted to how Lenti had shot Buchanan to death the previous night. Lenti said that, surrounded by the Hells Angels in the dimly lit games room of the Pro, he knew his life was in danger the instant he saw one of them flash a handgun. "All of a sudden, you see they're coming in, one, two, three, four, five, six, seven, eight surrounding me . . . I said, 'Excuse me, I gotta go.'"

He said he retreated to the lobby because he wanted his actions recorded on the hidden cameras he had helped install. "I went there for the camera. I went there because I wanted everybody to see that this guy's got a gun." When he was struck by Buchanan, Lenti said he realized that he would soon be beaten to death unless he did something. "When a one percenter hits you once, it's not going to stop there. They're going to beat you to death." He said someone flashed a pistol again, but he sounded confused about whether it was held by Buchanan or Verrelli, both of whom were stocky and short-haired. "I seen that guy pull it out. I went *boom, boom, boom, boom.*

"I just went for it," Lenti continued. "I shot him to death."

Lenti was transferred the next day to the Central East Correctional Centre in Lindsay, a couple of hours east of Toronto. He was placed in a tiny solitary cell in 8 Pod, which had ultra-high security. Authorities said it was for his own protection. In another part of the jail were Akleh and Stephenson, the Hells Angels who had been arrested for the supposed murder contract on his life. For his part, Lenti wanted to be one of the general population, in a wing with thirty-two other prisoners. He was a strong man, even though he was fifty-nine years old, and felt he could reason with the other prisoners—and, failing that, protect himself. But authorities worried he might never make it to his trial alive.[35]

Five days later, Carlo Verrelli was slumped in a wheelchair under a blanket, barely conscious, as he was wheeled into the Fratelli Vescio Funeral Home on Weston Road in Vaughan for Buchanan's funeral. The funeral marked the first time an Ontario Hells Angel had been killed by someone connected to another club, and Hells Angels from across Canada arrived on Harley-Davidson motorcycles and in sport utility vehicles—even a chartered bus—to pay their respects and show their strength.

Verrelli lived to attend the funeral because of the highly developed skills of a surgeon who treated bullet wounds to his arms, chest, abdomen and thigh, including two holes in his diaphragm. In the short time between the shooting and the funeral, he had been promoted to full-patch status in the Hells Angels as a testament to his efforts to save Buchanan. He would later tell a court that he had no memory of the night he almost lost his life and won his patch. Asked how he learned what had happened to Buchanan, Verrelli replied, "I read it in the paper . . . It kind of broke my heart and so I didn't continue reading."

The Hells Angels went into full damage-control mode, posting a statement on their website that pointed out that the Bandidos' mother chapter in Texas didn't recognize Frank Lenti or any of the Canadians who now called themselves Bandidos. "He is an imposter; what we refer [to] in the biker world as bogus. There are no Bandidos roaming the streets of Toronto or anywhere in Ontario. Those little men that pretend to be are frauds and not recognized by the real Bandidos Motorcycle Club." By this time, there were rumours that the Angels had already made plans to avenge the killing by arranging for "outside talent" to kill Lenti.

A few Bandidos and supporters countered with messages of their own in chat rooms, signing off "Free Bandido Cisco." In the months that followed, Lenti's life was lived alone in an eight-by-six-foot cell with a steel sink, bed and toilet in the Lindsay Jail. There was no radio, television, computer or desk in his cell, which he could easily pace across in three or four strides.

Food arrived on trays marked with other men's names, for fear the label FRANK LENTI would invite an attempt at poisoning. His only contact with other prisoners was by talking through a small open hatch in the door of his cell. He was allowed a subscription to the *Toronto Star,* as was ex-Toronto police officer Rick Wills, who had a cell two doors away. Wills was facing first-degree murder charges for beating his mistress to death, then stuffing her body into the wall of his home, where her remains liquefied. Now, Lenti's social life was effectively reduced to listening to Wills rant about how he couldn't stand *Star* columnist Rosie DiManno, who described him in print as "a narcissistic buffoon and a wicked man without a shred of decency" and asked readers, "How could .. . any sane woman, have loved such a rotter?" For his part, Wills raved through the bars of his cell that he couldn't stand to even look at DiManno's face as she sat in the courtroom and dismissed her as a "fucking witch."[36]

Twice a week, for periods of twenty minutes each,

Lenti was allowed to speak to visitors through a telephone hookup, separated from them by bulletproof Plexiglas. During one of his visits, Lenti tried to shrug off the suggestion that, even if he beat the second-degree murder charges for shooting Buchanan, his days were numbered. He spoke boldly about walking free after his trial and returning to the Club Pro, where he could hold court once again in the darkened games room, with his back to the emergency exit.

Frank Lenti travelled to and from court appearances in Newmarket in a convoy of a half-dozen vehicles, guarded by tactical offers with light, high-powered submachine guns. An officer gave him the option of wearing a bulletproof vest, like those worn by his police protectors.

"No, they'd use a rocket launcher if they did something," Lenti said.

"I wish you hadn't told me that," the officer replied.

Officers with assault rifles stood guard outside the Newmarket courtroom for his preliminary hearing on second-degree murder charges. Security was so tight that visitors had to show identification and sign a police information sheet, then remove their shoes so that they could be checked for weapons. Five associates of David (Dred) Buchanan showed up anyway. Under "organization" on the sign-in sheet, they wrote, "Hells Angels."

Senior Crown attorney Peter Westgate and defence lawyer Louie Genova faced the challenge of having to lead witnesses whose memories were particularly challenged. Shooting victim Carlo Verrelli of the West Toronto Hells Angels told the court he couldn't remember whether Buchanan had been a Hells Angel, nor could he recall the names of any members of their chapter.

"Have you always had memory problems?" Westgate asked in exasperation.

"I don't remember," Verrelli replied.

Westgate pressed on, asking, "Have you heard of the Bandidos?"

"I've watched many Mexican movies growing up," Verrelli replied, without a hint of a smile.

The longer Frank Lenti sat alone in his six-by-eight cell, the more he felt the urge to just plead guilty and get on with his life. The promise of brotherhood and open roads had pulled him into the one percenter biker life, but following its codes now meant that he was constantly alone and confined. As long as he remained in Lindsay, there was no hope he would ever be moved out of his segregation cell, except for his thrice-weekly showers, when he was watched by a guard, and his occasional twenty-minute blocks of yard time, when he paced alone in another concrete box.

Lenti was consoled by the news that, over the past few months, some members of the Hells Angels had approached his family, saying they didn't blame him for the shooting, that he'd done what he had to do to protect himself. And, like the true one percenter that he was, he hadn't ratted on anybody or cooperated with police, even though authorities would have dearly loved for him to talk.

If Lenti chose to fight the charges, there was the tempting thought that he might limp out of court a free man. He might successfully argue that he'd fired six bullets at the Hells Angels surrounding him in the lobby to protect his life. But what about the seventh and final bullet, fired point blank at Buchanan as he lay on the floor? Would a jury see this as the execution of a helpless man? Or would they agree with Lenti that Buchanan appeared to be reaching into his baggy pants for a hidden handgun?

In the end, Lenti pleaded guilty on April 14, 2008, to the reduced charge of manslaughter.[37] According to the agreed facts of the case, the chain of events that ended Buchanan's life began with Steven Gault's story to police that the Hells Angels had decided in June 2006 to murder Lenti for spurning their offer to join their club. "It was proposed that the agent kill Lenti and leave him in the middle of the highway in his [Bandidos] colours," the agreed statement said. "Lenti couldn't just disappear; he had to be found to prove a point." It was only after police alerted him to the alleged murder plot that Lenti began carrying a 9-millimetre weapon, the statement continued.

In the end, Mr. Justice Michael Brown judge decided a six-year prison term would be appropriate. "[The

shooting] did involve a measure of provocation," the
judge concluded shortly before Frank Lenti was led away
to prison in handcuffs.

In Oshawa that spring, Remond (Ray) Akleh of the Hells
Angels desperately needed to talk with Detective Todd
Dennis. Akleh's trial for conspiracy to murder his old
friend Frank Lenti was coming up later in the year, and
he needed to know that Dennis would protect a secret
they shared. It was so dangerous he hadn't even told his
lawyers, and Akleh needed to know Dennis wouldn't tell
anyone, whatever the pressure. He worried that just a few
words in open court would be the equivalent of pressing
a loaded gun to his own head and squeezing the trigger.

Akleh's secret was a deadly and bizarre one for a member of the elite Nomads chapter of the Hells Angels: he was
a police informant, reporting to Dennis under the code
name Lowdown. His informing had centred on Steven
Gault, whom Akleh considered an internal threat to the
Hells Angels. Akleh had gone first to the club with his sus-
picions that Gault was a police informant, and he refused
to take a cent for passing on information against Gault.
None of this would matter to some club members—nor
would it matter that Akleh felt his informing was essential
to protect his family from Gault, a bitter enemy. The one

percenter rules are clear: you don't inform to police. A rat is a rat is a rat, and rats who aren't killed can expect to be shunned, like someone expelled from a religious sect. "If it comes out, I'm fucked," Akleh told Dennis. "If it doesn't come out, I'm stuck here," he continued, referring to jail. He paused, reflected and saw only darkness. "I'm dead either way."

By November 7, 2008, Akleh worried that he might be facing a lengthy prison term. He was a fastidious family man who had never done any prison time. His stomach ulcers flared. He couldn't focus on his daily workouts at the gym, where he had once been able to bench-press a steroid-aided 470 pounds. His weight dropped from 210 to about 180 pounds, so that his shirts were now visibly loose around his neck. He had trouble sleeping.

Finally, he decided he had to play his trump card and declare publicly that he was a police informant. Officer Todd Dennis's police notes would back him up. One juror smirked and others looked stunned, as Akleh told an almost-empty courtroom that he lived the double life of an elite Hells Angels Nomad and a numbered police inform-ant. He testified that he first saw Dennis in the fall of 2002, when Gault was in court on charges of threatening the lives of Dennis and his family for giving him a speeding ticket. "He got emotional when he spoke about his wife and his kids," Akleh said of the police officer. "That they were being threatened."

The cop and the Hells Angel shared a common enemy in Gault, and their distaste for him was so strong that it pulled them together. "I seen him as a friend," Akleh said.

"Somebody I could trust and talk to." The court heard from the officer's notes, including a passage in which Akleh agreed to warn Dennis if he "received information of a hit on him or his family," and that he could expect "the same from us." Another entry in the officer's notes stated: "Says Steve [Gault] is a very crazy guy and will hurt somebody some day."

Akleh further told the court that he was trying to protect his friend Lenti from Gault, not murder him, and that he didn't particularly care about Lenti's efforts to revive the No Surrender Crew. "I never had a concern with Mr. Lenti," Akleh testified. "I didn't want anything to happen to Frank." Akleh's voice cracked as he told the court he believed he was now a target for a gangland hit from his former biker brothers. "I believe my life is in extreme danger now, and so is my family's," he told the court in a soft voice. He testified that he had taken out a life insurance policy, drafted a will, acquired a bullet-proof vest and built a steel fence around his home over the past few months. "I'm moving my family," Akleh said. "The house is for sale."

Then he slumped down and began to cry quietly.

On Sunday, January 18, 2009, after three days of deliberations, the jury was ready to announce its decision on the fates of Akleh and Stephenson. Relatives of the Hells Angels went silent and then began to sob as the jury foreperson said "Not guilty" to the charges of murder, conspiracy and counsel to commit murder of both men. The jury didn't believe they had plotted to murder Frank Lenti for trying to revive the Bandidos. It had all been just another scam by

Steven Gault, who sold out his biker brothers for the money he could make as a police agent.

Gault's betrayal had a deadly fallout. In the paranoia that followed the Akleh-Stephenson arrests, Frank Lenti had killed David Buchanan, thinking the Angel was part of a hit team and not just trying to rough him up. Now the rat Gault was a millionaire for his undercover work and testimony, even though the jury considered him a liar. Akleh and Stephenson were finally free to go home. The only person going to prison was Frank Lenti, the supposed target. Gault had set out to destroy his former Hells Angels brothers, but instead brought down the last of the Bandidos.

ACKNOWLEDGMENTS

There are many people to thank, including my former *Toronto Star* editor Richard (The Badger) Brennan, himself a Harley-Davidson enthusiast. The *Star*'s team covering the murders also included writers Betsy Powell, Nick Van Rijn, Rob Ferguson, Jim Rankin, Dale Brazao, the late John Duncanson, super-librarian Kathleen Power and her colleagues at the *Star* library. Assignment editor Phil Mascoll of the *Toronto Star* gave me the original call to cover this story, and I remain grateful to him. Steve Tustin, Graham Parley, Kevin Scanlon, Lynn McAuley, Janet Hurley, Jon Filson and Brian McAndrew are among those who kept me on it. I appreciate the decision of Tim Appleby of *The Globe and Mail* to *not* write a book himself. Two fine reporters, Jack Boland and Rob Lamberti of *The Toronto Sun,* provided insights into the No Surrender Crew. Liz Monteiro of the *Kitchener-Waterloo Record* is another valued colleague and friend. I particularly enjoyed covering the Remond Akleh–Mark Cephes Stephenson murder conspiracy trial with Jeff Mitchell of *Whitby This Week,* and the Frank Lenti proceedings with

Joe Fantauzzi of the York Region Newspaper Group. Jane Sims, Kate Dubinski and John Miner of *The London Free Press* were a pleasure to work alongside, as was sketch artist Karlene Ryan, Nick Paparella of A-Channel, Gary Ennett and Kerry McKee of CBC Radio and Allison Jones of the Canadian Press. I'm certain that no one—from criminals to judges—knows the goings-on at the London courthouse as well as Jane Sims.

Retired Sûreté du Québec Sergeant Guy Ouellette has been patient and entertaining over the years, while Antonio Nicaso, my valued friend and an internationally respected expert on organized crime, is always helpful when I want to put things in a global context. Like countless others in my line of work, I have nothing but admiration and respect for Michel Auger, whose work has made all journalists—and Canadians in general—safer. My agent, Daphne Hart, found an excellent home for this project and gave me the chance to work again with editor Jim Gifford. Nicholas Garrison was invaluable in helping me find a story amid a mountain of facts and anecdotes, and was also a pleasure to work with. It was also fun and educational to work on the website thebandidomassacre.com with Jefferson Rabb, who is truly great at his craft.

Mr. James French, formerly of Central Secondary School, encouraged my early efforts at journalism when I was attending school close to Weiner Kellestine's neighbourhood. I can't imagine a better English teacher. He helped me again as I was working on this story, with insights on themes like fratricide, regicide and jealousy in Shakespeare's works. The bikers in these pages played out their parts on a decidedly grubby stage, but it was their world nonetheless, and those themes apply to them as well. I'm indebted to Mr. French (it's hard to call a former teacher by his first name) for helping me contrast quotes by great thinkers like Shakespeare at the front of chapters, alongside utterances by the likes of Weiner Kellestine. Oddly enough, Mr. French was in the original jury pool for the Bandidos massacre trial.

While working on the book, I also had the pleasure of chatting with old London friends John Findley, Ross McLean, Cindy Moore and Bill Paul (my first editor, back at Central). In their own unique ways, John, Ross, Cindy and Bill each provided encouragement and insights that helped this project.

Numerous police officers, prosecutors, criminal lawyers, outlaw bikers and others also helped me, and I appreciate their support. Michael Demczcer got me reading Ernest Becker, which proved useful in trying to understand the one percenter world. Professor Ken Hardy of the Ivey School of Business at the University of Western Ontario was of great help in assessing the importance of "branding" in the outlaw biker world, as well as in mainstream corporations. John Douse, the father of murder victim Shawn Douse, reminded me of the human toll in this story, and of the deep and lasting pain that flows from a senseless act of violence. It was a pleasure to get to talk several times with Richard Jesso, the son of George (Pony) Jessome. (The family spells its name two different ways.) Richard's a decent, caring young man who reflects his father's finer qualities. The Douse family also showed enormous grace, under extremely difficult circumstances, in their encouragement for "Mary Thompson" to seek out a positive life. I was also impressed by the family of other victims, including that of Boxer Muscedere.

I'm grateful to J.B. for his insights, particularly on Taz Sandham, and to Don Norris for his historical perspective. Glenn (Wrongway) Atkinson struck me as someone who could have ended up teaching English himself, had his life taken a few different turns. My greatest helper was Julian Carsini (not his real name), who was also fun to chat with—almost on a daily basis—through the final year of research. I'm forever thankful that Glenn and "Julian" had both left the No Surrender Crew by the time of the massacre.

Due to the tensions of their varied lines of work, many people who helped me would appreciate not being acknowledged, and I respect that. For this reason, some sources are not thanked here publicly, but their help is enormously appreciated nonetheless. They know who they are.

Working on this book has continually reminded me of the need for family and of my good fortune. Everything I write has been influenced positively by my mother, the late Winona Edwards; my father, the late Kenneth Edwards; and, of course, Barbara, Sarah and James. My in-laws, Amund and Pauline Hanson, are also positive constants in my life. I feel blessed to have such a circle of love in my life. The addition of Eddie only makes my happy life happier.

ABBREVIATED CHRONOLOGY

1936—Outlaws Motorcycle Club forms in Chicago area as a racing, touring and partying fraternity.

1947—After a biker riot claims headlines, the president of the American Motorcycle Association tells the press that 99 percent of motorcyclists are law abiding. The Pissed Off Bastards of Bloomington, a California motorcycle club, love the quote and immediately sew badges on their leather jackets that read "1%er." Other particularly rebellious biker clubs join in, also adopting the patches. A year later, the Pissed Off Bastards change their names to Hells Angels, adopting the moniker of American World War II bomber crews.

Summer 1965—Former U.S. Marine Donald Eugene Chambers and fellow dockworkers in the small Texas fishing village of San Leon form a motorcycle club. The next summer, they began calling themselves the Bandidos. Chambers is originally an admirer of the Hells Angels, who have no chapters in the Texas Gulf area.

Friday, July 1, 1977—The U.S.-based Outlaws Motorcycle Club become the first international biker gang to move into Canada, patching over four chapters of the Satan's Choice club in Ontario and Quebec.

Monday, December 5, 1977—The Hells Angels move into Canada when the Montreal-based gang the Popeyes patch over—or switch allegiances—to their club. Hells Angels and Outlaws have a sometimes bloody rivalry.

Sunday, September 2, 1984 (Father's Day in Australia)—Three members of the Australian Comanchero Motorcycle Club, three Bandidos, and a fourteen-year-old girl are killed in a brawl involving guns and machetes at the Viking Tavern in the Sydney suburb of Milperra. The violence flowed from the decision of some Comancheros to leave their club and form the first international chapter of the Bandidos.

Sunday, March 24, 1985—Guy-Louis Adam, Guy Geoffrion, Laurent Viau, Jean-Pierre Mathieu and Michel Mayrand, formerly of the Montreal North chapter of the Hells Angels, are invited to a "church" or club meeting at the Angels' Lennoxville compound in Sherbrooke, Quebec, only to be slaughtered and dumped in the St. Lawrence River, wrapped in sleeping bags. Their crimes were excessive drug use, violence and stealing money from the club. After the killers go to prison, the compound is renovated and improved. Because of the high level of violence in the province, Quebec becomes known in the Canadian biker world as a "red zone."

June 1997—The Rock Machine Motorcycle Club is locked in a bloody war with the Hells Angels over drug-trafficking turf, and is badly outnumbered. Rock Machine founders Johnny Plescio, Fred Faucher and Robert (Tout Tout) Léger fly to Sweden to meet with Scandinavian members of the Bandidos, hoping to gain support from the international club. They're immediately ejected from the country by police.

July 1997—Hells Angels open new chapters in Alberta, based in Calgary and Edmonton.

Thursday, September 25, 1997—A truce is announced in the three-year-old Scandinavian war between the Bandidos and Hells Angels, after eleven people were killed and ninety-six were injured. Canadian Rock Machine members are impressed that the Bandidos stood up to the Hells Angels and survived.

Monday, September 7, 1998—Hells Angels open a Saskatchewan chapter, based in Saskatoon.

April 1999—The Rock Machine bolsters its strength, as the club is given hangaround status with the Bandidos Motorcycle Club. It is sponsored by European Bandidos, who are sometimes at odds with the club's Texas mother chapter. It is a complicated relationship, as the Canadians are still considered under the wing of Texas, even though their sponsors are from Scandinavia.

June 1999—The tiny Annihilators Motorcycle Club of southwestern Ontario folds into the much larger Loners club of Richmond Hill, north of Toronto. The Annihilators were led by Wayne (Weiner) Kellestine of Iona Station, and members included Kellestine's longtime friend Giovanni (John, Boxer) Muscedere of Chatham.

April 2000—Notes from Dany Kane, a Quebec member of a Hells Angels support club and police agent, record that David (Wolf) Carroll of the elite Hells Angels Nomads wants him to kill members of the Loners Motorcycle Club in the Greater Toronto Area, and has given him photographs of Loners to identify his targets. Shortly afterwards, Kane says that Carroll has aborted the plan, saying too many people know about it.

Friday, December 1, 2000—Ontario Rock Machine chapters become a probationary Bandidos chapter during a ceremony at a banquet hall on Jane Street in Vaughan, north of Toronto. The Loners provide security as forty-five probationary Bandidos patches are handed out. Shortly afterwards, Canadian Bandidos president Alain Brunette extends an olive branch to the rival Hells Angels, saying he and his Bandidos "want the situation to stay quiet for a long time."

Friday, December 22, 2000—The Hells Angels open a Manitoba chapter, patching over an existing club, the Los Bravos. This anchors their status as the dominant club iun the Prairies.

Friday, December 29, 2000—Some 168 members of Ontario motorcycle clubs—including the Satan's Choice, Para-Dice Riders, Lobos, Loners and Last Chance—arrive at the Hells Angels' bunker-like clubhouse in Laval, outside Montreal, to be granted membership in the Hells Angels. The Greater Toronto Area suddenly vaults from having no Hells Angels clubhouses to having the largest concentration of chapters in the world, with a half-dozen within an eighty-kilometre radius. Canada now has the second-highest number of Hells Angels in the world, behind only the U.S. Not all of the Toronto Loners or Para-Dice Riders are included in the "patchover."

Tuesday, May 22, 2001—In what is considered a hostile move against the Hells Angels, twelve members of the Loners chapters in Richmond Hill and Woodbridge, Ontario, become probationary Bandidos.

Saturday, December 1, 2001—Probationary Loners and Rock Machine members become full-patch members of the Bandidos, including Giovanni (John, Boxer) Muscedere, Luis Manny (Chopper, Porkchop) Raposo, George (Crash) Kriarakis, Frankie (Bam Bam, Bammer) Salerno and Wayne (Weiner) Kellestine.

Sunday, March 10, 2002—Police pull over a car on Highway 401 near Kingston, Ontario. One of the passengers, career criminal Daniel Lamer, opens fire and is killed. With him is Marc Bouffard, of the Hells Angels support club the Rockers, who is unharmed. In their car, police find four handguns, a bulletproof vest, silencer, balaclava and pictures of Bandidos Canada president Alain Brunette and his vehicle. They also find photos of several members of the Bandidos from southwestern Ontario, suggesting they were targeted for murder as well.

Spring 2002—Muscedere is promoted to vice-*presidente* of the Ontario Bandidos.

June 2002—Severely depleted by police raids, the Bandidos promote Muscedere to Canadian *presidente*. He has been an outlaw biker for only five years.

July 2004—Muscedere tours western Canada, hoping to pave the way for expansion.

August 2004—Kellestine is freed from prison after serving time for gun and drug charges, and is given the title of Bandidos Canada national sergeant-at-arms, or *sargento de armas*. He's uncomfortable that he now holds less power in the club than his former sidekick Muscedere.

Thursday, June 9, 2005—As part of a massive sweep, George (Bandido George) Wegers, *El Presidente* of the Bandidos Nation, is arrested in Washington State and charged with a long list of crimes, including kidnapping, drug trafficking, extortion and witness tampering.

Saturday, June 25, 2005—Michael (Taz, Tazman, Little Beaker) Sandham, president of the Winnipeg probationary chapter of the Bandidos, attends a party at Kellestine's farm near London, Ontario. Sandham, an ex-cop, goes home frustrated, after failing to elevate his chapter above probationary status.

Thursday, December 8, 2005—The badly burned body of drug dealer Shawn Douse is found northwest of Toronto. Shortly afterwards, police begin surveillance of Bandidos and associates in Keswick, north of Toronto.

Friday, February 3, 2006—Réjean Lessard is given temporary leave from a minimum-security facility in Laval, Quebec. Lessard, who had been known as "Zig-Zag" during his Hells Angels days, was serving five first-degree murder sentences for ordering the 1985 Lennoxville Massacre, in which five former members of the Laval chapter were murdered and dumped in the St. Lawrence River in sleeping bags. Lessard says he is now a vegetarian and a devout Buddhist, telling the National Parole Board, "You can't be a Buddhist and be in that milieu."

Saturday, April 8, 2006—Bodies of eight bikers connected to the No Surrender Crew of the Toronto area are found in vehicles abandoned off a farm laneway, near the hamlet of Shedden in southwestern Ontario. They had all been shot in the head, execution-style.

Thursday, September 28, 2006—Remond (Ray) Akleh, of the Hells Angels' elite Ottawa-based Nomads chapter, and Mark Cephes Stephenson, president of the Oshawa chapter, are charged with conspiring to murder Frank (Cisco) Lenti, who had been trying to restart the Bandidos Motorcycle Club in Canada after the Shedden Massacre. Police allege that the would-be hitman is Steven Gault, a Hells Angel who secretly received more than a million dollars as an undercover agent for police.

Friday, October 6, 2006—Bandidos *presidente* George Wegers pleads guilty to only one charge—racketeering—and is sentenced to twenty months in custody. With credit for the time he has already spent behind bars and fourteen other charges dropped, he is released in less than a month.

Saturday, December 2, 2006—Fearful that he's targeted for murder, Lenti opens fire on four bikers connected to the Hells Angels at Club Pro Adult Entertainment in Vaughan, where he provides security. He kills David (Dred) Buchanan and critically wounds Carlo Verrelli.

April 14, 2008—Lenti pleads guilty to manslaughter for killing Buchanan and to two counts of aggravated assault, for which he receives a six-year prison sentence.

Sunday, January 18, 2009—Akleh and Stephenson are each acquitted by a jury of all charges of plotting Lenti's murder.

Monday, February 23, 2009—Jury selection begins for the trial of six Bandidos and associates charged in the April 2006 massacre. There is a pool of two thousand prospective jurors, the largest jury pool in memory in Canada.

Tuesday, March 31, 2009—The trial of six men for the Bandido massacre begins, with Elgin County Crown attorney Kevin Gowdey telling a jury: "There was no gunfight. There was no flurry of bullets . . . One by one, the Bandidos were led to their deaths."

Friday, October 30, 2009—Each of the six men charged in the Bandido massacre is sentenced to life in prison after being found guilty of first-degree murder.

NOTES

Author's note: There are several different spellings of "Hells Angels." I chose to use the version without the apostrophe throughout this book to match the crests on the club members' vests.

(1) Peter Edwards, "It's a First: Mass Murder of 8 People South-west of Toronto," *Toronto Star*, April 22, 2007, B2.

(2) Information about the Shawn Douse murder came from the July 2007 preliminary hearing in Oshawa, Ontario, regarding the men charged with the crime.

(3) On April 28, 2000, the *Niagara Falls Review* reported that Francesco Salerno pleaded guilty to theft over $5,000 in connection with an incident at a Hy & Zel's drugstore on November 24, 1998, after he grabbed thirteen cartons of cigarettes and fled. The court heard Salerno wanted to sell the cigarettes to support his gambling addiction. "He came to the Niagara region to go to the casino and he lost money, to the extent that he didn't feel he'd be able to

make it home again," defence counsel Donald Wolfe told the court, describing Salerno as a recovering heroin addict who was trying to turn his life around with the help of Narcotics Anonymous, Alcoholics Anonymous and a methadone program. Judge Wayne Morrison sentenced Salerno to twenty days in jail, noting his criminal record included more than nineteen convictions on similar offences.

(4) Fullager was in a tense spot on August 1, 1995, when the Satan's Choice clubhouse a few doors from his home was hit by a rocket launcher. Underlying the tensions was a move by Lenti the previous year to quit the Loners and form a new group, the Diabolos. By 1995, Lenti was chatting with the Satan's Choice. The rocket-launcher attack came as Woodbridge Loners learned that Lenti would set up a Satan's Choice chapter in Woodbridge.

(5) Information regarding the history of the Frito Bandito character came from Don Markstein's Toonopedia website (http://www.toonopedia.com/frito.html).

(6) The Toronto Wild Ones were apparently not aligned with the Wild Ones of Hamilton, whose early members included Walter (Nurget) Stadnick. The Hamilton club came together a few years after its Toronto namesake.

(7) I spoke with Mario (The Wop, Mike) Parente for three hours on March 27, 2009, two weeks after criminal organization charges were dropped against him.

(8) The comments by Canadian biker Francesco (Cisco, Frank) Lenti were made to the author after Lenti's arrest on December 2, 2006, in Vaughan, Ontario, for the second-degree murder of Hells Angel David (Dred) Buchanan. A tape recording of Lenti's statement to police was played in court in Newmarket, Ontario, on September 24, 2007, during his preliminary hearing.

(9) At the same time that Gault was working against the Toronto-area Hells Angels, police had hooked up with the former sergeant-at-arms of the Downtown Chapter of the Hells Angels in Toronto. Dave (Shaky Dave) Atwell, who worked in security for visiting celebrities and ran a spy-gear shop, was Ontario Provincial Police Agent #3859. He earned at least $450,000 plus expenses for an eighteen-month-long operation called Project Develop, which began in the spring of 2005 and targeted Ontario Hells Angels.

(10) Ironically, some of the Harley-Davidson motorcycles driven by one percenters are former police motorcycles, which the bikers strip down and refurbish.

(11) I benefited from interviews with Normand Brisebois, Pierre Paradis and Gilles (Kid) Lalonde, all of whom were in the Bandidos or aligned with them in the Quebec biker wars.

(12) Daniel R. Wolf taught anthropology at the University of Prince Edward Island and his book *The Rebels*

(*see* Select Bibliograpy) is extremely insightful about the dynamics within an outlaw biker club in the era immediately before the Quebec biker wars. Wolf's book is highly recommended for anyone serious about this topic.

(13) While they were close neighbours geographically, the new Hells Angels chapters had distinctly different personalities. When the Greater Toronto Area Angels first gathered north of the city near Canada's Wonderland amusement park, Downtown Toronto member Donny Petersen arrived in a Corvette, as befitted his status as a master mechanic and a wealthy man. A little while later, a beat-up pickup truck came bouncing up to the compound and someone said, "Here's the guys from Keswick."

(14) Brian Beaucage moved from Kellestine's Holocaust to the Satan's Choice to the Loners. He survived a murder attempt on January 16, 1987, when he was shot twice in the chest while walking out of an east-end London, Ontario, strip club. However, on March 3, 1991, at the age of forty-three, he was hacked to death with an axe in a Toronto boarding house by a former friend in the Loners.

(15) I covered the David Kenneth (Sparky) O'Neill murder for the *Toronto Star*.

(16) Internal Hells Angels documents come from evidence given in the Project Tandem trials, including the statement of opinion of Detective Sergeant Kenneth Davis of the Biker Enforcement Unit, filed in September 2008.

(17) The Killerbeez Eastside was formed in May 2001, drawing members from Montreal and from the Oshawa area; it had about twenty members in total. The group was disbanded after Project Amigo in June 2002. The Killerbeez Westside was formed in November 2001, in Keswick. For about six months, both the Killerbeez Eastside and Westside were running, with about thirty-five members between them. Big Paul Sinopoli and Cameron Acorn were leading members of the Killerbeez Westside. Pierre (Carlitto) Aragon was a member of Killerbeez Eastside who moved up in early 2002 to become a Bandidos prospect. Acorn and Sinopoli became Bandidos prospects in late 2002, which effectively ended the Killerbeez Westside.

In April 2003, a half-dozen men tried to restart the Killerbeez Westside out of Toronto, but this attempt lasted until only December 2003, when the men were told to get motorcycles and become prospects for the No Surrender Crew. They didn't have motorcycles, and the idea fizzled.

On May 17, 2001, Eric Nadeau—a.k.a. Ratkiller, the police rat in the Bandidos world—sent this email to the Killerbeez message room: "HI TO ALL THE KILLERBEEZ AND TO YOU SCRATCH RESPECT *SALUT À TOUS LES KILLERBEEZ LACHER PAS MES BEST SALUT À ROCK ET TOUS LES BANDIDOS* 1.1.R. PEACE FOR EVERYBODY S.Y.1.B." "Scratch" was the nickname for a clubmate, while the rest of the message was a jumbled expression of his hopes for goodwill within the club.

(18) Some of Frank Lenti's criminal background is outlined in *Mafia Assassin: The Inside Story of a Canadian*

Biker, Hitman and Police Informer by Cecil Kirby with Thomas C. Renner (Toronto: Methuen, 1986).

(19) The Greek restaurant where the Bandidos used to meet has changed ownership and is now a yuppified "gastro pub and oyster bar."

(20) The Kellestine email is from *R. v. Michael Sandham et al* (the trial of the Bandidos for the Shedden Massacre).

(21) It shouldn't really come as a surprise that the ragtag Bandidos weren't well off financially. Authors Steven D. Levitt and Stephen J. Dubner reported on a similar phenomenon in *Freakonomics: A Rogue Economist Explores the Hidden Side of Everything* (New York: William Morrow, 2005). In chapter three, entitled "Why Do Drug Dealers Still Live with Their Moms?" they note a study by economist Sudhir Venkatesh on the crack-cocaine dealing Black Gangster Disciple Nation on Chicago's south side during the late 1980s and early 1990s. The study reveals that "officers" in the group made just $7 an hour, while foot soldiers earned an average of $3.30 an hour from dealing drugs, meaning they often had to supplement their crime with mainstream minimum-wage jobs. The hope of greater status and money drove them to work at a job that was statistically more dangerous than being an inmate on Texas's death row.

(22) The comments about the No Surrender Crew being busted down to probationary status, and about Kellestine

strongly opposing a shift to the Outlaws, are from Michael Sandham's December 29, 2007, statement to police.

(23) Evidence from *R. v. Michael Sandham et al* was essential here.

(24) Sandham's comments about the rumour of the No Surrender Crew patching over to the Outlaws were passed along to police after Sandham's arrest for the mass murder.

(25) Brett Gardiner had almost made it into Lenti's Loners, but things soured after the Ontario bikers felt he'd gone west for too long. After that, Gardiner spent some time with a little-known crew called the Pilgrims, which Lenti organized in Saskatchewan. This crew failed to gain a foothold, and Gardiner shuffled over to the Bandidos' orbit in Winnipeg.

(26) The phrase "calm rage" is from page 692 of *The Executioner's Song* by Norman Mailer (New York: Vintage International, 1979).

(27) I interviewed Kerry Morris on October 23, 2007.

(28) *R. v. Michael Sandham et al.*

(29) Pierre (Carlitto) Aragon's intercepted email is from *R. v. Akleh and Stephenson,* in a general overview of the Hells Angels and Bandidos. Donny Petersen's email was part of the evidence in the same court case.

(30) *R. v. Michael Sandham et al.*

(31) "Octagon" was also the code name for the conference held at the Chateau Frontenac hotel in Quebec City from September 12 to 16, 1944, in which the Allies—including Canadian Prime Minister William Lyon Mackenzie King, British Prime Minister Winston Churchill and U.S. President Franklin Roosevelt—agreed on Allied occupation zones in Germany.

(32) M.H. told the preliminary hearing into the Shedden Massacre that he met Quebec Hells Angels leader Maurice (Mom) Boucher in Winnipeg. Boucher's penchant for violence was dizzying, even in Quebec biker circles.

(33) Mike McIntyre, "Judge Jails Violent Home Invaders," *Winnipeg Free Press*, July 8, 2005, B1.

(34) I attended the trial on the dates mentioned.

(35) In September 2007, I attended the preliminary hearing for Lenti's case, involving the shootings of Buchanan, Verrelli and Carnegie. Here, I heard Club Pro workers and Carlo Verrelli of the Hells Angels describe the shooting early in the morning of December 2, 2006. I also spoke with Lenti from his jail cell about that night.

(36) Rosie DiManno, "Wills has assassinated the dead," *Toronto Star*, September 24, 2007, A2.

(37) The information about the meeting in June 2006 to recruit Frank Lenti into the Hells Angels and the plot to leave his body in the middle of a roadway are from the agreed statement of fact in the case in which Lenti pleaded guilty on April 14, 2008, in Newmarket, Ontario, to manslaughter and two counts of aggravated assault for the Club Pro shootings.

SELECT BIBLIOGRAPHY

Alcoba, Natalie, "'We Are Not Here to Judge,' Priest Says at Biker's Funeral," *National Post*, 19 April 2006.

Appleby, Tim, and Michael Den Tandt, "When Hell Comes to Town," *The Globe and Mail*, 17 July 2004.

"Bandidos on the Web," The Black Rod blog, comment posted 16 April 2006, <http://blackrod.blogspot.com/2006_04_01_archive.html>.

Barger, Ralph (Sonny), with Keith and Kent Zimmerman, *Hell's Angels: The Life and Times of Sonny Barger and the Hell's Angels Motorcycle Club* (New York: Harper Perennial, 2001).

Beaubien, Roxanne, "Big-City Crime a Jolt to London," *The London Free Press*, 3 January 1999.

Beaubien, Roxanne, "Biker Gang Leader Hit with Dozens of Charges," *The London Free Press*, 29 October 1999.

Bradley, Kim; Connor, Kevin; Lamberti, Rob; McLaughlin, Tracy; Cairns, Alan; Henry, Michele; Boland, Jack; and Godfrey, Tom, with files from Canadian Press, "Dead Men—Crooks and Good Guys: One Knew He'd Die Young, One Wanted Out," *The Toronto Sun*, April 11, 2006, page 36.

Campbell, Don, and Gary Dimmock, with files from Sarah Staples, "How a Career Criminal Fooled the System," *Ottawa Citizen*, 13 March 2002.

Castagna, Cary, and Bob Holliday, "From Texas, with Love," *Winnipeg Sun*, 20 September 2005.

Cernetig, Miro, and Peter Edwards, "Angels On the Brink," *Toronto Star*, 6 March 2004.

Cherry, Paul, "Peace Arch Was Meeting Place for Biker Accord," *The Gazette* (Montreal), 23 February 2004.

Cherry, Paul, "Slain Biker 'Prospect' Hailed from Cote St. Luc," *The Gazette* (Montreal), 12 April 2006.

Cherry, Paul, *The Biker Trials: Bringing Down the Hells Angels* (Toronto: ECW Press, 2005).

Chung, Andrew, "Crystal in the County," *Toronto Star*, 18 June 2005.

Dimmock, Gary, "Biker Killed in Shootout Was on Deadly Mission," *Ottawa Citizen*, 17 March 2002.

Dimmock, Gary, "Birth of the 'Bandidos Nation': Outlaw Bikers Speak of Peace with Rivals, but Police Fear War," *Ottawa Citizen*, 2 December 2001.

Dimmock, Gary, "Hells Angels 'Hit Squads' Target Rival Biker Gang," *Ottawa Citizen*, 27 March 2002.

Dimmock, Gary, "Lucky Luke's Climb to the Seat of Biker Power," *Ottawa Citizen*, 7 September 2004.

Dimmock, Gary, "Police Admit Biker War Has Spilled into Ontario," *Ottawa Citizen*, 6 December 2001.

Dimmock, Gary, "Raids Crush Biker Gang," *Ottawa Citizen*, 6 June 2002.

Duff-Brown, Beth, "Canada Slayings Suspect Said 'Respectful,'" Associated Press wire story, 11 April 2006.

Duncanson, John, "Slain Biker Buried in York," *Toronto Star*, 16 April 2005.

Duncanson, John, with files from Betsy Powell, "To Family, Biker Was 'Superman,'" *Toronto Star*, 18 April 2006.

Edwards, Peter, "Bikers Chided Informer over Cocaine," *Toronto Star*, 19 April 2008.

Edwards, Peter, "Hells' Rival Recruiting in GTA," *Toronto Star*, 5 April 2008.

Edwards, Peter, "Informer on the Run Is Suing Police," *Toronto Star*, 1 July 1996.

Fantauzzi, Joe, "Extra Precaution Needed if Biker Went to Trial," Yorkregion.com, 17 April 2008. < http://www.yorkregion.com/article/73169>.

Galbraith, John Kenneth, *The Scotch* (Baltimore: Penguin Books, 1966).

Herbert, John, "Beating Death Unsolved One Year Later," *The London Free Press*, 16 December 1999.

Herbert, John, "Body Only Half-Buried 'to Deliver a Message,'" *The London Free Press*, 18 December 1998.

Herbert, John, "Court Appearance Closely Watched," *The London Free Press*, 6 November 1999.

Herbert, John, "Death Linked to Area Killing," *The London Free Press*, 7 October 2000.

Herbert, John, "Did He Know Too Much?" *The London Free Press*, 28 September 2002.

Herbert, John, "Leads Sought in Murder: Police Release Photos of Murder Victim in Hopes of Collecting Clues," *The London Free Press*, 22 December 1998.

Herbert, John, "Murdered Millionaire Was Going to Florida," *The London Free Press*, 21 December 1998.

Herbert, John, "The Mysterious Life of a London Millionaire Ended in a Shallow Grave and Left Police with the Question: Who Killed Salvatore Vecchio?" *The London Free Press*, 9 January 1999.

Herbert, John, "Police Promise to Find Killer," *The London Free Press*, 19 December 1998.

Holliday, Bob, and Paul Turenne, "Ex-Cop Bust Shocks," *Winnipeg Sun*, 17 June 2006.

Hong, Rose, "SIU Concludes Morrisburg Shooting Investigation," Canada News Wire press release, 16 April 2002. <http://www.siu.on.ca/siu_publications_documentation_detai17d36.html>.

Kalogerakis, George, "And Then There Were Just Two," *The Gazette* (Montreal) website, 12 December 2000, < http://www.montreal-gazette.com/>.

Litwak, Leo E., review of *Hell's Angels: A Strange and Terrible Saga*, by Hunter S. Thompson, *The New York Times Review of Books*, 29 January 1967.

McCrindle, Kate, "'We're Loners, We Get Along,'" *The Chatham Daily News*, 2 December 1999.

Murray, Don, "Ex-Guard Jailed in Drug Bust," *London Free Press*, 11 September 1999.

National Parole Board of Canada, Records for Wayne Earl Kellestine, 20 January 1994 to 29 October 2003.

Oakes, Gary, "Murder Suspect Points Out Man He Says Did Killing," *Toronto Star*, 11 June 1982.

Official Harley-Davidson Website, The, (Milwaukee: H-D, 2001–2009). <www.harleydavidson.com>.

Palser, Lee, "Murdered Bandido Remembered Fondly: John 'Boxer' Muscedere," *National Post*, 18 April 2006.

Paradis, Pierre, *Nasty Business: One Biker Gang's Bloody War against the Hells Angels* (Toronto: HarperCollins, 2002).

Parker, Richard, *John Kenneth Galbraith: His Life, His Politics, His Economics* (New York: Farrar, Straus and Giroux, 2005).

Penn, Stanley, "The Wild Ones: Rise in Crime Ventures by Motorcycle Gangs Worries U.S. Lawmen," *The Wall Street Journal*, 11 January 1984.

Post, Jerrold M., "Substance Abuse: The High and the Mighty High," *The Washington Post*, 28 January 1990.

Rautigam, Tara, with the Canadian Press, "Bandidos Leader Recalled Fondly at Funeral," *The Globe and Mail*, 18 April 2006.

Richmond, Randy, "Blocking Bike Show Trouble Cost Cops $30,000," *The London Free Press*, 6 February 2002.

Richmond, Randy, "Cops Keep Rival Gangs Apart at Bike Show," *The London Free Press*, 3 February 2002.

Richmond, Randy, "'He Just Wanted to Retire,'" *The London Free Press*, 13 April 2006.

Richmond, Randy, "Kellestine Farm to Be Auctioned," *The London Free Press*, 27 June 2007.

Rohr, Richard, *Adam's Return: The Five Promises of Male Initiation* (New York: Crossroad Publishing Company, 2004).

Rook, Katie, "Neighbourhood of New Clubhouse—Good Idea, Bad Idea?" *National Post*, 7 October 2006.

Schuck, Paula, "Six Charged after Shooting," *The London Free Press*, 26 October 1999.

Sher, Jonathan, "Police in Kitchener Arrest Man Sought in Biker Shooting," *The London Free Press*, 3 November 1999.

Simpson, Lindsay, "Police 'Need a Scapegoat': Claim by Bikie Leader at Milperra Shooting Trial," *The Sydney Morning Herald*, 14 November 1986.

Simpson, Lindsay, and Sandra Harvey, "A Story of Bad Blood," *The Sydney Morning Herald*, 13 June 1987.

Simpson, Lindsay, and Sandra Harvey, *Brothers in Arms: The Inside Story of the Two Biker Gangs* (Crows Nest, New South Wales: Allen & Unwin, 1989).

Sims, Jane, "Biker Given 2 Years," *The London Free Press*, 18 July 2002.

Sims, Jane, "Career Criminal Breaton, 87, Died a Free Man," *The London Free Press*, 17 December 2008.

Sims, Jane, "Career Crook, 87, Vows to Go Straight," *The London Free Press*, 28 June 2008.

Sims, Jane, "Scenes from a massacre," *The London Free Press*, 29 May 2008.

Sims, Jane, "Still Not Old Enough to Know Better," *The London Free Press*, 13 December 2007.

Sims, Jane, "Veteran Criminal Marks 87th Birthday in Cell," *The London Free Press*, 28 May 2008.

Sims, Jane, "Veteran Jailbird Back behind Bars over Drug Charges," *The London Free Press*, 17 June 2008.

Sinnema, Jodie, "Gang May Seek Revenge for Double Slaying," *Edmonton Journal*, 2 February 2004.

Skelton, Chad, and Lori Culbert, "200 Attend Joey Campbell's Funeral," *Edmonton Journal*, 7 February 2004.

Skelton, Chad, and Lori Culbert, "Bandidos Motorcycle Club Sets Up 'Probationary' Chapter," *Edmonton Journal*, 21 February 2004.

Skelton, Chad, and Lori Culbert, "Police Fear B.C. Biker War," *The Vancouver Sun*, 30 July 2004.

Staples, Sarah, and Gary Dimmock, "Shooting Victim Was Warned to Stop Selling Drugs," *Ottawa Citizen*, 2 May 2002.

Thanh Ha, Tu, "Mourning and Mystery: How Did a Man from a Good Family Become Linked to a Biker Crew?" *The Globe and Mail*, 13 April 2006.

Thompson, Hunter S., *Hell's Angels: A Strange and Terrible Saga*
(New York: Random House, 1967).

Tzu, Sun, *The Art of War*, trans. Samuel B. Griffith (Vancouver: Blue
Heron Books, 2006).

Wilton, Katherine, "Montrealer 'Stood Out, Stood Up,' Family Says,"
The Gazette (Montreal), 13 April 2006.

Wilton, Katherine, with the Canadian Press, "Biker Remembered as
a Good Son," *The Gazette* (Montreal), 18 April 2006.

"Winnipeg Arrests Linked to Bandidos Massacre," *CBC.ca*, 21 June
2006. <http://www.cbc.ca/canada/toronto/story/2006/06/16/
to-bandidos20060616.html>

Winterhalder, Edward, *Out in Bad Standings: Inside the Bandidos
Motorcycle Club* (Owasso, Oklahoma: Blockhead City Press,
2005).

Wolf, Daniel R., *The Rebels: A Brotherhood of Outlaw Bikers*
(Toronto: University of Toronto

JUDICIAL PROCEEDINGS

R. vs. Akleh and Stephenson, the trials of Remond Akleh, of the
Ontario Nomads, and Mark Cephes Stephenson, of the Oshawa
Hells Angels chapter, on charges of conspiracy to commit murder
and counsel to commit murder. The trials were held in Whitby,
Ontario, from October 2008 to January 2009.

R. v. Lindsay, the trial against Hells Angels Steven Patrick Lindsay
and Raymond Lawrence Bonner. The trial was held in Barrie,
Ontario, in 2005.